Best wishes to
G. E. Maxon, my
favorite "71" pilot.

Jo. P. Dapheell.

U.S.
CIVIL
AIRCRAFT
VOL. 5

This work is dedicated to the preservation and perpetuation of a fond memory for the men and the planes that made a future for our air industry. And, to help kindle a knowledge and awareness within us of our debt of gratitude we owe to the past. . . . .

LIBRARY OF CONGRESS CATALOG CARD NUMBER 62-15967
COPYRIGHT© 1971 AERO PUBLISHERS, INC.

U.S. CIVIL AIRCRAFT

VOL. 5

(ATC 401-ATC 500)

By

JOSEPH P. JUPTNER

1971

ISBN-O-8168-9166-4

Aero Publishers, Inc.

329 Aviation Road
Fallbrook, California 92028

ACKNOWLEDGEMENTS

Any historian soon learns that in the process of digging for obscure facts and information, he must oftentimes rely on the help of numerous people, unselfish and generous people, many of whom were close to — or actually participated in — various incidents or events that make up this segment of history recorded here, and have been willing to give of their time and knowledge in behalf of this work. To these wonderful people I am greatly indebted and I feel a heart-warming gratitude; it is only fitting then that I proclaim their identity in appreciation.

Alfred V. Verville; H. Lloyd Child, Harold K. Phillips; Charles W. Morris; C. G. Taylor; W. U. Shaw; Theron K. Rinehart of Fairchild-Hiller Corp.; American Airlines: Robert L. Taylor of Antique Airplane assoc.; United Air Lines; Gene Kropf; Pan American World Airways; W. H. Weeks; John G. Leyden; the staff at Smithsonian Institution, National Air Museum; Ken Molson of Nat. Aviation Museum of Canada; Gordon S. Williams of The Boeing Co.; Sikorsky Aircraft Div.; Wanda R. Samford of Center, Tex. Chamber of Commerce; and the following group of dedicated aviation historians; Roger F. Besecker; Richard Sanders Allen; Wm. T. Larkins; Melba Beard; Erwin C. Eshelman; Robert W. Thompson; Chas. E. Lebrecht; Burton Kemp; Robert S. Hirsch; John E. Issitt; Everette J. Payette; Stephen J. Hudek; Henri D'Estout; Norman S. Orloff; Edward J. Gardyan; Chas. F. Schultz; Marion Havelaar; John W. Underwood; Peter M. Bowers; and Gerald H. Balzer.

FOREWORD

Statistics show us that 215 "aircraft companies" had been doing business in 1930 and by the end of 1931 this number had fallen to 110; of those that somehow remained the following year of 1932 was to take an additional toll. Where was it going, and where was it to end? Aircraft manufacture both big and little was slowly losing out to effects of the national depression, and many earned barely enough to pay the utilities that were necessary to stay open; but, optimists that they were, they hung on grimly by hook or by crook for better or for worse. Some of the grief and the sentiment they harbored within themselves for a way of life they hated to lose is reflected quite poignantly in the following ad: "A factory site and flying field bordering a railroad in southern Ohio, offered free if used for aviation purposes". We can see then that profit was not even considered; they just hated to see aviation give up and go under. At this point it is as if we were on the threshold of another era in aviation, or better to say we were standing on a ledge and viewing the crumpled ruins of a familiar industry down below us. Turning from this view with a heavy heart, we are conscious of seeing a new scene forming before us; we don't know yet if it will be any better, or if we will even like it, but surely it holds some promise — so we enter to find out where we fit.

Throughout the entire industry, what was left of it, everyone was finding it difficult to adjust; but spirits were not dimmed for very long, and morale was holding up. True, everyone was pining for happy days just gone by, but perhaps all was not lost yet. The light flivver-type monoplane just recently introduced was permitting many people to keep flying, and new pilots were even enticed into the fold occasionally. To a greater extent business-people were learning that it was a distinct advantage to own an airplane; airline passenger traffic was even increasing despite the decline in surface travel, and air-express shipments took a terrific jump in poundage. Selecting from a much wider variety of "strictly-for-sport" airplanes, the sportsman-pilots were now more active than ever, and every day some new job or errand for an airplane was being discovered. The flying-service operators suffered the biggest part of the blow, but many managed to stay in business by ingenuity; and automobile gas at "twelve for a dollar" allowed many of the week-end pilots to continue flying. By far the most widespread activity of this period was hangar-flying, and groups were mostly indulging in reminiscences of better days; but many future developments in aviation were also discussed and planned at these sessions.

A certain part of this great clan, undimmed by circumstances, still held onto sky-high adventure which lured them off on trans-oceanic flights, altitude records, endurance records, distance records, or speed records; and then still cast about for something more daring or new to do. Air-racing took on a new stature and became the means of harnessing ideas and energies that otherwise would have been dormant; and commercial aircraft development profited considerably from what was learned at the races. It also became a lot harder to recognize and identify the pioneer or the genius because they were all around as one of us; and even though aviation was to sink into still greater depths, everyone felt reasonably confident that soon it surely must be lifted to even greater heights. There was no premium to pay on dreams, so they all dreamed.

Jos. P. Juptner

TERMS

To make for better understanding of the various information contained herein, we should clarify a few points that might be in question. At the heading of each new chapter, the bracketed numerals under the ATC number, denote the first date of certification; any amendments made are noted in the text. Unless otherwise noted, the title photo of each chapter is an example of the model that bears that particular certificate number; any variants from this particular model, such as prototypes and special modifications, are identified. Normally accepted abbreviations and symbols are used in the listing of specifications and performance data. Unless otherwise noted, all maximum speed, cruising speed, and landing speed figures are based on sea level tests; this method of performance testing was largely the custom during this early period. Rate of climb figures are for first minute at sea level, and the altitude ceiling given is the so-called service ceiling. Cruising range in miles or hours duration is based on the engine's cruising r.p.m., but even at that, the range given must be considered as an average because of pilot's various throttle habits.

At the ending of each chapter, we show a listing of registered aircraft of a similar type; most of the listings show the complete production run of a particular type and this information we feel will be valuable to historians, photographers, and collectors in making correct identification of a certain aircraft by its registration number.

In each volume there are separate discussions on 100 certificated airplanes and we refer to these discussions as chapters, though they are not labeled as such; at the end of each chapter there is reference made to see the chapter for an ATC number pertaining to the next development of a certain type. As each volume contains discussions on 100 aircraft, it should be rather easy to pin-point the volume number for a chapter of discussion that would be numbered as A.T.C. #93, or perhaps A.T.C. #176, as an example. The use of such terms as "prop," "prop spinner," and "type," are normally used among aviation people and should present no difficulty in interpreting the meaning.

TABLE OF CONTENTS

A.T.C. # 401
(2-12-31)
C-W TRAVEL AIR, MODEL 12-Q

Fig. 1. The Curtiss-Wright model 12-Q with 90 h.p. Wright-Gipsy engine.

Like neat and fine-mannered cousins of a very well known family, Curtiss-Wright introduced a brand new line of "Travel Air" biplanes in 1931. A line certainly of different manner and personality, it still vaguely retained the flavor of family lineage and even some resemblance. The first of these selected for debut, and for the approval of the flying public, was a noisy, scampering machine called the "Sport Trainer" model 12-Q. As shown here in various views, this was an absolutely delightful airplane that was motivated into action by the sweet-running efforts of a 4 cyl. Wright "Gipsy" engine. Designed by Herb Rawdon and developed by Ted Wells especially for sport flying, with attributes calculated to qualify it also as a pilot-trainer, the sturdy frame was laid out with two roomy open cockpits. Bearing the fuselage with ease was a pair of rather stout wings well placed for visibility, offering ease of entry, and proportioned well for good behavior in flight. Added to this mechanical assemblage was the "Gipsy" engine. Like the popular "Cirrus" engine, the inline "Gipsy" was also a British-designed powerplant built in the U.S. under license, and both engines had an enthusiastic following. For those that would prefer the small American "radial" engine, Curtiss-Wright shortly offered this same basic airplane in the models 12-K and 12-W. Of

the 3 models built in this particular sport-trainer series, the 12-Q was the most numerous and it has often been said that it was no doubt the most fun.

Formally introduced at the Detroit Air Show for 1931, with conspicuous fanfare and great expectations, the brightly painted 12-Q stood as a trim open cockpit biplane with seating for two in tandem. With modest dimension and handy arrangement well suited for sport flying by the average owner-pilot, it fared well also in pilot-training by operators of small flying schools. For the flying school trade, the model 12-Q was available in somewhat of a stripped-down version, but several optional extras were available for the sport-flier owner. Powered with the 4 cyl. air-cooled inline Wright "Gipsy" L-320 engine of 90 h.p. at 2000 r.p.m., the perky 12-Q snorted and barked its way into making one believe that it was quite an airplane; reasonably stable and fairly responsive, it was great fun and a treat to fly. Lloyd Child, Curtiss-Wright test-pilot, made first-flights on the new 12-Q and spoke of it highly. The type certificate number for the model 12-Q was issued 2-12-31 and some 27 examples were built by the Travel Air Div. of the Curtiss-Wright Airplane Co., with examples well scattered throughout the country. Built for several months in the "Travel Air" plant at Wichita, Kans., this facility was closed by June of 1931 and later moved to the Curtiss-Wright plant in Robertson (St. Louis), Mo. on Lambert Field. At the Lambert Field plant, Curtiss-Wright was still employing about 500 people early in 1931, and "Junior" production was just getting into full swing.

Listed below are specifications and performance data for the model 12-Q "Sport Trainer" as powered with the 90 h.p. Wright "Gipsy" engine; length overall 21'5"; height overall 8'10"; wing span upper 28'10; wing span lower 26'4"; wing chord upper and lower 48"; wing area upper 113.4 sq.ft.; wing area lower 93 sq.ft.; total wing area 206.4 sq.ft.; airfoil clark Y-15; wt. empty 1071 lbs.; useful load 654 lbs.; payload with 33 gal. fuel 268 lbs. (1 pass. at 170 lb. & 98 lb. baggage); gross wt. 1725 lbs.; max. speed 105; cruising speed 88; landing speed 44; climb 600 ft. first min. at sea level; average take-off run 350-400 ft.; ceiling 12,000 ft.; gas cap. 33 gal.; oil cap. 2.5 gal.; cruising range at 6.5 gal. per hour 390 miles; price $3500. at factory field.

Construction detail and general arrangement was typical for all 3 models in the "Travel Air" 12-series, so description in the chapter for ATC # 406 will also apply here. Standard equipment on the model 12-Q included a wooden propeller, 6.50x10 semi-airwheels with brakes, brake pedals in rear cockpit only, dual controls, wiring for navigation lights, and a rubber-snubbed tail skid. Two parachutes at 20 lbs. each were part of the baggage allowance. Optional equipment included an electric engine starter for $175.00, a metal propeller for $200.00, brake pedals in front cockpit for $50.00, weather-proof engine cover for $8.00, weather-proof cockpit covers for $8.00, a head-rest fairing for rear cockpit cost $12.00, and two-tone color schemes other

than standard cost $50.00 extra. The next development in the Model 12 series was the 12-K as described in the chapter for ATC # 406 of this volume.

Listed below are Model 12-Q entries as gleaned from registration records:

X-430W;	Model 12-Q (12Q-2001)	Wright Gipsy
NC-438W;	" (12Q-2004)	"
NC-439W;	" (12Q-2005)	"
NC-440W;	" (12Q-2006)	"
NC-441W;	" (12Q-2007)	"
NC-442W;	" (12Q-2008)	"
NC-443W;	" (12Q-2009)	"
NC-444W;	" (12Q-2010)	"
NC-495W;	" (12Q-2022)	"
NC-496W;	" (12Q-2023)	"
NC-497W;	" (12Q-2024)	"
NC-498W;	" (12Q-2025)	"
NC-352M;	" (12Q-2026)	"
NC-414W;	" (12Q-2027)	"
NC-415W;	" (12Q-2028)	"
NC-416W;	" (12Q-2029)	"
NC-417W;	" (12Q-2030)	"
NC-418W;	" (12Q-2031)	"
NC-419W;	" (12Q-2032)	"
NC-11708;	" (12Q-2033)	"
NC-11709;	" (12Q-2034)	"
NC-11710;	" (12Q-2035)	"
NC-11711;	" (12Q-2036)	"
NC-11712;	" (12Q-2037)	"
NC-11713;	" (12Q-2038)	"
NC-11714;	" (12Q-2039)	"

Serial # 12Q-2010 unverified; ser. # -2021 unknown; as serial numbering ran concurrently for all models in the 12-series, some of the missing serial numbers in this listing were models 12-K and 12-W; ser. # -2031 and # -2038 later modified to 12-W; this approval for ser. # 12Q-2001 and up; approval expired 4-26-37.

Fig. 2. Perky 12-Q sport-trainer ushered in a new line of "Travel Air" biplanes by Curtiss-Wright.

A.T.C. # 402
(2-12-31)
STEARMAN "CLOUDBOY", 6-D

Fig. 3. Stearman model 6-D with 300 h.p. "Wasp Junior" engine.

Originally planned to offer both interesting and practical variety in a series of airplanes specifically designed for pilot-training, the model 6-D was introduced as yet another version in the "Stearman 6". Endowed with a stout airframe designed to easily absorb up through 300 h.p., it is interesting to note the number of modifications that finally appeared in this one basic design. It has always been a source of interest, and sometimes downright amazement, of the changes that can take place in an airplane simply by the change of engines. More likely than not, the airplane emerged as a *slightly* different personality, but in some cases the changes to its character were just short of amazing. This was the case of the Stearman model 6-D. With a 300 h.p. Pratt & Whitney "Wasp Junior" mounted in the nose, this craft abandoned its previous mild ways and became somewhat of a snorting charger; most airplanes have a few inherent talents that lay dormant and only added horsepower can bring them out to the surface. In the 6-D they were brought to notice with uninhibited vigor and clarity. For the sheer pleasure of rough-and-tumble flight the 6-D would have been an excellent mount

for the he-man sportsman-pilot, a ship that could be flown about in the blue skies with near-reckless abandon; this matching of mechanical and human personalities of like ilk, would have been a joy to see. Modified into this combination (6-D) from an earlier model 6-A, by replacing the 5 cyl. Wright engine with a 9 cyl. "Wasp Junior", only one example of this model was built. Likewise, one of the Army Air Corps models YPT-9 (similar to 6-A) was converted (1932) into a military counterpart of the 6-D, a basic-trainer designated the YBT-5. With a basic airframe so well adapted to modification and changes in powerplants, the "Stearman 6" was later developed into two more versions.

The Stearman model 6-D was an open cockpit biplane with seating arranged for two in tandem; specifically designed for pilot-training in the more advanced stages, the slab-sided frame and angular lines were devoted more to simplicity and rugged character. Powered with the 300 h.p. "Wasp Junior" engine, performance was naturally improved in all factors that rely on low weight per horsepower; as a consequence, take-off runs were shortened considerable, and climb-out was steep enough to fill a pilot with glee as he looked back at the disappearing airport. Basic flight maneuvers that were somewhat sedate and rather mild in the 6-A or 6-F, became breath-taking maneuvers in the 6-D. Backed by the extra muscle that directed its actions, the 6-D required more forceful attention, but its spirited behavior was ample reward for the effort. General behavior in the air or on the ground was a little more hairy-chested, but of no great consequence, if a pilot understood what he had to put up with. Built only in the one example, its operational history remains somewhere in the past, but the 6-D can at least be cited as a good example of the transformation that takes place in an airplane by doubling the power. The type certificate number for the model 6-D was issued 2-12-31 as manufactured by the Stearman Aircraft Div. at Whichita, Kansas.

Listed below are specifications and performance data for the Stearman model 6-D as powered with the 300 h.p. "Wasp Junior" R-985 engine; length overall 23-6"; height overall (tail up) 9'7"; wing span upper 32'0"; wing span lower 28'0"; wing chord upper & lower 60"; wing area upper 150.3 sq.ft.; wing area lower 121.9 sq.ft.; total wing area 272.2 sq.ft.; airfoil N-22; wt. empty 1952 lbs.; useful load 862 lbs.; payload with 65 gal. fuel 257 lbs. (1 pass. at 170 lb., 2 parachutes at 20 lb. each, and 47 lb. baggage); gross wt. 2814 lbs.; max. speed 137 (140 with speed-ring cowl); cruising speed 115; landing (stall) speed 55; climb 1250 ft. first min. at sea level; ceiling 18,100 ft.; gas cap. max. 65 gal.; oil cap. 6 gal.; cruising range at 16 gal. per hour 450 miles; price at factory first quoted as $10,500. later raised to $12,750.

The construction details and general arrangement of the 6-D were typical to that of the models 6-A and 6-F as described in the chapters for ATC # 365 and # 371 of U.S. CIVIL AIRCRAFT,

Vol. 4. Applicable data is also listed in chapters for ATC # 458 and # 459 of this volume. Other data pertinent to 6-D as follows: A stout outrigger landing gear of 85 in. tread used "Aerol" (air-oil) shock absorbing struts; wheels were 30x5 and Bendix brakes were standard equipment. A swiveling tail wheel was mounted at very end of fuselage for a longer wheel-base and better ground handling. Main fuel tank of 38 gal. capacity was mounted in the center-section panel of the upper wing; a direct-reading fuel gauge was visible from either cockpit. An auxiliary fuel tank of 27 gal. capacity was mounted high in the fuselage ahead of the front cockpit. A small baggage bin with allowance for 47 lbs. was in the turtle-back section behind the rear cockpit. The crank handle for the inertia-type engine starter was stowed upon top cowl on right-hand side of front cockpit. The lower wings had a wing-walk on either side and they were neatly faired at the fuselage junction. Interplane struts and all interplane bracing was of heavy gauge material to withstand the heavy stress of added power and acrobatic flying. Original installation of the R-985 engine used a large exhaust collector ring, but individual bayonet stacks were optional. Landing lights, navigation lights, a battery, and oil-cooling radiator were also optional. A metal propeller, hand crank inertia-type engine starter, brake pedals in both cockpits, dual controls, fire extinguisher, and first-aid kit were standard equipment. The next developments in the "Stearman 6" were the models 6-H and 6-L as described in the chapters for ATC # 458-459 of this volume.

Listed below is the only model 6-D entry in registration records:
NC-786H; Model 6-D (# 6001) Wasp Jr. 300
This approval for ser. # 6001 and up; ser. # 6001 also eligible for conversion to models 6-H or 6-L.

Fig. 4. 6-D did not radiate beauty, but slab-sided lines were functional.

Fig. 5. In 6-D doubling horsepower made startling difference in nature of "Cloudboy."

A.T.C. # 403
(2-21-31)
EMSCO MID-WING SPORT, B-7

Fig. 6. Emsco mid-wing model B-7 mounted a 5 cyl. Wright R-540 engine.

Except for the well-known Simplex "Red Arrow", mid-wing monoplanes were scarce and comparatively rare. Every now and again one would come out for a brief bow to the flying public, hoping for a friendly appraisal, and then have to quietly retreat to the sidelines. The previous "Cirrus Mid-Wing" by Emsco also made a brief appearance early in 1929, proclaiming itself noisily to one and all, but in spite of raucous flash and racy dash, it too failed to make the grade, soon becoming another has-been. When "Gerry" Vultee, former chief engineer at Lockheed, took on a similar position at Emsco, he was obliged to study the mid-wing design carefully to see what could be done to salvage it. Somewhat like a seamstress altering a poor-fitting garment, he refashioned the original concept extensively into an airplane that reflected a more practical, conservative style. Leveled especially at the sportsman-pilot, the design was altered specifically to the extent that normal flight would be more relaxed, more enjoyable, and sufficient horsepower was added to insure a high-caliber performance. As powered with the 165 h.p. Wright R-540 engine, the new model B-7 now posed as a sport-type airplane any sportsman would likely be proud to own; by specific design, it was dedicated to furnish him ample utility, but mainly with spirited and effortless flying pleasure. Introduced at a time when there was still some optimism left, in spite of the failing market, the B-7 "Sport" wait-ed hopefully to enter the stream of aviation, but the chance to enter never came.

The Emsco model B-7 was a sport-type mid-wing monoplane, with open cockpits that were arranged for seating two in tandem. Inheriting most of the peculiarities of the mid-wing configuration, the B-7 "Sport" was rather unhandy to get into or out of, making each flight a gymnastic ritual. Although having unlimited visibility upward, the broad wing blanked off a good portion of the visibility downward, mainly because of its close proximity to eye level. Some of this visibility downward was regained through small windows in the lower fuselage. Powered with the 5 cyl. Wright R-540 engine of 165 h.p., the B-7 boasted of a good performance throughout the entire range of normal flight. Arranged in good aerodynamic proportion, with well-placed areas of effective size, the "Emsco Mid-Wing Sport" displayed the ability for sure-footed character and a responsive nature. We can well imagine that this craft would have done well in the course of more normal times. The type certificate number for the mid-wing "Sport" model B-7 was issued 2-21-31 and it seems likely that only one example of this model was built by the Emsco Aircraft Corp. at Downey, Calif.

Listed below are specifications and performance data for the Emsco model B-7 as powered with the 165 h.p. Wright R-540 engine; length overall 23'9"; height overall 8'1"; wing span 36'0"; wing chord 72"; total effective wing area 194 sq.ft.; airfoil Clark Y; wt. empty 1492 lbs.;

Fig. 7. Early Emsco mid-wing mounted a 4 cyl. Cirrus engine.

useful load 608 lbs.; payload with 31 gal. fuel 214 lbs. (1 pass. at 170 lb. & 44 lb. baggage); gross wt. 2100 lbs.; max. speed 130 (with speed-ring cowl); cruising speed 110; landing speed 40; climb 1000 ft. first min. at sea level; climb to 8000 ft. in 10 min.; ceiling 18,000 ft.; an absolute ceiling of 25,000 ft. had been reached; gas cap. 31 gal.; oil cap. 5 gal.; cruising range at 9 gal. per hour 350 miles; price $5950. at factory field.

The fuselage framework was built up of welded chrome-moly steel tubing, lavishly faired to an elliptical section with wooden formers and fairing strips, then fabric covered. The cockpits were neatly upholstered and well protected by large windshields; small windows down low in the rear cockpit offered some visibility downward. A small baggage bin in the turtle-back section behind rear cockpit had allowance for up to 44 lbs.; two parachutes at 20 lbs. each, when carried, were part of the baggage allowance. The semi-cantilever wing framework was built up of heavy spruce spar beams with spruce and plywood truss-type wing ribs; the leading edges were covered with dural metal sheet and the completed framework was covered with fabric. The broad wing in two sections, was mounted approx. on the fuselage center-line, braced on upper and lower sides to steel tube cabanes with heavy streamlined steel wire. Two fuel tanks

were mounted in the root ends of each wing-half; the wing was streamlined into the fuselage junction by large metal wing-root fairings. The long-leg landing gear which fastened to the front spar mount and lower cabane, used "Aerol" shock absorbing struts; wheels were 24x4 or 26x4 and Bendix brakes were standard equipment. The unusual wheel fairings were built-up wooden assemblies that were covered with heavy doped fabric; although vulnerable to damage they were quite effective. A pair of 6.50x10 low pressure semi-airwheels with brakes were optional; in this case, the wheel fairings would not be used. The fabric covered tail-group was built up of welded steel tubing; the fin was ground adjustable and the horizontal stabilizer was adjustable in flight. A metal propeller, Eclipse hand-crank engine starter, wheel brakes, speed-ring engine cowl, dual controls, fire extinguisher, and first-aid kit were standard equipment. Navigation lights, a battery, Heywood engine starter, tail wheel, and extra instruments were optional. The next development in the Emsco "Mid-Wing Sport" series was the model B-7-C as described in the chapter for ATC # 424 of this volume.

Listed below is the only known entry for the Wright-powered model B-7:

NC-869N; Model B-7 (# 1) Wright R-540

As X-869N, ser. # 1 was first built up into model B-7 from an existing model B-4 airframe.

A.T.C. # 404
(3-7-31)
GEE BEE "SPORTSTER", D

Fig. 8. Gee Bee "Sportster" model D with 4 cyl. Menasco engine.

The Gee Bee "Sportster D" was another in a series of small high performance single-seaters, designed especially for the sportsman-pilot, a craft with but a singular purpose; a craft that came to life and flew just for him only. Together they would scoot merrily above the patchwork landscape as one, together they shared the pleasures, forging an intimate bond of understanding that soon flowered into mutual admiration. The Gee Bee "Sportster" was a mechanical contrivance, but we doubt if many pilots thought of it as such. Fashioned around a versatile basic airframe that could be fitted with various air-cooled inline or small radial engines, Gee Bee had an interesting selection of "Sportster" models to choose from. The "Sportster" model D, as shown, was no doubt the swiftest and the most capable of the bunch. Saucy, squat, and stubby, in a rather pleasing combination, it seemed ever eager to answer to the varied whims of the pilot. Be it on errand or just to some cloud-specked rendezvous, there they could communicate, and better appreciate the wonders of care-free flight. It mattered not whether a pilot flew it low, fast, and hard, or upside down, on end, or straight down, the "Sportster" always responded as if with glee. Strong of frame, strong of heart, and blessed with a very playful nature, the little "Sportster" was best described as an even match for the pilot who measured up to similar qualifications. There isn't any doubt that the single-seated Gee Bee was the very kind of airplane that hundreds of pilots often dreamed about, be-

cause it always attracted a swarm of interested onlookers wherever it went. Even as it sat, it fairly radiated fun and high adventure, but it was not the airplane many pilots could afford to own at this time. Candidly speaking, there's not much one could do with a Gee Bee "Sportster" but fly it and enjoy it. Comparatively rare because of the small number built, the Gee Bee "Sportster" series nevertheless sped their wings across a big chunk of sky to leave a trail of records in the record books. They also left a trail of fond and exciting memories in the hearts and minds of airmen who saw it or flew it.

The Gee Bee "Sportster" model D was a single-seated low winged wire-braced monoplane arranged specifically for the sporting pilot; it was well capable of fast cross-country trips to points at least 500 miles apart, or acrobatic nip-ups over the home-port for all to see. Because of its relatively high speed on nominal power, the "Sportster D" was a natural for closed-course air racing around the pylons, and it was just about the fastest stock airplane in its horsepower class. At the National Air Races for 1931 held at Cleveland, Ohio, Robert Hall flew the "Model D" to first place in the men's 400 cu. in. class, averaging over 128 m.p.h. In the men's race for the 650 cu. in. class, Lowell Bayles flew the same ship to 4th place. Mae Haizlip flew the "Sportster D" in the woman's 510 cu. in. class race to a very close second place at better than 1 29 m.p.h. Going all out in the woman's 650 cu. in. race, Mae Haizlip hustled to finish 2nd

Fig. 9. Racy lines of "Gee Bee D" devoted to speed-sport flying.

at nearly 132 m.p.h. Flashing around the pylons was great fun for this little craft, and its 4 cyl. Menasco C4-125 engine barked a strong tune as it joined in the fun. During the National Air Races for 1932, Wm. Rausch flew the "Sportster" D in the Leeds Trophy Race from New York to Cleveland, finishing 9th place in total points. In the Sohio Mystery Derby, Div. 2, Rausch finished 7th. Although often used for air-racing, more for the fun than the profit, the "Model D" was not basically a racing airplane; its prime stock in trade was its relatively high all-round performance. Climbing out of a field like a homesick angel, it could be at 12,000 ft. in 10 minutes; its excellent maneuverability could seduce the heart of a pilot in 5 minutes, and even at normal cruising speed, it could fly over 2 miles of scenery in much less than a minute. Powered with the 4 cyl. inverted Menasco "Pirate" C4-125 engine of 125 h.p., the "Model D" could easily have been the star of the Gee Bee "Sportster" lineup; it had the qualifications to swing it, but time and circumstance paid no heed to its future. Under the more favorable circumstances of another time, the playful "Sportster" could have graced the skies in good number, instead of the pitifully small number that were actually built. The type certificate number for the "Sportster" model D was issued 3-7-31; records indicate that only one example of this model was built by Granville Bros. Aircraft, Inc. on Springfield Airport in Springfield, Mass. "Gee Bee" airplanes had their big day at the National Air Races for 1931 when the barrel-shaped "Model Z" captured the famous Thompson Trophy Race; the chain of events that followed in the history of Granville Bros. Aircraft, saw the development of the most daring designs the air-racing fraternity had ever seen.

Listed below are specifications and performance data for the Gee Bee "Sportster" model D

as powered with the 125 h.p. Menasco "Pirate" C4 engine; length overall 17'3"; height overall 6'0"; wing span 25'0"; max. chord at root 52"; total wing area 95 sq.ft.; airfoil (NACA) M-6; wt. empty 922 lbs.; useful load 480 lbs.; payload with 37 gal. fuel 235 lbs. (pilot at 170 lbs. & 65 lbs. for parachute & baggage); gross wt. 1402 lbs.; max. speed 155; cruising speed 134; landing speed 53; climb 1550 ft. first min. at sea level; climb in 10 min. was 12,000 ft.; ceiling 20,000 ft.; gas cap. 37 gal.; oil cap. 3 gal.; cruising range at 7.5 gal. per hour 600 miles; price $4980. at factory field. The Menasco "Pirate" C4-125 engine was rated 125 h.p. at 2175 r.p.m., price was $1860.

The construction details and general arrangement of the "Sportster" model D was typical to that of the model E as described in the chapter for ATC # 398 of U.S. CIVIL AIRCRAFT, Vol. 4. The inverted Menasco engine installation in the model D was neatly cowled in, with internal baffles and cowling louvers to control the cooling airflow. A fuel tank mounted in each side of the stub-wing, fed fuel to a small gravity-feed tank mounted high in the fuselage by a hand-operated wobble pump. The carburetor and fuel line system were adapted to feed fuel properly even during inverted flight. A baggage compartment of 2 cu. ft. capacity, located just behind the firewall, had allowance for 35 lbs. The roomy cockpit was well protected by a large windshield, and a drop-down cowling panel offered easy step-over entry from the wing-walk. The interior was detailed with rich, durable upholstery, and several handy pockets for gloves, log-books, maps, etc. The fully streamlined landing gear of 62 in. tread used 20x9 low pressure "airwheels" and brakes were standard equipment. A metal propeller, navigation lights, and wheel pants were also standard equipment. An air-operated Heywood engine starter was optional. The horizontal stabilizer was adjustable

Fig. 10. Sportster D was familiar sight at the air races.

on ground only, so initial trim was selected by trial; longitudinal trim in flight was corrected by a bungee-cord adjustment on the joy-stick. Nine coats of Berryloid pigmented dope was applied in a choice of several two-tone colors; the familiar scalloped design was in the darker colors.

Listed below is the only known example of the "Sportster" model D:

NC-11043; Model D (# D-1) Menasco C4-125.

A.T.C. # 405
(3-17-31)
BUHL "BULL PUP", LA-1

Fig. 11. Buhl "Bull Pup" shown here during 1931 National Air Tour.

The big, stately Buhl "Airsedan" was well known about the country, establishing an enviable record for high-caliber performance, and exceptional reliability. Concentrating on these big cabin sesqui-planes for the past four years, it is hard to comprehend that an unusual little airplane such as the "Flying Bull Pup" had come from the same factory. As the market for the "Airsedan" type had already dwindled away to nothing, Buhl Aircraft was forced to come up with something soon, in order to stay in business. A careful study of the marketing trend pointed to only one practical alternative for Buhl, and that was to build a small light airplane for the growing band of flivver-plane enthusiasts. Sparked into action by the diversified talents of Etienne Dormoy, who always had something new up his sleeve, design discussions finally led to the development of a small single-seated monoplane. So, added now to the snow-balling flivver-plane movement was the Buhl "Flying Bull Pup", a distinctive shoulder-wing design developed primarily for sport flying. The maiden flight for the production prototype was on Jan. 7 of 1931. Formally introduced at the Detroit Air Show for 1931, the little monoplane created quite a stir at the exhibition and in the enthusiasm, some 290 orders were received during the week-long showing. With quantity production launched in April of 1931, fifty of the "Bull Pup" were built going into June. With a price-tag of $1250. at the factory, and also available on a $500.00 down payment with balance paid off in one year, the "Bull Pup" continued to sell fairly well into the year. A strong sales organization dotted the country, and many dealers bought them by the carload. Being a single-seated airplane, the

"Bull Pup" had its limitations of course, but that didn't seem to dampen the enthusiasm of those who owned and flew it. For economical flying to "build up time" or just for the sheer sport of it, the handsome "Pup" seemed to be the answer to many wishes. Finally built in over 100 examples into 1932, the steady pinch of the economic depression was making it almost impractical to continue production. In the ensuing years many of the "Bull Pup" had to be sidelined for one reason or another, but even at that more than 50 were still flying actively in 1939.

The experimental prototype "Flying Bull Pup" of 1930, which made its first-flight in October, was built along conventional construction principles with a fabric-covered welded steel tube fuselage; it was soon decided to use the all-metal semi-monocoque type of construction. This because of new fabricating methods developed at the Buhl Stamping works, which would actually speed up the production. Early tests had proven that the oval all-metal fuselage would "oil-can" under severe load, so Dormoy turned to his old friend Alfred Verville for help. Verville suggested the external longerons, a simple add-on which solved the ticklish problem. Meeting the need handsomely for this type of airplane the "Bull Pup" sold well through 1931, but orders were dwindling away by 1932. By year's end of 1932, Buhl Aircraft was slipping gradually, had already discontinued the "Pup", and was practically out of business. The development of a small two-place monoplane, a larger sport-type monoplane called the "Airster", and a two-place "pusher-type" autogiro had taken added toll financially, so Buhl was forced to some drastic measures. A year-end clearance

Fig. 12. Test pilot Jimmy Johnson flew prototype LA-1 on Jan. 1931.

sale offered new "Bull Pup" assemblies and parts, new Szekely engines and parts, raw materials, hardware stock and accessories, up to 50 per cent off list price. Bolstered temporarily by this added income Buhl hung on a while longer, but by September of 1933, after being in receivership since February, the entire inventory was up for sale. This now included various assembled and unassembled aircraft, new Szekely engines and parts, hardware stock and accessories, misc. raw materials, hand tools, machinery, and also the manufacturing rights to any or all of the Buhl airplane designs. Offered at 75 per cent below market value, this was indeed quite a bargain offering, but the crowds were not rushing in to buy. Eventually, most of this was sold off and Buhl Aircraft just slipped off quietly into the murk of past history. By 1934 a good used "Bull Pup" was selling from about $300. up to $500. at most, surely a graphic illustration of what was happening to the airplane market and aviation in general.

Differing from the rest in the light-plane field, the Buhl "Bull Pup" model LA-1 was a small shoulder-wing monoplane with seating only for one. Seated in an open cockpit amid the mountings of a wire-braced wing, the pilot had it all to himself. Flying alone, especially in an airplane that was limited to seating one, was a special kind of feeling, and to the "Bull Pup" pilot it was like sitting on top of the world. Powered with the 3 cyl. Szekely SR-3-0 engine of 45 h.p., the "Pup" had just about as much flash and dash as it was possible to muster with this amount of power. Light, deft, and dainty, the "Bull Pup" was a spritely vehicle and literally reveled under the guidance of a playful mood. Most of the "Pups" were privately owned and flown for sport, but several were on the flight-line of flying-schools for those students that were building up cheap solo-time. Early in the program the "Bull Pup" was offered with wings of optional area; small clipped-wings were for racing and sport, large-area wings for the high-altitude country, and standard size

wings for average flying in just about any part of the country. Except for an example or two, most of the "Bull Pups" were fitted with the standard (30 ft.) wings. The versatile LA-1 sometimes operated on skis, and a seaplane with twin-float gear was also available. In "dead-stick" landing contests during the National Air Races for 1931, Art Davis had captured first prize with a "Bull Pup" on one day, and Mrs. Art Davis captured second places on 3 different days; proving no less the predictable handling characteristics of this little airplane. Light and snappy with precise response, the "Bull Pup" had a rather infectious nature that created satisfied ownership and many thousands of happy flying hours. Several have been restored to flying condition in recent years, and the pilots are having a ball. The type certificate number for the "Bull Pup" model LA-1 series was issued 3-17-31 and at least 100 examples of this model were manufactured by the Buhl Aircraft Co. at Marysville, Mich. Lawrence D. Buhl was president; Etienne Dormoy was chief engineer; Cliff Jackson was asst. engineer; W. U. Shaw and John Easton were project engineers, and John O'Brien was general manager.

Listed below are specifications and performance data for the "Bull Pup" model LA-1 and LA-1A as powered with the 45 h.p. Szekely engine; length overall 19'0"; height overall 6'3"; wing span 30'0"; wing chord 55"; total wing area 122 sq.ft.; airfoil (NACA) M-12; wt. empty 550 lbs.; useful load 292 lbs.; crew wt. and payload with 10 gal. fuel 220 lbs. (pilot at 170 lb., 30 lb. baggage, 20 lb. parachute); gross wt. 842 lbs.; max. speed 95; cruising speed 80; landing speed 35; climb 800 ft. first min. at sea level; ceiling 14,000 ft.; gas cap. 10 gal.; oil cap. 6 qts.; cruising range at 3 gal. per hour 240 miles; price $1250. at factory field. Figures for LA-1B are typical except for the following; wt. empty 569 lbs.; useful load 281 lbs.; crew wt. and payload with 10 gal. fuel 209 lbs. (pilot at 170 lb., 19 lb. baggage, 20 lbs. for parachute); gross wt. 850 lbs.; oil cap. 7 qts.; no changes in perform-

Fig. 13. Trim lines of "Bull Pup" reveal reason for good performance.

Fig. 14. Striking view shows details of assembly.

ance figures. Twin-float seaplane in models LA-1S, LA-1SA, LA-1SB, eligible at 882 lbs. gross wt.; baggage allowance held to 10 lbs.; due to extra drag and weight of seaplane gear, performance figures would be slightly less than shown for landplane.

The ovoid semi-monocoque fuselage was built up of a riveted duralumin framework covered with formed sections of dural metal sheet. The pilot's cockpit was placed amidship between the wing spars for unlimited vision around and overhead, but much of the vision was restricted downward. Entry to the open cockpit, by clambering up and onto the wing, required a certain routine of practiced gymnastics, but hardly anyone complained about this. The small baggage bin was directly behind the seat. The fuel tank was mounted high in the fuselage just ahead of the cockpit; a "bobber-gauge" showed fuel content. The wing framework in two halves, was built up of solid spruce spar beams with spruce and plywood truss-type wing ribs; the leading edges were covered with dural metal sheet, and the completed framework was covered in fabric. Ailerons were of riveted duralumin construction, and covered with dural metal sheet. The wings, rigged to 3½ deg. of dihedral, were wire-braced to the apex of a steel tube cabane atop the fuselage on the upper side, and to the lower fuselage fitting on the underside. Bracing wires were of streamlined section, and of fairly heavy gauge. The long-legged landing gear used oleo-spring shock absorbing struts; taxiing loads were snubbed by several loops of rubber shock-cord. Tail skid was of the steel spring-leaf type. Low pressure Goodyear "airwheels" were 16x7-3 and wheel brakes were optional. As a seaplane the "Bull Pup" used Warner A-1680-B metal

floats; floats for the "Pup" weighed about 80 lbs., but weight of landing gear removed was deductable from that. Skis were often used for flying in winter. The fabric covered tail-group, with exception of the vertical fin, was built up of welded 1025 steel tubing; the horizontal stabilizer was adjusted for load trim on ground only. The vertical fin was a riveted duralumin framework covered with dural metal sheet, and built up as an integral part of the fuselage. A wooden Flottorp propeller, and Goodyear airwheels were standard equipment; wheel brakes were optional.

Listed below are Buhl "Bull Pup" entries as gleaned from registration records:

X-8459;	Buhl LA	(# 1)	Aeronca 26.
X-8460;	″	(# 2)	Szekely 45.
X-8461;	″	(# 3)	″
NC-11160;	Buhl LA-1	(# 101)	″
NC-11161;	″	(# 102)	″
NC-11162;	″	(# 103)	″
NC-316Y;	″	(# 104)	″

Serial # 1-2-3 were experimental prototypes; NC-317Y was ser. # 105 and numbers ran consecutively to NC-325Y which was ser. # 113; no listing for ser. # 114; NC-326Y was ser. # 115 and numbers ran consecutively to NC-368Y which was ser. # 157; no listing for ser. # 158; NC-370Y was ser. # 159 and numbers ran consecutively to NC-399Y which was ser. # 188; NC-12100 was ser. # 189 and numbers ran consecutively to NC-12111 which was ser. # 200; reg. no for ser. # 111, 160, 179, 186, 190, 194 unverified; X-12112 was Buhl LA-2 (# 201) with 4 cyl. Menasco engine; this approval for landplane ser. # 101 and up; this approval also for seaplane ser. # 113 and up; approval for "Bull Pup" manufacture expired 7-1-32.

A.T.C. # 406
(3-23-31)
C-W TRAVEL AIR, MODEL 12-K

Fig. 15. Curtiss-Wright model 12-K with 5 cyl. Kinner B5 engine.

For those that would prefer the new Model 12 "Sport Trainer" with an American "radial type" engine, instead of the inline Wright "Gipsy" as on the Model 12-Q, Curtiss-Wright offered the "Travel Air" model 12-K. This a spritely version that was powered with the 5 cyl. Kinner B5 engine of 125 h.p. Although typical in all respects from the firewall to the tail-post, the 12-K was altered a good deal by the Kinner engine, both in its appearance and behavior, with a noticeable increase in all-round performance. For some reason this particular version, although not especially unpopular in any sense, did not sell well; perhaps the $788.00 increase in delivered price was too steep to offset the slight gain there was in performance. What extras the model 12-K did have to offer were not really attractive nor necessary to the flying-school operator, and it is doubtfull if the average owner-pilot who flew just for sport, would care to go the extra expense. Then too, several other manufacturers were under-selling Curtiss-Wright with craft offering comparable or even much more value. The prospective buyer who could really afford to buy an airplane was something special during these times; he definitely could be very choosy about how he parted with his money. These grim hard facts, as unkind as they may seem to be, had ruined the future for many fine airplanes, and were the undeniable risks for manufacturers during these pinch-penny times. But, even

despite this sad-sounding note of truth, the Model 12-K was introduced as an interesting addition to this line of sport-craft, and is perhaps remembered well by those who had a chance to fly it.

Introduced closely onto the heels of the sassy 12-Q, the model 12-K was also an open cockpit biplane seating two in tandem, and was typical in all respects except for its engine installation. Because of the vast difference in the configuration of engines, the 12-K was altered somewhat in front, but otherwise, shared all the proportion and good features inherent to this basic design. Powered with the 5 cyl. Kinner B5 engine of 125 h.p., the extra horsepower translated easily into more of the get-up-and-go, a quickly noticeable increase throughout the whole performance range. With flight characteristics closely comparable to the other two models in this series, the 12-K was perhaps the more capable and the more responsive; it was probably a more suitable match for the rough and tumble type sportsman. The type certificate number for the Model 12-K was issued 3-23-31 and at least 2 examples of this model were built by the Travel Air Div. at Wichita, Kans. The Curtiss-Wright Airplane Co. at Robertson (St. Louis), Mo. was the parent company and handled all sales for "Travel Air" airplanes. Walter H. Beech was president; Ralph S. Damon was V.P. and general manager; Herb Rawdon and Ted Wells were project engineers for the "Travel Air" biplane development; H. Lloyd Child was test-pilot and chief engineer at St. Louis.

Listed below are specifications and performance data for the model 12-K "Sport Trainer" as powered with the 125 h.p. Kinner B5 engine; length overall 20'7"; height overall 8'10"; wing span upper 28'10"; wing span lower 26'4"; wing chord upper and lower 48"; wing area upper 113.4 sq.ft.; wing area lower 93 sq.ft.; total wing area 206.4 sq.ft.; airfoil Clark Y-15; wt. empty 1164 lbs.; useful load 636 lbs.; payload with 33 gal. fuel 238 lbs. (1 pass. at 170 lb. & 68 lb. baggage); gross wt. 1800 lb.; max. speed 112; cruising speed 95; landing speed 45; climb 800 ft. first min. at sea level; average take-off run 300-350 ft.; ceiling 14,000 ft.; gas cap. 33 gal.; oil cap. 4 gal.; cruising range at 7.2 gal. per hour 420 miles; price $4288. at factory field. As first tested in prototype with 100 h.p. Kinner engine, performance figures of the 12-K would be proportionately less.

The fuselage framework was built up of welded chrome-moly steel tubing in rigid truss form, faired to shape with wooden formers and metal fairing strips, then fabric covered. The cockpits were deep, roomy, and well protected by large windshields; dual controls were provided and the baggage compartment had allowance for 68 lbs. Two parachutes at 20 lbs. each, when carried, were part of the baggage allowance. The thick, robust wing panels were built up of solid (laminated) spruce spar beams with spruce and plywood girder-type wing ribs; the leading edges were covered with dural metal sheet, and the completed framework was covered in fabric. Ailerons of the Friese-type were in the upper wing panels only, actuated by a streamlined push-pull strut; the fuel tank was mounted in the center-section panel of the upper wing. The split-axle landing gear of 76 in. tread used oleo-spring shock absorbing struts and Zerk grease fittings were used at all points of wear; 6.50x10 semi-airwheels with brakes were standard equipment. Brake pedals were in the rear cockpit only, but brake pedals were available in the front cockpit for $50.00 extra. The rubber-snubbed tail skid swiveled through a limited arc for better ground handling. The fabric covered tail-group was built up of welded steel tubing and steel channel sections; the rudder had aerodynamic "balance", the fin was ground adjustable and the horizontal stabilizer was adjustable in flight. A wooden propeller, 6.50x10 semi-airwheels with brakes, dual controls, wiring for navigation lights, tail skid, a battery, and electric engine starter were standard equipment. A metal propeller for $200.00, extra brake pedals for $50.00, engine cover for $8.00, cockpit cover for $8.00, streamlined fairing for head-rest at $12.00, and two-tone color schemes other than standard were $50.00 extra. These details and arrangement, except where noted, apply to all 3 models in the 12-series. The next development in this series was the Model 12-W as described in the chapter for ATC # 407 of this volume.

Listed below are Model 12-K entries as gleaned from registration records:
NC-437W; Model 12-K (# 12K-2003) Kinner B5.
NC-445W;   "   (# 12K-2011)   "

C-W TRAVEL AIR, MODEL 12-W

Fig. 16. Curtiss-Wright model 12-W with 7 cyl. Warner "Scarab" engine.

As the third successive version in the Curtiss-Wright "Sport Trainer" 12-series, the Model 12-W was quite lady-like and definitely more on the deluxe side. Specifically, it incorporated features to make it somewhat more attractive to the sportsman-pilot and his particular needs, or as a good means of cheap travel and promotion for men of business. Because of its smaller diameter, the Warner "Scarab" engine was suitable for cowling-in, so it was shrouded with a deep-chord Curtiss-Wright version of the efficient NACA low-drag fairing; rounded out to blend in with the diameter up front, the fuselage now presented the look of fuller appearance. This combination of cowling and fairing promoted better airflow, so a small gain in speed was realized along with the better appearance. Some of the accessories and a few appointments that were optional extras on the two previous sport-trainer versions, were now standard equipment on the model 12-W. Proud to be a part of this particular combination, Warner Motors was one of the first to purchase the 12-W for promotion; one other was used for general-service by the Connecticut Dept. of Aero. Others were scattered about the country in service with private owners, generally for sport-type flying. Powered with the ever-popular Warner "Scarab" engine, the model 12-W enjoyed a good span of longevity, and several were still active 10 and 15 years later. Because of its responsive maneuverability and

particularly robust construction, the model 12-W was eligible for acrobatic training in the secondary stage of the Civilian Pilot Training Program. Had the price been more competitive during these tight-money times of the early thirties, it is very likely the model 12-W would have sold much better than it did, and would have been seen more often in far greater numbers.

The model 12-W was also a small open cockpit biplane with seating for two in tandem. It was basically similar to the two previous versions of the "Sport Trainer" except for its front-end modification that was more or less dictated by installation of the Warner engine. Quite presentable in its appearance, an appearance that now tended to be a good bit more feminine, the 12-W was always a lady and a particularly good choice for the average sportsman. Powered with the spunky 7 cyl. Warner "Scarab" engine of 110-125 h.p., the 12-W was able to kick out its heels in rather spritely performance, and the improved streamlines offered by the cowled engine added considerably to the available speed. Somewhat heavy for a ship of this size, any of the model 12 certainly had no tendency to float, but power was comfortably ample and flight characteristics were more like that of a bigger airplane. Responding well, reasonably stable, with good measure of performance, the 12-W was a finer example of the small sport-type biplane. The type certificate number for the

*Fig. 17. Model 12-W about to embark on
training flight.*

*Fig. 18. "Travel Air" lineage just faintly shows
through in this view of 12-W.*

model 12-W was issued 3-23-31 and some 12 or
more examples of this model were manufactured by the Travel Air Div. of the Curtiss-
Wright Airplane Co. at Wichita, Kans.

Listed below are specifications and performance data for the model 12-W "Sport Trainer"
as powered with the 110 h.p. Warner "Scarab"
engine; length overall 20'10"; height overall
8'10"; wing span upper 28'10"; wing span
lower 26'4"; wing chord upper and lower 48";
wing area upper 113.4 sq.ft.; wing area lower
93 sq.ft.; total wing area 206.4 sq.ft.; airfoil
Clark Y-15; wt. empty 1186 lbs.; useful load
614 lbs.; payload with 33 gal. fuel 216 lbs. (1
pass. at 170 lb. & 46 lb. baggage); gross wt.
1800 lbs.; max. speed 117; cruising speed 99;
landing speed 45; average take-off run 350-400
ft.; climb 780 ft. first min. at sea level; ceiling
15,000 ft.; gas cap. 33 gal.; oil cap. 4 gal.; cruising range at 6.5 gal. per hour 480 miles; price
$4455. at factory field.

Construction details and general arrangement
of the model 12-W was typical to that of the 12-K
as described in the chapter for ATC # 406 of
this volume. Standard equipment for the model
12-W included a wooden propeller, NACA-type
engine cowling, Eclipse electric engine starter,
a battery, 6.50x10 semi-airwheels with brakes,
brake pedals in rear cockpit only, dual controls,
head-rest fairing for rear cockpit, Travel Air
"Hydra-Flex" shock absorbing struts in landing
gear, 33 gal. fuel tank in center-section panel of
upper wing, large windshields, wiring for navigation lights, steerable tail skid, and a compass.
The following was available as optional equipment; brake pedals in front cockpit for $50.00,
metal panel cover for front cockpit, metal propeller for $200.00, steerable tail wheel, engine
cover for $8.00, cockpit cover for $8.00, and two-
tone colors other than standard were $50.00 ex-
tra. Aerodynamic geometry typical of all 3 models in the 12-series, included angle of incidence
none, interplane stagger was 28 in. positive, and
dihedral was 1½ degrees. The next development
in the Curtiss-Wright "Travel Air" series was
the model 16-K biplane as described in the chapter for ATC # 411 of this volume.

Listed below are model 12-W entries as
gleaned from registration records:

NC-434W; Model 12-W (12W-2002) Warner 110.
NC-493W;   "   (12W-2012)   "
NC-494W;   "   (12W-2013)   "
NC-410W;   "   (12W-2014)   "
NC-411W;   "   (12W-2015)   "
NC-412W;   "   (12W-2016)   "
NC-413W;   "   (12W-2017)   "
NC-408W;   "   (12W-2018)   "
NC-11700;   "   (12W-2019)   "
NC-11701;   "   (12W-2020)   "
NC-11815;   "   (12W-2040)   "
NC-11716;   "   (12W-2041)   "

Serial # -2020 also as NS-11701 with Conn.
Dept. of Aero.; ser. #-2017 in Alaska 1933; some
early 12-Q were later modified to 12-W; approval expired 4-26-37.

A.T.C. # 408
(3-27-31)
FAIRCHILD 22, MODEL C-7

Fig. 19. Fairchild 22 model C-7 with 75 h.p. Rover engine.

In the development of a new line of sport-trainer airplanes for 1930-31, Kreider-Reisner abandoned the standard open biplane configuration, and patterned a new craft in the increasingly popular "parasol" monoplane form. The plan to market an airplane that would be cheaper to build and to buy, dictated the design of a simpler, more efficient machine. This was to be a practical machine that could be produced quicker and easier, yet give the owner-pilot a comparatively good performing airplane with the best in dollar value. There are a lot of known and unknown factors as to what actually motivates people to buy a certain type airplane; it seemed that in their new Model 22, Kreider-Reisner (Fairchild) was happily on the right track, for a few years at least. Based on the theory that more customers would prefer to sacrifice some performance in the interests of greater operating economy, and thereby more flying time per dollar, Kreider-Reisner introduced their first Model 22 (C-7) with the 75 h.p. Michigan-Rover engine. The combination was a relatively sound formula and many interested inquiries soon turned into a handfull of orders, which was a happy circumstance in view of the slowly sagging market. Primarily an all-purpose sport plane for the average private-owner, the "Twenty Two" model C-7 also helped to revive the floundering business at some of the flight training schools.

As pictured here in the earliest prototype example (X-783W), the new model C-7 was powered for initial tests with the 80 h.p. A-S

"Genet" engine; by virtue of its low rounded tail and "radial" engine installation, it certainly presented a profile quite different from later production models. Perhaps for various reasons, some obvious and some not, the 5 cyl. "Genet" was not retained to power this new concept; a later development of this same airplane (also shown) now mounted the slender inline "Rover" engine, and the tail-group was modified to a more pleasant and efficient profile. At last in a rather happy combination that was just about right from any point of view, the Model 22 was certainly trim and rather girlish; from the outset it managed to pose prettily to catch the eye and fancy of flying-folk everywhere. For those that would prefer a little more pepper in the performance, and were willing to pay extra for it, Kreider-Reisner was soon developing some sportier versions of the "Twenty Two" with more horsepower.

Marketed by Fairchild Sales as the Model 22, the Kreider-Reisner model C-7 was a light parasol-type monoplane with seating for two in tandem. Arranged in a proportion that was mechanically practical as well as efficient, the trim C-7 was also one of the more handsome airplanes of this type. With the slender wing perched high above the fuselage, visibility was very good in most any direction, and movements into or around the airplane were quite handy and uncomplicated. Appointments and equipment included were consistent with requirements for the typical economy sport-plane, or perhaps a little better. Powered with the 4 cyl. inverted

Fig. 20. Louis Reisner and Sherman Fairchild discuss trim lines of model C-7.

inline "Rover" L-267 engine of 75 h.p., the C-7 offered a fairly lively performance that was more than ample for pilot-training, or just flying for fun. Pleasantly stable and responsive, the C-7 demonstrated inherent talents that could be easily brought to the fore with just a little more power. This particular version (C-7), although not numerous, remained quite popular and was in active service for a good many years. The type certificate number for the model 22-C7 was issued 3-27-31 and some 12 examples of this model were manufactured by Kreider-Reisner Aircraft Co., Inc.; a division of the Fairchild Aviation Corp. at Hagerstown, Md.

Listed below are specifications and performance data for the Fairchild 22 model C-7 as powered with the 75 h.p. Rover engine; length overall 22'0"; height overall 8'0"; wing span 32'10"; wing chord 66"; total wing area 170 sq.ft.; airfoil (NACA) N-22; wt. empty 870 lbs.; useful load 530 lbs.; payload with 21 gal. fuel 218 lbs.; gross wt. 1400 lbs.; max. speed 107; cruising speed 90; landing speed 43; climb 650 ft. first min. at sea level; ceiling 10,000 ft.; gas cap. 21 gal.; oil cap. 2 gal.; cruising range at 4.9 gal. per hour was 4 hours or 350 miles; following figures are for models with Rover rated at 78 h.p.

with metal propeller; wt. empty 902 lbs.; useful load 507 lbs.; payload with 21 gal. fuel 196 lbs.; baggage allowance 16 lbs.; gross wt. 1409 lbs.; all other figures more or less the same; price $2675. at factory. The Rover L-267 engine was rated 75 h.p. at 1975 r.p.m., and 78 h.p. at 2000 r.p.m.

The fuselage framework was built up of welded chrome-moly steel tubing in a combination of round and square section to make up better welded joints; the framework was heavily faired to a near-oval shape, then covered in fabric. Cockpits of 27x32 in. dimension were well protected and roomy, with parachute-type bucket seats; dual joy-stick controls were provided. Cockpit heaters were optional. The fuel tank of 21 gal. capacity was mounted high in the fuselage just ahead of the front cockpit; a direct-reading float-type gauge projected through the cowling. The parasol-type wing was perched high above the fuselage atop a splayed out cabane of streamlined steel tube struts, and braced to the fuselage by a vee of heavy-gauge streamlined steel tubes. Available as a one-piece or a two-piece unit, the wing framework was built up of laminated spruce spars fashioned to an I-beam section with spruce and plywood

Fig. 21. Fairchild 22 prototype first had 5 cyl. "Genet" engine.

Fig. 22. Parasol configuration of 22-C7 provided stable flight and excellent visibility.

wing ribs of Pratt truss form; the leading edges were covered with plywood sheet and the completed framework was covered in fabric. Full-span ailerons of narrow chord were entirely of riveted duralumin sheet construction. The one-piece wing was flat with no dihedral, and the two-piece wing was rigged with 1 or 1.5 deg. of dihedral. The sturdy outrigger landing gear of 91 ln. tread used oleo-spring shock absorbing struts; low pressure semi-airwheels were 6.50x10 equipped with brakes. The fabric covered tail-group, except for vertical fin, was built up of welded chrome-moly steel tubing; the horizontal stabilizer was adjustable in flight from either cockpit. The vertical fin was built up of wooden spars and ribs in a cantilever form to require no bracing. A wooden propeller, steel spring-leaf tail skid, Pyrene fire extinguisher, and a first-aid kit were standard equipment. A metal propeller, an 8x4 tail wheel, custom colors, and two-piece wings were optional. The next Fairchild development was the KR-135 sport biplane as described in the chapter for ATC

#415 also in this volume.

Listed below are Kreider-Reisner (Fairchild) model 22-C7 entries as gleaned from registration records:

NC-10760; Model C-7 (# 502) Rover 75.
NC-10774;   ”   (# 503)   ”
NC-10799;   ”   (# 504)   ”
      ;   ”   (# 505)   ”
NC-11606;   ”   (# 506)   ”
      ;   ”   (# 507)   ”
NC-11617;   ”   (# 508)   ”
NC-11618;   ”   (# 509)   ”
NC-11619;   ”   (# 510)   ”
NC-11620;   ”   (# 511)   ”
NC-11649;   ”   (# 512)   ”
NC-11650;   ”   (# 513)   ”

X-783W (probably ser. # 501) was prototype for C-7 series; reg. no. for ser. # 505 unknown; ser. # 506 modified into prototype for model C-7-A; ser. # 507 not listed, could be NC-11616; reg. no. for ser. # 510 unverified; ser. # 511 modified to C-7-A; this approval for ser. # 502 and up; approval for model C-7 expired 9-30-39.

Fig. 23. Head-on view of 22-C7 shows slender nose and wide landing gear.

Fig. 24. Neat installation of "Rover" engine offered ease of service.

A.T.C. # 409
(3-30-31)
FORD "TRI-MOTOR," 5-AT-D

Fig. 25. 5-AT-D preparing to load; note wing bins for mail and cargo.

Offhand and by casual glance it would appear that the new tri-motored 5-AT-D was little changed from that of its earlier sister-ships, but actually, the changes and improvements were quite numerous, and some were rather extensive. Perhaps the most significant change was a raising of the huge wing by 8 in. to create a deeper fuselage interior for more head-room when walking down the aisle. Because of this feature, the 5-AT-D was sometimes called the "high wing Ford." At this point, cabin interiors were progressively refined for more comfort, with decor of latest fashion; the "Club Model"

with its special convenience and rich appointments was the most elegant. Strangely enough, the first 4 of the 5-AT-D type were delivered to the Air Corps as the C-4A, to be used mostly as "command" transports. The first example for scheduled airline service went to NAT (National Air Transport) and another went to PAT (Pacific Air Transport), both lines receiving additional ships of this type within the year. The first "Club" model was delivered to the Dept. of Commerce for use by the Airways Div.; 3 other club models were built and one was later exported to China. The U. S. Navy and the

Fig. 26. Ford 5-AT-D on final assembly, behind it is rare 4-AT-F.

Fig. 27. 5-AT-D deluxe club-plane as delivered to
England.

Fig. 28. 5-AT-DS on Edo floats; operated in
Colombia, 1934.

Marine Corps each had one 5-AT-D where they were labeled the RR-5. The last example built of the 5-AT-D went to Pan American Airways, who then had two. Still "the queen of the airways" during this period, and a familiar sight where airliners gathered, the last of the Ford "Tri-Motor" flew majestically from coast to coast, but their days of reign were being numbered. By 1934 they were occasionally replaced by newer and faster twin-engined equipment, and some of the Fords began to slip off to foreign countries. One had gone to England, 3 had been shipped off to Colombia, and others that had been retired were taking up odd jobs here and there in the U.S. True-blue lady that she was, she gave way to progress graciously and quietly. For years the distinctive Ford "Tri-Motor" had played the part of a grand lady — the tall and buxom model 5-AT-D was perhaps the grandest of them all.

The Ford "Tri-Motor" model 5-AT-D was a high-winged all-metal cabin monoplane with seating arranged for 14 passengers and a crew of two. Interior appointments were quite pleasant and high-lighted in the latest fashion, with more efficient heating and ventilation to assure passenger comfort. Raising of the wing created more headroom in the cabin and promoted a feeling of spaciousness inside; truly the last word in airliner comfort and utility. Glistening in its polished aluminum skin, the Ford posed in a maternal beauty that instilled friendly confidence into passengers and pilots alike. Powered with 3 Pratt & Whitney "Wasp" engines of 420 h.p. each, the 5-AT-D only matched the earlier 5-AT-C (ATC # 165) in performance, but it did offer many other bonus values not found in the earlier 5-AT versions. Flight characteristics and general behavior were more or less comparable, with ability to operate well in and out of short fields. This feature was a blessing to operators that later used the Ford "Tri-Motor" for service in some of our neighboring countries. The type certificate number for the model 5-AT-D was issued 3-30-31 and 24 examples of this model were manufactured by the Stout Metal Airplane Div. of the Ford Motor Co. on Ford Airport in Dearborn, Mich.

Listed below are specifications and performance data for the Ford model 5-AT-D as powered with 3 "Wasp" engines of 420 h.p.

each; length overall 50'3"; height overall 12'8"; wing span 77'10"; wing chord at root 156"; wing chord at tip 92"; total wing area 835 sq. ft.' airfoil "Ford" # 2 (modified Goettingen); wt. empty 7840 (8320) lbs.; useful load 5660 (5680) lbs.; payload with 277 gal. fuel 3386 (3406) lbs. (14 passengers at 170 lb. each & 1006-1026 lbs. baggage-cargo); payload with 355 gal. fuel 2920 (2940) lbs. (14 passengers & 540-560 lbs. baggage-cargo); gross wt. 13,500 (14,000) lbs.; wts. in brackets are revised allowable wts.; max. speed (speed-ring cowlings on outboard engines) 150; cruising speed 122; landing speed 64; climb 1050 ft. first min. at sea level; climb to 8000 ft. in 10 min.; ceiling 18,050 ft.; gas cap. normal 277 gal.; gas cap. max. 355 gal.; oil cap. 34 gal.; cruising range at 66 gal. per hour 475-625 miles; price $50,000. at factory field.

The construction details and general arrangement of the model 5-AT-D were typical to that of the 5-AT-C as described in the chapter for ATC # 165 of U.S. CIVIL AIRCRAFT, Vol. 2. The following details pertain to the

Fig. 29. Interior view shows added head-room and
seating for eleven passengers.

Fig. 30. One of the last 5-AT-D, this example also exported to So. America.

5-AT-D, but in some cases were available also as modifications on earlier models. Internal structure was now coated with a zinc-chromate primer and sprayed with aluminized lacquer. The interior was sound-proofed, heavily insulated, and windows were one-piece panes of shatter-proof glass. Ventilation with individual preference adjustment was provided at each window, and cabin heaters were now more efficient and of higher capacity. The pilot's cabin was now closed off with a bulkhead door, and a console panel was equipped with latest pilot aids; some of the later versions had slanted windshields to eliminate night-time glare. Entry to the main cabin was by a large rectangular door, which was a distinguishing feature on the 5-AT-D. Previous Fords had the rounded entry door. Commercial models had speed-ring cowlings on the outboard engines, while the Army and Navy versions had "speed-rings" on all 3 engines. Metal bins in the wing, outboard from the engines, had allowance for 400 lbs. of baggage and cargo. The "Club" models all had large streamlined "wheel pants", and extensive landing gear fairing for an increase in speed; the standard models had only metal fenders to protect propellers from flying debris. The landing gear now employed large "Aerol" (air-oil) shock absorbing struts; wheels were 44x10 and Bendix brakes were standard equipment. Metal propellers, inertia-type engine starters, tail wheel, dual wheel controls, and navigation lights were also standard equipment. The next development in the tri-motor Ford was the model 13-A as described in the chapter for ATC # 431 of this volume.

Listed below are Ford model 5-AT-D entries as gleaned from registration records:

AC31-401;	5-AT-D	(# 5-AT-91)	3 Wasp 420.
AC31-402;	"	(# 5-AT-92)	"
AC31-403;	"	(# 5-AT-93)	"
AC31-404;	"	(# 5-AT-95)	"
NC-424H;	"	(# 5-AT-97)	"
NC-431H;	"	(# 5-AT-98)	"
NC-432H;	"	(# 5-AT-99)	"
NC-433H;	"	(# 5-AT-100)	"
NS-1:	"	(# 5-AT-101)	"
NC-435H;	"	(# 5-AT-102)	"
NC-436H;	"	(# 5-AT-103)	"
NC-437H;	"	(# 5-AT-104)	"
A-9205;	"	(# 5-AT-105)	"
NC-439H;	"	(# 5-AT-106)	"
NC-440H;	"	(# 5-AT-107)	"
NC-9653;	"	(# 5-AT-108)	"
NC-9654;	"	(# 5-AT-109)	"
NC-9655;	"	(# 5-AT-110)	"
NC-434H;	"	(# 5-AT-111)	"
NC-438H;	"	(# 5-AT-112)	"
A-9206:	"	(# 5-AT-113)	"
NC-9657;	"	(# 5-AT-114)	"
NC-9658;	"	(# 5-AT-115)	"
NC-9659;	"	(# 5-AT-116)	"

Serial # 91, 92, 93, 95, with Army Air Corps as C-4A; ser. # 99, 101, 107, 112, were "Club". models; ser. # 100 modified to model 13-A; ser. # 101 with Dept. of Commerce; ser. # 105 with Marine Corps as RR-5; ser. # 109 had geared "Wasp" engine in nose; ser. # 112 had modified vertical fin and rudder; ser. # 113 with U.S. Navy as RR-5; ser. # 114 later as (5-AT-DS) seaplane on Group 2-504; ser. # 116 was last Ford "Tri-Motor" built.

Fig. 31. Revealing view of PCA-2 "autogiro" with Wright R-975 engine. Giro used to cover special news events.

The "autogiro" was an exciting newcomer to the American skies; because of its "rotary wing", and the phenomenal things claimed and proven that it was able to do, it was about the most interesting development in aviation during 1930-31. Pitcairn, who possessed manufacturing and licensing rights for the revolutionary "whirly bird", spent a few years developing workable prototype models. They proudly announced their offering of a 3-place utility model for the commercial market in 1931. Because of the novelty of this type aircraft, with its terrific promotional value, large, well-known business-houses were the first to place orders. The "Detroit News", a newspaper long the champion for aviation, had distinction of buying the first commercial autogiro (a Pitcairn PCA-2) in this country; because of the autogiro's peculiar abilities, the "News" giro was used for difficult photowork and specialized news coverage. Other famous-name companies followed quickly with orders for the 3-place PCA-2. Such companies as Standard Oil of N.Y. (Socony), "Sealed Power" Piston Ring Co., the Champion Spark Plug Co., Beechnut Packing Co., and others were enjoying the benefits of its promotional value. One was delivered in Canada for specialized use on wheels or skis. The U.S. Navy bought a PCA-2 (XOP-1) early in 1931, and after

tests decided to order two more for use on aircraft carriers. The NACA also ordered one for test flying and research into flight with the rotary wing.

Because the "autogiro" was just now on the threshold of its life as a fully practical flying-machine in a new guise, it was only natural that pilots would try for records and other outstanding flights. Amelia Earhart, well-known and accomplished aviatrix, climbed high over Willow Grove, Pa. on 4-8-31 to set an altitude record of 18,415 ft., and then flew the "Beechnut" 'giro to a cross-country record. Capt. Lewis A. Yancey who flew a similar PCA-2 for Champion Spark Plug, later (9-25-32) raised the altitude record to 21,500 ft. over Boston, Mass. While on an extensive tour, Yancey demonstrated the autogiro's ability to operate from a confined area by landing and taking off from down among Yosemite Park's 3000 ft. cliffs, cliffs that frowned above the valley floor with menace on all sides. All companies that owned autogiros kept them on tour constantly in all parts of the country and even abroad; some went into Cuba, various parts of the Caribbean, into Yucatan and Mexico, with newspapers headlining their activities every day. With 20 or more of the model PCA-2 in constant service over varied terrain in climates of all kinds, it is commendable that the autogiro

Fig. 32. PCA-2 of Detroit News over crowd at Detroit City Airport.

proved itself so gallantly under the interested and watchful eyes of the whole world.

Juan de la Cierva's first theoretical conception of an aircraft with freely rotating wings was in 1920, when he became convinced that safety in flight must somehow be divorced from the necessity for continuous high speeds to maintain flight. After intensive study and experiments with models, the first full-sized "autogiro" was built in 1922 for study; this was followed early in 1923 by the first machine to fly under full control of the pilot. The first flight of the so-called "autogiro" on Jan. 17 of 1923 in Madrid, Spain was only a hop of some 200 yards, but it was an epochal triumph. After that first flight, experimental work was continued, and during the next 5 years some 70 machines had been built and flown, each incorporating some improvement or refinement of design. The first autogiro flight in America was on Dec. 19 of 1928, by now with a craft of practicability, but it still had to taxi around the field to gather proper rotating speed for its rotor blades. After development of a self-starter for the rotor blades, the giro could run up its rotor to proper r.p.m. while the engine was being warmed up. As full throttle was applied, the wheel brakes were released, and the giro would jump off into a 30 yard take-off with a very steep climb-out, even on a still day. Climbing quite rapidly at a rather steep angle, but with very low forward speed, the autogiro was thus able to operate out of areas generally forbidden to ordinary airplanes.

As a flying-machine, the "autogiro" differs basically from all other aircraft in the source of

its lifting capacity; the sustaining lift is created primarily by rotating "airfoiled" blades which take the place of a fixed wing or wings as in a normal airplane. There is no time when the supporting rotation of the blades can be stopped while the machine is in the air; their rotating motion is produced solely by an air pressure caused by movement of the 'giro in any direction, whether climbing, in level flight, in a normal glide, or a steep vertical descent. In this way, the supporting rotation of the blades is independent of the engine, whose sole function therefore is to propel the machine forward. The autogiro presented flying characteristics not heretofore achieved by normal aircraft; it could take off after a very short run, then immediately assume a steep climbing angle to clear obstacles. If need be, the autogiro could quickly check its forward speed and gently descend in front of any obstacle it could not clear. With power off and "stick" full back, the descent was about 15 ft. per second. In level flight it could fly along well over 100 m.p.h., and as slow as 25 m.p.h., or even brought to a standstill to hover for just a moment. It could bank and turn quite slowly without the fear for loss of forward speed, even with a dead engine. Nearly fool-proof as compared to an ordinary airplane with fixed wings, the autogiro generally could be flown with less instructing time and less operating skill, once the mechanics of this machine was understood.

The Pitcairn-Cierva model PCA-2 was the first autogiro approved by the government, a utility craft that seated 3 in open cockpits. The

Fig. 33. PCA-2 poking along at low level to attract attention; people ran out to watch "wind-mill" plane.

fuselage followed lines similar to that of a 3-seated airplane, but with a pylon structure in front to support the 45 ft. diameter rotor. A smáll fixed-wing added modestly to the lifting area, but was used primarily as a stabilizer and for attachment of the ailerons; this wing also provided a place to mount the unusually wide landing gear, and offered a convenient walk-way for occupants entering or leaving the cockpits. Powered with the 9 cyl. Wright R-975 engine of 300 h.p., the PCA-2 could clip along at speeds of nearly 120 m.p.h., or dilly-dally along at 25. It is understandable that an autogiro could be satisfactorily flown with minimum instruction or flying technique, but only a thorough understanding of the machine, and a superb handling technique could bring out all the amazing performance this craft was actually capable of. Modified slightly from the earlier PCA-1 version, the higher-powered PCA-2 was built in some 20 or more examples and nearly every one was a headliner at one time or another. The approved type certificate for the model PCA-2 was issued 4-2-31 and it was manufactured by the Pitcairn-Cierva Autogiro Co., a div. of Pitcairn Aviation, Inc. on Pitcairn Field in Willow Grove, Pa.

Listed below are specifications and performance data for the model PCA-2 as powered with the 300 h.p. Wright R-975 engine; fuselage length overall 23'1"; height overall (tail down) 13'0"; rotor dia. 45'0"; rotor blade chord 22'; rotor blade area 159.5 sq.ft.; fixed-wing span 30'0"; wing chord at root 52"; wing chord at tip 30"; fixed wing area 88 sq.ft.; wing airfoil (NACA) M-3 modified; wt. empty 2093 lbs.; useful load 907 lbs.; payload with 52 gal. fuel 375 lbs. (2 pass. at 170 lb. each & 35 lb. baggage); gross wt. 3000 lbs.; max. speed 118; cruising speed 98; landing speed 20-25; climb 800 ft. first min. at sea level; service ceiling 15,000 ft.; gas cap. 52 gal.; oil cap. 6.5 gal.; cruising range at 16 gal. per hour 290 miles; price $15,000. at factory field. The PCA-2 as later fitted with the Wright R-975-E2 engine of 420 h.p. was called the PA-21. All data as listed above would still apply except for generous increases in performance.

The construction details and general arrangement of the Pitcairn model PCA-2 is typical to

Fig. 34. Pitcairn PCA-2 in Canada; novelty of 'giro exploited in advertising.

that of the PCA-3 as described in the chapter for ATC # 446 of this volume. Most information and descriptive data listed here would be applicable to both models unless otherwise noted. The rotor blades were of course the most conspicuous part of the autogiro; rigged from the pylon with a slight droop when at rest, the blades were started into rotation through a clutch, gearbox, and shaft, driven by the engine. Shaft-drive of the rotor was disengaged for flight. The fixed wing of modest area was actually called the "lateral stabilizer", and it supported the large Friese type ailerons which imparted a banking motion in turns, and kept the rotor level in normal flight. Containing 5 deg. of dihedral through the main portion of the wing's span, the wing tips had highly exaggerated dihedral for added stability. The unusual landing gear had a tread of 159 in. with "oleo" shock absorbing legs of long travel; wheels were 8.50x10 and brakes were provided. Two fuel tanks were mounted low in the fuselage under the front seat to keep fluctuating fuel load on the center of gravity. An extra 20 gal. fuel tank was available to extend the range. The baggage compartment of 3.3 cu. ft. capacity was located in the turtle-back section behind the rear seat. A metal propeller, and Heywood engine starter were standard equipment. Dual controls, parachute flares, and navigation lights were optional. The next development in the Pitcairn autogiro was the smaller

PAA-1 as described in the chapter for ATC # 433 of this volume.

Listed below are model PCA-2 entries as gleaned from registration records:

NC-784W; PCA-2 (# B-5) Wright R-975.
NC-799W;   "   (# B-6)   "
NC-10761;   "   (# B-7)   "
NC-26;   "   (# B-8)   "
NC-10768;   "   (# B-9)   "
NC-10780;   "   (# B-12)   "
NC-10781;   "   (# B-13)   "
NC-10785;   "   (# B-14)   "
NC-10786;   "   (# B-15)   "
NC-10787;   "   (# B-16)   "
NC-10788;   "   (# B-22)   "
NC-10789;   "   (# B-23)   "
NC-10790;   "   (# B-24)   "
NC-10791;   "   (# B-25)   "
NC-11608;   "   (# B-26)   "
NC-11609;   "   (# B-27)   "
NC-11610;   "   (# B-28)   "
NC-11611;   "   (# B-29)   "
NC-11613;   "   (# B-31)   "

Pitcairn autogiro serial numbering was consecutive as mfgd., regardless of model, so some of the missing ser. numbers in the list above were models PAA-1; as NR-784W, ser. # B-5 later as 2 pl. with 400 h.p. Wright engine; ser. # B-8 later as NC-2624; ser. # B-15 later as CF-ARO in Canada; some of the listed PCA-2 were later modified to model PA-21 by installation of 420 h.p. Wright R-975-E2 engine; this approval for ser. # B-5 and up; approval expired 9-30-39.

Fig. 35. Curtiss-Wright model 16-K with 5 cyl. Kinner B5 engine.

Stemming from the basic design of the series-12 "Sport Trainer", Curtiss-Wright (Travel Air Div.) developed a version called the "Light Sport", a craft in many ways similar, but with added arrangement in the fuselage forward to carry two passengers instead of just one. Not having much luck in selling the 2-place model 12-K trainer, the added versatility of the 2-3 place model 16-K was perhaps a mild stimulant to sales; therefore, the Kinner-powered "Light Sport" went on to do somewhat better in enticing a few buyers. In general, the Model 16 was not quite as lean and bouncy as the "Twelve" because of a little more cross-section and added weight, but it was the better buy for the flying-service operator as well as the sportsman. Actually it only cost some $200.00 more to buy this 3-place airplane, as compared to buying the 2-place trainer, but in these times of cutrate prices and marked-down inventories, neither version was considered an exceptional bargain. The Kinner B5 engine as mounted in the 16-K developed 125 h.p. at 1925 r.p.m. and cost $1585.00 complete with exhaust collector ring. Some quick figuring reveals that this left some $2900.00 for the rest of the 16-K, a margin of profit somewhat fatter than the normally riduculous average for these times. Nevertheless, nearly a dozen of the Model 16-K were built and sold to sportsmen and operators, well scattered around the country.

The model 16-K "Light Sport" was an open cockpit biplane seating 2 or 3, and was typical of the Travel Air "Sport Trainer" except for the modification necessary to allow seating for an extra passenger. Two people could be stuffed into the front seat, but it was better for all concerned if they were on the smaller side. Well equipped with accessories and other pilot aids, the delivered price was somewhat high, but ease of operation, more utility, and better enjoyment was the benefit. Powered with the 5 cyl. Kinner B5 (R-440) engine of 125 h.p., the model 16-K still had power reserve to turn in a very creditable performance without the penalty of higher operating costs. Burdened slightly by the weight of an extra passenger, the 16-K at gross loading was not quite as bouncy as the lighter 12-K, but the difference between them was only slight. Because of its suitable strength and flight characteristics, the model 16-K was also eligible to be used for acrobatic flight training in the secondary phase of the Civilian Pilot Training Program. Blessed with a robust construction that was over-strength for all normal usage, the "Sixteen" stood up well to hard service, many for 10 years and more. The type certificate number for the model 16-K was issued 4-7-31 and some 11 or more examples of this model were built by the Travel Air Div. of the Curtiss-Wright Airplane Co. at Wichita, Kan. Once again Herb Rawdon and Ted Wells had teamed up on the design-development of the new 16 series.

Listed below are specifications and performance data for the model 16-K "Light Sport" as powered with the 125 h.p. Kinner B5 engine; length overall 20'7"; height overall 8'10"; wing span upper 28'10"; wing span lower 26'4"; wing chord upper and lower 48"; wing area upper 113.4 sq.ft.; wing area lower 93 sq.ft.; total wing

Fig. 36. Low-drag "Townend ring," an optional feature on 16-K for slight boost in speed.

area 206.4 sq.ft.; airfoil Clark Y-15; wt. empty 1176 lbs.; useful load 774 lbs.; payload with 33 gal. fuel 376 lbs. (2 pass. at 170 lb. each & 36 lb. baggage); gross wt. 1950 lbs.; max. speed 112; cruising speed 95; landing speed 48; average take-off run 350-400 ft.; climb 750 ft. first min. at sea level; ceiling 12,500 ft.; gas cap. 33 gal.; oil cap. 4 gal.; cruising range at 7.2 gal. per hour 420 miles; price $4488. at factory field.

The construction details and general arrangement of the model 16-K were basically typical to that of the 12-K as described in the chapter for ATC # 406 of this volume. Standard equipment for the 3-seated 16-K included a baggage locker in dash-panel of front cockpit with allowance for up to 36 lbs., dual controls with the front set quickly removable, 6.50x10 semi-air-wheels with brakes, brake pedals in rear cockpit only, head-rest fairing for rear cockpit, a 33 gal.

fuel tank in center-section panel of upper wing, a wooden propeller, Eclipse electric engine starter, battery, wiring for navigation lights, and a steerable tail wheel. Optional equipment included a metal propeller for $200.00, brake pedals in front cockpit for $50.00, engine cover $8.00, cockpit cover for $8.00, two-tone colors other than standard were $50.00 extra. A custom made speed-ring engine cowling was later available for $60.00. An extra 20 gal. fuel tank was available for installation in the front cockpit; no passengers were then carried. Goodyear "air-wheels" with brakes were also optional. By May of 1931 some 95 airplane "types" had been certificated with the various Kinner engines since 1928; this tally had slowed its pace considerably for the next few lean years. The next development in the 16-series was the Model 16-W as described in the chapter for ATC # 429 of this volume.

Listed below are Model 16-K entries as gleaned from registration records:

NC-446W; Model 16-K (16K-2001) Kinner B5.
NC-421W;   "   (16K-2003)   "
NC-422W;   "   (16K-2004)   "
NC-407W;   "   (16K-2005)   "
NC-409W;   "   (16K-2006)   "
NC-11703;   "   (16K-2007)   "
NC-11704;   "   (16K-2008)   "
NC-11705;   "   (16K-2009)   "
NC-11706;   "   (16K-2010)   "
NC-11707;   "   (16K-2011)   "
NC-11718;   "   (16K-2012)   "

Approval for the Model 16-K expired on 4-26-37.

Fig. 37. 16-K was 3-seated version of sport-trainer series.

Fig. 38. Waco model QDC with Continental A-70 engine. Prototype airplane shown.

The plump and stubby model QDC was Waco Aircraft's initial entry since 1924 into the cabin airplane field, a progressive line of high-performance cabin biplanes that extended into the next ten years. Sensing the trend towards cabin airplanes with seating for 4 or 5, the actual break-through for "Waco" into this field was really quite simple. Using the basic "Model F" design, the fuselage sides were extended to the upper wing, the closed-in interior was then rearranged to seat four, and thus, we might say, evolved the model QDC. It was not all this simple of course, but the basic "Waco" biplane configuration was certainly ideal as a starting point. Designing to a proven formula that had established the "Waco" biplane high among the leaders in all-purpose airplanes, the cabin-type QDC took its place in line to uphold this tradition. Fairly small and light, the new QDC seated four nicely, and the 165 h.p. Continental engine provided sufficient power for a satisfactory performance. As a family-type airplane that could operate on a relatively small budget, or as an economical vehicle for the businessman, the QDC had much in its favor at this time. Happy with the new combination and anxious to help promote its future, Continental Motors acquired the second ship off the line,

and sent it on tour. Formally introduced at the Detroit Air Show for 1931, many marveled at the new cabin-type "Waco", and it was certainly impressing people favorably. Initial sales of the cabin four-seater (QDC) started off well, and surprisingly, kept side-by-side pace with the open 3-seater (QCF) to the end of the year. Actually, Waco Aircraft never did discontinue the open-cockpit biplane, but from here on in, its popularity was waning and the "Cabin Waco" was soon to elbow its way to the forefront.

The Waco model QDC was a fairly small cabin biplane arranged to seat four; purposely kept small in overall dimension, the allotted cabin space was cozy, but not intimate. An extension of the cabin windows beyond the trailing edge of the upper wing provided excellent visibility to the rear, and provided a suitable form where the fuselage made the transition from a rectangle to a roughly oval shape. With its useful load well grouped and also well arranged, there was a surprising amount of room for an airplane as close-coupled as this one. Powered with the 7 cyl. Continental A-70-2 engine of 165 h.p., the model QDC used every horsepower sparingly and wisely to turn in a very good performance. Based on average cost per seat-mile, the economical utility

Fig. 39. Chubby arrangement of QDC seated four in comfort.

of the QDC posed as ideal for the private-owner flyer, and especially as used in general-purpose work. Being closely akin to the Model F for 1931 (QCF), the new Model C (QDC) of course shared many of its personality traits, so it too was rather easy to fly and a pleasure to operate from the smaller fields. The type certificate number of the model QDC was issued 4-8-31 and some 32 examples of this model were manufactured by the Waco Aircraft Co. at Troy, Ohio. Popularity and a rugged character naturally promoted its longevity, so it is commendable that 23 of this particular model were still flying actively in 1939.

Listed below are specifications and performance data for the Waco model QDC as powered with the 165 h.p. Continental A-70-2 engine; length overall 23'2"; height overall 8'5"; wing span upper 33'3"; wing span lower 28'2"; wing chord upper & lower 57"; wing area upper 134 sq. ft.; wing area lower 111 sq. ft.; total wing area 245 sq. ft.; airfoil Clark Y; wt. empty 1530 (1541) lbs.; useful load 977 (1040) lbs.; payload with 40 gal. fuel 540 (602) lbs.; baggage allowance 30 (94) lbs.; gross wt. 2507 (2581) lbs.; wts. in brackets as later revised for allowable increases; max. speed (with speeding-ring cowling) 116; cruising speed 102; landing speed 48; climb 750-700 ft. first min. at sea level; ceiling 14,000 ft.; gas cap. 40 gal.; oil cap. 3.5-

Fig. 40. Rear-view windows on QDC offered 360° vision.

Fig. 41. First "Waco" cabin biplane was built in 1924, also featured good visibility.

4.25 gal.; cruising range at 9.5 gal. per hour 400 miles; price $5985. at the factory field. Amended allowance later boosted gross wt. to 2652 lbs.; revised wts. as follows; wt. empty 1550; useful load 1102; payload 660; gross wt. 2652 lbs. Oil cap. increased to 4.25 gal. The max. allowable wts. had some detriment to overall performance.

The fuselage framework was built up of welded chrome-moly steel tubing, heavily faired to shape with wooden formers and fairing strips, then fabric covered. The cabin interior was neatly upholstered, with seating arranged for four; two sat in front on individual seats and two sat on a bench-type seat in back.

A large door on left-hand side provided easy entry to any seat. An abundance of window area provided excellent visibility, and windows on the sides could be rolled down; a throw-over control wheel provided control from either front seat. The passenger baggage was stowed in a compartment behind the rear seat, with an allowance for up to 80 lbs; a 14 lb. tool kit roll was stowed under rear seat. The wing framework was built up of solid spruce spar beams with spruce and plywood truss-type wing ribs; the leading edges were covered with dural metal sheet and the completed framework was covered in fabric. Ailerons were connected

Fig. 42. Minimum dimension and absence of useless weight provided QDC with excellent performance on 165 h.p.

together in pairs, and each was a metal-framed structure covered with corrugated "Alclad" metal sheet. Fuel tanks of 20 gal. cap. each were mounted in the root end of each upper wing half; float-type fuel gauges were visible from the cabin. The vee-legged landing gear of 72 in. tread used oleo & spring shock absorbing struts; 7.50x10 semi-airwheels with brakes were standard equipment. A large swiveling tail wheel was provided for easier ground handling. The fabric covered tail-group was built up of welded steel tubing; the horizontal stabilizer was adjustable in flight and elevators had aerodynamic balance "horns". A Hartzell wooden propeller, Heywood engine starter, speed-ring engine cowl, a hot-shot battery, navigation lights, a compass, wheel brakes, and a swing-over control wheel were standard equipment. A metal propeller and wheel pants were optional. The next development in the Waco cabin biplane was the 1932 model UEC as described in the chapter for ATC # 467 of this volume.

Listed below are model QDC entries as gleaned from registration records:

NC-11250; Model QDC (# 3454) A-70-2
NC-11244;   "   (# 3455) "
NC-11428:   "   (# 3498) "
NC-11434;   "   (# 3499) "
NC-11435;   "   (# 3500) "

NC-11439; **Model QDC** (# 3501) **A-70-2**
NC-11437;   "   (# 3502) "
NC-11443;   "   (# 3503) "
NC-11438;   "   (# 3504) "
NC-11446;   "   (# 3505) "
NC-11447;   "   (# 3506) "
NC-11441;   "   (# 3507) "
NC-11449;   "   (# 3508) "
NC-11457;   "   (# 3509) "
NC-11460;   "   (# 3510) "
NC-11463;   "   (# 3511) "
NC-11470;   "   (# 3513) "
NC-11473;   "   (# 3514) "
NC-11471;   "   (# 3515) "
NC-11480;   "   (# 3516) "
NC-11474;   "   (# 3544) "
NC-11477;   "   (# 3545) "
NC-11486;   "   (# 3546) "
NC-11489;   "   (# 3547) "
NC-12427;   "   (# 3548) "
NC-12429;   "   (# 3549) "
NC-12430;   "   (# 3550) "
NC-12431;   "   (# 3551) "
NC-12432;   "   (# 3552) "
NC-12436;   "   (# 3578) "
NC-12438;   "   (# 3579) "
NC-12441;   "   (# 3581) "

This approval for ser. # 3454 and up; 11250 (ser. # 3454) as "ODC" with Kinner C5-210 engine in 1933; this approval expired 9-30-39.

Fig. 43. Sioux Coupe 90-A with Brownback "Tiger" 90 engine actually similar to Kari-Keen shown.

There is actually very little of significance to say about the Sioux "Coupe", except that it was a slightly warmed-over "Kari-Keen" 90 offered in the selection of 3 different engines. Originally designed by Swen Swanson, the "Kari-Keen" was redesigned slightly in 1930 by engineers Gazely and LaSha to a somewhat improved offering that actually met with little success. Reorganized early in 1931 as the Sioux Aircraft Corp., the perky "Coupe" remained more or less the same except that it was now available with a greater selection of engines. It was often theorized among aircraft manufacturers that buyers had an unwavering preference for certain engines, so the keynote to more aircraft sales would seem to be the offering of several combinations more apt to appeal to the different buyers. This theory quite apparently did nothing to enhance the future of the Sioux "Coupe". Being a direct kin of the popular "Kari-Keen" monoplane, the Sioux "Coupe" was very much a good airplane and perhaps would have enjoyed acceptance and some national success had economic conditions been more favorable. Apparently only one example of the model 90-A was built and it was modified from a "Kari-Keen" 90 (ser. # L-306) that was already partially completed; normally it would have been powered with the Lambert 90 engine, but the

"Tiger 90" was installed instead. The rugged character of the "Coupe" and its sly infectious nature had tendency to promote its longevity; those few that were built in this newer series since 1930, enjoyed long periods of active service.

The Sioux "Coupe" model 90-A was a light high-winged cabin monoplane with side by side seating for two in plenty of room and good comfort. A rather chummy and lady-like type of airplane, it was very often described as easy to like. Of course, the most distinguishing feature first seen on the little "Coupe" was its broad cantilever wing, a stout wooden framework of thick and robust proportion, the likes of which had been introduced earlier on the "Kari-Keen". A wing of this type was not usually employed on a high-winged airplane so small, therefore it was quite conspicuous. The powerplant selected for the Sioux "Coupe" model 90-A was the interesting 6 cyl. Brownback (Light) "Tiger" of 90 h.p., a twin-row package of power that offered a good lively performance with smoothness and unstrained ease. By any yardstick of comparison, this craft was a sensible combination that had much to its credit. Ironically enough the "Tiger" 90 engine soon acquired a shaky future and was discontinued from active production by 1932; this was actually of little matter to the Sioux 90-A because it was on its last legs also. Together they quietly slipped away into the shadow of the side-lines. The type certificate number for the Sioux "Coupe" model 90-A was issued 4-8-31 and possibly no more than one example of this model was built by the Sioux Aircraft Corp. at Sioux City, Iowa.

A published report of the period stated that the Kari-Keen Aircraft Co., after falling into serious financial difficulty, was acquired intact in Nov. of 1930 by the C. F. Lytle Investment Co. of Sioux City, Iowa. Reorganized shortly after with new capital as the Sioux Aircraft Corp., the plant and its facilities were scheduled to re-open in Jan. of 1931. Experimental work was then in process to develop 3 new versions of the basic "Coupe", the models 90-A, the 90-B, and the 90-C. By mid-year of 1931 all 3 versions had been certificated and were scheduled for production on demand. The Sioux "Coupe" 90 (formerly the Kari-Keen 90) with the 5 cyl. Lambert 90 engine was still available on order.

Listed below are specifications and perform-ance data for the Sioux "Coupe" model 90-A as powered with the 90 h.p. Brownback (Light) "Tiger" engine; length overall 23'0"; height overall 7'4"; wing span 30'0"; wing chord at root 90"; wing chord at tip 54"; total wing area 150 sq.ft.; airfoil "Eiffel" 385; wt. empty 1015 lbs.; useful load 533 lbs.; payload with 25 gal. fuel 195 lbs. (1 pass. at 170 lbs. & 25 lb. bag-gage); gross wt. 1548 lbs.; max. speed 115; cruis-ing speed 100; landing speed 45; climb 850 ft. first min. at sea level; ceiling 14,000 ft.; gas cap. 25 gal.; oil cap. 2.5 gal.; cruising range at 5.5 gal. per hour 400 miles; price $3355. at factory with Goodyear airwheels and brakes.

The construction details and general arrange-ment of the model 90-A were typical to that of the "Kari-Keen" 90 as described in the chapter for ATC # 331 of USCA/C, Vol. 4. The only major changes that would be required in the model 90-A would be a revised engine mount to fit the "Tiger" 90, and other minor modifica-tions necessary to this particular combination. No other published technical data was avail-able. The next development in the Sioux "Coupe" series was the model 90-B as de-scribed in the chapter for ATC # 414 of this volume.

Listed below is the only known "Sioux" model 90-A.

NC-10544; Model 90-A (# L-306) Tiger 90. This approval expired 7-1-33; ser. # L-306 re-registered to Sioux Aircraft Corp. as "identi-fied" airplane 7-15-33; 10544 (ser. # L-306) still owned and operated by Sioux Aircraft Corp. through 1934.

A.T.C. # 414
(4-8-31)
SIOUX "COUPE", 90-B

Fig. 44. Sioux Coupe 90-B with Warner 90 engine actually similar to Kari-Keen shown. Difference was in engine installation only.

Extensive research into reams of published data, and interrogation of several likely individuals had failed to turn up very much fact or even fancy about the rare Sioux "Coupe" model 90-B. It is only known as fact that the 90-B was typical of the new "Coupe" series for 1931, and was powered with the 5 cyl. Warner "Junior" engine of 90 h.p. Whether this model was developed from partially constructed "Kari-Keen" airframes that were left over, or was built up from scratch, also could not be determined. In registration listings awarded to the Sioux Aircraft Corp. this model (90-B) was labeled the "Coupe Jr.", and the model 90-C as powered with the 7 cyl. Warner "Scarab" engine of 110 h.p., was labeled the "Coupe Sr.". Manufacturer's serial numbering for both these models was in the 400-block, so we can at least assume they probably were developed by Sioux Aircraft, and not left-overs from Kari-Keen. Both the models 90-B and 90-C were developed and approved before mid-year 1931; all the evidence available would indicate that only one of each was built, and the firm was all but folded up again by year's end. Although there was no active production, Sioux Aircraft was not entirely disbanded yet, and both the 90-B and 90-C were still registered to the company into 1934. Approval had expired for all "Sioux" models by 7-1-33, so we can then assume this was the end of the line for manufacture at least.

The Sioux "Coupe Jr." model 90-B was a high-winged cabin monoplane with side by side seating for two. Ably supported by a stout tapered cantilever wing it was basically typical of the earlier "Kari-Keen 90" and the Sioux "Coupe" 90-A, except perhaps for some minor changes necessary to this particular combination. Powered with the 5 cyl. Warner "Junior" (series 40 or 50) engine of 90 h.p., the all-round performance of the 90-B would be at least comparable to either the Kari-Keen 90 or the Sioux 90-A. As powered with the 7 cyl. Warner "Sca-

rab" engine of 110 h.p., the model 90-C of course had the benefit of 20 h.p. extra for a much better performance. Described as basically typical of the original Swanson (Kari-Keen) design, the 90-B and 90-C no doubt were inherently well-mannered airplanes that performed very well. The type certificate number for the Sioux "Coupe Jr." model 90-B was issued 4-8-31 and only one example of this model was built. The "Coupe Sr." model 90-C was built on a Group 2 approval numbered 2-356.

Listed below are specifications and performance data for the "Sioux" model 90-B as powered with the 90 h.p. Warner "Junior" engine; (the following data has not been verified, so a certain amount of it is qualified assumption); length overall 23'0"; height overall 7'4"; wing span 30'0"; wing chord at root 90"; wing chord at tip 54"; total wing area 150 sq.ft.; airfoil "Eiffel" 385; wt. empty 992 lbs.; useful load 530 lbs.; payload with 25 gal. fuel 195 lbs. (1 pass. at 170 lbs. & 25 lb. baggage); gross wt. 1522 lbs.; max. speed 115; cruising speed 98; landing speed 45; climb 850 ft. first min. at sea level; ceiling 14,000 ft.; gas cap. 25 gal.; oil cap. 2.5 gal.; cruising range at 5.5 gal. per hour 400 miles; price at factory approx. $3500.

No factual data for construction details or general arrangement was available so we can only assume again that the model 90-B was typical of the "Kari-Keen" 90 as described in the chapter for ATC # 331 of USCA/C, Vol. 4, or the "Sioux" model 90-A as described in the chapter for ATC # 413 of this volume. From all facts rumored or implied, there is very little reason to believe that the "Sioux" varied to any extent from the previous "Kari-Keen".

Listed below are 90-B and 90-C entries as gleaned from registration records:
NC-10721; Model 90-B (# 401) Warner 90.
NC-10735; Model 90-C (# 402) Warner 110.
This approval expired 7-1-33.

A.T.C. # 415
(4-9-31)
FAIRCHILD (PILGRIM), KR-135

Fig. 45. Inline engine enhances trim lines of Fairchild KR-135.

The Fairchild (Pilgrim) model KR-135 was basically a KR-21 series biplane in all respects, except that it was specifically modified to serve as a flying test-bed for the newly developed Fairchild 6-390, an inverted inline air-cooled engine. Because of its particularly robust frame and rugged character, the basic KR-21 sport-biplane was a logical choice for in-flight testing and further development of this new power-plant. Operating the engine repeatedly at per-formance maximums or even beyond, would then not be so apt to instigate troubles in the structure of the airplane; this would allow more time for study of the engine and any of its own arising problems. Just 6 months or so previous to this (KR-135) development, Fairchild had built a similar model in the KR-125 (refer to ATC # 368 of USCA/C, Vol. 4). The earlier KR-125 was not entirely satisfactory because of its excess weight causing a high weight per horsepower ratio, a weight penalty that was a detriment to its performance potential. Most of the weight increase seems to have been caused by added equipment, and some enlargement of the basic design. Designed by a Mr. Dykman as an Army-type trainer, the KR-125 was retained for a time to perform various services around the plant in Farmingdale. With 200 hours on the engine, the plane was finally sold and it is at least commendable that in 6 years of flying, over 1000 hours were accumulated without replacing an engine part. Whereby the KR-125 was modi-fied from the standard layout of the KR-21 in

landing gear geometry, wing layout, and in some of the interplane bracing, the new KR-135 held more closely to the standard KR-21 con-figuration. Also, a better shaped cowling over the engine section showed more study and better planning for control of engine temperatures; a functional shape too that greatly enhanced the beauty of this new combination. With its engine installed in Nov. of 1930, the first KR-135 was flown some 150 hours and then sold to Roland Palmedo of Hicksville, L.I. About April of 1932 the second KR-135 was sold to Charles S. Glenn as personal transportation in the line of busi-ness. Flown extensively throughout the south and southwest into 1936, the combination ac-cumulated nearly 500 hours without any major service or repair to the engine. Finally, a major overhaul at that time cost only $129.43! Excep-tionally smooth-running because of the inherent dynamic balance of the 6 cyl. inline engine, the Fairchild 6-390 had many other good features to its credit. Later known as the popular "Rang-er" engine, with power output progessively in-creased to some 200 h.p., this engine was in-stalled in many and varied airplane models in the next ten years.

As shown here in varied views, the Fair-child (Pilgrim) model KR-135 was an open cock-pit biplane with seating for two in tandem; basic-ally, it was typical of the KR-21 series sport-biplane (by Kreider-Reisner) except for its en-gine installation and whatever modifications were necessary to this particular combination.

Fig. 46. Fairchild 6-390 engine provides streamlining and improved visibility in KR-135.

Because only 2 or possibly 3 airplanes of this type were built, and because no detailed operating records or lore were available, we can only assume that its performance and general behavior would match that at least of the KR-21-B. There is every reason to believe that the talents of this airplane, merged with those of this fine engine, surely translated into a combination of pleasure and fine performance. Considerably lighter when empty than the previous KR-125, and operating at a gross weight some 145 lbs. less, the new KR-135 immediately poses as a more sprightly airplane with noticeable increases in the performance that would be affected by weight. Powered with the inverted 6 cyl. Fairchild 6-390 engine of 125 h.p., this installation promoted better visibility over the nose, and a more streamlined appearance in the all-important front end. Performance figures for the KR-135 were listed as identical to that of the KR-21-B, but this would seem rather conserva-

tive for a craft that definitely shows aerodynamic improvement. The type certificate number for the model KR-135 was issued 4-9-31 and at least 2 or 3 examples of this model were built; engine installations and subsequent testing of the KR-135 were performed at Fairchild Div. and the American Airplane & Engine Corp. at Farmingdale, L.I., N.Y. This was actually a Fairchild project that was inherited by the American Airplane & Engine Corp.

After corporate manipulations that were sometimes described as legal hokus-pokus, the Fairchild Airplane & Engine Co. became the American Airplane & Engine Corp. in April of 1931. The Fairchild monoplanes were then labeled the "Pilgrim" and the most notable development of this new company was the "Model 100-A", a development of the earlier "Fairchild 100". Later in the year, the Fairchild 6-390 engine became the "Ranger", and a 12 cyl. version was also under development. Officers of

Fig. 47. KR-135 was KR-21 airframe adapted to new Fairchild inline engine.

Fig. 48. Fairchild 6-390 later became famous "Ranger" engine.

the American Airplane & Engine Corp. were F. G. Coburn as president, with Virginius E. Clark as V.P. and chief engineer. Richard H. Depew, Jr. had been with Fairchild and then with American Airplane & Engine Corp. in various capacities (test pilot, chief pilot, sales manager, sales engineer, etc.) from 1923 until May of 1932. Leaving "American" he demonstrated Pitcairn autogiros, but later went back to his first love, selling Fairchild airplanes. Starting his flying career in 1911, by 1934 he already had 23 years of flight in his bulging log-books, and had flown well over 100 different airplanes. Following the forming of "American" the Kreider-Reisner Div. was still retained by Sherman Fairchild and they were soon going into quantity production of their new "Model 22".

Listed below are specifications and performance data for the Fairchild (Pilgrim) model KR-135 (P-135) as powered with the 125 h.p. Fairchild (Ranger) engine; length overall 21'6"; height overall 8'6"; wing span upper 27'0"; wing span lower 24'6"; wing chord both at root 57"; wing chord both at tip 42"; wing area upper 107 sq.ft.; wing area lower 86 sq.ft.; total wing area 193 sq.ft.; airfoil USA-45 modified; wt. empty 1155 lbs.; useful load 590 lbs.; payload with 30 gal. fuel 218 lbs. (1 pass. at 170 lb. & 48 lb. baggage); gross wt. 1745 lbs.; max. speed 116; cruising speed 93; landing speed 51; climb 750 ft. first min. at sea level; climb to 6100 ft. in 10 mins.; climb to 10,000 ft. in 20 mins.; ceiling 14,900 ft.; gas cap. 30 gal.; oil cap. 3-4 gal.; cruising range at 7 gal. per hour 380 miles; price not announced.

The construction details and general arrangement of the model KR-135 (P-135) were typical of the KR-21-B as described in the chapter for ATC # 363 (USCA/C, Vol. 4). The most notice-able change in the KR-135 was of course the inverted inline engine installation, which was completely cowled in and baffled internally for proper cooling. Numerous louvers provided the proper hot-air outlet. Because no cylinders protruded from the cowling as they would in a "radial" engined installation, the visibility was much better across and around the nose. The oil supply tank was mounted into the belly of the fuselage, just behind the engine; an oil cooler core was used to regulate the oil temperature. Max. baggage allowance was 48 lbs., but no baggage was allowed when two parachutes (40 lbs.) were carried. Dual controls were provided and lower wing had wing-walk on either side for entry. The fuel tank was mounted in the center-section panel of the upper wing; a float-type fuel gauge was visible from either cockpit. The landing gear of 61 in. tread was fitted with oleo-spring shock absorbing struts; wheels were 24x4 and Bendix brakes were standard equipment. Low pressure semi-air-wheels with brakes were later optional. A metal propeller, and hand-crank inertia-type engine starter were also standard equipment. The next "Pilgrim" development was the model 100-A as described in the chapter for ATC # 443 of this volume.

Listed below are model KR-135 entries as gleaned from registration records:
NC-248V; KR-135 (# S-1052) Fairchild 6-390.
NC-963V;   "   (# S-1054)   "
Serial numbers have sometimes been listed as # S-1502 and # S-1504; this approval for ser. # S-1052, # S-1054, # 7000 and up; registration number for ser. # 7000 unknown; ser. # S-1052 mounted engine # 7, and ser. # S-1054 mounted engine # 11; this approval expired 9-30-39.

A.T.C. #416
(4-9-31)
WACO, MODEL QCF

Fig. 49. Waco model QCF with Continental A-70 engine.

Following the basic pattern of the successful "Model F" of 1930, Waco Aircraft continued in their established tradition of building practical all-purpose biplanes. Now more than ever, the new F-line continued to serve the flying-service operator and the owner-pilot, in a utility unmatched by anything the industry had to offer. A generous boost in horsepower sharpened the performance throughout the normal range, allowing some increase in payload and cruising range as well. A studied, practical application of the added horsepower fostered a combination that proved to be just about the best airplane available for all-purpose use; almost immediately, flying-service operators, owner-pilots, and even the sportsman-pilot, were giving voluntary testimony of their satisfaction with this airplane. Powered with the popular Continental A-70-2 engine of 165 h.p., the model QCF still followed the original "F" concept quite closely, and as a result, was arranged to handle its useful load in a compact and handy manner. Trim, deft, and playful, the QCF operated just about anywhere and was well represented in metropolitan and small-town areas alike. The first model QCF to be rolled off the production line was delivered to Continental Motors on May 12 of 1931 for test and promotion; to veteran flier "Tex" LaGrone, sometime in 1932, went the honors of buying the last QCF off the line. By this time, several other new stars in the Waco biplane line-up were hogging the limelight in a strong bid for attention. Of the 31 or so model

QCF that were built in about a year's time, it is flattering testimony indeed that 26 of these were still flying actively in 1939. In more recent years the QCF has been avidly searched by "antiquers," and has been restored in several examples.

The Waco model QCF was an open cockpit biplane with seating arranged for three; sensibly arranged with its useful load in a well distributed, compact form, the pudgy QCF was not penalized by excess weight, nor cumbersome dimension. Never choosy either as to chore or place of operation, the QCF was just about as happy working out of a small pasture-strip, as anywhere else; for increased utility it was also eligible as a seaplane on "Edo" floats. With a hardy and dutiful nature more attuned to handle the everyday chores of the flying-service operator, there was still a playful streak in its nature that appealed to those who flew only for the sport of it. Often used in pilot-training the nimble QCF was eligible also for the acrobatic stages of flight training in the CPTP program. Powered with the 7 cyl. Continental A-70 (Series 2) engine of 165 h.p., this craft was blessed with the combination of top-notch performance at a very reasonable price. Flight characteristics were deft and nimble, mixed with a sprinkling of considerate traits that added up to both profit and flying pleasure. Whether in the air or on the ground, its everyday behavior was quite honest, easily predictable, and it seemed to display a genuine concern for all

Fig. 50. QCF was 1931 version of famous "Waco F" series.

those involved in its operation or its well being. The 3-place open all-purpose biplane was by now a slowly dying breed, and for all practical purposes based on usefulness per dollar, the QCF must be considered as one of the very best of this type. The type certificate number for the model QCF was issued 4-9-31 and some 31 examples of this model were manufactured by the Waco Aircraft Co. at Troy, Ohio.

Listed below are specifications and performance data for the Waco model QCF as powered with the Continental A-70-2 engine of 165 h.p.; length overall 20'4"; height overall 8'9"; wing span upper 29'7"; wing span lower 27'5"; wing chord upper & lower 57"; wing area upper 130.4 sq. ft.; wing area lower 111 sq. ft.; total wing area 241.4 sq. ft.; airfoil Clark Y; wt. empty 1317-1336 lbs.; useful load 864 lbs.; payload with

39 gal. fuel 430 lbs. (2 pass. at 170 lb. each & 90 lb. baggage); gross wt. 2181-2200 lbs.; max. speed (with speed-ring cowl) 125; cruising speed 108; landing (stall) speed 40; climb 1000 ft. first min. at sea level; climb to 8000 ft. in 10 min.; ceiling 15,000 ft.; gas cap. 40 gal.; oil cap. 3.75 gal.; cruising range at 9 gal. per hour 430 miles; price $4985. at factory field. On aircraft equipped with metal propeller, speed-ring cowling, Heywood engine starter, navigation lights, a battery, and wheel pants, the wts. were 1418 lbs. empty, useful load was 882 lbs., payload with 40 gal. fuel was 442 lbs. (including 90 lbs. baggage), and max gross wt. was allowed to 2300 lbs. The following figures are for seaplane on Edo L-2260 twin-float gear; wt. empty 1535 lbs.; useful load 845 lbs.; payload with 40 gal. fuel 405 lbs. (including 65 lbs. baggage);

Fig. 51. 1931 Model QCF offered improved performance for all-purpose service.

Fig. 52. QCF shown used by Continental Motors in promotional service.

gross wt. 2300 lbs. Landplanes of 2300 lb. gross and seaplanes at 2380 lb. gross would suffer proportionate decreases in performance.

The fuselage framework was built up of welded chrome-moly steel tubing heavily faired to a well-rounded shape with wooden formers and fairing strips, then fabric covered. A door on the left-hand side offered easy entry into the front cockpit, and entry to the pilot's cockpit was an easy step-over from the wing-walk. A 15 lb. tool kit roll was stowed in dash-panel of the front cockpit, and the main baggage compartment, located in the turtle-back section behind rear cockpit, had allowance for 75 lbs. Two parachutes at 20 lbs. each, when carried, were part of the baggage allowance. The seaplane version had allowance for 65 lbs. baggage which included a 15 lb. anchor stowed in front cockpit, and 50 lbs. in rear baggage compartment. The wing framework was built up of solid spruce spar beams with spruce and plywood gusseted wing ribs; the leading edges were covered with dural metal sheet, and the completed framework was covered in fabric. Metal-framed ailerons were covered with corrugated duralumin sheet and fastened together in pairs with a streamlined steel push-pull strut. The fuel tank was mounted in the center-section panel of the upper wing; a large cut-out with hand-holds in trailing edge of the upper wing offered visibility upward and easier entry to the rear cockpit. The robust landing gear of 72 in. tread, unlike any that Waco had used before, was built up with faired vees on either side, using oleo-spring shock absorbing struts; wheels were 6.50x10 and brakes were standard equipment. The fabric covered tail-group was built up of welded steel tubing; the elevators had aerodynamic "balance horns," and the horizontal stabilizer was adjustable in flight. A Hartzell wooden propeller,

Heywood engine starter, navigation lights, speed-ring engine cowl, compass, tail wheel, and wheel brakes were standard equipment. A gray, black, vermillion, or silver fuselage, with silver wings, were standard color schemes. A metal propeller, electric engine starter, a battery, landing lights, dual controls, 7.50x10 semi-airwheels with brakes, streamlined wheel pants, and skis, were optional. The model QCF (ser. # 3554 and up) were eligible as seaplane on Edo L-2260 twin-float gear; ser. # 3453 through # 3553 were also eligible upon proper fuselage modification. The next development in the new F-series was the model PCF as described in the chapter for ATC # 453 of this volume.

Listed below are model QCF entries as gleaned from registration records:

Registration	Model	Serial	Type
X-11241;	Model QCF	(# 3453)	A-70-2.
NC-11247;	"	(# 3487)	"
NC-11427;	"	(# 3488)	"
NC-11273:	"	(# 3489)	"
NC-11426;	"	(# 3490)	"
NC-11429;	"	(# 3491)	"
NC-11430;	"	(# 3492)	"
NC-11431;	"	(# 3494)	"
NC-11444;	"	(# 3495)	"
NC-11445;	"	(# 3496)	"
NC-11440;	"	(# 3497)	"
NC-11442;	"	(#)	"
NC-11450;	"	(# 3534)	"
NC-11451;	"	(# 3535)	"
NC-11461;	"	(# 3536)	"
NC-11465;	"	(# 3537)	"
NC-11454;	"	(# 3538)	"
NC-11453;	"	(# 3539)	"
NC-11455;	"	(# 3540)	"
NC-11468;	"	(# 3541)	"
NC-11472;	"	(# 3542)	"
NC-11459;	"	(# 3543)	"
NC-12433;	"	(# 3553)	"
NC-11469;	"	(# 3554)	"
NC-11479;	"	(# 3556)	"
NC-11484;	"	(# 3558)	"
NC-11478;	"	(# 3559)	"
NC-11485;	"	(# 3560)	"
NC-11481;	"	(# 3561)	"
NC-11482;	"	(# 3562)	"
NC-11496;	"	(# 3566)	"
NC-11488;	"	(# 3567)	"
NC-12428;	"	(# 3569)	"
NC-11487;	"	(# 3570)	"
NC-11490;	"	(# 3572)	"
NC-13028;	"	(# 3573)	"

This approval for ser. # 3453 and up; ser. no. for NC-11442 unknown; approval expired 9-30-39.

A.T.C. # 417
(4-10-31)
OVERLAND "SPORT", MODEL L

Fig. 53. Overland "Sport" model L with 70 h.p. LeBlond engine.

Overland's rather timid entry into the sport-flying class was the "Sport" model L; basically, it was a small open cockpit biplane that thrived very well in combination with the efforts of a 70 h.p. LeBlond 5DE engine. Not having any particular stand-out features, in its outward appearance, the "Sport L" however inherited some fairly pleasant features in its character, and general behavior. Initially planned, designed, developed, and hurriedly built by a band of fliers, it was naturally endowed with certain qualities, qualities that seasoned pilots felt should be incorporated into a sport-type airplane. Willing to sacrifice some of the fine-edge of high performance for numerous features far dearer to the heart of the average owner-pilot, the "Overland" series were more apt to provoke smiles rather than any excitement. Whether the feeling was mutual the country over, we have been unable to determine, but in the general vicinity of Omaha it was known as the "Sweetheart of the air". Like most good airplanes, its utility offered some use beyond the sport-type category, so the "Sport" was often used in pilot-training. Built in very small number, and not generally known beyond the sphere of its birth-place, the "Overland" however did leave a good operational record; some examples of this model were reported flying actively for many years around Denver and in N. Dakota.

The original Overland "Sport" as also shown here, was designed by Harold K. Phillips, a versatile man whose aeronautical experience dated back to 1922 at the Nebraska Aircraft Co. (Lincoln-Standard) plant in Lincoln. Here he had intimate occasion to rub elbows with other early greats such as Ray Page, Otto Timm, Swen Swanson, Auggie Pedlar, Chas. Lindbergh, and others. When Otto Timm returned to California, Phillips had taken over as super-intendent of manufacturing and maintenance. Coming to Overland Airways of Omaha in 1928, Phillips also held down the same position. Offering to fill the need for a safe and sane sport-trainer, Harold Phillips, drawing from his wealth of experience, commenced the design of a little two-seated biplane to be powered with the LeBlond 60 engine. From the time the design was sketched on paper, on the 15th of March, the completed airplane was rolled out and test-flown only two months later. Test hops one after the other that day, were testimony to Phillips' good judgment and sound design; more than 15 pilots flew the little ship that first day, and all tendered smiles as they voiced their approval. With a crew of some 12 men, production plans called for the construction of 2 more planes of this type; one was powered with a 55 h.p. Velie engine, and the other powered with a LeBlond 60. Three more airplanes had also been started and were on the

Fig. 54. First 3 Overland sport-trainers had LeBlond 60 engines.

floor in different stages of construction. Disagreement with management's policy had caused H. K. Phillips to finally leave Overland Airways, and the 3 initial examples of the "Sport" never did reach government approval tests.

After Phillips had left to take a position with Rapid Air Lines of Omaha, "Chet" Cummings was hired in by Overland Airways to continue the "Sport" project. Wallace C. "Chet" Cummings will be remembered as designer of the original Mohawk "Pinto", and the Watkins "Skylark". It is only natural that Cummings, also a man of extensive experience, would want to inject some of his own ideas into the Phillips design; his obvious modifications to the "Sport" did change the face of things. An increase in interplane gap, a pronounced "wash-out" of the wing tips, a deepening of the fuselage cross-section, and redesign of the tail-group altered the general appearance somewhat; it is doubtful if any of these changes were necessarily for the better. The flight characteristics were altered, of course, and this was cause for some mixed feelings. The first Overland "Sport" as redesigned by Cummings, received a Group 2 approval numbered 2-289 (1301 lbs. gross wt.) issued on 10-17-30 for serial # 114 and up; this approval was superseded by ATC # 417 issued on 4-10-31.

The Overland "Sport" model L was a smallish open cockpit sport-type biplane with seating for two in tandem. Abbreviated in dimension the "Sport" was, however, arranged in such manner as to allow the room, comfort, and protection of a larger ship. Somewhat heavier now than its prototype, the Model L had to have just a little more power to achieve a comparable performance. Powered now with the improved 5 cyl. LeBlond 5DE engine of 70 h.p., performance was satisfactory through the full range of flight, and good economy allowed extra hours of flying time. Concerted efforts to find someone familiar with the flight characteristics and general behavior of the new redesigned "Sport" only lead back to the fact that it inherited most of the fine qualities of its earlier sister-ship; this a craft which won for itself by acclaim, the title as "sweetheart of the air". Had the new Overland "Sport" been introduced much earlier, chances are good that it would have enjoyed a far wider acceptance, but the market in 1931-32 for airplanes of this type was certainly not conducive to any great future. The type certificate number for the "Sport" model L was issued 4-10-31 and at least 3 examples of this model were built by Overland Airways, Inc. at Omaha, Nebr. Roy Furstenberg was president; J. B. Caldwell was V.P.; Royal DeVol was sec. & treas.; and Harold K. Phillips was general manager and chief engineer until leaving the company to be replaced by Wallace C. "Chet" Cummings. "Sport" production as such, was no doubt terminated some time in 1932, but the approval for this model remained in force until 9-30-39. Available records do not reveal if additional examples of this model were built into the latter date.

Listed below are specifications and performance data for the Overland "Sport" model L as powered with the 70 h.p. LeBlond 5DE engine; length overall 17'10"; height overall 7'2"; wing span upper 27'4"; wing span lower 26'4"; wing chord upper & lower 44"; total wing area 180 sq. ft.; airfoil USA-27; wt. empty 904 lbs.; useful load 462 lbs.; payload with 18 gal. fuel 176 lbs.; gross wt. 1366 lbs.; max. speed 100; cruising speed 85; landing speed 38; climb 650 ft. first min. at sea level; ceiling 12,500 ft.; gas cap. 18 gal.; oil cap. 2 gal.; cruising range at 4.6 gal. per hour 300 miles; price $2895. at factory. Dimensions as listed above were taken from the earlier model, so Model L may actually vary slightly from figures given. All other data applies specifically to Model L.

Fig. 55. Overland "Sport" prototype with Harold K. Phillips in foreground.

The 5 cyl. LeBlond 5DE engine, developing 70 h.p. at 1950 r.p.m., cost $1050. at factory.

The fuselage framework was built up of welded chrome-moly and 1025 steel tubing, faired to shape with wooden fairing strips, then fabric covered. The open cockpits were deep and well protected by a high cowl line, and large windshields; a small baggage locker with allowance for 6 lbs. was in the dash-panel of the front cockpit. Access to either cockpit was an easy step-over from wing-walk of the lower wing. The wing framework in 4 panels, was built up of solid spruce spar beams, with spruce and plywood truss-type wing ribs; the leading edges were covered with plywood sheet to preserve the airfoil form, and the completed framework was covered in fabric. The upper wing provided an extra large cut-out for visibility upward, and unhampered access to front cockpit; the fuel tank was mounted in the center-section panel. Large ailerons were on the lower panels only. Interplane struts and bracing were typical of the normal practice; rigging of the Model L employed a pronounced "wash-out" of the wing tips, probably to pro-

mote a more progressive "stall" in the wing cellule. The long-leg landing gear of 72 in. tread used oleo-spring shock absorbing struts; wheels were 26x4 with no brakes. the tail skid was of the steel spring-leaf type. The fabric covered tail-group, now of revised shape and dimension, was built up of welded steel tubing; the fin was ground adjustable and the horizontal stabilizer was adjustable in flight. A wooden propeller, dual controls, fire extinguisher, and exhaust collector ring were standard equipment. Low pressure 6.50x10 semi-airwheels, navigation lights, battery, and bayonet-type exhaust stacks were optional.

Listed below are all Overland "Sport" entries as gleaned from registration records:

X-315 H; Sport 60 (# 111) LeBlond 60.
   - 92 M;   ”   (# 112) Velie 55
X-315 V;   ”   (# 113) LeBlond 60.
NC-10491; Model L (# 114) Leblond 70.
NC- 972 N;   ”   (# 115)   ”
NC- 506 Y;   ”   (# 116)   ”

This approval for serial # 114 and up; approval expired 9-30-39.

A.T.C. # 418
(4-14-31)
SIKORSKY "AMPHIBION", S-41-A

Fig. 56. Sikorsky S-41-A with 2 Hornet B engines was bigger sister-ship to famous S-38.

Successful development of the Hornet-powered S-38-BH (ATC # 356) proved several things for Sikorsky. Other than international recognition for an outstanding performance, Sikorsky gained proof also that the basic S-38 design, with added dimension and more power in its frame, would be capable of handling worthwhile increases of paying load, and at better speeds. The idea for a slightly larger craft of this same basic type led directly to the successful development of the 16-passenger model S-41. Developed primarily for the Pan American Airways System the new amphibious S-41, as compared to the popular S-38, was a noticeably larger ship with increased seating and capable of extended cruising range. Dispensing with the familiar lower wing, as on the S-38, the S-41 became a parasol monoplane of some 7 ft. more span, but of less wing area; this denotes the increasing trend in the industry to higher wing loadings for the larger transports. Standing some 2 foot taller now, and some 5 feet longer, the S-41 was also some 1500 lbs. heavier empty, carried a half-ton more in payload, and topped off at about 2500 lbs. heavier at gross weight. Capt. Boris Sergievsky, Sikorsky's talented test-pilot, reportedly flew the first example of the S-41 from the factory to Santiago, Chile in just over 62 hours; the frustrating return trip by boat and rail took him 19 days! Operating with Pan Am on its far-flung Caribbean system, the S-41 was also used by Pan Am for a time on a route from Boston

to Halifax. In prototype, as is usually the case, the S-41 was a much lighter and more nimble ship; added equipment and successively greater allowable loads in the S-41-A and S-41-B versions were certainly favorable to its utility as a transport, but slightly detrimental to its original performance.

The Sikorsky "Amphibion" model S-41-A was a high-wing parasol monoplane of the flying-boat type with a spidery arrangement that was typical of the earlier S-38. The large bulky hull had maximum seating capacity for 16, but seating was often traded in favor of more fuel to extend the range on certain routes. Having a retractable wheeled undercarriage, the S-41 was introduced late in 1930 as the world's largest amphibian airplane; this distinction it did not hold for long. Powered with 2 Pratt & Whitney "Hornet B" engines of 575 h.p. each, the performance was more than adequate for the type of service it was performing in the Caribbean Sea. In some instances the S-41 operated as a pure "flying boat" with its landing gear removed; in this case it would trade the saving in weight for more paying load, more range, or just better performance. Designed to fit a particular need at a particular time, the S-41 could not cope for long with the rapid changes in Pan America's ever-expanding system; just about the time it got going good it was already outmoded by the need for larger equipment. As a result of this, only a few of this version were built. The model S-41 in prototype

Fig. 57. Navy version of S-41 was RS-1, in role as amphibious transport.

was first approved on a Group 2 memo numbered 2-286 and issued 10-14-30. The type certificate number for the model S-41-A was issued 4-14-31 and probably no more than 4 or 5 examples of this model were manufactured by Sikorsky Aviation Corp. at Bridgeport, Conn. As a division of the United Aircraft & Transport Corp., F. W. Neilson was president and general manager, Igor Sikorsky was V.P. and chief engineer, and W. A. Bary was V.P. in charge of production.

Listed below are specifications and performance data for the Sikorsky model S-41-A as powered with two 575 h.p. "Hornet B" engines; length overall 45'2"; height overall (wheels down) 15'3"; wing span 78'9"; wing chord 115"; total wing area 729 sq. ft.; airfoil "Sikorsky GS-M"; wt. empty 8100 lbs.; useful load 5700 lbs.; payload with 380 gal. fuel 2780 lbs. (14 pass. & 400 lbs. baggage-mail); payload with 550 gal. fuel 1760 lbs. (10 pass. & 60 lb. baggage); gross wt. 13,800 lbs.; max. speed 133; cruising speed 115; landing speed 66; climb 876 ft. first min. at sea level; ceiling 16,000 ft.; gas cap. normal 380 gal.; gas cap. max. 550 gal.; oil cap. 40 gal.; cruising range at 56 gal. per hour was 5 to 8 hours, or 575-920 miles; price $62,500. at factory ramp.

Fig. 58. S-41-A offered increased capacity and better performance.

Fig. 59. Versatility of S-41-A adaptable to land or water.

The stubby two-step hull was a riveted dura-lumin structure covered with a riveted skin of "Alclad" metal sheet; all seams were sealed with fabric strips saturated in marine glue. The hull was divided into 3 water-tight compartments above the floor line, and into six water-tight compartments below the floor. The pilot's compartment seated two, and the main cabin seated up to 14 in various arrangements; cabin access was by way of a large hatch in the aft end. A small compartment in the stern provided lavatory and toilet facilities; a compartment in front of pilot's station was provided for stowing baggage and cargo, while anchor and mooring gear were stowed up front in the nose. Cabin windows were fixed and adjustable louvers provided ventilation as needed; cabin heaters were optional. Dual controls were of the swing-over wheel type. The thick semi-cantilever wing in 3 sections, was built up of riveted duralumin truss-type spar beams and similar wing ribs; the completed framework was covered with fabric. Two large fuel tanks were mounted in the center-section panel of the wing, and each pontoon was fitted with an 85 gal. fuel tank for extra range. Fuel was pumped from the pontoons to the gravity-feed wing tanks by an engine-driven pump or an emergency hand pump. An oil tank was mounted in each engine nacelle; nacelles were streamlined pods fastened slightly below underside of the wing. The fabric covered twin-tailed control group was fastened to two outrigger booms that were attached to the rear wing spar, and braced to the hull by struts. Fitted with oleo-spring shock absorbing struts, the retractable landing gear was operated to up or down position by a hydraulic hand-pump; 40x10 low pressure semi-airwheels were fitted with Sikorsky multiple-disc hydraulic brakes. Adjustable metal propellers, electric inertia-type engine starters, navigation lights, a battery, throw-over control wheel, hydraulic wheel brakes, anchor, and mooring gear were standard equipment. Cabin heaters, night-flying equipment, and speed-ring engine cowlings were optional. The next Sikorsky development was the huge 4-motored "Clipper" model S-40 described in the chapter for ATC # 454 of this volume.

Listed below are model S-41 entries as gleaned from registration records:

NC- 41V; S-41   (# 1100-X) 2 Hornet B.
NC- 60V; S-41-A   (# 1100-X2)   "
NC-784Y; S-41-B   (# 1105)   "

No listing for ser. # 1103, # 1104; ser. # 1100-X variously as S-41, S-41-A, S-41-B; ser. # 1105 as S-41-B on Group 2 approval 2-286; ser. # 1100-X bought by Pan American on 9-26-30 for $63,000.; ser. # 1105 bought 7-31-31 for $62,000. and operated in the Caribbean; an S-41-A was delivered to Pan American 8-27-34 and operated in South America.

A.T.C. # 419
(4-15-31)
BIRD, MODEL CJ

Fig. 60. Bird model CJ with 170 h.p. Jacobs LA-1 engine.

The handsome "Bird" model CJ might very well be the best airplane Bird Aircraft had ever built; from assessment and comparison of ability and virtues, that opinion would be rather hard to form easily but we can at least say that the CJ was the last standard model in production. First introduced among such stars as the "Bird" C, CK, and BW, the model CJ took its place gingerly in the lineup to be duly recognized. As brought out early in 1931, this model mounted the 7 cyl. Jacobs LA-1 engine of 150 h.p.; the price-tag on the shiny offering read $4480. The Jacobs engine was rerated a month later to 170 h.p., and in this new combination, the price of the CJ took a jump to $4995. For an all-purpose biplane that probably leaned more heavily to the sport-plane category, the $5000. tab restricted its sales somewhat in those days of skidding economy. To warrant its consideration then, by those that could yet afford a ship of this type, the CJ was bedecked with much of the finery that was usually provided only as extra equipment. Of the small number that were built, one CJ was owned and flown by a lady sportsman-pilot; one example enjoyed the sporting touches of a panel-covered front cockpit, lower wing roots neatly faired into the fuselage, and other minor finishing touches that together in-

creased its cruising speeds. It is hard to predict what the future of the model CJ would have been in more normal times, perhaps it would have been very popular and built in a large number; it was every bit a "Bird" and it surely shared all the fine qualities this airplane series has been noted for.

For Bird aircraft, the period of 1930-31 was one producing several interesting developments. Announced and shown at the annual Detroit Air Show for 1931, was the Bird model E. This was a 4-5 place cabin biplane that at first flush promised to be one of the most interesting models in the company's line-up. Powered with a 125 h.p. Kinner B5 engine, the model E was said to have hauled 4 big people in unbelievable performance. This was the talk at the show. For reasons unknown, further development of this promising version was quietly dropped, but it was still offered late in 1931 for $4895. The trusty Bird model A with the Curtiss OX-5 engine was still available at this time, and the price by now had dropped to $1995. As shown, the brawny-looking model F was another development during this period; powered with a 225-300 h.p. Packard Diesel engine, it was offered as a high-performance sport-plane for two, or as a single-seated mail-cargo plane. Its fur-

Fig. 61. Bird CJ adapted to all-purpose service, but largely used for sport.

ther development was also dropped. Perhaps the last development by Bird, the 3-place model CC was powered with the 6 cyl. Curtiss "Challenger" engine of 185 h.p.; it was hangared in New York for general use by the Curtiss-Wright Flying Service. Despite all that "Bird" had to offer, sales had taken a drastic drop and production lines fizzled to a halt; no amount of sales promotion seemed to be of any help. Battling valiantly to overcome effects of the entrenched depression, Bird Aircraft finally had to give up in late 1932. All manufacturing had ceased, and the corporation was sold to the Perth-Amboy Title Co. of New Jersey. Early in 1933, the Speed Bird Corp. of Keyport, N.J. was formed

to serve all "Bird" aircraft owners with spare parts, repairs, and maintenance service. Later in 1933, this company designed and developed a two-place side-by-side sport-trainer powered with the 90 h.p. Lambert engine. Called the "Speed Bird", it was faithfully fashioned in the familiar lines of the "Bird" biplane, but its future more or less withered on the vine. Of the 200 or so "Bird" biplanes that were built in the five-year period to 1932, some 120 were still flying actively in 1939. There is work afoot to ressurect many of these fine airplanes, and the number that are already flying is lasting tribute to the pioneers of another generation.

The Bird model CJ was an open cockpit bi-

Fig. 62. The rare Bird model E carried four on 125 h.p. Lack of finances curtailed further development.

Fig. 63. Packard diesel-powered Bird model F shown here as mail-plane, convertible also to two-seated sport-plane.

plane with seating arranged for three. Basically an airplane for the chores of all-purpose service, it was, however, slanted more to the requirements of the sportsman-pilot. Typical of other "Bird" models, its main claim to fame and separate identity was the installation of the new Jacobs radial engine. Powered with the 7 cyl. Jacobs LA-1 engine of 150-170 h.p., its useable performance range was outstanding among other craft of this type. Enjoying the feel of more power than any other "Bird" on the production line, the "CJ" had a range of performance from slow speed to high speed, that in the hands of a good pilot, could make even an "autogiro" blush with envy. Favoring the tastes of the sportsman, the CJ was fitted with a "speed-ring" cowling over the Jacobs engine, it was equipped with wheel brakes and engine starter, neater interior appointments, extra equipment, and accessories to aid the pilot for better operation. By any standards of comparison, the Bird model CJ was a truly fine airplane and clearly one of the best airplanes available in this particular class. At this time, all "Bird" models were available on the time-payment purchase plan; 40% was required as down payment and the balance was spread over a 12 month period. The type certificate number for the model CJ was issued 4-15-31 and some 6 examples of this model were built by the Bird Aircraft Corp. at Glendale, Long Island, N.Y.

Listed below are specifications and performance data for the Bird model CJ as powered

with the 170 h.p. Jacobs LA-1 engine; length overall 22'9"; height overall 8'6"; wing span upper 34'0"; wing span lower 25'0"; wing chord upper 69"; wing chord lower 48"; wing area upper 184 sq.ft.; wing area lower 82 sq.ft.; total wing area 266 sq.ft.; airfoil USA-40B modified; wt. empty 1413 lbs.; useful load 832 lbs.; payload with 45 gal. fuel 370 lbs. (2 pass. at 170 lb. each & 30 lb. baggage); gross wt. 2245 lbs.; max. speed 126; cruising speed 109; landing speed 38; climb 980 ft. first min. at sea level; climb to 8000 ft. in 10 min.; ceiling 18,000 ft.; gas cap. 45 gal.; oil cap. 3 gal.; cruising range at 9 gal. per hour 490 miles; price early models at factory with Jacobs 150 at $4480.; price later models at factory with Jacobs 170 at $4995.

The construction details and general arrangement of the Bird model CJ was typical to that of the models BK, C, and BW. The bottom fuselage on the CJ was faired out a little fuller, and head-rest fairing was extended nearly to base of the vertical fin; lower wing roots were sometimes faired-in to the fuselage junction with a stream-lined fillet. A baggage bin with allowance for 30 lbs. was located in the turtle-back section behind the rear cockpit; two metal peg-steps afforded better entry to either cockpit. The fuel tank was mounted high in the fuselage just ahead of the front cockpit; a direct-reading fuel gauge projected through the cowling. The cross-axle landing gear of 66 in. tread used oleo-spring shock absorbing struts; low pressure "semi-airwheels" were 7.50x10 and brakes were provided. A metal propeller, speed-ring engine cowl, Heywood engine starter, navigation lights, dual controls, a compass, cockpit covers, fire extinguisher, and first-aid kit were standard equipment.

Listed below are model CJ entries as gleaned from registration records:
NC-851W; Bird CJ (# CJ-7001) Jacobs 170.
NC-854W;   "   (# CJ-7002)   "
NC-990M;   "   (# CJ-7003)   "
NC-999M;   "   (# CJ-7004)   "
NC-2103;   "   (# CJ-7005)   "
NC-13225;   "   (# CJ-7006)   "
NR-855W; Bird E   (# 6001) Kinner B5-125.
X-790N;   Bird F (# 8001) Packard Diesel.
X-789N;   Bird CC (# 9001) Curtiss R-600.
Serial # 6001 (Model E) later as 1 pl.; ser. # 8001 as 2 pl. sport, or 1 pl. mail; ser. # 9001 (Model CC) as 3 pl. on Group 2 approval # 2-441; approval for model CJ expired 3-3-33.

Fig. 64. Stinson SM-6000-B with three 215 h.p. Lycoming engines; also known as "Model T."

Comparatively low-priced and quite economical for the amount of work it could perform, the Stinson tri-motored "Model T" (SM-6000-B) found ready favor with new and expanding airline systems across the country. Century Airlines was, of course, equipped with the new transport, so was the Century-Pacific line, and later they were put into service by the N.Y.-Philadelphia & Washington Line, the Pennsylvania Air Lines, the American Airways, Transamerican, Chicago & Southern, Eastern Air Transport, and Delta Air Lines; one tri-motored SM-6000-B even got over to the Philippine Islands for air line service there. Century Airlines as organized by E. L. Cord, used the SM-6000-B on the route from Cleveland to St. Louis, with stops at Toledo, Detroit, and Chicago. The Century-Pacific line, also an E. L. Cord venture, served a route from San Diego to San Francisco for a short time. Early in 1932 the Century and Century-Pacific lines, through some corporate manipulations, were absorbed into the workings of the American Airways system; thus "American" inherited some 24 tri-motored SM-6000-B and 3 Stinson "Junior" in the deal. Stately, confidence-inspiring, hardy, and very dependable, the SM-6000-B served the various airlines faithfully for several years; when retired from regular service most were relegated to further service on lesser lines, or to "barnstorm" the countryside in the mid-thirties. These barnstorming tours, very much like those of the gipsy-fliers in the decade previous, were a haphazard living at best but the cheap joy-rides brought many people their first airplane ride, winning over many new converts to air-travel. Excellent performance, inherent safety, and a compatible nature helped to promote the popularity and the longevity of the SM-6000-B, so we find that at least 25 examples were still flying actively in 1939, and some even for years afterwards.

The Stinson tri-motored model SM-6000-B (Model T) was a large high-winged cabin monoplane of the transport type with various seating arrangements for 6 to 10 passengers. The model SM-6000-B1 was the all-passenger version seating 10 passengers and a pilot; arranged with coach-style interiors, this version allowed just short of 25 lbs. of baggage per person. The model SM-6000-B2 as the mail-passenger version was the more popular, with arrangements for 8 or 9 passengers and bins for up to 350 lbs. of mail and baggage. Extensively upgraded from the earlier SM-6000 "Airliner", the SM-6000-B now had provisions for extra equipment, more pilot aids, more comfort for the passengers, including washroom and lavatory, and other progressive modifications that added to its usefulness in airline service. With all passenger seating removed, the SM-6000-B was also eligible as a cargo-carrier. For the business man, special "Club" interiors were available to seat from 6 to

Fig. 65. SM-6000-B served Cleveland-Pittsburgh-Washington route for Pennsylvania Air Lines.

8 passengers in varying degrees of deluxe comfort, for just traveling in style or for conducting business enroute. As powered with three 9 cyl. Lycoming R-680 engines of 215 h.p. each, the SM-6000-B delivered a performance that certainly belied its well-apparent bulk. With a low-drag speed-ring cowling shrouding each of its engines, and large streamlined fairings over the big wheels, this craft could maintain a top speed of 146 m.p.h. With a fair amount of power reserve, the tri-motored SM-6000-B could maintain an altitude of 6000 ft. with any two of its engines, even when fully loaded. A take-off run of about 700 ft. and a landing run of about 400 ft.

was not particularly essential for airline work, but it was particularly appreciated later on by pilots barnstorming out of small turf-covered fields. Typical of all Stinson monoplanes, the big SM-6000-B cooperated with the pilot to perform an admirable job, no matter what the chore. Many pilots to this day have a soft spot in their hearts for the big, good-natured SM-6000-B. The type certificate number for the tri-motored SM-6000-B was issued 4-23-31 and at least 40 examples of this model were manufactured by the Stinson Aircraft Corp. at Wayne, Mich.

Listed below are specifications and performance data for the Stinson model SM-6000-B

Fig. 66. Transamerican crew prepare to move Stinson T into hangar for service.

Fig. 67. SM-6000-B retired from airline service shown here during barnstorming tour through Indiana in mid-1930.

as powered with 3 Lycoming R-680 engines of 215 h.p. each; length overall 42'10"; height overall 12'0"; wing span 60'0"; wing chord 105"; total wing area 490 sq.ft.; airfoil Goettingen 398; (following wts. apply specifically to SM-6000-B1); wt. empty 5670 lbs.; useful load 2930 lbs.; payload with 160 gal. fuel 1680 lbs.; payload with 110 gal. fuel 1980 lbs. (10 pass. at 170 lb. each & 280 lb. baggage); gross wt. 8600 lbs.; max. speed 138; cruising speed 115 (2 engines cowled, no wheel pants); max. speed 146; cruising speed 122 (3 engines cowled and wheel pants); landing speed 60-65; climb 1000 ft. first min. at sea level; climb to 10,000 ft. in 30 min.; ceiling 14,500 ft.; gas cap. max. 160 gal.; oil cap. 15 gal.; cruising range at 35 gal. per hour 350 miles; price $25,900. at factory in 1931, lowered to $19,500. early in 1932; (the following wts. apply specifically to SM-6000-B2); wt. empty 5758 lbs.; useful load 2842 lbs.; payload with 110 gal. fuel 1892 lbs. (9 pass. at 170 lb. each & 362 lbs. mail-baggage); gross wt. 8600 lbs.; above listed performance figures apply to SM-6000-B2 also. Gross wt. allowance later boosted to 8800 lbs. with approved modifications.

The fuselage framework was built up of welded chrome-moly (4130) steel tubing,

Fig. 68. SM-6000-B as deluxe club-plane offered plush appointments and special conveniences.

Fig. 69. SM-6000-B retired from airlines were popular for charter flights.

faired to shape with formers and fairing strips, then fabric covered; the whole forward section to a point just behind the pilot station was covered in removable duralumin metal panels. The pilot's compartment had optional seating for 1 or 2 pilots, with either single or dual controls. The main cabin area normally had seating arranged for 10 passengers (SM-6000-B1); by eliminating one or two of the front passenger seats, the space could be converted with metal bins to carry mail-cargo and baggage. To provide easier access to pilot's cabin and cargo bins up forward, a door installation on right side front was available. All windows were of shatter-proof glass, and any window could be opened for ventilation throughout length of the cabin; cabin lights and ventilators were also provided. Main cabin entry door was to the rear on right side. The wing framework in two halves, was built up of chrome-moly steel tube spar beams that were welded into Warren truss girders, with wing ribs riveted together of square duralumin tubing; the leading edges were covered with dural metal sheet and the completed framework was covered in fabric. A fuel tank of 60 gal. cap. and one of 20 gal. cap. was mounted inboard in each wing half. The engine nacelles were mounted into a truss connecting the wing bracing struts, and from this extended the landing gear system using "Aerol" shock absorbing struts. The wheels were normally 36x8 and Bendix brakes were standard equipment; low pressure 35x15-6 Goodyear "airwheels" were optional.

The fabric covered tail-group was built up of welded 4130 and 1025 steel tubing; both vertical fin and horizontal stabilizer were adjustable for trim during flight. Adjustable metal propellers, electric engine starters, a battery, generator, navigation lights, lighted instrument panel, a tail wheel, fire extinguishers, chrome-plated cabin hardware, and speed-ring engine cowls were standard equipment. Low pressure airwheels, wheel pants or wheel fenders, cabin heaters, lavatory room, one-way or two-way radio installation, night-flying equipment, dual wheel controls, and custom interiors were optional. The next development in the Stinson "Tri-Motor" was the model U as described in the chapter for ATC # 484 of this volume.

Listed below are SM-6000-B entries as gleaned from registration records:

NC-11118;	SM-6000-B (# 5015)	3 Lyc. 215
NC-11122;	” (# 5016)	”
NC-11124;	” (# 5017)	”
NC-11119;	” (# 5018)	”
NC-11120;	” (# 5019)	”
NC-484Y;	” (# 5020)	”
NC-11153;	” (# 5021)	”
NC-11155;	” (# 5022)	”
NC-11170;	” (# 5023)	”
NC-11174;	” (# 5024)	”
NC-11175;	” (# 5025)	”
NC-11176;	” (# 5026)	”
NC-11177;	” (# 5027)	”
NC-10804;	” (# 5028)	”
NC-10807;	” (# 5029)	”
NC-10808;	” (# 5030)	”
NC-10809;	” (# 5031)	”
NC-10810;	” (# 5032)	”
NC-10811;	” (# 5033)	”
NC-10813;	” (# 5034)	”
NC-10814;	” (# 5035)	”
NC-10860;	” (# 5036)	”
NC-10818;	” (# 5037)	”
NC-10822;	” (# 5038)	”
NC-10823;	” (# 5039)	”
NC-11167;	” (# 5040)	”
NC-10840;	” (# 5041)	”
NC-10843;	” (# 5042)	”
NC-10844;	” (# 5043)	”
NC-10845;	” (# 5044)	”
NC-10846;	” (# 5045)	”
NC-10847;	” (# 5046)	”
NC-10858;	” (# 5047)	”
NC-10872;	” (# 5048)	”
NC-10871;	” (# 5049)	”
NC-10894;	” (# 5050)	”
NC-10891;	” (# 5051)	”
NC-10892;	” (# 5052)	”
NC-10893;	” (# 5053)	”
NC-12168;	” (# 5054)	”
NC-12130;	” (# 5055)	”
NC-12135;	” (# 5056)	”

Serial # 5015 was 9 pl. Club Model; ser. # 5036 was 8 pl. Club Model; all others were either 11 pl. all-passenger type, or 8-9-10 pl. mail-passenger versions at different times; ser. # 5033 to Honduras in 1932; this approval expired 5-1-33.

Fig. 70. Lockheed "Orion" 9 amid California setting preparing to load; planes offered
"three-mile-a-minute" service.

Billed as the "fastest airliner in the world", the new Lockheed "Orion" was a basic evolution from the earlier "Sirius" and the "Altair"; actually, the prototype "Orion" was called the "6 passenger Sirius" at times, and also the "Altair D". Knowing they had a shiny new star in their famous lineup of stars, Lockheed soon named it the "Orion". Seeking speed and more speed, Temple Bowen, whose Bowen Air Lines were striving to be the "world's fastest airline" on a 945 mile route from Texas to Oklahoma, took delivery of the first two "Orion 9" to come off the line. New York & Western Airlines ordered the next two, and Asa Candler, Jr. a millionaire sportsman, ordered the next as an executive transport for his own use. Two more of the fast "Orion 9" went to Continental Airways, and one went to the Ludington Line. Walter T. Varney, pioneer airmail operator on the west coast, was miffed because of the trespass by Century-Pacific Airlines in "his territory". Vowing to compete by getting the fastest commercial passenger-carrying airplane on the market, Varney wrote a check for six of the fast-flying "Orion". Air travelers were quickly drawn to the romance of the speedy "Orion" and basked in its leather-upholstered comfort; built of wood and thickly padded with insulation and upholstery, the "Ori-

on" was surprisingly free of much motor noise and vibration. Sharing the prime feature that was first introduced on the "Altair", the "Orion" landing gear retracted up flush with the wing's under-surface; this virtually eliminated the parasitic drag caused by wheels, braces, and struts, that hung down into the airstream. The "clean" underside boosted speeds by up to 25 m.p.h. It is ironic that all the major carriers were skeptical of the "Orion" and its disappearing undercarriage, so the smaller airlines were the first to take advantage of its higher cruising speeds. It was almost unbelievable that 4 routes were offering 180 m.p.h. schedules, while the rest were still plodding along at 100. By 1933, the big airline systems were willing to trust the proven "Orion", and were ordering the faster, more powerful models.

The beautiful Lockheed "Orion" model 9 was a roundish low-winged cabin monoplane with seating arranged for seven. As usual, Lockheed was prone to lead with a "first", and the "Orion" was the holder of several. Airlines that first used the "Orion" were boasting of "fastest schedules in the world", but like any innovation, it was not without its problems; rectifying the problems, both operational and mechanical as they came up, it was not long before

*Fig. 71. Retractable landing gear on "Orion" boosted top speed nearly 20 m.p.h.; known as
fastest transport in the world.*

the "Orion" became known as the finest air-liner of its type. Powered with the Pratt & Whitney "Wasp" SC of 450 h.p., the new model 9 was favorably comparable in performance to any other of the wooden "Lockheeds", except that its ace-in-the-hole for more speed was the folding landing gear and some other minor aerodynamic refinements. Staunch, stable, and of predictable nature, pilots actually enjoyed flying the "Orion" and jumped at the chance every time. Up to now, every Lockheed "type" (be it Vega, Air Express, Sirius, etc.) was a record-breaker of one sort or another, and the swift "Orion" was no exception; its baptism to contest was in the first Bendix Trophy Race of 1931. Closely behind Jimmie Doolittle in his special "Laird" racer, one "Orion", averaging nearly

200 m.p.h., finished second and another finished third. Inter-city records were being set almost daily, and no matter where the "Orion" went it had a habit of getting there faster. The type certificate number for the "Orion" model 9 was issued 5-6-31 and 14 examples of this model were manufactured by the Lockheed Aircraft Co. at Burbank, Calif., a division of the Detroit Aircraft Corp. As of mid-1931, some 150 employees were still kept busy working at Lockheed, but the future for some was becoming rather uncertain.

Listed below are specifications and performance data for the "Orion" model 9 as powered with the 450 h.p. "Wasp" SC engine; length overall 27'10"; height overall 9'3"; wing span 42'10"; wing chord at root 102"; wing

Fig. 72. Varney Speed Lines used "Orion" 9 for service into Mexico.

Fig. 73. "Orion" 9 modified for air-express service from coast to coast; service was fast but line unsuccessful.

chord at tip 62"; mean wing chord 84.7"; total wing area 284 sq.ft.; airfoil at root Clark Y-18; airfoil at tip Clark Y-9.5; wt. empty 3250 lbs.; useful load 1950 lbs.; payload with 115 gal. fuel 1020 lbs. (6 pass. at 170 lb. each & no baggage); payload with 100 gal. fuel 1110 lbs. (6 pass. at 170 lb. each & 90 lb. baggage); gross wt. 5200 lbs.; max speed 210 at 6000 ft.; cruising speed 180; landing (stall) speed 64; climb 1200 ft. first min. at sea level; ceiling 20,500 ft.; gas cap. normal 100 gal.; gas cap. max. 125 gal.; oil cap. 9-12 gal.; cruising range at 24 gal. per hour was 4-5 hours, or 650-800 miles; price $25,000. at factory field. Added equipment raised empty wt. of planes in service to 4320 lbs., and a 30 lb. increase in useful load brought gross wt. to an allowable 5400 lbs.; some changes in performance would be noted.

Typical of all woden Lockheeds, the "Orion" fuselage was a cigar-shaped all-wood monocoque structure with appropriate cut-outs for the wing, door, windows, and pilot's cabin. Arranged for six in rather close quarters, the cabin was insulated and richly upholstered in real leather. Cabin entry door was on the right side, and baggage was stowed in a compartment behind the rear seat, with access from inside or out. The pilot's compartment was high up in front, and was protected by a sliding canopy. The tapered cantilever wing was built up of spruce and plywood box-type spar beams, with laminated spruce and plywood wing ribs; of all-wood construction, the completed framework was covered with plywood sheet. The retracting undercarriage folded up inwardly into recesses in the underside of the wing; the gear was operated by a hydraulic hand-pump and was normally retracted in about 30 seconds. The landing gear locked automatically in either the up or down position with signal lights indicating its position. With a tread of 139 in., the landing gear was equipped with oleo shock absorbing struts; 9.50x12 wheels were fitted with 11x12 tires and AP brakes were standard equipment. The cantilever tail-group was an all-wood structure covered with plywood sheet; the horizontal stabilizer was adjustable in flight. An adjustable metal propeller, inertia-type engine starter, swiveling tail wheel, and wheel brakes were standard equipment. Cockpit and cabin heat, navigation lights, a battery, and custom color schemes were optional. The next development in the "Orion" was the Cyclone-powered model 9-B as described in the chapter for ATC # 462 of this volume.

Listed below are "Orion" model 9 entries as gleaned from registration records:

X-960Y;	Orion 9 (# 168) Wasp SC-450.	
NC-964Y;	" (# 169)	"
NC-975Y;	" (# 172)	"
NC-984Y;	" (# 173)	"
NC-988Y;	" (# 174)	"
NC-991Y;	" (# 175)	"
NC-12220;	" (# 177)	"
NC-12221;	" (# 178)	"
NC-12223;	" (# 181)	"
NC-12224;	" (# 182)	"
NC-12225;	" (# 183)	"
NC-12226;	" (# 184)	"
NC-12227;	" (# 185)	"
NC-12228;	" (# 186)	"

Serial # 169, 174, with Pan American in 1934; ser. # 172-173 modified into all-cargo carriers; ser. # 181 later as XA-BHA; ser. # 182 later as XA-BHB; ser. # 183 later as XA-BHC; ser. # 185 later as XA-BHD; ser. # 186 later as XA-BHE; ser. # 173-174 as 3-5 pl. on Group 2 approval # 2-367; ser. # 175, 177, destroyed 1932 in hangar fire; ser. # 178 crashed 11-5-31, as washout.

A.T.C. # 422
(5-9-31)
DOUGLAS "DOLPHIN", MODEL 1

Fig. 74. Douglas "Dolphin" model 1 with 2 Wright R-975 engines; "Dolphin" was excellent "boat" and a good airplane.

Douglas Aircraft made its re-entry into the commercial airplane market with the introduction of its new "Dolphin" monoplane; compared to what Douglas had been building previously, the twin-engined "Dolphin" stood on the plant floor as a very strange craft indeed. Standing on its wheels as a sturdy "amphibian" of the flying-boat type, one that could absorb hard knocks in all kinds of service, the "Dolphin" model 1 posed staunchly as the first of a new and hardy breed. Doubly suitable as a light passenger-transport, or as an "air yacht" for the moneyed sportsman, it is faintly suggestive that the rugged "Dolphin" was also planned to appeal to the various government services. One of the first "Dolphin" to be put into commercial service was used on the Wilmington-Catalina Airline, a flight of some 20 miles that was then the shortest scheduled commercial route. Leaving the California mainland at Wilmington, the 12 min. flight terminated in Avalon Bay at the Isle of Catalina. Although normally carrying 8, the popularity of these flights soon prompted modifications to the "Dolphin" that allowed 10 passengers, baggage, and 2 pilots. These were the "Model 1 Spl." and business on the line was so good that a sister-ship was put into service soon after. Versatile, extremely rugged, and a good performer, the "Dolphin" model 1 was appraised by the Army, Navy, and Coast Guard: orders were soon placed by each of the services for custom-built versions to fit their needs.

Douglas Aircraft laid claim to 15 orders in 1931, but most of these must have gone to the "services" because only a few "commercial" orders were recorded. The "Dolphin" model 1 with its 300 h.p. engines was the first in a long line of some very interesting and resourceful machines.

The Douglas "Dolphin" model 1 was a cabin monoplane of the flying-boat type with a retracting undercarriage to permit operations off land or water. The deep and broad metal hull was spaciously arranged for the seating of 8. Designed to take the buffeting of heavy waters, the sturdy hull was arranged in 3 water-tight compartments with ample space for a variety of appointments. The 2 engines were mounted high above the stout cantilever wing on a system of braces in a tractor fashion; the engine nacelles were cleverly tied together with a small wing that added rigidity to the trusses, and also provided some extra lift. The high mounting of the engines provided comfortable clearance and distance from the whirling propellers, and kept propellers away from damaging water-spray. The retracting long-leg landing gear folded up and out of the way for operations on water, and could be easily lowered for operations on land. Wing-tip floats helped to keep the hull on an even keel, and prevented wings from heeling into the water. Powered with two 9 cyl. Wright "Whirlwind" R-975 engines of 300 h.p. each, the performance of the "Dolphin" was exceptional for a craft of this type, but must have been

Fig. 75. Douglas "Dolphin" in story-book setting on Catalina Island.

somewhat marginal with "one engine out". Flight-tested first in Sept. of 1930, and tested rigorously for the next 8 months, it had been claimed that the "Dolphin" could fly safely on one of its 300 h.p. engines; it must have been a scary and sweaty task. With this aside, the "Dolphin" was however a very good airplane and a very good boat, lending itself to all sorts of rigorous service. For a 4-ton airplane, this craft was quite deft on land or water, and pleasantly maneuverable in the air. The type certificate number for the "Dolphin" model 1 was issued 5-9-31 and some 4 or more examples of this

model were manufactured by Douglas Aircraft Co., Inc. on Clover Field in Santa Monica, Calif.

Listed below are specifications and performance data for the Douglas "Dolphin" model 1 as powered with 2 Wright R-975 engines of 300 h.p. each; length overall 44'4"; height overall 14'7"; main wing span 60'0"; wing chord at root 132"; wing chord at tip 87"; main wing area 515 sq.ft.; aux. wing span 20'0"; aux. wing chord 30"; aux. wing area 47 sq.ft.; total wing area 562 sq.ft.; airfoil main wing Clark Y-18 at root, and Clark Y-9 at tip; airfoil aux. wing Clark Y; wt. empty 5610 lbs.; useful load 2590 lbs.;

Fig. 76. Prototype "Dolphin" during early test-flights.

Fig. 77. "Dolphin 1 Special" flew ferry-trip from Wilmington, Cal. to Catalina Island.

payload with 155 gal. fuel (2 pilots) 1180 lbs. (6 pass. at 170 lb. each & 160 lb. baggage); payload with 180 gal. fuel (2 pilots) 1030 lbs. (6 pass. & no baggage); gross wt. 8200 lbs.; max. speed (with speed-rings) 141; cruising speed 115; landing speed 62; climb 750 ft. first min. at sea level; ceiling 16,000 ft.; gas cap. normal 155 gal.; gas cap. max. 180 gal.; oil cap. 18 gal.; cruising range at 36 gal. per hour 450-525 miles; price $35,000. at factory field. Prototype airplane was 400 lbs. lighter, so performance would be affected accordingly.

The two-step boat-type hull was a duralumin semi-monocoque structure divided into 3 main water-tight compartments; emergency exit was provided by 3 external hatches. The main cabin was normally arranged with 6 adjustable seats that were provided with head-rests for comfort; 3 large windows lined each side and center window of each side was removable for escape. A large external hatchway, beyond the wing's trailing edge, provided easy entry to the main cabin. A lavatory and toilet equipment could be fitted in the space to rear of the main hatchway. Two baggage compartments of 30 cu.ft. capacity total, were provided; one up front of pilot's station had allowance for 100 lbs., and one to rear of cabin had allowance for 50 lbs. The pilot's cabin for two, was high up front ahead of the wing; a sky-light hatchway provided entry or exit. Dual wheel controls were standard equipment for normal operations. The tapered cantilever wing was built up of laminated spruce box-type spar beams with spruce and plywood truss-

type wing ribs; the completed framework was covered with spruce plywood sheet. Two fuel tanks of 90 gal. capacity each were mounted in the wing flanking each side of the hull; a 9 gal. oil tank was mounted in each nacelle. The long-leg retractable landing gear used Gruss oil-spring shock absorbing struts; wheels were 36x8 and Bendix brakes were standard equipment. The landing gear was operated into up or down position by either pilot with a hydraulic hand-pump the landing gear position was visible at all times. The tail-group was a riveted duralumin structure covered with "Alclad" metal sheet; the horizontal stabilizer was adjustable in flight and all movable surfaces had aerodynamic balance. Metal propellers, electric engine starters, a battery, generator, fire extinguishers, anchoring and mooring gear, wheel brakes, tail wheel, and dual controls were standard equipment. Toilet-lavatory equipment, and custom interior arrangements were optional. The next "Dolphin" development was the model 3 as described in the chapter for ATC # 432 of this volume.

Listed below are "Dolphin" model 1 entries as gleaned from registration records:
X-145W; Dolphin 1 (# 1-A-703) 2 Wright R-975.
NC-967Y;   ”   (# 999)   ”
NC-12212;   ”   (# 1002)   ”
NC-12243;   ”   (# 1003)   ”
Serial # 999 and # 1002 modified to model 1 Special on Group 2 approval # 2-366 as 12 pl. for air-ferry; Y1C-21 a military version of "Dolphin 1", Army Air Corps had 8 in 1932.

A.T.C. # 423
(5-12-31)
STINSON "JUNIOR", MODEL S

Fig. 78. The popular Stinson "Junior" S with 215 h.p. Lycoming engine.

The four-seated Stinson "Junior" model S for 1931-32 was but very little changed from the SM-8 of 1930, but it was loaded with little improvements. Comparatively speaking, the SM-8 "Junior" was a very good airplane, a terrific bargain, and was selling like hot-cakes; perhaps it was only logical then to keep on building the so-called hot-cakes. Already popular with men of business, the flying-service operator and the family-man who flew for the sport, the "Junior" in the new S-version took on some added chores now to prove its terrific utility. The "New S" was the so-called Stinson "Air Taxi" and charter-flight operators were scattered in all parts of the country. Unusual for an airplane of this modest size, the "Model S" even took on the role of airliner. Several small airlines sprang up in the most likely and unlikely spots to offer scheduled and non-scheduled runs, most often to connect passengers with main-line systems. Frequent shuttle-runs were also offered in many areas where high-capacity equipment would not be feasible nor profitable. Many of these small airlines had only one airplane, but others had as many as 2 or 3. Most of the operators maintained their "Air Taxi" on the line in constant readiness, and were ready to go most anywhere on a few moments notice. Without a doubt the best buy in the country for a four-place cabin airplane at this time, sales for the new "Junior S" held up well in spite of the steadily sinking economy. John C. Kelley, as traveling sales manager for Stinson, was busy flying and kept in constant touch with area representatives; together they sold a lot of Stinson airplanes. Probably built in well over 100 examples there were still at least 70 of the "Junior S" version flying actively in

1939. One example with the same owner over the years was still going strong in 1959.

The Stinson Junior-type "model S" was a high-winged cabin monoplane with seating arranged for four, all in an environment that was pleasantly comfortable, practical, and quite serviceable. One would think that an airplane of this type with a price-tag of less than $5000. would surely have to sacrifice something for the sake of economy, but this certainly was not true of the new "Stinson S". Features of convenience and finery, as introduced in this basic "Junior" design a year previous, were all retained in full with perhaps a little more stress on being more serviceable and more practical. With an airplane that was now 111 lbs. heavier empty, with the useful load cut by 41 lbs. and loaded gross weight heavier now by 70 lbs., the "model S" cancelled out this slight penalty by carrying 11 gal. less fuel. This short-coming was of small consequence in view of the fact that a 50 gal. fuel load still allowed a cruising range of some 400 miles. Frequent and extended use in all kinds of service was actually hard on an airplane's innards, so it is commendable to say that the "model S" wore very well and bore its accumulated years lightly. Powered with the popular 9 cyl. Lycoming R-680 engine of 215 h.p., the new "S" delivered a very good performance and certainly was not choosy about its chore or base of operations; a short sod-strip or a long paved runway, it mattered little to this amiable craft. Slanted toward business-men and private-owners, as well as the flying-service operators, this airplane was purposely designed as a strong, safe, and easy to fly airplane. Of very good nature, the "Junior S" like its earlier

Fig. 79. At less than $5000 Stinson S was biggest bargain of 1931.

sister-ships, was very patient and made great allowances for abuse or error. The enviable safety record and the interesting, almost unbelieveable lore left behind by the Stinson "Junior" type was not shared by too many other airplanes. The type certificate number for the Stinson "Model S" was issued 5-12-31 and at least 100 examples of this model were manufactured by the Stinson Aircraft Corp. at Wayne, Mich.; a division of the Cord Corp.

Listed below are specifications and performance data for the Stinson "Model S" as powered with the 215 h.p. Lycoming engine; length overall 28'11"; height overall 8'9"; wing span 42'1"; wing chord 75"; total wing area 235 sq.ft.; airfoil Clark Y; empty wt. 2172 lbs. (wt. empty includes speed-ring, starter, & battery); useful load 1093 lbs.; payload with 50 gal. fuel 585 lbs. (3 pass. at 170 lb. each & 75 lb. baggage); gross wt. 3265 lbs.; max. speed (with speed-ring) 128; cruising speed 105; landing (stall) speed 48; climb 750 ft. first min. at sea level; ceiling 13,500 ft.; gas cap. 50 gal.; oil cap. 4-5 gal.; cruising range at 12 gal. per hour 400 miles; price at factory field $4995. in 1931, lowered to $4595. in 1932. Price delivered on west coast $4962. in 1932. Gross wt. of seaplane version was 3520 lbs. with 65 lbs. allowed for baggage and gear; as fitted with Edo P twin-float gear, price was $6695.

The fuselage framework was built up of welded chrome-moly and mild-carbon steel tubing,

Fig. 80. Stinson "Jr. S" was popular as air-taxi.

faired to shape with wooden and metal formers, wooden fairing strips then fabric covered. The cabin interior was plainly neat and upholstered in various fine serviceable fabrics. All windows were of shatter-proof glass; the front side-panels at pilot's station could be lowered or slid back when necessary. The cabin walls were sound-proofed and well insulated with added provisions for cabin heat and ventilation. A small skylight in the forward roof offered visibility upward. A large door and a convenient step on either side offered easy exit or entry. Front seats were individual, the rear seat was of the bench type, and a baggage compartment of 7 cu.ft. capacity with allowance for up to 75 lbs. was accessible from inside or out. The wing framework was built up of solid spruce spars routed to an I-beam section with Hyblum metal and stainless steel wing ribs; the leading edges were covered with dural metal sheet and the completed framework was covered in fabric. Wing bracing struts were large diameter steel tubes encased in balsa-wood fairings shaped to an Eiffel 380 section; the faired struts added to the lift and lateral stability. On later-type struts the bracing tubes were faired with metal ribs and fabric covered. Fuel tanks were mounted in the root end of each wing half flanking the fuselage; fuel-level gauges were in easy view. The outrigger landing gear of 115 in. tread used oleo-spring shock absorbing struts; 8.50x10 low pressure semi-airwheels were fitted with brakes. Brake pedals were on left side for pilot only, but available for right side also. Fittings were also provided for the installation of Edo P twin-float seaplane gear. The fabric covered tail-group was built up of welded steel tubing; the fin was ground adjustable and the horizontal stabilizer was adjustable in flight. Standard color scheme was black and red, however some were finished in two-tone dark green with light green; custom colors were optional. A metal propeller, electric engine starter. and navigation lights were standard equipment. A speed-ring engine cowling, wheel pants for main

wheels and tail wheel, metal fairings on landing gear struts, landing lights, parachute flares, 73 gal. fuel capacity, reclining chair in right front side, 25x11-4 Goodyear airwheels, skis, and Edo P floats were optional. The next development in the basic Stinson "Junior" series was the model W as described in the chapter for ATC # 435 of this volume.

Listed below is partial listing of "model S" entries as gleaned from registration records:

NC-11172; Model S (# 8000) Lyc. 215.		
NC-10816;	"	(# 8002)	"
NC-10819;	"	(# 8003)	"
NC-10817;	"	(# 8004)	"
NC-10820;	"	(# 8005)	"
NC-10821;	"	(# 8006)	"
NC-8445;	"	(# 8007)	"
NC-10824;	"	(# 8008)	"
NC-10825;	"	(# 8009)	"
NC-10827;	"	(# 8010)	"
NC-10828;	"	(# 8011)	"
NC-10826;	"	(# 8012)	"
NC-8463;	"	(# 8013)	"
NC-10829;	"	(# 8014)	"
NC-8462;	"	(# 8015)	"
NC-8464;	"	(# 8016)	"
NC-11164;	"	(# 8017)	"
NC-11163;	"	(# 8018)	"
NC-11165;	"	(# 8019)	"
NC-11166;	"	(# 8020)	"
NC-11169;	"	(# 8021)	"
NC-11168;	"	(# 8022)	"
NS-72;	"	(# 8023)	"
NC-10830;	"	(# 8024)	"
NC-10832;	"	(# 8025)	"
NC-10831;	"	(# 8026)	"
NC-10833;	"	(# 8027)	"
NC-10834;	"	(# 8028)	"
NC-10835;	"	(# 8029)	"
NC-10836;	"	(# 8030)	"
NC-12141;	"	(# 8093)	"
NC-10875;	"	(# 8101)	"
NC-12158;	"	(# 8209)	"

This approval for ser. # 8000, 8002, and up; this approval expired 9-30-39.

Fig. 81. Emsco B-7-C mid-wing with Continental A-70 engine.

With a basic design and airframe easily adapt-ed to several different powerplant installations, Emsco introduced a companion model in the mid-wing "Sport" series. Now as the model B-7-C, the new "Sport" was powered with the 7 cyl. Continental A-70 engine of 165 h.p. The A-70 engine had been gaining favor steadily as a smooth, reliable powerplant, so its installation in the Emsco mid-wing was calculated as a favorable move. The new combination turned out to be a compatible mating that tended to bring out some of the better traits of the Emsco "Sport"; although comment on the B-7-C was very favorable from those who knew it, its fu-ture was not a very bright promise. Leveled es-pecially at the flying sportsman, with a price-tag just short of $6000., its possibilities for sale were limited to a very small band of customers at this particular time. So far the Emsco mid-wing "Sport" series were available in two mod-els, and these were represented by only one ex-ample of each; still another model was later in-troduced as the B-7-CH with a 6 cyl. Curtiss "Challenger" engine. By that time Emsco was seriously thinking of closing its doors. Those who can remember will surely agree that some of the most beautiful airplanes of this period came out of the Emsco factory in Downey.

Development continued on several diverse models through 1931, in effort to come up with something that might sell, but the cash register showed "no sale" more often than not. By June of 1931, in effort to recapture some of its huge investment, Emsco was selling off surplus en-gines, accessories, and all sorts of hardware and raw stock. It was easy to see that the end was drawing near. With hardly enough to keep him busy, and somewhat enamored with ambitious plans of his own, Gerry Vultee left Emsco by Sept. of 1931 to be replaced by T. V. Van Stone. With a design proposal for an all-metal high-speed transport monoplane already in his hip-pocket, Vultee was backed for this new project by E. L. Cord interests. A model B-9 and B-10 by Emsco were believed to be the last develop-ments, and chief engineer Van Stone had naught to do then but wait around for the end. The end came in about Feb. of 1932; Emsco quit the busi-ness, closed its books, and vacated their beauti-ful plant in Downey. Very soon a portion of the plant was reopened temporarily by the Cham-pion Aircraft Corp. for the manufacture of light training airplanes, and engines. H. S. "Dick" Myhres, formerly with Simplex and also the "Cycloplane" venture, spark-plugged this new company, but it quietly folded up before the year was out.

As shown here in varied views, the Emsco "Sport" model B-7-C was also a mid-wing mono-plane with open cockpits arranged for the seat-ing of two in tandem. Definitely slanted to ap-peal to the sportsman, the B-7-C was finished off in manner pleasing to the discriminate buy-er, and equipped with extras that would make its operation more practical and enjoyable. As powered with the 165 h.p. Continental A-70 (Series 2) engine, the "Sport" delivered a rela-tively above-average performance. Arranged in

Fig. 82. B-7-C shown here as true mid-wing; large wing blanked-off view downward.

good aerodynamic proportion with large effective areas, the B-7 was docile when checked and quite spirited when spurred. Outside of a few minor annoying traits, directly attributed to the "center-wing" design, the Emsco "Sport" was an excellent airplane. The type certificate number for the Emsco model B-7-C was issued 6-2-31 and only one example of this model was built by the Emsco Aircraft Corp. at Downey, Calif.

E. M. Smith was president; Gerard F. Vultee was chief engineer, replaced later by T. V. Van Stone.

Listed below are specifications and performance data for the Emsco "Sport" model B-7-C as powered with the 165 h.p. Continental A-70-2 engine; length overall 23'9"; height overall 8'1"; wing span 36'0"; wing chord 72"; total effective wing area 194 sq.ft.; airfoil Clark

Fig. 83. Emsco B-7-C developed especially for the sportsman-pilot.

Fig. 84. Emsco B-8 "Flying Wing" developed for long-distance flights.

Y; wt. empty 1490 lbs.; useful load 610 lbs.; payload with 31 gal. fuel 216 lbs. (1 pass. at 170 lb. & 46 lb. baggage); gross wt. 2100 lbs.; max. speed 130 (with speed-ring cowl & wheel pants); cruising speed 110; landing speed 40; climb 1000 ft. first min. at sea level; climb to 8000 ft. in 10 min.; ceiling 18,000 ft.; gas cap. 31 gal.; oil cap. 5 gal.; cruising range at 9 gal. per hour 350 miles; price $5900. at factory field with standard equipment.

The construction details and general arrangement of the model B-7-C were typical to that of the model B-7 as described in the chapter for ATC # 403 of this volume. Some applicable data for the B-7-C as follows. Fuel tanks were mounted in the root ends of the two-piece wing; a small gravity-feed fuel tank was mounted high in the fuselage ahead of front cockpit. The wing was faired into the fuselage junction by large metal wing-root fillets. A small baggage bin behind rear cockpit had allowance for up to 46 lbs.; two parachutes at 20 lbs. each, when carried, were part of the baggage allowance. The long-leg landing gear used "Aerol" (air-oil) shock absorbing struts; wheels were 26x4 and Bendix brakes were standard equipment. Low pressure 6.50x10 semi-airwheels with brakes were optional, and in this case, the unusual wheel fairings were not used. A metal propeller, Eclipse hand-crank engine starter, speed-ring engine cowl, dual controls, fire extinguisher, and first-aid kit were standard equipment. Navigation lights, a battery, Heywood air-operated engine starter and tail wheel were optional. The next development in the Emsco "Sport" mid-wing monoplane series was the model B-7-CH as on Group 2 approval numbered 2-396.

Listed below is the only known entry for the model B-7-C:
NC-969Y; Model B-7-C (# 1) A-70-2.

A.T.C. # 425
(6-4-31)
CURTISS-WRIGHT "SEDAN", 15-N

Fig. 85. Curtiss-Wright "Sedan" model 15-N with 210 h.p. Kinner C5 engine.

Like several others, Curtiss-Wright tried earlier (as the Curtiss-Robertson Div.) to meet Stinson's competition by pitting the 4-place "Robin" (4C-1A) against the popular SM-8 "Junior"; the uneven match was hardly a decent contest. Prompted into further action, there was a hurried development of the "Sedan" model 15, a craft which fared only a little better in the market for this type of airplane. Using the Travel Air "model 10" monoplane (ATC # 278) as a handy basis for the new development, only such changes were incorporated that would allow more efficient production and quicker assembly; a cabin windshield of simpler shape, a landing gear of simpler geometry, and other logical short-cuts that would not detract from reliability nor performance were some of the changes. These savings in the building and assembly time were then reflected in the lowered delivered price. Not skimping in materials, structure, appointments, or equipment, the "model 15" was certainly good value for the money, but it could hardly cope with prevailing cut-rate prices of other manufacturers. As an example in point, the Stinson "Junior" S for 1931, also a typical 4-place cabin monoplane, delivered for $4995. with a 215 h.p. engine! Introduced by Curtiss-Wright with tongue-in-cheek for $6950., it was soon evident that a price reduction was quickly in order; the new price of $5100. for the 15-N was more attractive but just about break-even money. Powered with the big 5 cyl. Kinner C5 engine of 210 h.p., the model 15-N was not particularly popular nor successful; this because the well-spaced jolts of the "big Kinner" produced uncomfortable and even damaging vibrations,

both to human temperament and the airplane's structure. Somewhere along the line at different times, most of the 15-N were gradually modified to the Wright-powered model 15-D.

The Curtiss-Wright "Sedan" model 15-N was a fairly large high-winged cabin monoplane arranged with comfortable seating for four. Interior appointments, general workmanship, and the equipment included was far better than one would expect in a craft that was held to rock-bottom price. Arranged and fitted primarily for the sportsman who required more seating capacity, the "Sedan" did not, however, shy away from hard work and was well suited for rugged all-purpose service. Powered with the big Kinner C5 engine of 210 h.p., the 15-N had ample muscle to turn in a very good performance, getting into and out of small 'fields with remarkable dexterity and ease. Flight characteristics were described as quite good, and general behavior was perhaps about average for a ship of this type. The type certificate number for the model 15-N was issued 6-4-31 and 3 examples of this model were manufactured by the Curtiss-Wright Airplane Co. at Robertson (St. Louis), Mo.

Listed below are specifications and performance data for the "Sedan" model 15-N as powered with the 210 h.p. Kinner C5 engine; length overall 30'5"; height overall 8'10"; wing span 43'5"; wing chord 74"; total wing area 240 sq.ft.; airfoil Travel Air # 2 (modified Goettingen 593); wt. empty 2081 lbs.; useful load 1198 lbs.; payload with 60 gal. fuel 630 lbs. (3 pass. at 170 lb. each & 120 lb. baggage); gross wt. 3279 lbs.; max. speed 125; cruising speed 105; landing speed 53; average take-off run 580

Fig. 86. A large airplane, the 15-N offered plenty of room.

ft.; climb 700 ft. first min. at sea level; ceiling 13,000 ft.; gas cap. 60 gal.; oil cap. 5 gal.; cruising range at 12 gal. per hour 475 miles; price at factory first quoted as $6950., lowered to $5100. in April of 1931. The 5 cyl. Kinner C5-210 (R-715) was rated 210 h.p. at 1900 r.p.m.; price was $2250. with exhaust collector ring.

The fuselage framework was built up of welded chrome-moly steel tubing into a rigid truss, heavily faired to shape with formers and fairing strips, then fabric covered. With interior arranged for four, there were two individual seats in front and a bench-type seat in back; a large rectangular door and a convenient step offered easy exit or entry. Large windows were of shatter-proof glass, and some slid open for extra ventilation; cabin heat was available. A large baggage compartment with allowance for up to 120 lbs. was behind the rear seat, with small bins under the front seats for tools and other sundry items. Dual control was provided with a swing-over wheel, but dual control wheels were also available. The wing framework was built up of solid spruce spar beams with spruce and plywood truss-type wing ribs; the leading edges were covered with dural metal sheet and the completed framework was covered in fabric. The wings were braced to the fuselage by heavy steel tube struts, that were faired to an airfoil shape. The fuel tanks were mounted in the root end of each wing-half flanking the fuselage. The simple tripod landing gear used oleo-spring shock absorbing struts; low pressure semi-airwheels with brakes were standard equip-

ment. Brake pedals were provided at pilot's station only, but were available for right-hand side also. The fabric covered tail-group was built up of welded steel tubing; the fin was ground adjustable and the horizontal stabilizer was adjustable in flight. A metal propeller, Eclipse electric engine starter, a battery, tail wheel, wheel brakes, navigation lights, and a throw-over control wheel were standard equipment. Optional equipment included dual wheel controls for $50.00, engine cover for $10.00, retractable landing lights mounted in the wings for $200.00, and two-tone colors other than standard were $100.00 extra. Goodyear 25x11-4 low pressure "airwheels" were also optional.

Listed Below are model 15-N entries as gleaned from registration records:

NC-448W; Model 15-N (15N-2002) Kinner C5.
NC-10927;   "   (15N-2202)   "
NC-11862;   "   (15N-2208)   "

Fig. 87. Utility of 15-N adaptable to many uses.

A.T.C. # 426
(6-10-31)
CURTISS-WRIGHT "SEDAN", 15-C

Fig. 88. Curtiss-Wright "Sedan" model 15-C with 185 h.p. Curtiss "Challenger" engine.

With liberal borrowing from the design and general make-up of the "Travel Air" model 10 monoplane, the "Sedan" model 15-C was closely akin and introduced at Wichita as the first version in this new cabin-type series. Powered with the tried and true 6 cyl. Curtiss "Challenger" (R-600) engine of 185 h.p., with ample seating for four big people, the model 15-C posed well as a good choice for the private-owner or the flying-service operator. A good performance range with relatively low operating costs were its best points of consideration, but delivered price, while more than reasonable for value received, was not competitive enough to stand up against other similar offerings then on the market. Introduced early in 1931 with a let's-try-it attitude for $6370., the shrugs of prospective buyers forced a hurried cut to $4595. At this price there was some scattered interest and a few sales, but not enough to make any appreciable showing. Designed and engineered by Walter Burnham, the "Sedan" model 15 appears to have borrowed better features from the 4-place "Robin", and numerous features from the various successful "Travel Air" monoplanes. With all this ancestry in its rugged innards, the "Fifteen" was bound to distinguish itself as a fine airplane, and it did, but in very small number. Of the 15 or so that were built in all, most were still in operation some 10 years later.

The Curtiss-Wright "Sedan" model 15-C was a high-winged cabin monoplane with uncramped seating for four, enveloped in practical and suitable tasteful surroundings. A rather large vehicle for an airplane of this type, the lean and lanky 15-C was arranged for stretch-out comfort, with ample room for a lot of baggage, and added equipment. Chosen primarily for economy of operation, the 185 h.p. Curtiss "Challenger" engine offered no great reserves in power, but it did turn in a creditable performance. Everyday operation in all-purpose service out of small fields was taken in stride, and leisurely cross-country jaunts could be stretched to 500 miles and more. Able to carry 120 lbs. of personal baggage, with provision for convenient pilot-aids such as engine starter, wheel brakes, and tail wheel, the 15-C was a good example of the ideal family-type airplane. Flight characteristics had that smooth big-ship feel, with good stability for a solid and comfortable ride. Rugged in its character and quite agile in spite of its size, the "Fifteen" performed its varied duties amiably, and wore very well in extended service. The type certificate number for the Model 15-C was issued 6-10-31 and some 9 or more examples of this model were manufactured by the Curtiss-Wright Airplane Co. at Lambert Field in Robertson (St. Louis), Mo.

Listed below are specifications and per-

Fig. 89. View shows functional simplicity of "Sedan" design. Model 15-C shown.

formance data for the "Sedan" model 15-C as powered with the 185 h.p. Curtiss "Challenger" engine; length overall 30'5"; height overall 8'10"; wing span 43'5"; wing chord 74"; total wing area 240 sq.ft.; airfoil Travel Air # 2 (modified Goettingen 593); wt. empty 2083 lbs.; useful load 1198 lbs.; payload with 60 gal. fuel 630 lbs. (3 pass. at 170 lb. each & 120 lb. baggage; gross wt. 3281 lbs.; max. speed 115; cruising speed 97; landing speed 53; average take-off run 640 ft.; climb 600 ft. first min. at sea level;

ceiling 12,000 ft.; gas cap. 60 gal.; oil cap. 5 gal.; cruising range at 10 gal. per hour 525 miles; price first quoted at $6370., lowered to $4595. in April of 1931.

The construction details and general arrangement of the model 15-C were typical to that of the 15-N as described in the chapter just previous. The following, while applicable to the model 15-C, were also typical of the 15-N and the 15-D. Entry to the cabin was by way of a large centrally located rectangular door, and a con-

Fig. 90. 15-C stood up well in all sorts of hard service; shown here during 1935.

Fig. 91. Wheel pants and landing lights on 15-C were optional extras.

venient step on the right-hand side. A large vee-type windshield of flat plane offered undistorted view, and an extension of this upward into a forward skylight offered vision overhead. A throw-over wheel offered dual control, but dual control wheels were available for $50.00 extra. A large baggage compartment with allowance for up to 120 lbs. was behind the rear seat and accessible from inside or out; small bins under each front seat were suitable for tool kits and other airplane-operating paraphenalia. The oleo-spring landing gear was fitted with low pressure semi-airwheels, and brakes were standard equipment; 25x11-4 Goodyear "airwheels" were optional. The oleo-legs were fastened to a cantilever portion of the front wing-bracing strut; Zerk grease fittings were provided at points of wear. Cowling panels were quickly removable for inspection or maintenance to the engine, and the engine was often shrouded with a Curtiss-type "speed-ring" fairing. The airframe was bonded and shielded for radio. A metal propeller, electric inertia-type engine starter, a battery, navigation lights, dual controls, and a tail

wheel were standard equipment. Optional equipment included a speed-ring cowl for $75.00, retractable landing lights mounted in the wing for $200.00, engine cover for $10.00, and two-tone colors other than standard were $100.00 extra. The next development in the "Sedan" model 15 series was the Wright-powered 15-D as described in the chapter for ATC # 444 of this volume.

Listed below are model 15-C entries as gleaned from registration records:

X-436W;	Model 15-C	(15C-2001)	Curtiss R-600
NC-10928;	"	(15C-2203)	"
NC-11805;	"	(15C-2204)	"
NC-11806;	"	(15C-2205)	"
NC-11807;	"	(15C-2206)	"
NC-11861;	"	(15C-2207)	"
NC-11864;	"	(15C-2210)	"
NC-12302;	"	(15C-2211)	"
NC-12303;	"	(15C-2212)	"

Serial # 2001, 2203, 2206, 2207, later modified to 15-D; ser. # 2212 later modified to 15-D and registration number changed to NS-4Y; approval for this model expired 4-26-37.

Fig. 92. Spartan model C2-60 with 55 h.p. Jacobs L-3 engine.

While Spartan Aircraft was finishing up on the last 3 or 4 examples of their big, beautiful (C4 and C5) high-winged monoplanes, they began installing jigs and tooling for the first batch (25) of the little C2-60 trainer. How they came to choose this particular configuration is a small mystery, but "Spartan" could always be credited with the courage to choose diversification in the various models they had developed. Well versed in the requirements an airplane would have to meet to pay off on the flight-line of a flying school, Spartan no doubt considered the trend to lighter aircraft and cheaper operating costs. While these considerations were becoming more attractive to the average flying-school operator, owner-pilots were also beginning to shop more frequently in the light-plane field; hence, the model C2-60 was developed with this in mind as a craft suitable for both training or for sport. Suggesting more heft than it actually had, the C2-60 "sport-trainer" was a rather large airplane that incorporated several innovations. Oddly enough, the long and narrow wing was fastened to the belly in a low-wing position, and braced to the fuselage by steel wires, as if it were a "racer". Contemporary race-plane influence must have suggested the landing gear configuration also, but it was a practical and sensible choice, especially with wire wing-bracing trusses. The side-by-side seating in the open cockpit was more compatible to pilot training, and also a more friendly arrangement for communication during sport-flying. Because of its generous dimensions, which brought along with them the penalty of some extra weight, the C2-60 required a little more power than the average light airplane; going the unusual just

a step further, the C2-60 was powered with the newly introduced 3 cyl. Jacobs engine. The 55 h.p. "Jacobs" was also unusual in many ways, but it seemed quite happy in its mating with the new "Spartan" monoplane. Production of the C2-60 was well on its way in June of 1931, and deliveries were soon scattered to all parts of the country by year's end; some were used strictly for sport and some were kept busy in pilot training. Spartan's own flying school division, one of the largest in the country, used several of the C2-60 for primary training, and some of these ships were still at it in 1937. One example of the C2-60, by now some 35 years old, was restored to fly again and now stands quietly in an air museum.

The Spartan model C2-60 was a light low-winged monoplane with side-by-side seating for two in a chummy open cockpit. Developed as a combination sport-trainer it was somewhat larger and heavier than the average light-plane, and dared to deviate somewhat from the conventional. Standing stiff-legged and rather squat, with its slender wings outstretched like a sail-plane, it seemed to confirm the first creeping thought that here was an airplane more at home aloft than on the ground. As a primary trainer for teaching the rudiments of pilot training, it was both tolerant and reasonably unforgiving; as a sportster it offered a serene and intimate look into air-adventure and the fleeting beauties of unregulated flight. Powered with the 3 cyl. Jacobs L-3 engine of 55 h.p., the C2-60 used this power rather wisely and delivered a performance better than usually expected by pilots flying it for the first time. Take-offs required only a hop, skip, and a jump, the climb-out was

Fig. 93. Cockpit of C2-60 rather chummy for two large people.

surprisingly good, and all the rest was fun. Because of the stiff-legged landing gear, that relied only on the "give" in the roly-poly Goodyear "airwheels" to absorb the shock, good landings required a certain technique; some found this rather offensive, others did not. Flight characteristics were fairly nimble and quite enjoyable, but the C2-60 was restricted from horseplay or any intentional acrobatics. Spartan Aircraft had great hopes for their little monoplane, but it was hard to foresee into the changing market of this period; as a result, production of the C2-60 was comparatively small and spread rather thinly over the country. The type certificate number for the model C2-60 was issued 7-1-31 and some 16 or more examples of this model were manufactured by the Spartan Aircraft Co. in Tulsa, Okla. Lawrence V. Kerber was president, and Rex B. Beisel was V.P. in

charge of engineering. Lawrence Vincent Kerber was not just an everyday president; in 1927 he was appointed as professor of applied aeronautics at the University of Michigan. This talent was no doubt helpful to Spartan's trusted reputation in aircraft manufacture.

Listed below are specifications and performance data for the Spartan model C2-60 as powered with the 55 h.p. Jacobs L-3 engine; length overall 22'5"; height overall 6'11"; wing span 40'0"; wing chord 54"; total wing area 162 sq.ft.; airfoil Clark Y; wt. empty 731 lbs.; useful load 464 lbs.; payload with 15.5 gal. fuel 190 lbs. (1 pass. at 170 lb. & 20 lb. baggage); gross wt. 1195 lbs.; max. speed 93; cruising speed 81; landing speed 39; climb 750 ft. first min. at sea level; ceiling 13,000 ft.; gas cap. 15.5 gal.; oil cap. 6 qts.; cruising range at 3.5 gal. per hour 320 miles; price $2245. at factory with

Fig. 94. Spartan C2-60 developed for primary flight-training; large dimension induced gentle behavior.

Fig. 95. C2-60 landing gear and wing bracing influenced by racing-plane designs.

a metal propeller and exhaust collector ring. The gross wt. allowance was later raised to 1215 lbs. to allow installation of coupe-top.

The fuselage framework was built up of welded (4130) chrome-moly and 1025 steel tubing with gusset plates at all highly stressed points; the framework was faired to shape with formers and fairing strips, then fabric covered. The open cockpit was deep and well protected with easy step-over entry from the wing-walk on either side; a small baggage bin was provided in the dash-panel. When two parachutes were carried no baggage was allowed. A coupe-top canopy (20 lbs.) was later available for comfort in cold-weather flying. The slender wing framework, in two halves, was built up of solid spruce spar beams with spruce and plywood truss-type wing ribs; the leading edges were covered with dural metal sheet and the completed framework was covered in fabric. Wing bracing was provided by streamlined steel wires, both above and below, in conjunction with the landing gear bracing truss. Rigging of the wing provided 2 deg. of incidence, and 4 deg. of dihedral. The stiff-legged landing gear of 90 in. tread, consisted of two N-type steel tube assemblies with forks at the front end to mount 19x9-3 Goodyear airwheels; no other shock absorption was provided. Criss-cross wires braced the landing gear which provided brace points for the wing, and steel tube struts braced the truss from above. The fuel tank was mounted high in the fuselage, slightly ahead of the cockpit, and the oil tank was mounted ahead of the

firewall. The fabric covered tail-group was built up of welded steel tubes and steel channel sections; the vertical fin and horizontal stabilizer were adjustable for trim on the ground only. The later models were provided with a novel bungee-trim (Trim-Control) on the joy-stick. A metal propeller, exhaust collector ring, a fire extinguisher bottle, and a fuel shut-off were standard equipment. A wooden propeller and coupe-top canopy were optional. Standard color schemes were all maroon, or maroon fuselage with orange-yellow wings. The next Spartan development was the "Executive" of 1937.

Listed below are Spartan C2-60 entries as gleaned from registration records:

NC-11000; C2-60 (# J-1) Jacobs 55.
NC-11015;   ”   (# J-2)   ”
NC-11016;   ”   (# J-3)   ”
NC-11021;   ”   (# J-4)   ”
NC-11022;   ”   (# J-5)   ”
NC-11023;   ”   (# J-6)   ”
NC-11900;   ”   (# J-7)   ”
NC-11901;   ”   (# J-8)   ”
NC-11902;   ”   (# J-9)   ”
NC-11903;   ”   (# J-10)   ”
NC-11904;   ”   (# J-11)   ”
NC-11905;   ”   (# J-12)   ”
NC-11906;   ”   (# J-13)   ”
NC-11907;   ”   (# J-14)   ”
NC-11908;   ”   (# J-15)   ”
NC-11909;   ”   (# J-16)   ”

There was a C2-60 as -992N, serial number unknown; this approval for ser. # J-2 and up; this approval expired 9-30-39.

A.T.C. # 428
(6-18-31)
FLEET, MODELS 8 and 9

Fig. 96. Fleet model 8 powered with Kinner B5 engine; model 8 seated three.

The brawny "Fleet" biplanes had been built more or less the same through some 7 different models since the "Husky Junior" of 1928, but the Models 8 and 9 as discussed here, were a pleasing departure in many respects. The Model 8 "Sport" for instance was unusual in the fact that it was a 3-place version. With a fully-faired fuselage of higher profile and of deeper cross-section, two people could be stuffed into the front cockpit, but it was better for both concerned if they were not too large. The airplane itself would be much happier about it also. Leveled especially at the sport-flyer, the "Eight" offered the bonus of carrying 3 instead of 2, with nearly the performance of the two-seater. Two of the Model 8 were operated by the State Police of New York in various facets of law enforcement; others were operated by owner-pilots for what might be termed as all-purpose service, and some just for sport. Perhaps one of the handsomest in the "Fleet" lineup was the Model 8, however, it did not sell to any great extent and remained rather scarce in number. The Model 9 "Sport" also a handsome airplane closely resembled the 8, but it was a slightly lighter airplane and only had seating arranged for two. Suitable as a pilot-trainer also, the Model 9 was, however, fancied up quite a bit and therefore was more of an offering for the sportsman pilot. Both the 8 and 9 were longer, stood up taller, and reflected more "class" than any of the previous "Fleet" models. More rounded now and of fuller form, the 8 and 9 by comparison, had more of a feminine character than the bony-looking Models 1, 2, and 7. It is quite possible that, had the price-tag been more in keeping with what the average sport-flyer could afford, the 8 and 9 would have easily tripled in numbers built. Holding up well through the years, at least one Model 8 and one Model 9 have been carefully restored to fly again.

Both of these new "Fleet" models were open cockpit biplanes of a similar pattern; the Model 8 was arranged to seat three and the Model 9 was arranged to seat two. As the only models built by Fleet Aircraft that were primarily leveled at the sport-flyer, these models were actually known as the "Sport 8" and the "Sport 9." Designed to cater to the whims and fancies of the average owner-pilot, both models had neatly upholstered interiors, were finished off in more of a "civilian look," and were equipped with extra conveniences and pilot aids as standard equipment. Powered with the 5 cyl. Kinner B5 engine of 125 h.p., performance of either model was quite good and actually a little better than the conservative figures listed here. Flight characteristics and general behavior were likened to that of a much heavier ship, but both were still quite nimble in spite of that. Of typical Fleet construction, both models were also capable of absorbing rough treatment, either air-wise or otherwise. The only handicap these two models suffered were the many sport-fliers who were interested in buying but had empty pockets. The type cer-

Fig. 97. Fleet model 9 powered with Kinner B5 engine; Model 9 seated two.

tificate number for the Fleet models 8 and 9 was issued 6-18-31 and some 16 of the "Sport 8" and 25 of the "Sport 9" were manufactured by Fleet Aircraft, Inc., a division of the Consolidated Aircraft Corp. at Buffalo, New York. Lawrence D. Bell was president; Ray P. Whitman was V.P.; and Joseph Marr Gwinn, Jr. was chief of engineering. By 1933, Fleet Aircraft was discontinued as such, and as an economy measure, was absorbed into the workings of the Consolidated Aircraft Corp.; a reshuffle of company officers brought on added duties for some and dismissal for others.

Listed below are specifications and performance data for the 3-seated "Fleet" model 8 as powered with the 125 h.p. Kinner B5 engine;

length overall 22'10" (this figure is variable because of rudder shapes); height overall 8'3"; wing span upper and lower 28'0"; wing chord upper and lower 45"; wing area upper 99.7 sq.ft.; wing area lower 94.7 sq.ft.; total wing area 194.4 sq.ft.; airfoil Clark Y-15; wt. empty 1283 (1300) lbs.; useful load 702 (700) lbs.; payload with 39 gal. fuel 269 (267) lbs.; gross wt. 1985 (2000) lbs.; figures in brackets were amended allowable wts.; max. speed 115; cruising speed 95; landing (stall) speed 55; climb 520 ft. first min. at sea level; ceiling 10,000 ft.; gas cap. max. 39 gal.; oil cap. 3.2 gal.; cruising range at 7.8 gal. per hour (1780 r.p.m.) was 420 miles; price $5585. at factory. It was possible for the Model 8 to carry two pas-

Fig. 98. Model 8 was rare version in popular Fleet series, also the most handsome.

Fig. 99. Fleet model 9 in Dept. of Commerce service.

sengers averaging 170 lbs. each, if fuel load was held to about 25 gal. The Model 8 was not in regular production by 1933.

Listed below are specifications and performance data for the 2-seated "Fleet" model 9 as powered with the 125 h.p. Kinner B5 engine; length overall 22'10" (this figure is variable because of rudder shapes); height overall 8'2"; wing span upper and lower 28'0"; wing chord upper and lower 45"; wing area upper 99.7 sq.ft.; wing area lower 94.7 sq.ft.; total wing area 194.4 sq.ft.; airfoil Clark Y-15; wt. empty 1253 (1278) lbs.; useful load 694 (689) lbs.; payload with 39 gal. fuel 259 (254) lbs.; gross wt. 1947 (1967) lbs.; figures in brackets for amended allowance; max. speed 115; cruising speed 95; landing (stall) speed 54; climb 540 ft. first min. at sea level; ceiling 10,400 ft.; gas cap. 39 gal.; oil cap. 4 gal.; cruising range at 7.8 gal. per hour (1780 r.p.m.) was 420 miles; price $5185. at factory. Model 9 not in regular production by late 1933.

Except as noted, all data listed here will apply to both Model 8 and 9. The fuselage framework was built up of welded chrome-moly steel tubing, faired to a well-rounded shape with wooden fairing strips, then fabric covered. Sport-type cockpits were deep, roomy, and well protected by a high profile cowl and large windshields; interiors on both models were neatly upholstered. The front cockpit opening on the Model 8 was slightly larger to accommodate two people. The baggage compartment was just behind the rear cockpit with a metal panel door on left-hand side; 2 parachutes at 20 lbs. each were part of the baggage allowance. Baggage allowance was 50 lbs. on the Model 9, but none was allowed on the Model 8 when carrying 3 people. The thick, robust wing framework was built up of heavy-sectioned laminated spruce spar beams with wing ribs riveted together of dural metal stampings; the leading edges were covered with dural metal sheet and the completed framework was cov-

Fig. 100. Fleet 8 leveled at the sportsman. A Fleet with 3 seats was unusual.

Fig. 101. Fleet model 9 on Edo pontoons; shown here in setting of Pacific northwest.

ered in fabric. The lower wing was in 2 sections, and the upper wing was a one-piece section. The main fuel tank was mounted in the center portion of the upper wing; a float-type fuel gauge was visible from either cockpit. A large cut-out in trailing edge of upper wing allowed easier entry to front cockpit with added visibility upward; large ailerons were on the lower wing panels only. Interplane struts were N-type of heavy gauge streamlined steel tubing, and interplane bracing was of heavy gauge streamlined steel wire. The landing gear of 77 in. tread was a departure from normal Fleet practice having oleo-spring shock absorbing struts on rear legs of outer vees; wheels on the 8 were 7.50x10 and 6.50x10 on the 9 with semi-airwheels and brakes as standard equipment on both models. The Model 9 had brake pedals in both cockpits, with this convenience optional on the Model 8; a swiveling tail wheel was standard for both. The Model 9 was also available with "Edo" Model I twin-float gear. The fabric covered tail-group, now of more effective shape and area, was built up of welded chrome-moly steel tubing and sheet steel channel ribs; the fin was ground adjustable and the horizontal stabilizer was adjustable in flight. Another departure from normal Fleet practice was the "non-lifting" horizontal stabilizer as used on both the 8 and 9. A metal propeller, Heywood engine starter, hot-shot battery, wheel brakes, and navigation lights were standard equipment. 7.50x10 semi-airwheels with brakes were optional for the Model 9. The Model 9 (2-seater) was still listed as in production into 1933, but the Model 8 (3-seater) had already been discontinued. The next Fleet biplane development was the 160 h.p. Model

11 described in the chapter for ATC # 526.

Listed below are Model 8 entries as gleaned from registration records:

X-344N; Model 8 (# 800) Kinner B5.
NC-941V;   "   (# 801)   "
NC-953V;   "   (# 802)   "
NS-69V;   "   (# 803)   "
NS-68V;   "   (# 804)   "
NC-70V;   "   (# 805)   "
NC-71V;   "   (806)   "

Serial # 803-804 operated by State Police of New York; this approval for ser. # 800 through # 815; identity for serial numbers beyond # 806 unknown.

Listed below are Model 9 entries as gleaned from registration records:

X-345N; Model 9 (# 500) Kinner B5.
NC-937V;   "   (# 501)   "
NC-938V;   "   (# 502)   "
NC-939V;   "   (# 503)   "
NC-940V;   "   (# 504)   "
NS-36;   "   (# 505)   "
NS-37;   "   (# 506)   "
NC-65V;   "   (# 507)   "
NC-66V;   "   (# 508)   "
;   "   (# 509)   "
NC-67V;   "   (# 510)   "

Serial # 505-506 operated by Dept. of Commerce; ser. # 505-506 later as NC-13920 and NC-13921; ser. # 508 owned by A. Felix Dupont; registration number for ser. # 509 unknown; ser. # 510 later as seaplane on Edo model I floats per Group 2 approval # 2-443; this approval for ser. # 500 through # 524; identity of serial numbers beyond # 510 unknown; approval for both model 8 and 9 expired 4-6-39 due to sale to Brewster Aero. Corp. of Long Island City, New York.

A.T.C. # 429
(6-18-31)
C-W TRAVEL AIR, MODEL 16-W

Fig. 102. Curtiss-Wright model 16-W with 125 h.p. Warner engine; 16-W was 3-seated version of sports-trainer series.

As a direct kin to the Curtiss-Wright series-12 sport trainer, and a companion offering with the model 16-K, very little else of any consequence can be said about the three-place 16-W. Powered with the 7 cyl. Warner "Scarab" engine, it was introduced as another version in the new "Light Sport" series. Almost identical to the 12-W sport-trainer, and costing only $133.00 more, the 16-W was broadened ever so slightly to make room for an extra passenger, thereby offering a little more in utility. Extra utility to a flying-service operator or private-owner was still reason enough to help sway his judgment in the buying of an airplane. Mainly because of the large variety of airplanes that were available at this time to a limited market, the 16-W "Light Sport" found literally no customers. Primed with pride and reasonably hopeful expectations earlier in 1931, Curtiss-Wright (Travel Air Div.) actually found but little demand for their models 12 and 16. None of these models were continued in production during 1932, however, the 16-W was later modified into a craft suitable for military-type primary training. Because of good solid value at a low-budget price, with features slanted to definite service needs, this redesigned 16-W was groomed for export to the smaller foreign countries.

The Curtiss-Wright "Light Sport" model 16-W was also an open cockpit biplane seating 2 or 3, and was otherwise similar to the 16-K except for its engine and cowl installation. Both of the model 16 (16-K and 16-W) were rather small airplanes for the carrying of three, so larger people found the quarters quite chummy in the front cockpit. With controls installed in the front cockpit, it was also suitable for pilot-training. Of robust frame and hardy character, the "Light Sport" took hard service in its stride and held up under it exceptionally well. Powered with the 7 cyl. Warner "Scarab" engine of 110-125 h.p., the 16-W delivered bonus performance for general-purpose use, and also for sport flying. Flight characteristics were pleasant with good response, and in general, it had the feel of a much bigger airplane. The type certificate number for the model 16-W was issued 6-18-31 and only one of this model was manufactured by the Travel Air Div. of the Curtiss-Wright Airplane Co. By June of 1931 some 475 people were employed by Curtiss-Wright, showing a gradual thinning out since the first of the year.

Listed below are specifications and performance data for the model 16-W "Light Sport" as powered with the 110 h.p. Warner "Scarab" engine; length overall 20'10"; height

Fig. 103. Export-trainer version of 16-W offered to foreign countries.

overall 8'10"; wing span upper 28'10"; wing span lower 26'4"; wing chord upper and lower 48"; wing area upper 113.4 sq.ft.; wing area lower 93 sq.ft.; total wing area 206.4 sq.ft.; airfoil Clark Y-15; wt. empty 1177 lbs.; useful load 773 lbs.; payload with 33 gal. fuel 375 lbs. (2 pass. at 170 lb. each & 35 lb. baggage); gross wt. 1950 lbs.; max. speed 117; cruising speed 99; landing speed 48; average take-off run 475 ft.; climb 650 ft. first min. at sea level; ceiling 12,500 ft.; gas cap. 33 gal.; oil cap. 4 gal.; cruising range at 6.5 gal. per hour 450 miles; price $4588. at factory field. Later eligible with re-rated 125 h.p. Warner engine, showing slight performance increases.

The construction details and general arrangement of the model 16-W was similar to that of the 16-K as described in the chapter for ATC # 411 of this volume. A baggage bin was located in the dash-panel of front cockpit with allowance for up to 35 lbs. Dual controls were provided with the front set quickly removable; all movable control surfaces were fastened to ball-bearing hinges. The landing gear was provided with Zerk grease fittings. Low pressure

6.50x10 semi-airwheels were equipped with brakes; brake pedals were in rear cockpit only, but available in front cockpit for $50.00. A head-rest fairing for rear cockpit, a wooden propeller, NACA-type engine cowling, Eclipse electric engine starter, a battery, wiring for navigation lights, and a steerable tail wheel were standard equipment. Optional equipment included a metal propeller for $200.00, weather-proof engine cover for $8.00, a weather-proof cockpit cover for $8.00, and two-tone colors other than standard were $50.00 extra. Goodyear "airwheels" with brakes were also available. The next Curtiss-Wright development in the new "Travel Air" biplane series was the model A-14-D "Sportsman" as described in the chapter for ATC # 442 of this volume.

Listed below is the only known 16-W entry as gleaned from registration records:
NC-420W; Model 16-W (16W-2002) Warner 110-125.
Each aircraft of the 16-W type built after 12-20-40 must, prior to certification, satisfactorily pass inspection for workmanship, materials, and conformity.

A.T.C. # 430
(6-20-31)
FRANKLIN "SPORT", 90

Fig. 104. Franklin "Sport 90" with 90 h.p. Lambert engine.

The Franklin "Sport 90" would not necessarily catch your eye quickly, it didn't quite stand out in form enough for that, but yet, it was somehow not like other sport biplanes of this particular period. It looked pot-bellied, somehow good-natured, and you almost felt as if you'd seen at least parts of it somewhere before. Perhaps its form was inspired by the angles of some, and the curves of others, but altogether it was pretty much a configuration unto itself, once you took the time for a more searching look. Designed specifically as a sport-trainer, the "Franklin 90" held sufficient appeal to the average sporting pilot, one that would enjoy flight in a smallish biplane promising tough character, and a reasonable tolerance to what it was asked to perform. Comparatively stubby, fat and a little sassy, the "Sport 90" had to be firmly flown from the ground up and then back again, but it was not wayward and responded readily to the guidance of the average pilot. Developed and introduced at a time certainly not conducive to a very bright future, the Franklin "Ninety" was generally unknown and built only in small number; beyond the sphere of where it was born it didn't get a fair chance to acquaint itself with all those who would have enjoyed owning and flying it. In time, the few that were built of this model were pretty well scattered around the country. It is commendable to the design at least that one or two examples of this sport-biplane have been faithfully restored and are flying again in recent years.

The basic design for the "Franklin" sport-biplane was originally conceived in Rockford,

Ill. by Jos P. Bauer and an associate. Vener Eichholtz, formerly the postmaster at Zelianople, Penna., displayed an interest in the new design, and ventured out to secure some financial backing from W. E. Barrow in Franklin, Penna. Setting up shop in an old wooden building adjoining the Joy Mfg. Co. the small group had a prototype rolled out for test-flight in Feb. of 1930. With open-cockpit seating for two, and powered with the 5 cyl. Velie engine of 55 h.p., the "Model A" was introduced as a small sport-biplane that would operate efficiently on nominal power. Running rigid tests and adding little improvements as they went on, a second example was built; the 3rd ship was finally certificated (8-4-30) for manufacture on a Group 2 approval numbered 2-246. Organized as the Franklin Aircraft Corp. in Feb. of 1930, the company went on to build 6 more of the Model A with the 65 h.p. Velie M-5 engine, and one Model B with the 70 h.p. LeBlond 5DE engine. Concentrating on the Model A through 1930 and into 1931, Franklin Aircraft introduced the new "Sport 90" early in the year. Basically typical of the Model A, but faired out to a more buxom profile with added strength in its frame, and enjoying the extra horsepower provided by the Lambert 90 engine, the "Sport 90" was sharply improved in performance and utility. The "Ninety" remained in token production through 1932 and into 1933, but customer orders were coming few and far between. In Feb. of 1933 an advertisement read as follows: "Latest Franklin "Sport 90", about 20 hours total time on airframe and engine, fully equipped for $1500.00 cash"! It takes but little

Fig. 105. Buxom lines of "Sport 90" harbored rugged frame and hardy nature.

imagination to ascertain that an ad for a bargain such as this just about heralds the end of the line for Franklin Aircraft Corp.

The Franklin "Sport 90" was an open cockpit sport-biplane with seating arranged for two in tandem. Close-coupled in a buxom form that limited its overall size, the improved "Ninety" was primarily designed as a sporting machine, but could double in duty as a pilot-trainer. It had also been used in fact to haul joy-ride passengers at 2 and 3 dollars a flight; the 3-dollar flight had a flip or two thrown in. Arranged about short aerodynamic moment arms the "Sport 90" tended to be of playful nature, but its stability was quite normal and its response was excellent. As powered with the 5 cyl. Lambert R-266 engine of 90 h.p., the "Sport" delivered good performance, and economy of operation was an added bonus. Bred to operate from the smaller fields the "Ninety" was quite at home "out in the country"; with a full fuel load, both cockpits occupied, and heading into a gentle breeze, it would break ground easily in less than 350 feet. Climb-out was rather generous and landing speed was a gentle 40 m.p.h. or less. Overall

Fig. 106. Franklin "Sport 90" was fine example of the light sport biplane.

Fig. 107. Grassy fields held no qualms for "Sport 90."

flight characteristics were described as enjoyable and its general behavior was rather tom-boyish, certainly well within the requisites of a good sport-type airplane. The type certificate number for the "Sport 90" was issued 6-20-31 and at least 6 examples of this model were manufactured by the Franklin Aircraft Corp. at Franklin, Penna. W. E. Barrow was president; Jos. P. Bauer was V.P., general manager and sales manager; Vener F. Eichholtz was secretary-treasurer; L. G. Felderman was chief engineer; Art Rosa was supt. of manufacturing, and Jack Falkner was test pilot.

Listed below are specifications and performance data for the Franklin "Sport 90" as powered with the 90 h.p. Lambert R-266 engine; length overall 19'6"; Height overall 7'9"; wing span upper 26'0"; wing span lower 24'0"; wing chord upper & lower 48"; wing area upper 100.5 sq. ft.; wing area lower 84.5 sq. ft.; total wing area 185 sq. ft.; wt. empty 885 lbs.; useful load 539 lbs.; payload with 24 gal. fuel 210 lbs. (1 pass. at 170 lbs. & 2 parachutes at 20 lb. each); gross wt. 1424 lbs.; max. speed 115; cruising speed 95; landing speed 38; climb 900 ft. first min. at sea level; climb to 8000 ft. in 10 min.; ceiling 10,000 ft.; gas cap. 24 gal.; oil cap. 2 gal.; cruising range at 5.5 gal. per hour 375 miles; price $3350. at factory. The Lambert 90 (R-266) engine developed 90 h.p. at 2375 r.p.m.; price was $1460. crated for delivery.

The fuselage framework was built up of welded 4130 and 1025 steel tubing into a rigid Warren truss, heavily faired with wooden formers and fairing strips, then fabric covered. The deep, roomy cockpits were an easy step-over from the lower wing, bucket seats were formed for a parachute pack, and the interior was neatly upholstered; dual joy-stick controls were provided. Two parachutes at 20 lbs. each were part of the payload allowance. The gravity-feed fuel tank was mounted high in the fuselage ahead of the front cockpit; a direct-reading

fuel gauge projected up through the cowling. The wing framework in 4 panels and a center-section was built up of solid spruce spar beams with spruce and plywood-gussted truss-type wing ribs; the leading edges were covered with dural metal sheet and the completed framework was covered with fabric. Long span, large area ailerons were on the lower panels only. Normal rigging was as follows: angle of incidence 2.5 deg. in upper wing and 2 deg. in lower wing; stagger was 20 in. positive; no dihedral in upper wing, lower wing at 2 deg. Interplane struts were of streamlined steel tubing, and interplane bracing was of heavy-gauge streamlined steel wire. The long-legged landing gear used oleo-spring shock absorbing struts; low pressure semi-airwheels were 6.50x 10 and wheel brakes were optional. Goodyear "airwheels" with AP brakes were also optional. The tail skid was of the steel spring-leaf type with removable shoe. The fabric covered tail-group was built up of welded 4130 and 1025 steel tubing; the fin was ground adjustable and the horizontal stabilizer was adjustable in flight. A metal propeller, engine exhaust collector ring, dual controls, a battery, navigation lights, 6.50x10 tires, a compass, fire extinguisher, a Stromberg fuel filter, and first-aid kit were standard equipment. A Heywood air-operated engine starter, wooden propeller, bayonet-type engine exhaust stacks, Goodyear airwheels with brakes, and custom colors were optional.

Listed below are "Sport 90" entries as gleaned from registration records:

NC-10765; Model 90 (# 101) Lambert 90.
NC-10792;　　　"　　　(# 102)　　　"
NC-10779;　　　"　　　(# 103)　　　"
NC-11601;　　　"　　　(# 104)　　　"
NC-13139;　　　"　　　(# 105)　　　"
NC-13271;　　　"　　　(# 106)　　　"

Some of the earlier Model A were later modified to Model 90 specs; this approval for ser. # 101 and up; this approval expired 9-30-39.

A.T.C. # 431
(6-22-31)
FORD "TRI-MOTOR", 13-A

Fig. 108. Ford model 13-A had 575 h.p. "Cyclone" in nose and a 300 h.p. Wright R-975 under each wing.

Perhaps the most significant reason for development of the tri-motored Ford model 13-A was its planned entry in the up-coming National Air Tour for 1931. As formally shown at the Detroit Air Show for 1931, held in April, it must have at least drawn some comment because of its lop-sided powerplant combination. From July 4 to 25 it was flown by Harry Russell with a flair, and it did win the cross-country "tour" of that year, averaging better than 143 m.p.h. around the 4858 mile circuit. As the 7th of these annual reliability tours, that year's (1931) contest was announced as the last, and the huge Edsel

B. Ford Trophy was permanently awarded to the Ford Motor Co. Starting out as a standard model 5-AT-D, the 3 "Wasp" engines were removed and replaced by 2 Wright J6 engines of 300 h.p. each in the outboard nacelles, with a whopping 575 h.p. Wright "Cyclone" engine mounted in the nose; in this combination it became the one-only model 13-A. It has been hinted time and again that this sort of combination was particularly favored by the "tour formula", but without actual proof, this can only be speculation. It is possible the 13-A as such might have been intended for service in Bolivia, but ap-

Fig. 109. Ford model 13-A during 1931 National Air Tour. Tour originated from
Ford Airport in Dearborn, Mich.

Fig. 110. Winner of the National Air Tour for 1931 the 13-A was then dismantled and converted to model 5-AT-D.

parently it was changed back to model 5-AT-D standards and sold to Pan American-Grace Airways. Flying then with 3 "Wasp" engines, it operated in South America from 1932 to 1935.

The Ford "Tri-Motor" model 13-A was a high-winged all-metal cabin monoplane with seating for 14 passengers and a crew of two. Stemming as a modification of that model in the first place, it can be considered as basically typical of the 5-AT-D. A distinguishing feature of the 13-A would no doubt be the big "Cyclone" engine mounted in the nose. Carefully faired to eliminate as much of the parasitic drag as would be practical, the 13-A was among the fastest in the "Ford" line-up. Powered with two 9 cyl. Wright J6 (R-975) engines of 300 h.p. each, and one Wright "Cyclone" (R-1820-E) engine of 575 h.p., little else can be said of this lone example. Basically similar to the 5-AT-D, we can assume that flight characteristics and general behavior of the 13-A were more or less typical; there is no reason to assume that the peculiar power combination had any effect, either complimentary or detrimental. Failure of the big center engine on a take-off with gross load would have caused a near 50 per cent loss in power, and many anxious moments. The type certificate number for the model 13-A was issued 6-22-31 and only one example of this model was built by the Stout Metal Airplane Div. of the Ford Motor Co. on Ford Airport in Dearborn, Mich. Edsel B. Ford was the president; Wm. B. Mayo was V.P. and general manager.

Listed below are specifications and performance data for the Ford model 13-A with a total of 1175 h.p.; length overall 50'3"; height overall 12'8"; wing span 77'10"; wing chord at root 156"; wing chord at tip 92"; total wing area 835 sq.ft.; airfoil Ford # 2 (modified Goettingen); wt. empty 7632 lbs.; useful load 5368 lbs.; payload with 277 gal. fuel 3128 lbs. (14 pass. at 170 lb. each & 748 lb. baggage); payload with 355 gal. fuel 2658 lbs. (14 pass. & 278 lb. baggage); gross wt. 13,000 lbs.; max. speed 150; cruising speed 122; landing speed 60; stall speed 64; climb 1000 ft. first min. at sea level; climb to 7800 ft. in 10 min.; ceiling 18,000 ft.; gas cap. normal 277 gal.; gas cap. max. 355 gal.; oil cap. 30 gal.; cruising range at 58 gal. per hour 550-680 miles; price not announced. Weights listed above as revised 6-30-31; previous wts. were empty 8135 lbs., useful load 5315 lbs., gross wt. 13,500 lbs. Performance figures and payload were proportionately affected.

The construction details and general arrangement of the model 13-A were typical to that of the 5-AT-D as described in the chapter for ATC # 409 of this volume. All 3 engines of the 13-A were shrouded with Townend-type "speed-ring" cowlings which added measurably to the top speeds. Speeds up to 170 m.p.h. were attributed to this model, but that doesn't seem likely; 160 m.p.h. would be easier to believe. The big "Cyclone" engine mounted in the nose alternately used either a 2-bladed propeller, or a 3-bladed one. The landing gear of 18 ft. 6 in. tread was carefully streamlined and wheels were encased in large tear-drop wheel pants. Adjustable metal propellers, 3 inertia-type engine starters, wheel brakes, tail wheel, and navigation lights were standard equipment. The next development in the Ford "Tri-Motor" was the model 4-AT-F as described in the chapter for

Fig. 111. Ford model 13-A held up by "giant" during Detroit Air Show for 1931;
single-engined 8-A freighter on floor.

ATC # 441 of this volume.

Listed below is the only example of the Ford model 13-A:

NC-433H; Model 13-A (# 13-A-1) 3 Wright eng.

This particular airplane started out as a 5-AT-D (# 5-AT-100); after cancelling 13-A development, it was modified at factory back to 5-AT-D standards.

A.T.C. # 432
(6-29-31)
DOUGLAS "DOLPHIN", MODEL 3

Fig. 112. Douglas "Dolphin" 3 on ramp at Pratt & Whitney engine factory. "Wasp Junior" engines powered the model 3.

Coming down the assembly line along with some of the "Dolphin 1", the Douglas "Dolphin 3" was a nearly identical sister-ship except for the brand of its engines. While rubbing wing-tips with some of its kin, the first example in this series languished in the fact it was ordered and being built for Powell Crosley, Jr. the noted manufacturer and a rabid flying sportsman. As a rather special version of the "Dolphin 3" type, this particular craft was arranged for six, and boasted of a plush yacht-like interior; in fact, it was Crosley's "air yacht" that had winged him to all parts of the country. Appropriately named "LesGo", the "Dolphin" was often seen at many aviation gatherings, and many lakes and waterways had felt the splash of its metal bottom. Normally offered as an 8-place transport, the "Dolphin 3" was a worthy companion model to the similar "Dolphin 1", and selection of either would be at best an eeny-

Fig. 113. "Dolphin 3" with Dornier DO-X in background; "Lesgo" shown was owned by Powell Crosley, Jr.

Fig. 114. Dolphin 3 ("Lesgo") shown here during 1931 National Air Races; heavy ship was mired in mud.

meeny-miney-moe choice. Powered with 2 Pratt & Whitney "Wasp Junior" R-985 engines of 300 h.p. each, the "Dolphin 3" was also closely appraised by the Army Air Corps and 2 were ordered in 1932 as the Y1C-26. A beautiful, aristocratic airplane, and a tough, versatile boat, the "Dolphin 3" almost too soon had to bow out in favor of similar Douglas examples of this type, but with more horsepower.

The Douglas "Dolphin 3" was a high-winged amphibious monoplane of the flying-boat type with seating arranged for six to eight. Typical of the "Dolphin 1", the new "Dolphin 3" varied only in the engines that were installed, these being Pratt & Whitney instead of Wright. The spacious hull interior was normally to carry 8 as a coach-type transport, but various optional seatings and appointments were available on order. Making its debut to a very cautious market, the "Dolphin," however, took on weight and power as the years went by, and finally evolved into one of the aristocrats in commercial and sport aviation. Powered with two "Wasp Junior" engines of 300 h.p. each, the "Dolphin 3" offered ample performance with a broad range of utility; as a four-ton airplane that was far from compact in its proportion, the "Dolphin" was surprisingly nimble and it never shied away from a tough job. The type certificate number for the "Dolphin 3" was issued 6-29-31 and perhaps no more than one commercial example of this model was manufactured by Douglas Aircraft Co., Inc. on Clover Field in Santa Monica, Calif. Donald W. Douglas was president; Harry H. Wetzel was V.P. and general manager; J. H. Kindelberger was V.P. in charge of engineering; Carl A. Cover was V.P. in charge of sales; Carl Cover, a talented pilot of extensive experience, also made many of the experimental test flights.

Listed below are specifications and performance data for the Douglas "Dolphin" model 3 as powered with 2 "Wasp Jr." R-985 engines of 300 h.p. each; length overall 44'4"; height overall 14-7"; main wing span 60'0"; wing chord at root 132"; wing chord at tip 87"; main wing area 515 sq.ft.; aux. wing span 20'0"; aux. wing chord 30"; aux. wing area 47 sq.ft.; total wing area 562 sq.ft.; airfoil main wing Clark Y-18 at root, and Clark Y-9 at tip; airfoil aux. wing Clark Y; wt. empty 5872 lbs.; useful load 2328 lbs.; payload with 150 gal. fuel (2 pilots) 948 lbs. (4 pass. at 170 lb. each with 268 lb. baggage & extra equipment); payload with 120 gal. fuel (2 pilots) 1128 lbs. (6 pass. & no baggage); gross wt. 8200 lbs.; max. speed (with speed-rings) 141; cruising speed 115; landing speed 62; climb 750 ft. first min. at sea level; ceiling 16,000 ft.; gas cap. max 180 gal.; oil cap. 16 gal.; cruising range at 36 gal. per hour 450 miles; price $35,000. at factory field.

The construction details and general arrangement of the "Dolphin 3" was typical to that of the "Dolphin 1" as described in the chapter for ATC # 422 of this volume. Following data applies to both models, unless otherwise noted. The boat-like hull, which was thoroughly tested in the wind-tunnel and in water-tanks, was of the so-called "free bottom" type so that much of the water suction was eliminated for quicker take-offs. Structural strength of the hull and the wing were sufficient to permit operations in rough waters and heavy seas; water-tight compartments were sufficient to forestall sinking in the case of hull damage. As a precaution, five emergency exits were available to avoid isolating occupants from escape. Fabric covered ailerons were of the slotted-hinge type for better lateral control; the fabric covered rudder and

Fig. 115. U.S. Coast Guard version of the Dolphin 3.

elevators also used the offset hinge-line for aerodynamic balance. Two small fins were mounted atop the stabilizer to provide additional fin area. The retracting landing gear folded up out of the way for water operations, but its parasitic drag was ever-present; optional wheel streamlines (pants) offered a slight reduction in this drag. Normally, baggage allowance was 150 lbs., but could be adjusted to varying loads. Metal propellers, speed-rings, electric engine starters, a battery, generator, exhaust collector rings, fire extinguishers, anchoring and mooring gear; wheel brakes, tail wheel, and dual controls were standard equipment. Navigation lights, wheel streamlines, toilet-lavatory equipment, custom interior arrangements, and custom appointments were optional. For yet another development in the "Dolphin" series, refer to ATC # 505.

Listed below is the only known commercial entry for the "Dolphin 3":

NC-982Y; Dolphin 3 (# 1001) 2 Wasp Jr. 300.

Army Air versions of the "Dolphin 3" were the Y1C-26 and Y1C-26A; approval expired 9-30-39.

PITCAIRN "AUTOGIRO", PAA-1

Fig. 116. Pitcairn model PAA-1 with 125 h.p. Kinner B5 engine.

While the earlier PCA-2 was landing on White House lawns to receive awards, flying in and out of big city downtown areas, setting numerous records, landing and taking off from crowded water-front piers, and other such stunts to demonstrate the autogiro's practicability, Pitcairn had already developed the smaller PAA-1 to fit the more modest requirements of the average private-owner. For sport-flying of a general nature, the modestly powered PAA-1 offered less performance, but its economy of upkeep and operation was better suited to the owner-flyer who just flew for fun. In instances where high performance was of no great consequence, and cheaper utility was more desirable, the PAA-1 was also used for forest-fire spotting, aerial photography, and specialized news-gathering. Allowing a good deal less dependence on flying skills and handling technique, the autogiro proved very useful for these various jobs, jobs that often required deliberate concentration on happenings of great interest. A good deal smaller and naturally lacking the flash and dash of the more powerful PCA-2, the diminutive PAA-1 was nevertheless all "autogiro" and offered all the advantages peculiar to this type of craft, only in smaller measure.

The Pitcairn model PAA-1 was a sport-type autogiro with open cockpits arranged to seat two in tandem. Characteristic of its bigger (PCA-2) sister-ship, the PAA-1 was more or less similar in a scaled-down fashion. Powered with the 5 cyl. Kinner B5 engine of 125 h.p., the mild-mannered PAA-1 was no great charger, but it had surprising ability and adequate performance. At a nice and easy 75 m.p.h., the range was about 250 miles, but the nature of the autogiro prompted one to snoop around and drop into places generally overlooked by airplane-pilots. In some instances, leisurely across country flights took on the ups and downs of a yo-yo. Designed for sport-flying, the PAA-1 offered the distinctive novelty of flying an "autogiro" on expenditures just a little more than a comparable airplane. It is quite unfortunate that the small sport type autogiro was introduced at a time when the country was skidding into the depths of an economic "depression"; it is easy to predict that had the aircraft market upheld a more normal stature, the small autogiro would have attained a much brighter future. The type certificate number for the model PAA-1 was issued 7-8-31 and some 25 examples of this model were manufactured by Pitcairn Aircraft, Inc. in Willow Grove, Penna. Veteran James G. Ray was chief test-pilot, and Walter C. Clayton was the chief engineer for autogiro development. Harold F. Pitcairn and his associates were presented with the Collier Trophy in April of 1931 for development work responsible for the design of a practical commercial autogiro, an award for the greatest achievement in aviation during 1930.

Fig. 117. PAA-1 was developed for the sportsman-pilot of more modest means.

Mixed among the earlier developments of the Pitcairn "autogiro" was the PC-2-30 (X-759W) a light two-place open sport-type powered with a 110 h.p. Warner "Scarab" engine; a companion model to the PAA-1 was labeled the PAA-2 and it was powered with the 4 cyl. inverted inline Martin-Chevrolair engine of 120 h.p. Following the development of the PA-18 and PA-19, the PA-20 was introduced as an improved version of the PAA-1; the model PA-21 was introduced as a 420 h.p. version of the PCA-2, and the PA-22 was an experimental cabin sport-type powered with a 75 h.p. Pobjoy en-gine. Identity of the PA-23 is unknown, and the PA-24 was developed as an improved version of the PA-20. By this particular time, Pitcairn was already experimenting with the direct-control autogiro, requiring no fixed wing, and also a roadable model with folding rotor blades.

Listed below are specifications and per-formance data for the model PAA-1 as powered with the 125 h.p. Kinner B5 engine; fuselage length overall 18'7"; overall height (tail down" 11'0"; rotor dia. 37 ft.; rotor blade chord 18.6"; rotor blade area 108 sq.ft.; fixed-wing span 22'9";

Fig. 118. Early Cierva "Autogiro" with Juan de la Cierva on left and Harold F. Pitcairn in center.

fixed-wing chord (constant) 30"; fixed-wing area 51.6 sq.ft.; fixed-wing airfoil Goettingen 429 modified; wt. empty 1178 lbs.; useful load 572 lbs.; payload with 27 gal. fuel 214 lbs. (1 pass. at 170 lbs. & 44 lb. baggage); gross wt. 1750 lbs.; max speed 90; cruising speed 75; landing speed 20-25; climb 550 ft. first min. at sea level; service ceiling 10,000 ft.; gas cap. 27 gal.; oil cap. 3.5 gal.; cruising range at 7.5 gal. per hour was 250 miles; price $6750. at factory field. A later improved version of the PAA-1 was called the PA-20 with gross wt. boosted to 1800 lbs. The PA-20 was basically similar to the PAA-1, but was redesigned slightly to present a cleaner aerodynamic arrangement for a slight increase in performance, and a much better outward appearance. Some of the PAA-1 were eligible for modification to PA-20, and most PAA-1 and PA-20 were eligible for modification to the higher-powered (160 h.p.) PA-24.

The deep fuselage framework was built up of welded square and round section chrome-moly steel tubing, generously faired into a streamlined section with duralumin fairing strips, then fabric covered. The large cockpits were deep and well protected, providing a large door on left side for easy entry to the front seat. Each cockpit was upholstered neatly, and dual controls were provided. A small baggage bin of 1.9 cu. ft. capacity was located behind the rear seat; baggage allowance was 44 lbs. which included 2 parachutes at 20 lbs. each, when carried. The rather small fixed-wing was built up of spruce and plywood box-type spar beams with I-type wing ribs of plywood webs and spruce flanges; the full-length ailerons were also of wooden construction, and the completed wing framework was covered in fabric. The rotor system, mounted on a tripod pylon placed over the front cockpit, consisted of 4 blades mounted on a freely rotating hub. An articulating joint was used at the base of each blade. Anti-droop cables provided support for the blades while at rest, and inter-bracing cables kept the rotor blades 90 deg. apart. A rotor starter driven by the engine, through a multi-disc clutch and over-running drive unit, was used to bring the rotor blades to proper r.p.m. for take-off. The rotor starter was used only to bring blades up to proper speed, and was disengaged prior to taking off. The rotor blades were each built up of a long

steel tube spar, plywood ribs, and covered in fabric. The unusual landing gear of 120 in. tread, was a bird-cage affair of streamlined steel tubing and streamlined steel wire; shock absorbers were long-travel oleo-spring legs. Low pressure 6.50x10 semi-airwheels were provided with brakes; a rubber-snubbed tail skid swung through 360 deg. A gravity-feed fuel tank of 27 gal. capacity was mounted high in the fuselage just behind the firewall. The fabric covered tail-group was built up of welded steel tubing; the horizontal stabilizer was adjustable in flight. A wooden propeller, Heywood engine starter, dual controls, navigation lights, and wheel brakes were standard equipment. A metal propeller was optional. The next development in the Pitcairn "autogiro" was the model PCA-3 as described in the chapter for ATC # 446 of this volume.

Listed below are model PAA-1 entries as gleaned from registration records:

X-10770;	PAA-1	(# C-17)	Kinner B5.
NC-10771;	"	(#C-18)	"
NC-10773;	"	(# C-19)	"
NC-10772;	"	(# C-20)	"
NC-10769;	"	(# C-21)	"
NC-11625;	"	(# C-32)	"
NC-11626;	"	(# C-33)	"
NC-11627;	"	(# C-34)	"
NC-11628;	"	(# C-35)	"
NC-11629;	"	(# C-36)	"
NC-11630;	"	(# C-37)	"
NC-11631;	"	(# C-38)	"
NC-11632;	"	(# C-39)	"
NC-11633;	"	(# C-40)	"
NC-11634;	"	(# C-41)	"
NC-11635;	"	(# C-52)	"
NC-11636;	"	(# C-53)	"
NC-11637;	"	(# C-54)	"
NC-11638;	"	(# C-55)	"
NC-11639;	"	(# C-56)	"
NC-11640;	"	(# C-57)	"
NC-11641;	"	(# C-58)	"
NC-11642;	"	(# C-59)	"
NC-11643;	"	(# C-60)	"
NC-11648;	"	(# C-72)	"

This approval for ser. # C-19, C-21 and up; ser. # C-19, C-32 thru C-37, C-39, C-40, C-52 thru C-56 were as PAA-1 only; ser. # C-38 and C-41 later modified to PA-24; ser. # C-57 thru C-61 later as PA-24; reg. no. for ser. # C-61 unknown; this approval expired 9-30-39.

A.T.C. 434
(7-9-31)
REARWIN "JUNIOR", 3000

Fig. 119. Rearwin's entry in light-plane field was "Junior" 3000 with 45 h.p. Szekely engine.

Rearwin Airplanes, Inc. hadn't fared too well with their beautiful "Ken-Royce" biplane; it was clearly the outstanding airplane of its type, but the market for this type of airplane had all but vanished, so only 6 of the sport-biplanes were actually built. Still confident he could make a go of it, and still desiring to continue in the aircraft business, Rae Rearwin studied the budding light-plane movement. Never one to fear competition, he decided to enter the fracas, and to try his luck with a small tandem-seated monoplane that could sell for less than $1500. Powered with the 3 cyl. Szekely SR-3-0 engine of 45 h.p., the new "Rearwin" faced the world about mid-year as the "Junior" model 3000. Missing the estimated $1500. price-tag by nearly $300., the perky "Junior" was still good value for the money, and scattered signs of interest soon turned into firm orders; not many, but at least encouraging. Suitably arranged as a training craft that offered minimal operating costs, several were soon seen on the flight-lines of various flying schools. A few were also used by flying clubs that had banded together to enjoy cheaper flying time, and one was used in Texas for aerial photography work; a few others were week-end darlings of private-owners who flew only for the sport. The Rearwin "Junior" was a nice little airplane; it looked well, behaved quite well, and made many friends as it went, but the continued popularity of the pixie-like "Aeronca", and the comical Curtiss-Wright "Junior" left very little of the market for Rearwin to share with other light-plane makers.

In Jan. of 1931, D. H. Webber placed an advertisement in a national aviation magazine offering the sale of a new light-plane design, complete with engineering and production data. It is believed that Rearwin bought this project, and Doug Webber came along with the deal as the chief engineer. Rolling out the quickly-built prototype a few months later, it needed no practiced eye to see that Rearwin's new "Junior" was very little more than a slightly refined (American Eagle) "Eaglet". Noel Hockaday and Doug Webber, who together had also conceived the "Eaglet", were once again teamed up in the development of the new "Junior". Ralph Hall, who had been thoroughly captivated by the earlier "Eaglet", also made first flights on the Rearwin "Junior". A new light-plane engine called the "Poyer" had also been developed during this time in one corner of the plant; this 3 cyl. radial engine of 40 h.p. was installed in the second airplane (labeled model 3001), but the development pains that beset any newly designed engine, caused its removal and tests were continued with an engine of another make. Several "Junior" airframes were also built, but left unassembled pending certification of the model 3000 in July. With only a small tricle of orders coming in the Rearwin work-force had been kept to a bare minimum; even Rearwin's two teenaged sons would pitch in to help complete an order.

The trim Rearwin "Junior" model 3000 was a conventional parasol-type monoplane with seating for two in tandem; normally it was flown with open sides, but a light detachable enclosure could be fitted to keep out the bite of the cold winter winds. Standing tall and rather spindly, it didn't quite have that flivver-plane look, but its ample proportions did not amount to very much weight either. Although quite toy-like throughout its frame and appointments, by comparison with 3 other popular light-planes, Rearwin's

"Junior" was the heaviest of them all; the extra weight was allotted to a husky frame, fuel for greater cruising range, and slightly more useful load. Much like all of the popular light airplanes, the "Junior" was a bag of fun and easy to fly, once the pilot learned that a cartain new technique was required to fly it properly; like other light-planes it also had its inherent limitations, but a strong frame and a robust character did permit a certain amount of levity and mild mistreatment. Powered with the 3 cyl. Szekely SR-3-0 engine of 45 h.p., the "Junior" 3000 came up with adequate performance for its intended purpose, it afforded an hour's flying pleasure for just a few dollars; easy-going and friendly, an hour's flight was usually enough to promote understanding and a happy association. Rolled out into a market that was slowly beginning to disappear, the Rearwin "Junior" looked around longingly for some customers; only a few stopped to buy, and the rest walked slowly by. The type certificate number for the "Junior" model 3000 was issued 7-9-31 and some 17 examples of this model were manufactured by Rearwin Airplanes, Inc. on Fairfax Field in Kansas City, Kansas. Rae A. Rearwin was president; Albert R. Jones was V.P.; R. S. Rearwin was secretary; and Douglas H. Webber was chief of engineering. Noel Hockaday, a versatile craftsman in many fields, was largely concerned with much of the design and development.

Listed below are specifications and performance data for the Rearwin "Junior" model 3000 as powered with the 45 h.p. Szekely engine; length overall 21'11"; height overall 7'6"; wing span 36'0"; wing chord 60"; total wing area 179.5 sq. ft.; airfoil (NACA) M-series; wt. empty 569 lbs.; useful load 430 lbs.; payload with 12 gal. fuel 177 lbs. (1 pass. at 170 lb. & 7 lb. baggage); gross wt. 999 lbs.; later models when operating with enclosure, eligible with 15 lbs. baggage at 1040 lbs. max. gross wt.; max. speed 85; cruising speed 75; landing speed 30-35; climb 680 ft. first min. at sea level; ceiling 15,000 ft.; gas cap. 12 gal.; oil cap. 6 qts.; cruising range at 2.75 gal. per hour 300 miles; price $1795. at factory field. The Szekely SR-3-0 engine developed 45 h.p. at 1750 r.p.m.; price was $625. at the factory.

All models of the Rearwin "Junior" were typical of each other from the engine firewall back, so detailed data of construction and arrangement for the model 4000 (ATC #469) will apply for the model 3000 also. The wide split-axle landing gear of 72 in. tread used 16x7-4 low pressure airwheels; no wheel brakes were provided. The baggage allowance of 7 lbs. (behind rear seat) was hardly enough for more than a tool-roll on early models, but later models were eligible with 15 lbs. baggage and a winter enclosure at 1040 lbs. max. gross weight. The detachable enclosure was of light steel tube framing covered with pyralin sheet; an optional extra, it did provide some protection against cold weather. The 12 gal. fuel tank was mounted high in the fuselage just behind the firewall, and offered 4 hours of flying time. The cockpit interior was not overly spacious, but there was room enough for two, even while wearing bulky clothing and parachutes. A generous cut-out in trailing edge of the wing offered visibility upward from the rear seat; dual-stick controls were provided, and the horizontal stabilizer was adjustable in flight. The next development in the Rearwin "Junior" series was the model 4000 as described in the chapter for ATC #469 of this volume.

Listed below are "Junior" model 3000 entries as gleaned from registration records:

X-507Y;	Model 3000	(# 201) Szekely 45.
X-508Y;	" 3001	(# 202) Poyer 40.
NC-535Y;	Model 3000	(# 203) Szekely 45.
NC-536Y;	"	(# 204) "
NC-537Y;	"	(# 205) "
NC-553Y;	"	(# 206) "
NC-538Y;	"	(# 207) "
NC-539Y;	"	(# 208) "
NC-554Y;	"	(# 209) "
NC-555Y;	"	(# 210) "
NC-556Y;	"	(# 211) "
NC-557Y;	"	(# 212) "
NC-11056;	"	(# 213) "
NC-11057;	"	(# 214) "
NC-11058;	"	(# 215) "
NC-11059;	"	(# 216) "
NC-11092;	"	(# 218) "

This approval for ser. # 203 and up; ser. # 201-202 eligible when modified to conform; ser. # 202 (as # 202-A) modified to 4000; ser. # 212 later modified to 4000; ser. # 216 modified to 3100 with 50 h.p. Szekely engine; ser. # 217 mfgd. as 4000; ser. # 218 last example of model 3000; approval expired 11-5-36.

A.T.C. # 435
(7-14-31)
STINSON, MODEL W

Fig. 120. Stinson model W was deluxe "Junior" with 300 h.p. "Wasp Jr." engine.

The "Junior-type" model W was a rather rare and unobtrusive machine in the look-alike family of Stinson single-engined monoplanes. With not very much showing to distinguish itself from some of its sister-models, it could very well be mistaken for the SM-7B, and very often was. As an improved offering for 1931-32, the Model W was more or less a compromise of what they were asking for in a ship of this particular type. The Model W was a companion offering to the popular Model S, but Stinson spiced the flavor of its utility and performance with a generous increase in power. Without hardly being noticeable the Model W was now longer, a little bit taller, and a good bit heavier. Lavishly equipped with durable deluxe appointments and a sprinkling of extra equipment, she was also heavier when sitting empty. More available payload was more often favored against longer range, so the Model W swapped fuel for some 100 lbs. extra in payload allowance. Although the loaded gross weight was now some 150 lbs. more, this didn't seem to have any appreciable effect on its performance; "Stinsons" were like that. As a consequence, the Model W was a very attractive choice in a sporty four-place high-performance cabin airplane, whether for business or sport, and sold for the ridiculous figure of less than $9000. General Electric, a faithful Stinson cus-

tomer for several years, used a modified Model W for electronic testing and research. Along about this time it was said that Stinson Aircraft, and especially Wm. A. Mara, was anxious to get away from the ill-fitted "Junior" designation, they felt the name was becoming entirely unsuited for their four-place monoplane series. Actually they had long ago outgrown the early "Junior" concept of 1928. The models S and W for 1931-32 were not technically listed as "Juniors", but it was rather hard for people to break away from the popular name.

The husky Stinson Model W was a strut-braced high wing cabin monoplane with seating arranged in style and comfort for four. Basically fashioned in the popular "Junior" concept, the Model W, however, was a larger and heavier airplane that was equipped with tasteful interior appointments and numerous extras to aid the pilot. Specifically, it was aimed directly at the sportsman-pilot, the well-to-do family man or the business executive; in short, it was for those who wouldn't quibble over paying a little more for a much better airplane. Powered with the 9 cyl. Pratt & Whitney "Wasp Junior" (R-985) engine of 300 h.p., the Model W literally surged with the extra power and delivered a cabin-plane performance that one couldn't help but admire. Catering as it did to a limited clientele, this

Fig. 121. Stinson model W offered high performance for business or sport.

craft was also offered later as a one-seated cargo-plane to broaden its chances in the market, but only a very small number were built in all. As one of the lesser-known models in the so-called Stinson "Junior" line-up, the Model W was perhaps the best. The type certificate number for the Model W was issued 7-14-31 and perhaps no more than 5 examples of this model were manufactured by the Stinson Aircraft Corp. at Wayne, Mich. Edward A. Stinson was president; Wm. A. Mara was V.P.; B. D. DeWeese was general manager, and A. H. Saxon was chief engineer.

Listed below are specifications and perform-ance data for the Stinson Model W as powered with the 300 h.p. "Wasp Junior" (R-985) engine; length overall 30'10"; height overall 8'11"; wing span 42'1"; wing chord 75"; total wing area 235 sq.ft.; airfoil Clark Y; wt. empty 2379 lbs; useful load 1271 lbs.; payload with 73 gal. fuel 610 lbs. (3 pass. at 170 lb. each & 100 lb. baggage); gross wt. 3650 lbs.; max. speed (with speed-ring) 143; cruising speed 122; landing speed 60; climb 950 ft. first min. at sea level; ceiling 18,000 ft.; gas cap. normal 73 gal.; gas cap. max. 90 gal.; oil cap. 7 gal.; cruising range

Fig. 122. Rebuilt "Stinson W" shown at Spokane in 1959.

at 18 gal. per hour 470 miles; basic price $8995 at factory field; empty wt. listed above includes speed-ring cowling, streamlined pants on all wheels, strut fairings, retractable landing lights, engine starter, and a battery. Oddly enough, all these were optional extras added to the basic price.

The construction details and general arrangement of the Model W was typical to that of the Model S (ATC # 423), and the many other "Junior" models described previously. With a good allowance of useful load to play with, it was possible to include many extras to further improve comfort, utility, and operation. Convenient steps and wide entry doors were on both sides; cabin dimensions were ample and seating was well-positioned for comfort. All windows were of shatter-proof glass; ventilation and heat were provided for all-weather cabin comfort. A baggage compartment of 7 cu. ft. capacity, with allowance for up to 100 lbs., was accessible from the inside or out. Three of the seats could be quickly removed for hauling package cargo; a special cargo-plane with reinforced floors and tie-down hooks was also available. The normal fuel capacity was 73 gal., but an extra tank boosting fuel load to 90 gal. was optional; no baggage was allowed with the greater amount of fuel. The wide-track oleo-spring landing gear was fitted with 8.50x10 low pressure semi-airwheels and

brakes were standard equipment. The wheels could be encased in streamlined wheel pants for more speed, or fitted with fenders when operating out of unimproved landing fields. The swiveling tail wheel could also be fitted with a streamlined (pant) fairing. To present a more finished appearance, many of the strut fittings for wings and landing gear were neatly faired over with metal streamlined cups or cuffs. A metal propeller, navigation lights, electric engine starter, and battery were standard equipment. A speed-ring engine cowl, wheel streamlines, wing-mounted retractable landing lights, dual wheel controls, and parachute flares were usually fitted, but were listed as extra or optional equipment. The next Stinson development was the four-place Model R as described in the chapter for ATC # 457 of this volume.

Listed below are Model W entries as gleaned from registration records:

NC-10849;	Model W	(# 3050)	R-985-300.
NC-12177;	"	(# 3051)	"
NC-12160;	"	(# 3052)	"
NC-12144;	"	(# 3053)	"
NC-12146;	"	(# 3054)	"

Serial # 3053 operated by General Electric for electronic research as 3-place; this approval for ser. # 3050 and up; this approval expired 3-22-34.

A.T.C. # 436
(7-16-31)
C-W "TRAVEL AIR SEDAN", A-6-A

Fig. 123. Travel Air "Sedan" model A-6-A with 450 h.p. "Wasp" engine.

The story of the Curtiss-Wright A-6-A "Sedan" might very well begin about two and one-half years previous with the development of the "Wasp-powered" model A-6000-A. Basically a "Travel Air" 6000-series monoplane, this big, buxom beauty had space, comfort, and remarkable ability for a varied line of service; several airlines were using the A-6000-A, so were several business-houses, and at least one private-owner used his plane strictly for sport. As a versatile light transport the hard-working A-6000-A left very little to be desired, but even the simple passing of time seems to breed a yearning for some change and improvement. Inheriting this "Travel Air" design Curtiss-Wright management was no doubt hard put to find any large areas calling for improvement, but normal progress in some two years time at least upheld the excuse for change. Using the model 6-B (ATC # 352) as a pattern to go by, the first and most noticeable change wrought into the new A-6-A was the big bulge-type cabin enclosure in front; calculated to improve the range of visibility and extend head-room for the pilots, the super-imposed "veranda" somehow distracted from the flowing lines of its former beauty. Added to the apparent bulkiness was a sizeable increase to the gross weight allowance, so the A-6-A must have suffered for this to some extent and lost some of its former agility. Using the large interior dimensions to fuller advantage, more seating was arranged, so available capacity was now stretched to eight places; any variety of loads were available to the pilot sim-

ply by the juggling of fuel load, baggage load, and whether he chose to have a co-pilot or not. On the face of it then, the new A-6-A might be credited for offering an extension in utility, and some operating improvement, but there seemed to be no urgent reason to go to all the bother; this especially for a market that could offer no future for very many such airplanes. The lone "model A-6-A" served handily in varied duties at the Curtiss-Wright plant, but its final disposition is unknown.

The Curtiss-Wright model A-6-A "Sedan" was a big high-winged cabin monoplane with seating arranged for up to 8 places; with the installation of toilet facilities and the use of a co-pilot, passenger seating was held to five. To the biggest extent the new A-6-A was still quite typical of the earlier "Travel Air" A-6000-A (ATC # 116), except for numerous modifications calculated to improve its operation and general utility. With several improvements in the pilot's cockpit, in the main cabin interior, to the ventilating and heating systems, provisions for a chemical toilet, and some changes to the basic outward configuration, the A-6-A weighed in over 100 lbs. heavier when empty. Nearly 250 lbs. was added to the useful load, so all this added up to some 350 lbs. heavier at fully loaded weight. As a consequence, this was some detriment to the overall performance, but not of any appreciable note. Inheriting a gentle and obedient nature from its earlier sister-ships, the A-6-A was rugged enough to wear well in hard service, and useful enough to stretch its life-span over a

*Fig. 124. A-6-A was improved version of earlier 6000 series. Curtiss-Wright planned production,
but only one was built.*

period of many years. Powered with the 9 cyl. Pratt & Whitney "Wasp" C1 engine of 420 h.p., the A-6-A had no great power reserve, but it used the available horsepower very efficiently. The type certificate number for the Model A-6-A "Sedan" was issued 7-16-31 and only one example of this model was built by the Travel Air Div. of the Curtiss-Wright Airplane Co. of Robertson (St. Louis), Mo.

Listed below are specifications and performance data for the model A-6-A "Sedan" as powered with the 420 h.p. "Wasp" C1 engine; length overall 32-5"; height overall 9'6"; wing span 54'6"; wing chord 84"; total wing area 340 sq.ft.; airfoil either a Clark Y-15 or a Goettingen 398; wt. empty 3332 lbs.; useful load 2268 lbs.; payload with 130 gal. fuel and 2 pilots 1088 lbs. (6 pass. & 68 lb. baggage); gross wt. 5600 lbs.; max. speed (with speed-ring) 144; cruising speed 120; landing (stall) speed 65; climb 850 ft. first min. at sea level; ceiling 17,000 ft.; gas cap. 130 gal.; oil cap. 8 gal.; cruising range at 25 gal. per hour 600 miles; price approx. $18,000. at factory field. Outside of data from CAA Manual, all other data not verified with manufacturer's reports.

The construction details and general arrangement of the model A-6-A were mostly typical to that of the A-6000-A as described in the chapter for ATC # 116. Much of the descriptive data for the model 6-B on ATC # 352 will also apply. Among the changes wrought into the A-6-A, the bulge-type front cabin enclosure at the pilot station was the most apparent; tending to be unsightly, the enclosure however did improve the range of visibility, and extended head-room for the pilots. Inside cabin dimensions of 112x52x36 in. allowed ample seating for 8 places, or a variety of other loading configurations; ample room was available for installation of radio gear and lavatory facilities. Equipped with dual "Dep" wheel controls, this ship was normally operated by two pilots. An extension to the fuselage length could only be linked to the statement, "it seemed to be about a foot longer". The wing seemed to be similar to earlier "Travel Air" design, but random data seems to differ on the "airfoil" used; it could have been either the Clark Y-15 or the Goettingen 398. The wing bracing truss and landing gear trusses were similar to early types. Two fuel tanks of 130 gal. total capacity were mounted in the root ends of each wing-half; fuel-level gauges were visible from the cockpit. The fabric covered tail-group was shaped differently, with areas distributed in different proportion. A metal propeller, electric engine starter, navigation lights, a battery, wheel brakes, and dual controls were standard equipment. Landing lights, flares, radio gear, generator, and speed-ring cowling were optional.

Listed below is the only known Model A-6-A entry:

NC-469W; Model A-6-A (A6A-2009) Wasp C1.

This approval for # A6A-2009 and up; approval expired 7-1-32.

A.T.C. # 437
(7-17-31)
KELLETT "AUTOGIRO", K-2

Fig. 125. Kellett "Autogiro" model K-2 shown here in prototype.

The Autogiro Co. of America, which owned and controlled all the patent rights, issued licenses for the manufacture of the "autogiro" here in the U.S.A. Kellett was the only other qualified manufacturer to actively participate in this new venture of bulding the remarkable wind-mill airplanes. Whereas the Pitcairn firm built a variety of sport and utility models, Kellett built a model that was primarily for sport-flying in this new dimension. Introduced late in 1930, the new Kellett model K-2 was a high back slab-sided machine that had the sturdy look of a very functional piece of flying machinery. Although similar in general mechanical arrangement to the well-rounded "Pitcairn" machines, the "Kellett" reminded one of a chummy "roadster" for two that was sure to provide open-air fun, and all sorts of adventure. While the K-2 was definitely slanted towards the sport-flier, its unusual abilities were also easily converted to some of the more utilitarian uses; a noted western prospector used his K-2 to increase the scope of his day's work in the desert and mountains. In many respects, the autogiro was more naturally adaptable to many chores not particularly suitable to the normal fixed-wing airplane. Sharing also the ability to take off from small hemmed-in places, and able to land almost vertically on the proverbial dime, the Kellett K-2 was capable of outstanding performance feats also, especially when handled by a pilot well-versed in attaining its maximum potential. A rather unusual incident, well worth relating here, involved a Kellett K-2 that had run out of

fuel, because of stiff headwinds, during a flight at dusk. Far from an airport and over dark, unfamiliar terrain, there was nothing to do but go down. Heading into the stiff breeze and establishing minimum forward speed, the wind-milling autogiro descended slowly and almost vertically for some 2000 feet; it landed with a heavy plop in a farmer's backyard. Luckily, there was no damage and it was just happy coincidence of course that the descending autogiro selected such a likely landing place. Basking in the publicity that was accorded the "autogiro" nationally during this period, the Kellett K-2 was well received and soon began making its appearance here and there across the country. Because of its peculiar nature the Kellett's habitat was more likely to be someone's backyard lawn than an airport.

The Kellett model K-2 was a bulky sport-type autogiro with seating arranged side by side for two in an open cockpit; a convertible coupe-top canopy was available for quick installation to those desiring a little more comfort in cold weather. Basically possessing all the unusual characteristics of the autogiro, the model K-2 was primarily designed for sport flying; the airframe was beefy with ample strength to withstand the escapades that were normally attributed to the flying "sport". Powered with the 7 cyl. Continental A-70-2 engine of 165 h.p., the K-2 had sufficient performance for the average sportsman, one who had no particular yen to charge off into the blue like a screaming eagle. For those that did wish to emulate the eagle,

Fig. 126. View of K-2 shows basic workings of autogiro concept.

and there were several, Kellett offered the improved K-2-A with a 210 h.p. Continental engine. All of the K-2 were eligible for this K-2-A modification, and several K-2 owners took advantage of the sizeable boost in all-round performance. In general, the Kellett K-2 was a sturdy knock-about type of ship with a rather friendly manner, and was never too fussy about its chore or treatment. Mild-mannered and reasonably docile as the model K-2, as the K-2-A

Fig. 127. Kellett K-2 taking off from pier in Atlantic City.

Fig. 128. Kellett K-2 also offered with coupe-top for cold weather.

type with its extra 45 h.p., it had more nerve and more verve in its mode and its behavior. Comparable in price to a normal fixed-wing airplane of similar power and seating, the Kellett K-2 should have sold well among the flying sportsmen; that it did not is one of the many riddles of this particular time. The type certificate number for the Kellett model K-2 was issued 7-17-31 and some 12 examples of this model were manufactured by the Kellett Aircraft Corp. at Philadelphia, Penna.

Listed below are specifications and performance data for the Kellett model K-2 as powered with the 165 h.p. Continental A-70-2 engine; length overall 19'6"; height overall 12'4"; rotor dia. 41'0"; rotor blade chord 23"; rotor disc area 1320 sq.ft.; rotor turns 130 r.p.m. at cruising speed; fixed-wing span 26'0"; fixed-wing chord 54"; fixed-wing area 100 sq.ft.; fixed-wing air-foil RAF-30; wt. empty 1551 [1518] lbs.; useful load 649 [682] lbs.; payload with 35 gal. fuel 238 [270] lbs.; gross wt. 2200 lbs.; wts in brackets for open-cockpit model; max. speed 100 [95]; cruising speed 82 [78]; landing speed 15-20 [10-15]; speeds in brackets for open-cockpit model; climb 650 ft. first min. at sea level; service ceiling 9000 ft.; gas cap. 35 gal.; oil cap. 4 gal.; cruising range at 11 gal. per hour 250 miles; price $7885. at factory for open model, and $8255. at factory for coupe model.

The fuselage framework was built up of welded round and square steel tubing, faired out to a rounded shape and fabric covered. The spacious open cockpit seated 2 side by side, with a large entry door on the right side; a baggage compartment of 5.5 cu.ft. capacity was mounted low behind the seat with access from the outside. Two parachutes when carried, were part of the

Fig. 129. Cold weather no problem for K-2, but high winds were shunned.

68 lb. baggage allowance. All examples beyond the prototype dispensed with the high turtle-back, and a demountable coupe-type canopy was available for cold-weather flying. Fuel tanks of 28 and 7 gal. capacity were mounted low in the fuselage under the seat. The fixed-wing framework was built up of spruce and ply-wood box-type spar beams, with spruce and ply-wood wing ribs; the leading edges were covered with plywood sheet and the completed frame-work was covered in fabric. The 4-bladed rotor system was mounted on a tripod pylon, running in a large ball-bearing hub; various cables kept the blades 90 deg. apart, and also limited the droop. A mechanical rotor starter was used to bring blades up to proper r.p.m. for take-off; a rotor brake was also provided. The rotor blades were built up of round chrome-moly steel tube spars and plywood ribs of symmetrical section; the leading edges were covered with plywood sheet and the completed blade framework was covered in fabric. The unusual landing gear truss of 144 in. tread used long-travel (10 in.) oleo shock absorbing legs; wheels were 7.50x10 and brakes were provided. A full-swivel tail wheel was also provided. The fabric covered tail-group was a built-up structure of wooden

spars, formers, and ribs; the horizontal stabilizer was adjustable in flight. A metal propeller, Hey-wood engine starter, a rotor starter, compass, and dual controls were standard equipment. A coupe-type canopy was available installed for $370.00 extra. The next development in the Kellett autogiro was the model K-3 as described in the chapter for ATC # 471 of this volume.

Listed below are model K-2 entries as gleaned from registration records:

X-10766;   Model K-2 (# 1) Continental A-70.
NC-10767;   ”   (# 2)   ”
NC-11666;   ”   (# 3)   ”
NC-11667;   ”   (# 4)   ”
NC-11668;   ”   (# 5)   ”
NC-11683;   ”   (# 6)   ”
NC-11685;   ”   (# 7)   ”
NC-11686;   ”   (# 8)   ”
NC-11687;   ”   (# 9)   ”
NC-11691;   ”   (# 10)   ”
NC-12603;   ”   (# 11)   ”
NC-12605;   ”   (# 12)   ”

Serial # 2 and # 12 later modified into model K-3; ser. # 4, 7, 9, 10, later as model K-2-A; ser. # 3 later modified into model K-4; models K-2-A on Group 2 approval numbered 2-431; this approval (ATC # 437) for ser. # 1 through # 12.

A.T.C. # 438
(7-21-31)
FAIRCHILD 22, MODEL C-7-A

Fig. 130. Fairchild 22-C7A with 95 h.p. Cirrus Hi-Drive engine; inline engine enhances slender beauty.

The trim Rover-powered model C-7 did an excellent job of setting the stage and gaining attention for the new "Fairchild 22" series, but soon had to bow out and step aside for the improved "Twenty Two" that came along with more to offer. The relentless demand for a little more horsepower, a little more performance and added finery, quickly came to overshadow the singular consideration of operating economy. In this new model labeled the C-7-A, the Fairchild 22 now had available some 20 h.p. extra by installation of the 4 cyl. inverted inline Cirrus "Hi-Drive" engine of 95 h.p. Every bit as trim and handsome as its earlier sister-ship, of course, the impish C-7-A was bolstered in spirit by this added muscle, and it wasn't long in catching the eyes of the average flying public. To any owner-pilot who particularly favored the open monoplane type, and was in the market for an airplane with good looks, a spirited performance and operating convenience, all with a reasonably low price-tag, the new "Twenty Two" (C-7-A) would be hard to pass up as a first choice. Well adapted also to pilot-training, the C-7-A was soon on the flight-line at several flying-schools; at least two of these were fully equipped for "blind flight" training under the hood. One example of this model, in a slightly modified form, was delivered to the NACA laboratories on Langley Field early in 1932; this ship was specifically selected for flight-testing various "slot" and "flap" configurations in conjunction with wing dihedral changes. These tests were part of that never-ending search to find a practical combination for the fool-proof

airplane. Accepted quickly and cheerfully, holding up very well in popularity, and steadily in production into 1933, the C-7-A was improved periodically as time went by; the later versions were perhaps the handsomest example of the parasol monoplane type.

The Kreider-Reisner (Fairchild 22) model C-7-A was a light parasol-type monoplane with seating arranged for two in tandem. Arranged in a proportion of dimension and shape that was practical as well as efficient, the trim and girlish C-7-A was also one of the more eye-catching airplanes of this particular type. With its light slender wing perched high atop the slender fuselage, visibility was exceptional in most directions, and access into or around the airplane was handy and uncomplicated. A few added appointments and some extra equipment in the C-7-A were consistent with normal demands for the typical light sport-plane. Powered now with the popular 4 cyl. Cirrus "Hi-Drive" (inverted) engine of 95 h.p., the model C-7-A (Fairchild 22-C7A) offered a more lively performance that was nearly ideal for the average sporting-pilot who flew for the fun of it; flying schools welcomed the added performance also to teach pilots the more advanced maneuvers and piloting techniques. Pleasantly stable, and responsive to even the lightest touch, the C-7-A was widely considered as a treat to fly; it certainly confirmed the fact that the "model 22" design harbored many inherent talents that were best brought out by added power. This second version of the "Twenty Two" became popular quickly and was well scattered around the coun-

Fig. 131. Lively nature of 22-C7A popular among sport-pilots.

try; several were exported to foreign countries. The popularity of this model and its hardy character in normal service tended to promote its longevity, so it is understandable that perhaps 40 of these were still flying actively in 1939. The type certificate number for the model C-7-A (Fairchild 22-C7A) as landplane and seaplane was issued 7-21-31; some 58 or more examples of this model were manufactured by the Kreider-Reisner Aircraft Co., Inc. at Hagerstown, Maryland.

Listed below are specifications and performance data for the Fairchild 22 model C-7-A as powered with the 95 h.p. Cirrus Hi-Drive engine; length overall 21'8"; height overall 8'0"; wing span 32'10"; wing chord 66"; total wing area 170 sq.ft.; airfoil (Navy-NACA) N-22; wt. empty 926 [940] lbs.; useful load 574 [610] lbs.; payload with 21 gal. fuel 259 [295] lbs.; 2 parachutes at 20 lbs. each as part of payload; gross wt. 1500 [1550] lbs.; max. speed 114; cruising speed 94; landing speed 42-45; stall speed 45-47; climb 750-725 ft. first min. at sea level; ceiling 13,000-12,500 ft.; gas cap. 21 gal.; oil cap. 2.5 gal.; cruising range at 6 gal. per hour 290 miles; price at factory first as $2775., soon

Fig. 132. Fairchild 22-C7A on Edo floats.

Fig. 133. A 22-C7A in Canada.

raised to $2975., and lowered to $2275. in 1933. Wts. shown in brackets are for C-7-A with sport-type landing gear and the max. allowable gross wt. Model C-7-A also eligible for 1550 lbs. gross wt. to allow the installation of metal propeller, hand crank inertia-type starter, a battery, and navigation lights. Seaplane gross wt. at 1550 lbs. with Edo I-1835 twin-float gear, a metal propeller, hand crank inertia-type starter, navigation lights, and battery. The Cirrus Hi-Drive

engine developing 95 h.p. at 2100 r.p.m., cost $895.00 crated for delivery.

The construction details and general arrangement of the model C-7-A was typical to that of the C-7 as described in the chapter for ATC # 408. Typical of all models in the 22-series, the fuselage framework was built up of welded chrome-moly (4130) steel tubing in a combination of square and round section; this was to provide easier, better, and stronger welds,

Fig. 134. Special 22-C7A used by NACA for testing of slats, flaps, and changes in dihedral.

especially where the tubes joined in a multiple cluster. All welds were sand-blasted before painting or plating. Brake pedals were in the rear cockpit only, but optional for installation in the front cockpit also for $25.00. A fuel level float-gauge was visible from either seat. Also available as an option was a sport-type landing gear of 7'7" tread; the center-vees were faired over and 6.50x10 semi-airwheels were encased in streamlined "pants"; wheel brakes were standard equipment. A steel spring-leaf tail skid was standard, but an 8x4 tail wheel was optional. The seaplane version of the C-7-A, as equipped with Edo I-1835 floats, had metal propeller, a hand crank inertia-type engine starter, navigation (position) lights, and a battery. The optional one-piece or two-piece wing employed built-up spars of I-beam section, using a spruce center-web and heavy spruce capstrips; a spar of this type is lighter and considerably stronger. Pratt-truss wing ribs of spruce members and plywood gussets were designed to load factor of 9, weighing but 5 oz. each; each rib could sustain at least 500 lbs. The leading edges were covered with dural metal sheet and the completed framework was covered in fabric; the complete wing weighed only 172 lbs. Ailerons were covered with corrugated dural metal sheet most ends to link up with push-pull tubes coming directly out of the cockpit. Linking geometry provided differential action, and each aileron was interchangeable from one side to other. The standard color combinations, in a 9-coat finish, were an International-Orange fuselage and Ivory wing, or Insignia-Blue fuselage and Army-Navy yellow wing; striping on fuselage was same color as the wing. Optional two-color combinations were $40.00 extra. Other optional extras included Edo twin-float gear for $975.00, an Eclipse hand-crank engine starter for $133.00, low pressure Goodyear 19x9-3 airwheels were $25.00 extra, navigation (position) lights for $25.00, sport-type landing gear with wheel pants for $150.00, and a metal cover for front cockpit at $15.00. The next development in the Fairchild 22 was the Menasco-powered model C-7-B as described in the chapter for ATC # 483 of this volume.

Listed below are C-7-A entries as gleaned from registration records:

NC-11606; C-7-A (# 506) Hi-Drive 95.
NC-11620;   "   (# 511)   "
NC-11651;   "   (# 1001)   "
NC-11652;   "   (# 1002)   "
NC-11653;   "   (# 1003)   "
NC-11678;   "   (# 1004)   "
NC-11677;   "   (# 1005)   "
NC-11679;   "   (# 1006)   "
NC-11676;   "   (# 1007)   "
NC-11696;   "   (# 1008)   "
NC-11697;   "   (# 1009)   "
NC-11698;   "   (# 1010)   "
NC-11699;   "   (# 1011)   "
NC-12600;   "   (# 1012)   "
NC-12649;   "   (# 1029)   "
NC-12650;   "   (# 1030)   "
CF-ARG;   "   (# 1038)   "
NC-13194;   "   (# 1049)   "
NC-2816;   "   (# 1053)   "
NC-2853;   "   (# 1054)   "
NC-2871;   "   (# 1055)   "
NC-2872;   "   (# 1056)   "

Serial # 506 and 511 modified to C-7-A from C-7; ser. # 1005 also on floats; ser. # 1016 not listed; NC-12611 was # 1013; NC-12612 was # 1014; NC-12613 was # 1015; NC-12614 was # 1017; NC-12621 was # 1018 and numbers ran consecutively to NC-12625 which was # 1022; NC-12638 was # 1023 and numbers ran consecutively to NC-12641 which was # 1026; ser. # 1027-1028 not listed; NC-12672 was # 1031 and numbers ran consecutively to NC-12674 which was # 1033; NC-12687 was # 1034 and numbers ran consecutively to NC-12690 which was # 1037; NC-13100 was # 1039 and numbers ran consecutively to NC-13103 which was # 1042; ser. # 1043 not listed; NC-13160 was # 1044 and numbers ran consecutively to NC-13164 which was # 1048; ser. # 1050-1051 and 1052 not listed; ser. # 1031, 1032, 1036, 1040, 1041 unverified; ser. # 1037 later had Menasco B4-95 on Group 2 approval; ser. # 1038 operated in Canada; several of the C-7-A were exported; this approval for ser. # 506, 511, 1001 and up; this approval expired 7-1-35.

A.T.C. # 439
(7-31-31)
ALEXANDER "FLYABOUT", D-1

Fig. 135. Alexander "Flyabout" model D-1 with Continental A-40 engine.

By the time the revolutionary Alexander "Bullet" was tested, approved, and ready to market, the company began to feel the financial drain its development had caused. A disappearing market for the standard "Eaglerock" biplane series failed to help matters any, and together this instigated plans for something that would sell; a small light-weight monoplane seemed the most likely. Both Ludwig Muther and Dr. Max Munk had already left the company's employe by mid-1930, and young Proctor Nichols was moved up to chief engineer. Discussions and drawing-board sessions among Nichols and some of his associates led to the formulation of a basic design that became the flivver-type "Flyabout". As introduced at the Detroit Air Show early in 1931, the Alexander "Flyabout" model D-1 was the first side-by-side cabin monoplane in the light-plane (under 1000 lbs.) class, and soon after became the first airplane to be certificated with the new 4 cyl. Continental A-40 engine. "Fly cheaply with 2 people and a puppy aboard on less than 40 horsepower", thus read Alexander ads of the period. Operational tests in the high altitudes of Colorado, and thereabouts, soon proved that the sum total of 37 h.p. was a bit shy for peace of mind in the mountainous western country. An increase in the available horsepower was inevitable, so only 3 or 4 examples of the model D-1 were built, and most of these were soon after modified to mount an engine of greater power. The model D-1 was still offered through 1934, but apparently buyers shunned it for the more powerful model.

The Alexander "Flyabout" model D-1 was a snub-nosed squat high-winged cabin monoplane with seating arranged side-by-side for two, all closed-in for comfort. Not a small airplane by any means, the "Flyabout" offered sufficient room for two, and the operating utility of a good stout airframe. Powered with the new 4 cyl. (flat 4) Continental A-40 engine of 37 h.p., there was no power reserve to speak of, but the performance of this combination was very good within limits; economy of operation was its cardinal feature. The Continental A-40 engine, developing 37 h.p. at 2550 r.p.m. burned only 2.8 gallon of fuel at hard cruise, or over 25 miles to the gallon. Of good aerodynamic proportion, the D-1 flew honestly, easily, and precisely, with no especial skills required for satisfactory operation. Its gentle nature in this and succeeding models was a treat for student pilots, and the private-pilot who only took a turn or two about the country-side on week-ends. The type certificate number for the "Flyabout" model D-1 was issued 7-31-31 and no more than 3 or 4 examples of this model were manufactured by the Alexander Aircraft Co. at Colorado Springs, Colo. Development of a companion model to the D-1 was already under way, but Alexander was slowly failing from the drain of expenses and was seriously thinking of giving up, for a time at least.

Listed below are specifications and per-

Fig. 136. Flyabout D-1 as later converted to D-2.

formance data for the "Flyabout" model D-1 as powered with the 37 h.p. Continental A-40 engine; length overall 21'9"; height overall 5'9"; wing span 37'10"; wing chord 60"; total wing area 175 sq. ft.; airfoil (NACA) M-6; wt. empty 573 lbs.; useful load 389 lbs.; payload with 7 gal. fuel 170 lbs.; gross wt. 962 lbs.; max. speed 80; cruising speed 70; landing (stall) speed 28; climb 350 ft. first min. at sea level; service ceiling 8500 ft.; gas cap. 7 gal.; oil cap. 4 qts.; cruising range at 2.8 gal. per hour 175 miles; price $1465. at factory.

The husky fuselage framework was built up of welded (4130) chrome-moly and 1025 steel tubing, slightly faired to a rounded rectangle shape, then fabric covered. The large cabin entry door was on the left side, and side-by-side seats were slightly staggered for a little more shoulder room; the windshield and the large windows were of pyralin, with a skylight in the cabin roof for vision overhead. Cabin dimensions of 60 in. long x 30 in. wide x 41 in. high offered leg-room for larger people and a small baggage bin behind the seats. The wing framework was built up of spruce box-type spar beams with spruce truss-type wing ribs of "I" section; the leading edges were covered with dural metal sheet and the completed framework was covered with fabric. The wing was bolted to top longerons of the fuselage frame and braced by parallel steel tube struts of streamlined section. The fuel tank was mount-

ed behind the engine firewall and a float-type fuel-level gauge was visible from the cabin; one gallon of oil was carried in the engine sump. The split-axle landing gear of 54 in. tread used rubber shock-cord to snub the bumps on the prototype airplane, but this was found unnecessary, so subsequent examples used the rigid stiff-legged gear. The 16x7-3 Goodyear "airwheels' were found to be sufficient for absorbing the normal shock; the spring-leaf tail skid swiveled for better ground handling, but no wheel brakes were provided. The fabric covered tail-group was built up of welded steel tubing; the horizontal stabilizer was adjustable for load trim on the ground only. The steel tube engine mount was easily detachable to allow the mounting of different engines. A wooden propeller, dual controls, and Goodyear "airwheels" were standard equipment. The next development in the little "Flyabout" was the model D-2 as described in the chapter for ATC # 449 of this volume.

Listed below are Flyabout model D-1 entries as gleaned from registration records:

X-447V Model D-1 (# 3000) Cont. A-40.
          ;   "   (# 3001)   "
NC-528Y;   "   (# 3002)   "
NC-11061;   "   (# 3003)   "

No listing for ser. # 3001; ser. # 3002 and # 3003 later modified to model D-2 by installation of 45 h.p. Szekely engine.

Fig. 137. Curtiss-Wright "Kingbird" D-3 was improvement over earlier D-2; two exported to Turkey.

The Curtiss "Kingbird" was a rather unusual medium-sized transport designed especially to operate safely in the case of failure to one engine; the remaining engine was quite capable to sustain near-normal flight to a haven of refuge. Aerodynamic arrangement has always been important in multi-engined designs, so Curtiss engineers ran numerous tests to find the ideal concept. Deciding on a small "twin", the engines were placed so far forward and so close together that the center-line of thrust moved laterally only a small degree in single-engined operation. Introduced first to the market as the D-1 (ATC # 347) with two Wright 225 h.p. engines, the power reserve was found to be too scant, so a power increase was in order. As the model D-2 (ATC # 348), the "Kingbird" mounted two Wright 300 h.p. engines, with a resulting increase in performance and much better behavior with "one engine out". Eastern Air Transport eventually received 14 of the model D-2, which served the eastern seaboard route for several years. In the latter part of 1931, Curtiss-Wright was grooming a new improved "Kingbird" as the model D-3; with an eye to still greater performance and more power reserve, the new D-3 mounted two 330 h.p. engines and carried only six passengers. This particular "Kingbird" has such an obscure past at this date, that even those closely connected with the project had trouble remembering the whys and wherefores of this last model. Only skimpy accounts from sundry sources were available to throw some light

of understanding on the model D-3. Basically the D-3 was a counterpart to the successful D-2, except that it mounted the newer more powerful engines, and some of the seats were removed to make way for baggage and mail. Designed as a small airliner that could operate flexibly and cheaply, it was reported that two of this model were purchased by the government of Turkey in 1932, for the first Turkish airline which was to inaugurate service early in 1933. These two "Kingbirds" were the initial equipment delivered to this line, and more orders were to follow. It is doubtful if they did. One example of the new model D-3 was registered here in the U.S. to Curtiss-Wright, and by 1935 it had not yet been sold. There was no evidence of additional craft of this type. With plans already afoot for larger and faster aircraft, the American airlines would certainly not be in the market at this date for a craft of the "Kingbird" type.

The Curtiss-Wright "Kingbird" model D-3 was a medium size twin-engined high wing cabin monoplane with seating arranged for six. Descriptive reports all agree that it was basically similar to the earlier model D-2, except for newer more powerful engines and a slight re-arrangement of the interior. Seating was limited to 5 passengers and a pilot, with a bin in the rear corner for 259 lbs. of baggage and mail. A larger fuel load and provisions for toilet equipment hint strongly that the D-3 was designed to operate with a greater range. Powered with two Wright R-975-E engines of 330 h.p. each, reports state that performance and general behavior of the new D-3 was comparable or perhaps just a little better than the earlier D-2; the power increase affected the speeds very little, and was almost absorbed by the increase in gross weight. The only known example of the D-3 here in the U.S.A. was operated by the Curtiss-Wright Corp., and it was equipped with "fenders" and big roly-poly Goodyear "airwheels", because it was said to operate very often away from the home field. Registered to Curtiss-Wright consecutively into 1935, the final disposition of this craft is not known. The type certificate number for the "Kingbird" model D-3 was issued 8-6-31 and perhaps no more than 3 examples of this model were manufactured by the Curtiss-Wright Airplane Co. on Lambert Field in Robertson (St. Louis), Mo. At this particular time the work force at the St. Louis Div. was normally about 200 people, with laid-off personnel being called up as needed on different projects, projects which were many and varied. Drawing a fair work-load from the large number of "types" that were being produced, Curtiss-Wright bided its time while waiting for an improvement in the condition of the nation's economy.

Listed below are specifications and performance data for the "Kingbird" model D-3 as powered with two 330 h.p. Wright R-975-E engines; length overall 34'9"; height overall 10'0"; wing span 54'6"; wing chord 100"; total wing area 405 sq.ft.; airfoil Curtiss C-72; wt. empty 4215 lbs.; useful load 2385 lbs.; payload with 166 gal. fuel 1109 lbs. (5 pass. at 170 lb. each & 250 lb. mail-baggage); gross wt. 6600 lbs.; max. speed 142; cruising speed 122; stall speed 65; landing speed 62; climb 1000 ft. first min. at sea level; ceiling 16,000 ft.; gas cap. 166 gal.; oil cap. 14 gal.; cruising range at 36 gal. per hour 550 miles; basic price at factory approx. $25,000. This data not verified with manufacturer's reports.

The construction details and general arrangement were typical to that of the models D-1 and D-2; for data and a complete description that would basically apply to the D-3 also, refer to chapters for ATC # 347-348 of USCA/C, Vol. 4. The cabin was equipped with ventilation, cabin heaters, and toilet-lavatory facilities. The "oleo" landing gear was fitted with 30x13 Goodyear airwheels with brakes; metal fenders were provided to protect propellers from mud and flying debris during take-off, landing, and taxiing. The engines were shrouded with Townend-type low drag cowlings (Curtiss speed-rings) for added speed and better airflow distribution. Adj. metal propellers, electric engine starters, a battery, generator, navigation lights, landing lights, and parachute flares were standard equipment. The next C-W development was the Deluxe Sportsman model A-14-D as described in the chapter for ATC # 442 of this volume.

Listed below is the only known "Kingbird" model D-3 entry:

NC-11816; Model D-3 (# 2016) 2 Wright 330.

This approval for ser. # 2016 and up; approval expired 4-26-37.

Fig. 138. Ford model 4-AT-F was larger version of earlier 4-AT-E.

Progressive development in the popular Ford "Tri-Motor" was often so subtle that succeeding models of a series showed very little discernable difference, a difference hardly noted, or only by a closer examination. A good example in point was the model 4-AT-F. Resembling the the earlier A-AT-E in very many ways, the model 4-AT-F harbored many changes and improvements that had little to do with its general outward appearance. Extensively refined in overall detail, the 4-AT-F was perhaps the finest example in the smaller 4-AT series, and it was also the last one built. Initial flight testing began on July 27 of 1931 and its certificate of approval was awarded about two weeks later. Sometime later in that year the single 4-AT-F was exported to Spain for airline service. With the coming of the civil war in Spain, it was hastily commandeered and pressed into service with the Spanish Air Force. After the war, still hale and hearty, it was returned back to airline service with the Iberia line, serving actively until some time in 1945. Details of its existence beyond that are unknown, but its known 14 years of existence were certainly interesting and quite eventful.

The Ford "Tri-Motor" model 4-AT-F was a high-winged all-metal cabin monoplane normally seating 12 passengers with a crew of two, in an interior arrangement substantially improved both in decor and in comfort. Cabin ventilation was improved, cabin heating was more efficient, and interior appointments were more comfortable and more decorative. Exact details on much else of the ship's makeup and character are either vague or unknown, but the 4-AT-F has always been described as the finest example in the 4-AT series. Considerably heavier when empty, with more allowance for useful load, the loaded gross weight was increased by better than 800 lbs. Powered with three 9 cyl. Wright J6 (R-975) engines of 300 h.p. each, the gross weight increase seemed to have very little effect on the general performance. Aerodynamic improvements to the engine nacelles, the landing gear assembly, and the use of "speed ring" cowlings on the outboard engines boosted the available speed range by a noticeable margin. It can be assumed that flight characteristics and general behavior were similar or perhaps somewhat better than in earlier models typical of this (4-AT) series. The type certificate number for the model 4-AT-F was issued 8-10-31 and only one example of this model was built.

Listed below are specifications and performance data for the Ford model 4-AT-F as powered with 3 Wright J6 engines of 300 h.p. each; length overall 49'10"; height overall 11'9"; wing span 74'0"; wing chord at root 156"; wing chord at tip 92"; total wing area 785 sq.ft.; airfoil Ford # 2; wt. empty 6929 lbs.; useful load 4071 lbs.; payload with 231 gal. fuel 2171 lbs. (12 pass. at 170 lb. each & 131 lb. baggage); gross wt. 11,000 lbs.; max speed 138; cruising speed 113; landing speed 59; climb 900 ft. first min. at sea level; climb 7000 ft. in 10 min.; ceiling 14,000 ft.; gas cap. normal 231

Fig. 139. Tri-motored 4-AT-F as operated on Spanish airline.

gal.; oil cap. 24 gal.; cruising range at 45 gal. per hour 540 miles; price $40,000. at factory with standard equipment.

The construction details and general arrangement of the model 4-AT-F was typical to that of other models in the 4-AT series, especially the 4-AT-E (ATC # 132). Cabin windows were now one-piece panes of shatter-proof glass, with ventilating slots of more efficient design. A large heat-muff from the center engine, provided abundant and more efficient cabin heat. Engine nacelles were profusely louvered for heat expulsion, generally cleaned-up for less drag, and speed-ring cowlings on outboard engines added considerably to the top speed. The landing gear of 16'9" tread was equipped with 40x10 wheels and brakes were standard equipment. Metal fenders protected whirling propellers from debris churned up by the wheels. The fuel capacity was divided among 3 tanks mounted in the wing, and were often filled to less than full capacity to allow an increase in the payload. An oil tank of 8 gal. capacity was mounted in each engine nacelle. Metal propellers, inertia-type engine starters, a tail wheel, dual controls, and navigation lights were standard equipment. The model 4-AT-F was also available with 3 P & W "Wasp

Junior" engines of 300 h.p. each, but none of this version were built.

Listed below is the only model 4-AT-F entry: NC-9656; Model 4-AT-F (#4-AT-71) 3 Wright 300. This ship registered also as EC-RRA and EC-WIO on Spanish airlines, as 42-8 with the Spanish Air Force, and as EC-BAB for the Iberia line, also in Spain; ship believed destroyed in 1948.

On Sept. of 1932, Ford finally ceased all manufacture of the "Tri-Motor". The reason for this decision were many and varied, but the most decisive factor was perhaps the general business depression, which showed no signs of easing up. Building the Ford "Tri-Motor" had not been a profitable venture, and continued building could hardly be expected to write off any more of the losses. The doors were slammed shut on Jan. 8 of 1933. By then, some 200 of the famous "Tin Goose" had already been built, large airlines continued to use them into the late thirties, 47 were still flying actively in 1955, and a handful of the old die-hards were still flying in the sixties. It is hard to predict the closing chapter of the illustrious Ford "Tri-Motor", it may go on for years yet, but wherever old airline pilots gather, it is sure to be a spirited topic of reminiscence and discussion.

Fig. 140. Curtiss-Wright model A-14-D with Wright R-760-E engine.

Designed especially to take best advantage of the low-drag NACA "radial engine" cowling, the new Travel Air (Curtiss-Wright) "Sportsman" was faired out neatly in soft rounded curves and smooth flowing lines. Rather big and roundish in front to match the cowling diameter, the rest of the fuselage tapered back into very slender lines. Fitted with a pair of thin, slender wings that were easy on the drag, this combination was inherently lively and capable of rather outstanding speeds. Posing with a thin-legged almost girlish look, the "Sportsman" model A-14-D was definitely a craft with appeal to the sportsman-pilot, one who would offer it a man's affection with pampered care. No doubt suitable for promotion of a specialized form, the A-14-D was also selected as a machine of business. The Union Oil Co. of Calif. who had a special liking for "Travel Air" airplanes, traded their two older models in on two of the speedy "Sportsman Deluxe". Other examples of the flashing A-14-D must have been divided among sportsman-pilots because it is hard to conceive a ship of this type performing all-purpose duties for some fixed-base operator.

The Curtiss-Wright (Travel Air) "Deluxe Sportsman" model A-14-D was an open cockpit biplane with seating for 3, and although larger, was patterned somewhat after the 12-series sport-trainer. Although the "Sportsman" actually had room enough to carry 3, it was most often seen with the front cockpit covered over to take advantage of the speed gain. From its big round cowling in front, down its tapering fuselage to its slender wings, the A-14-D reflected speed in its every line. Built especially for the sportsman-pilot, there is no doubt that it also offered a fair share of utility, but its main forte was speed and cruising range. Powered with the 7 cyl. Wright J6 (R-760-E) engine of 240 h.p., the A-14-D had more than enough muscle in its frame to deliver a very good performance. The earlier "Travel Air" model 4-D (ATC # 254) was distant kin and might be likened as a similar type of airplane to the A-14-D, but the personalities of the two certainly had nothing much in common. Flight characteristics and general behavior of the new "Deluxe Sportsman" were sometimes described as not typically "Travel Air", but in any case were still quite typical for an airplane of this new specialized type. Certain techniques required to bring out the full potential in this craft, usually promoted a somewhat remarkable performance. The type certificate number for the "Sportsman" (Speedwing) model A-14-D was issued 8-13-31 and some 7 or 8 examples of this model were manufactured by the Curtiss-Wright Airplane Co. at Robertson (St. Louis), Mo.

As described and pictured here, it is plain to see that the new Curtiss-Wright "Sportsman" (Speedwing) was not typically a "Travel Air" as most knew it; Fred Landgraf, who was project engineer on the 14-series, might very well

Fig. 141. A-14-D "Sportsman" as shown at Detroit Air Show for 1932.

be the underlying reason for it. Earlier, Fred Landgraf was associated with the development of the "Eaglerock" (Alexander) biplane, and more recently he had designed the "Ken-Royce" (Rearwin) biplane; it takes only casual scrutiny to discover that a little of each was subtly incorporated into the new "Sportsman". This striking resemblance is most noticeable in the Challenger-powered model 14-C, which was first of the "Sportsman" series. Earliest versions of the A-14-D were somewhat lighter and called "Sportsman Deluxe"; later versions were heavier, better equipped, refined for more speed, and as such they fell heir to the name of "Speed-

wing". The "Speedwing" design became the logical basis for the famous "Osprey" fighter-bombers that were exported to foreign countries, and the A-14-D itself was still offered in 1935 with a 285 h.p. Wright engine.

Listed below are specifications and performance data for the model A-14-D as powered with the 240 h.p. Wright R-760-E engine; length overall 23'7"; height overall 9'1"; wing span upper 31'0"; wing span lower 23'7"; wing chord upper 60"; wing chord lower 48"; total wing area 247 sq.ft.; airfoil (NACA) N-9; wt. empty 1755 lbs.; useful load 995 lbs.; payload with 58 gal. fuel 431 lbs. (2 pass. at 170 lb. each & 91

Fig. 142. Ideal for sport, the A-14-D featured high speeds and extended range.

Fig. 143. Union Oil Co. used A-14-D for test and promotion.

lbs. baggage); gross wt. 2750 lbs.; max. speed 150; cruising speed 130; landing speed 56; climb 1100 ft. first min. at sea level; ceiling 17,000 ft.; gas cap. 58 gal.; oil cap. 4.75 gal.; cruising range at 13 gal. per hour 540 miles; price first quoted at $8750., later raised to $10,895. The following figures are for later examples with revised wts.; wt. empty 1772 lbs.; useful load 1098 lbs.; payload with 58 gal. fuel 534 lbs. (2 pass. & 194 lbs. baggage); gross wt. 2870 lbs.; max. speed 155; cruising speed 135; landing speed 60; climb 1000 ft. first min. at sea level; ceiling 16,100 ft.; all other figures same; price $10,895. at factory field.

The fuselage framework was built up of welded chrome-moly steel tubing, lavishly faired with formers and fairing strips to a near-oval section, then fabric covered. The pilot's cockpit was deep and well protected by a 3-piece Tri-Plex shatter-proof windshield; a large baggage compartment was behind the rear cockpit with a locking type access door on the right side. Brake pedals were in the rear cockpit only, but available in the front cockpit also for $50.00 extra. The front cockpit seated two and could be covered over with a metal panel when not in use. There was a small baggage bin in dash-panel of the front cockpit, and dual controls were available. The large NACA cowling that shrouded the engine was removable in 4 sections for quick maintenance and easy inspection. The wing framework was built up of solid spruce spar beams with web-type spruce wing ribs; the wing ribs were closely spaced (8 in.) to preserve the airfoil form across the span, and the completed framework was covered in fabric. Large Friese-type ailerons were in the upper wing panels. A 35 gal. fuel tank was mounted high in the

fuselage just ahead of the front cockpit; a 23 gal. tank was mounted in the center-section panel of the upper wing. The lower wings were faired into the fuselage junction with a streamlined metal fillet, and there was a wing-walk on either side. The split-axle landing gear of 18 in. tread used oleo (Hydra-Flex) shock absorbing struts; low pressure 8.00x10 semi-airwheels with brakes were standard equipment. The fabric covered tail-group was built up of welded chrome-moly steel tubing; the rudder had aerodynamic balance, the fin was ground adjustable, and the horizontal stabilizer was adjustable in flight. A metal propeller, Eclipse electric engine starter, navigation lights, a battery, tail wheel, a metal front cockpit cover, head-rest for rear cockpit, and lighted instrument panel were standard equipment. Optional equipment included a weather-proof cover for rear cockpit at $10.00, retractable landing lights at $200.00, and two-tone colors other than standard were $100.00 extra. Brackets were available for mounting of radio and parachute flares. The next development in the Curtiss-Wright "Speedwing" (Sportsman) series was the model B-14-B as described in the chapter for ATC # 485 of this volume.

Listed below are A-14-D entries as gleaned from registration records:

NC-449W; A-14-D (A14D-2001) Wright 240.
NC-12307;   ”   (A14D-2006)   ”
NC-12310;   ”   (A14D-2007)   ”
NC-12323;   ”   (A14D-2008)   ”
NC-12329;   ”   (A14D-2009)   ”

This approval for ser. # 2001, 2002, 2004, and up; registration numbers for ser. # 2002, 2004, 2005, unknown; ser. # 2007-2008 with Union Oil Co.; approval for A-14-D expired 9-30-39.

Fig. 144. Pilgrim model 100-A with 575 h.p. Hornet B engine as used by American Airways.

All the years that the "Model 100-A" was parading around as a "Pilgrim" it really was of "Fairchild" kin; in fact, it was a direct descendant of the "Fairchild 100" (ATC # 390) that had been introduced less than a year previous. Linked to the needs of more payload at greater speeds, the early "One Hundred" was developed into a very useful machine, but a future of its own died in the making. Plagued by the "depression" in this country at the time, the Fairchild corporate structure certainly had its ups and downs, finally emerging as the American Airplane & Engine Corp. In a logical course of continued development, the "Fairchild 100" design was revived to set the stage for a very successful and popular design concept. Drawing pointers from the specifications laid down by a ready-made customer within the big corporation, the basic "100" design was altered, modified, and improved for even greater utility as a transport. Now as the "Pilgrim 100-A", its buxom form fairly bulged with carrying capacity for mail, passengers, and air-express, with only a slight detriment to the original performance. Powered also with the big 575 h.p. "Hornet B" engine, the big ten-place monoplane was soon coming off the assembly line for delivery to American Airways, another division of the huge parent corporation. All examples of the 100-A were finally delivered to American Airways, and they were used on various portions of their coast-to-coast system. Serving efficiently and profitably for several years, the "Pilgrim 100-A" were all retired from American Airways service

in 1934 when larger and faster transports were placed into use. But this was certainly not the end for the "Pilgrim", no, this was only the beginning.

In 1933 American Airways had loaned one of its veteran 100-A, which had already seen many hours of hard service on its routes, to Adm. Richard E. Byrd for his 2nd South Pole Expedition. Christened "Miss American Airways", it was hoisted ashore in Jan. of 1934, and immediately pressed into cargo-hauling service. Hauling a ton of supplies on each trip, it flew a shuttle-run from the Bay of Whales to the Byrd camp on Little America. During the course of the expedition the "Pilgrim" was also used for photographic work and some exploration, often in temperatures 40 deg. below zero. Several other planes that accompanied the expedition, were lost because of various mishaps, but the rugged "Pilgrim" was returned to the U.S. to fly again. Another of the venerable 100-A, after being retired from American Airways service, was employed as a work-horse transport in the bush-country of Alaska and the U.S.; on its 30th birthday and still in excellent flying condition, it was finally retired and donated back to American Airlines to be placed in their museum. In the museum it stands as a silent tribute to aeronautical science of years gone by.

The most interesting part in the life of the average "100-A" came after they were retired from airline service in the U.S. Several of these were shipped to Alaska for use by Alaskan Airways, a subsidiary of American Airways; these were

Fig. 145. 100-A offered pilot a commanding view of any situation.

later bought up by Pan American Airways and operated on their Pacific-Alaska division. At least 9 of the 100-A had found their way to varying services in Alaska, operating very successfully under the most trying conditions. The various operators were happy for the exceptionally good payload capacity, maintenance to the rugged old ships was very nominal even in rough service, and from the pilot's viewpoint, especially under adverse conditions, the old "Pilgrim" was hard to beat. Some had already served in Alaska for 15 years and were still going strong. One operator who was equipped with modern transports for his scheduled runs, still kept a 100-A, already a 25-year-old veteran, on stand-by duty for specialized jobs, jobs not many other airplanes could hope to perform.

The "Pilgrim" model 100-A was a high-winged cabin monoplane of large and buxom proportion that had seating arranged for ten; as a transport for passengers, mail, and express-cargo, it was primarily designed for the shorter routes. Of slightly larger size than the earlier "Fairchild 100", the 100-A retained most features, plus the addition of modifications to structure and arrangement that would be more suitable to handling larger payloads. Nine passen-

gers were seated comfortably in the main cabin while passenger baggage was stowed in the plane's bulging belly; a large compartment under the pilot's cabin floor was used for stowing mail and cargo. The pilot's station high up front gave him a commanding view of his surroundings from take-off to the landing, and pilots were ready with praise for this thoughtful feature. Powered with the big 9 cyl. Pratt & Whitney "Hornet B" engine of 575 h.p., the 100-A converted this power into a surprising performance. Its broad wing could lift large payloads out of small fields, thereby permitting operations into and out of airfields that were often little more than a grassy pasture. Its rugged structure could withstand a terrific beating, so there was no need to back away from any chore. Designed with some thought in mind for the mechanic who would have to maintain and service it, all accessories and other components were readily accessible for repair or replacement, thereby cutting operating costs and time away from the flight line. Flight characteristics and general behavior were such that pilots actually jumped at the chance to fly the "Pilgrim", and had naught but praise for its nature and ability. Not fussy or critical even under the most trying

*Fig. 146. Rare shot shows 100-A with 968V on rudder and 997V on right wing,
denoting parts of two different airplanes.*

Fig. 147. Buxom lines of 100-A were bulging with carrying capacity.

circumstance, it has been said the 100-A would still fly almost normally even with more than an inch of ice on the wing's leading edge; it is not hard to comprehend why pilots put such a trust into the ability of this craft. The "Pilgrim" 100-A was first approved on a Group 2 memo numbered 2-365, and the type certificate number was issued 8-21-31; sixteen examples of this model were manufactured and all were delivered to American Airways. Established by mid-year of 1931 in the former plant used by the Fairchild Airplane Mfg. Corp. at Farmingdale, L.I., N.Y., the American Airplane & Engine Corp. was concentrating its production on the 100-A for American Airways. As a manufacturing division of the huge Aviation Corp., G. G. Coburn was president; V. E. Clark and Thurman Bane were V.P.; while Virginius E. Clark was also the chief engineer.

Listed below are specifications and performance data for the "Pilgrim" model 100-A as powered with 575 h.p. Hornet B engine; length overall 38'1"; height overall 12'3"; wing span 57'0"; wing chord 8'4"; total wing area 459 sq.ft.; airfoil Goettingen 398; wt. empty 4362 lbs.; useful load 3388 lbs.; payload with 120 gal. fuel 2408 lbs. (9 passengers at 170 lb. each & 878 lb. baggage-mial-cargo); payload with 150 gal. fuel 2228 lbs. (9 passengers at 170 lb. & 878 lb. baggage-mail-cargo); payload with lbs.; max. speed 136; cruising speed 118; stalling speed 65; climb 800 ft. first min. at sea level; ceiling 13,600 ft.; gas cap. normal 120 gal.; gas cap. max. 150 gal.; oil cap. 12 gal.; cruising range at 32 gal. per hour 410-510 miles; price not announced.

The fuselage framework was built up of welded steel tubing in various grades, faired to shape with duralumin formers and fairing strips, then fabric covered. The main cabin compartment was arranged to seat nine passengers; the front seat faced backwards seating 3

Fig. 148. 100-A retired from airline use were very popular "in the bush country."

across, and 6 individual seats faced forward. Entry to the main cabin was by two large doors in the rear; toilet equipment was provided to rear of cabin compartment. The pilot's cabin up forward was elevated above the main cabin level to a point of better visibility, with a separate entry door on the right side. A large metal-lined compartment for mail and express cargo was under the pilot's floor, with an access door on the right side. Passenger baggage was stowed in three compartments provided in the belly of the fuselage; additional storage for 60 lbs. was provided under the front passenger seat. The semi-cantilever wing framework in two halves, was built up of welded steel tube girder-type spar beams, with wing ribs of riveted dural tubing; the leading edges were covered with dural metal sheet and the completed framework was covered in fabric. Fuel tanks were mounted in each wing-half, flanking the fuselage. The wide tread landing gear was of the outrigger type using oleo-spring shock absorbing struts; 36x8 Bendix wheels with brakes were standard equipment, and 35x16-6 Goodyear "airwheels" with brakes were optional. A 10x3 full swivel tail wheel was also fitted. The fabric covered tail-group was build up of duralumin spars and ribs in a riveted structure; the rudder and elevators were aerodynamically balanced for lighter stick loads, and the horizontal stabilizer was adjustable in flight. An adjustable metal propel-

ler, speed-ring engine cowling, two-way radio gear, navigation lights, landing lights, parachute flares, a battery, generator, tool kit, first-aid kit, 3 fire extinguishers, and cabin heaters were standard equipment. The next development in the "Pilgrim" 100-series was the Cyclone-powered model 100-B as described in the chapter for ATC # 470 of this volume.

Listed below are "Pilgrim" model 100-A entries as gleaned from registration records:

NC-968V; 100-A (# 6601) Hornet B-575.
NC-997V;   ”   (# 6602)   ”
NC-707Y;   ”   (# 6603)   ”
NC-708Y;   ”   (# 6604)   ”
NC-709Y;   ”   (# 6605)   ”
NC-710Y;   ”   (# 6606)   ”
NC-711Y;   ”   (# 6607)   ”
NC-712Y;   ”   (# 6608)   ”
NC-713Y;   ”   (# 6609)   ”
NC-714Y;   ”   (# 6610)   ”
NC-982M;   ”   (# 6611)   ”
NC-732N;   ”   (# 6612)   ”
NC-733N;   ”   (# 6613)   ”
NC-734N;   ”   (# 6614)   ”
NC-735N;   ”   (# 6615)   ”
NC-736N;   ”   (# 6616)   ”

Serial # 6605, 6608, 6609, converted to model 100-B in 1934; ser. # 6611 as X-982M with geared Wright "Cyclone" for test, later modified to 100-A and delivered to American Airways; this approval expired 9-1-33.

A.T.C. # 444
(8-22-31)
CURTISS-WRIGHT "SEDAN", 15-D

Fig. 149. Curtiss-Wright "Sedan" model 15-D with 240 h.p. Wright R-760-E engine.

At the top of the line in the 15-series, the Curtiss-Wright model 15-D "Sedan" offered all the best that only comes with a boost in power, and the resulting increase in performance. Typical of both the models 15-C and 15-N, the 15-D was also adaptable to general-purpose service, but its custom-like qualities and topnotch performance were much more attractive to the flying sportsman. As a family-type airplane the spirited 15-D was an attractive vehicle to the flying family of four, a family that would enjoy comfortable and relatively speedy cross-country hops to out-of-the-way places on errand or on promise of interest. Having need for an airplane that would take him easily to every section of the state, David S. Ingalls, formerly Asst. Sec. of the Navy for Aeronautics, used a 15-D "Sedan" to great advantage while campaigning for the governorship of Ohio. Even the smallest and most remote airports in the state were visited. Fitted with the new 7 cyl. Wright R-760-E engine of 240 h.p., the model 15-D was fortunate to inherit a lot of its better characteristics from the earlier "Travel Air" monoplane model 10-D, so quite naturally, it too was easily adapted to specialized "bush country" service; a 25 year-old veteran (XB-DEE) of this particular "Sedan" model (15-D) was reported still flying actively (1957) in Mexico. Such service is certainly an acid-test for the character and personality of any aircraft. A more recent example, restored as a 15-D, has spent much of its time towing gliders, and hauling sky-divers (parachutists) to their aerial jump-off point.

The Curtiss-Wright "Sedan" model 15-D was a fairly large high-winged cabin monoplane of rather plain and uncomplicated lines; arranged with comfortable seating for four big people, it also provided suitably tasteful appointments and accommodation. Interior appointments, general workmanship, and the equipment that was included were just about as one would expect for a craft leveled primarily at the sportsman; altho' arranged and fitted primarily for the flying sportsman, the "Sedan", however, did not shy away from hard work. It easily and quite handily doubled in duty at general-purpose service. Powered with the new Wright R-760-E engine of 240 h.p., the 15-D had sufficient power reserve to turn in a rather exciting performance, getting in and out of small tight fields fully loaded, even at the higher altitudes, with remarkable aplomb and ease. Flight characteristics were generally described as sharp and quite lively, with a general behavior that was somewhat sporty, but easy enough to cope with by even the average pilot. Lighter, leaner, and more lanky, the 15-D still showed its unmistakeable lineage from the earlier 10-D, but an impartial overall comparison of the two craft would probably now give the 15-D the slight edge. The type certificate number for the "Sedan" model 15-D was issued 8-22-31 and some 7 examples of this model were built by the Curtiss-Wright Airplane Co. at Robertson (St. Louis), Mo. The "Sedan" was discontinued early in 1932.

Listed below are specifications and performance data for the model 15-D as powered with

Fig. 150. Model 15-D "Sedan" reminiscent of earlier "Travel Air" 10 D.

the 240 h.p. Wright R-760-E engine; length overall 30'5"; height overall 8'10"; wing span 43'5"; wing chord 74"; total wing area 240 sq. ft.; airfoil Travel Air #2 (modified Goettingen 593); wt. empty 2121 lbs.; useful load 1198 lbs.; payload with 60 gal. fuel 630 lbs. (3 pass. at 170 lb. each & 120 lb. baggage); gross wt. 3319 lbs.; max. speed (with speed-ring) 135; cruising speed 115; landing speed 55; average take-off run full load 525 ft.; climb 800 ft. first min. at sea level; ceiling 16,000 ft.; gas cap. normal 60 gal.; oil cap. 5 gal.; cruising range at 13 gal. per hour 460 miles; price $9600. at factory field. Later 15-D was eligible with 80 gal. fuel and 3360 lb. gross weight.

The construction details and general arrangement of the "Sedan" 15-D was typical to that of the models 15-N and 15-C as described in the chapters for ATC # 425-426 of this volume. Dual "Dep" wheel controls were normally mounted on a Y-type column, but separate wheel controls were available for $50.00 extra; the right-hand wheel was removable when not in use. The large baggage compartment behind the rear seat had allowance for up to 121 lbs., and was accessible from the inside, or through a large door on the outside. Normal fuel capacity was 60 gal., but two 40 gal. fuel tanks were available to replace the two 30 gal. tanks; both tanks were provided with fuel level gauges. A Curtiss-type "speed-ring" engine cowl shrouded the engine for better airflow distribution and a slight gain in speed. Low pressure semi-airwheels with brakes were normally used, but 25x11-4 Goodyear airwheels

Fig. 151. "Sedan" prototype converted to 15-D, used for glider-tow in Seattle, 1966-67.

with brakes were optional; skis for winter-flying were also eligible. The airframe was bonded and shielded for radio and brackets were provided for the mounting of radio gear; a full complement of night-flying equipment was also available. A metal propeller, speed-ring engine cowl, Eclipse electric engine starter, navigation lights, a battery, generator, tail wheel, cabin heater, and a dual-wheel control column were standard equipment. An oil-cooling radiator, fire extinguisher, parachute flares, engine cover for $10.00, retractable landing lights mounted in wing for $200.00, and two-tone colors other than standard for $100.00 were optional.

Listed below are model 15-D entries as gleaned from registration records:

NC-10928; Model 15-D (15D-2203) Wright 240
NC-11807;   ”   (15D-2206)   ”
NC-11861;   ”   (15D-2207)   ”
NS-3Y;   ”   (15D-2209)   ”
NS-4Y;   ”   (15D-2212)   ”
NC-12304;   ”   (15D-2213)   ”
NC-12314;   ”   (15D-2214)   ”

Serial # 2203 and # 2206 first as 15-C; ser. # 2212 first as 15-C (NC-12303) modified to 15-D (NS-4Y); ser. no. for XB-DEE unknown; this approval expired 4-26-37.

A.T.C. # 445
(8-25-31)
CYCLOPLANE, C-1

Fig. 152. Cycloplane solo-trainer with 22 h.p. Cyclomotor "twin."

The flivverish looking "Cycloplane" mono-plane was a rather unusual flying-machine in many ways, and unusual too in the fact that it was part of a "package deal" in a newly devised system of pilot-training. Based largely on the theory that many more people would learn to fly if they could dispell their fears of leaving the ground, it was believed that an easy-step method would actually entice more people into learning to fly airplanes. With several taxi-planes developed by mid-1930, large crowds gathered every week-end to watch the ground-flying demonstrations. Interested spectators were of course informed of the gradual step-by-step training that would eventually lead to actual solo-flight. The "Cycloplane" solo-trainer powered with a 22 h.p. "Cyclomotor" was then demonstrated as the final step in the flight-course, a transition from the taxi-planes into a glider-type airplane that now actually took off from the ground. A net-work of these schools were planned for installation all over the country; a few were actually in business, but the idea did not catch on to any extent. Those people who did want to learn to fly, went to regular flying schools anyhow, seeing no reason to spend some of their time and money on winged go-carts that never left the ground.

O. L. Woodson, reputable airplane designer, and H. S. "Dick" Myhres, a colorful and talented test-pilot, revived the idea of the Penguin-type ground-trainer, such as was used by some pilot-training schools in the early part of World War 1. Devising a method of self-training that actually required 3 different machines, the prospective student was first taken out for a few short trial runs in a dual-controlled ground trainer. This was to show him the basic mechanics of flying an airplane. He was then allowed to "solo" for a time in the single-place ground trainer until he began showing some proficiency. The "instructor" just watched and supervised his runs; a student's ventures around the field in the taxi-plane were regulated by throttle-stops with throttle openings gradually increased as the fledgling-pilot gained confidence and experience. When nervousness subsided and good knowledge was demonstrated as to what all the controls were for, and what they would do, the student was ready for short solo-flights in the "Cycloplane". The "Cycloplane" was sort of a real-airplane version of the two previous machines, a slow-flying, slow-landing affair with "a lot of sail". First flights were about 50 yards just a few feet off the ground, and well within the length of the runway, or perhaps a wobbly circuit around the field. As more daring was gained by more experience, students ventured higher and farther from the field, but by then they were usually ready and willing to fly a regular airplane.

The "Cycloplane" model C-1 was a single-place ultra-light open cockpit monoplane of unusual configuration. Basically a powered-glider, the occupant sat up front in a covered pod, with the engine mounted high out in front of him. A small windscreen protected him somewhat from the fumes and oil splatterings caused by the two-stroke cycle engine. The "Cyclo-plane" was really not much of an airplane in the normal sense, because of its extremely light weight and large areas; fair-weather flying was no doubt a lark, but gusty winds could create serious operating problems. The "Cycloplane"

Fig. 153. Cycloplane prototype first used two-stroke cycle "Cleone" twin.

C-1 as powered with the 2 cyl. two-cycle "Cyclo-motor" of 22 h.p., was a special kind of flying fun that certainly had some merit, but very little practical purpose. Taking off easily on just a waft of wind, the climb-out was slow and steady; it has been reported that altitudes up to 12,000 ft. had been reached. This would no doubt be an interesting way to spend an hour. With a cruising speed of some 50 m.p.h. and a range of some 200 miles, it was best not to consider any extensive cross-country flying. Landing normally at 20-25 m.p.h., it was possible at times to land most anywhere with virtually no ground run. In spite of

its singular purpose and very limited utility, the "Cycloplane" did have its merits and its own special kind of importance in light-airplane development. The model C-1 was first approved on a Group 2 memo numbered 2-352 for the first 3 airplanes. A type certificate number was issued 8-25-31 for airplanes # 4 and up. In all, some 6 examples of this model were manufactured by the Cycloplane Co., Ltd. of Los Angeles Calif. O. L. Woodson and H. S. Myhres were managing officers. By 1932, all production had ceased at the Cycloplane facility. and Dick Myhres organized the new Champion Aircraft

Fig. 154. After student mastered ground-trainer, he graduated to Cycloplane shown above.

Fig. 155. Initial "hops" were in two-place trainer to learn use of controls.

Corp. to build two models of a new light-plane design. Quarters were taken up in a corner of the recently vacated "Emsco" plant in Downey, Cal.

Listed below are specifications and performance data for the "Cycloplane" model C-1 as powered with the 22 h.p. "Cyclomotor"; length overall 19'7"; height overall 93"; wing span overall 40'0"; wing chord 60"; total wing area 193 sq. ft.; airfoil Goettingen 398; wt. empty 430 lbs.; useful load 240 lbs.; this included 7 gal. fuel, 1 gal. oil, pilot at 170 lb. & parachute or 1-way radio at 20 lb.; gross wt. 670 lbs.; max. speed 65; cruising speed 50; landing speed 20-25; climb 450 ft. first min. at sea level; ceiling 10,000 ft.; gas cap. 7 gal.; oil cap. 1 gal.; cruising range at 1.75 gal. per hour 200 miles; price at factory included package deal of one "Cycloplane", a single-seated taxi-plane, and data for the system of flight-training. A taxi-plane powered by "Cyclomotor", with 25 ft. wing span, weighing 250 lbs. empty, sold for $895. The price of the "Cycloplane" varied at around $1400. The model A2-25 "Cyclomotor", developing 22.5 h.p. at 2300 r.p.m., sold for $327.50.

The fuselage framework was a simple backbone truss of welded steel tubing, with a metal-framed fabric covered pod in front to house the single seat. Entry was an easy step from the ground, and the occupant was protected by a small windshield in front. No baggage was allowed, but a parachute or 1-way radio was eligible as part of the useful load. The wing framework in two halves, was built up of solid spruce spar beams, with spruce and plywood truss-type wing ribs; the completed framework was covered with fabric. The wings were wire-braced to a vee-type cabane on the upper side, and to lower fuselage longerons on the underside. The engine was mounted approx. at the wing's leading edge, and the fuel tank was mounted in roof of the cabin area. The long-leg landing gear used steel-spring shock absorber units; wheels were of the Goodyear "airwheel" type with no brakes. A tail skid or tail wheel was optional. The fabric covered tail-group was built up of welded steel tubing, providing adjustments for flight trim on the ground only. A wooden propeller, Goodyear airwheels, and tail skid were standard equipment. A tail wheel was optional.

Listed below are Cycloplane C-1 entries as gleaned from registration records:

X-144W; Model A-1 (# 101) Cleone 22.
X-970; Model C-1 (# 1) Cyclomotor 22.
NC-996Y; " (# 2) "
NC-12202; " (# 3) "
NC-12215; " (# 4) "
NC-12253; " (# 5) "

Serial # 101 first as model A-1 with 22 h.p. Cleone engine, later modified to C-1 with 22 h.p. Cyclomotor; ser. # 1-2-3 on Group 2 approval 2-352; this approval for ser. # 4 and up; approval expired 9-30-39.

A.T.C. # 446
(8-25-31)
PITCAIRN AUTOGIRO, PCA-3

Fig. 156. Pitcairn model PCA-3 with "Wasp Junior" engine, a rare version of Autogiro series.

To demonstrate some of the remarkable things possible with an "autogiro", one of these craft was landed on the lawn of the White House in Washington, D.C. Yet another took off from a city street in downtown Philadelphia, flew over to and landed on a New York City pier to pick up Juan de la Cierva; it had landed there to pick up the autogiro's inventor as he disembarked from the steamer that had brought him from Europe. Boarding the 'giro they took off from the crowded pier and flew back to Philadelphia where Harold Pitcairn awaited their arrival. For some time flights such as these were considered as nothing more than "stunts" and front-page news; in a sense they were just that, but doing this sort of thing almost daily for a year or more, soon proved that unusual operations such as these were not necessarily stunts but only a practical application of the autogiro's remarkable capabilities.

By the ending of 1931, more than 350 business firms were using company-owned airplanes in the development and promotion of their business ventures; a good many used the "autogiro" because of its tremendous publicity value. The United Aircraft & Transport Corp. (UA&T), one of the largest combines in American aviation, decided they too should have an autogiro, at least for its promotional value. Pratt & Whitney engines were manufactured by a division of the

UA&T Corp., so the 300 h.p. "Wasp Junior" was naturally selected to power a new windmill-craft on order from Pitcairn-Cierva. Mounting the "Wasp Junior" (R-985) engine in their standard 3-place model, Pitcairn labeled it the model PCA-3, and it differed only from the PCA-2 in its engine installation. James Ray, veteran pilot, delivered the new PCA-3 to the UA&T base at Hartford, Conn.; it was to be used primarily by the research division for various experimental testing, among which was the testing of a new variable-pitch propeller. Offered tentatively as a companion model to their popular PCA-2, Pitcairn Aircraft, however, built only a few examples of the PCA-3. For nearly two years the PCA-3 at UA&T served rather quietly at varied duties, and probably paid for itself many times over in its experimental value. By July of 1933, with only some 60 hours of total time on its airframe and engine, the UA&T Corp. offered their one-only PCA-3 in like-new condition at the bargain price of $5000. for a quick sale. Final disposition of this rare craft is unknown.

The Pitcairn-Cierva model PCA-3 was an autogiro of the utility class that seated three, all in open cockpits. The fuselage followed lines similar to that of a 3-seated airplane, especially typical of the PA-8 "Mailwing". The model PCA-3 was more or less identical to the PCA-2, de-

Fig. 157. Early Pitcairn "giro" over New York City.

scribed here earlier, except for its engine installation, and whatever modifications were necessary for this combination. Powered with the 9 cyl. Pratt & Whitney "Wasp Junior" (R-985) engine of 300 h.p., the PCA-3 could clip along at speeds up to 120 m.p.h., or dilly-dally along at 25. The only notable example of this version was in service at "United Aircraft", mainly for engine and propeller tests. Whereas most of the PCA-2 were head-liners, and frequently front-page news, the PCA-3 received scant coverage and very little is known about its service life, or if it participated in any interesting escapades. Being practically identical to the model PCA-2 (ATC # 410), we can assume that the PCA-3 was its match in performance and behavior. As equipped with a variable-pitch propeller, it is quite possible that the PCA-3 was capable of a more flexible and much better performance. The type certificate number for the model PCA-3 was issued 8-25-31 and perhaps no more than 2 examples of this model were built by the Pitcairn-Cierva Autogiro Co.,Willow Grove, Penna.

Listed below are specifications and performance data for the model PCA-3 as powered with the 300 h.p. "Wasp Junior" engine; length overall 23'1"; height overall 13'4"; rotor dia. 45'0"; rotor blade chord 22"; rotor blade area 159.5 sq.ft.; fixed wing span 30'0"; wing chord at root 52"; wing chord at tip 30"; fixed-wing area 88 sq.ft.; fixed-wing airfoil (NACA) M-3 modified; wt. empty 2121 lbs.; useful load 942 lbs.; payload with 52 gal. fuel 408 lbs. (2 pass. at 170 lb. each & 68 lb. baggage); gross wt. 3063 lbs.; max. speed 120; cruising speed 100; landing speed 20-30; climb 800 ft. first min. at sea level; service ceiling 15,000 ft.; gas cap. 52 gal.; oil

cap. 6 gal.; cruising range at 16 gal. per hour 300 miles; price $15,000. at factory.

The construction details and general arrangement as listed here, will apply to both models PCA-2 and PCA-3, unless otherwise noted. The fuselage framework was built up of welded 4130 steel tubing of square and round section, heavily faired to a well-rounded shape with duralumin fairing strips, then fabric covered. Following the lines of the PA-8 "Mailwing", the cockpits were quite deep and well protected; the pilot's seat in the rear was adjustable and two passengers sat side-by-side in the front cockpit. The front cockpit could be quickly covered when not in use. A baggage compartment of 3.3 cu.ft. capacity, mounted in the turtle-back section, had allowance for up to 68 lbs.; parachutes were deducted from the baggage allowance when carried. The tapered fixed-wing was built up of spruce and plywood box-type spar beams, with spruce and plywood web-type wing ribs; the leading edges were covered with plywood sheet, the Friese-type ailerons were of wooden framework, and the completed wing was covered with fabric. The unusually wide and spidery landing gear of 159 in. tread used oleo shock absorber legs that were incorporated into a very unusual wing-bracing truss; low pressure wheels were 8.50x10 and brakes were provided. A full-swivel tail skid or a tail wheel were also provided. The 4-bladed rotor system was mounted on a tripod pylon, and rotated freely on a ball-bearing hub; a mechanical starter shaft was used to bring rotor blades to proper rotational speeds for take-off. A rotor-brake actuated by the pilot after landing was used to stop rotor. The rotor blades consisted of a steel tubular spar, with wooden blade ribs fastened to its length at intervals; the leading edges were covered with plywood sheet and the completed blades were then covered in fabric. The fabric covered tail-group was build up of welded steel tubing; the horizontal stabilizer was adjustable in flight. Two fuel tanks were mounted low in the fuselage under the front seat to avoid fluctuating fuel loads from shifting the center of gravity point. An extra 20 gal. fuel tank was available to extend the range. A metal propeller was standard equipment. Electric or air-operated engine starter, fire extinguisher, navigation lights, landing lights, parachute flares, and dual controls were optional. Other details pertaining to both models were noted in the coverage for ATC # 410. The next development in the Pitcairn autogiro was the two-place model PA-18 as described in the chapter for ATC # 478 of this volume.

Listed below is the only PCA-3 entry appearing in registration records:

NC-11612; Model PCA-3 (# E-45) Wasp Jr. 300. Serial # E-43 was another example of the model PCA-3, but registration number is unknown; ser. # E-45 eligible with controllable propeller for service testing; this approval expired 9-30-39.

Fig. 158. Aeronca "Cadet" model C-1 with 36 h.p. Aeronca engine; C-1 developed especially for sport.

A slow searching walk-around would soon reveal that the model C-1 "Cadet" was no ordinary "Aeronca"; true enough, it bore similar lines to the newer "Scout", but there was also a certain grace to the way it stood, almost as if in a pugnacious manner. Developed as a special breed of airplane in the "Aeronca" line, the trim "Cadet" was the so-called "clipped wing model" that did away with nearly 30 sq. ft. of wing area; this was calculated to boost top speeds and accelerate response in the various rotational maneuvers. To provide the extra muscle that was almost mandatory in an airplane of this type, the C-1 "Cadet" mounted the bigger Aeronca E-113 engine of 36-40 h.p. Knowing full well that pilots would tend to take advantage of the extra speed and sharper response, thereby forcing the "Cadet" into above-normal stresses, designers beefed-up many points of the airframe to provide an average safety factor of 8.5 as a precaution. Promising early to fulfill a special need in the lightplane field, the "Cadet" was put through an extensive testing program, and all hands were jubilant with its performance and behavior. Perhaps a little more restraint would have been wiser, but in the flush of victory it is impossible to be complacent or worry about the course of events. Conrad Dietz, V.P., general manager, and sporting pilot, was greatly affect-

ed by the sassy "Cadet" and fairly reveled in its performance; it was to be his nemesis. Veiled reports dictated by sadness reveal little of any detail except that an extreme maneuver of sorts caused the gyrating "Cadet" to fold up its wings. Dietz plunged on to his death. A stunning blow, this naturally halted any further progress on the "Cadet" development program, and eventually the idea was discontinued entirely. Two other examples of the C-1, already built, were reportedly crated and stored. Despite these grim developments, the little "Cadet" must not stand naked to be judged by this alone; certainly it was a graceful expression in a new concept that was only stifled by the fickle course of fate.

The Aeronca model C-1 "Cadet" was a small wire-braced high winged monoplane with seating arranged for one. The fuselage frame and interior was quite typical to that of the newer "Scout", but the "clipped" wing changed its overall appearance and its behavior by a great deal. For the special use intended, that broad span of standard wing was hardly necessary, so 3.5 ft. were taken off from each tip for considerably less drag and a better aerodynamic proportion. As a sportsman's airplane that would certainly be used on occasion for air-racing and often for acrobatic flying, the C-1 "Cadet" mounted the bigger Aeronca E-113 engine of 36-40 h.p.; for a trim 700-pound

Fig. 159. Wings of "Cadet" were "clipped" for more speed.

airplane this was to be quite sufficient. That the little C-1 was fast and highly maneuverable there is no doubt, and lacking any other factual reports, we must still assume that the "Cadet" could easily stir a man into considerable exhuberance simply by its special nature. Predictions of what might have been seem idle at this point, but an airplane such as the nimble "Cadet" surely could have found great favor among the sporting pilots. The type certificate number for the "Cadet" model C-1 was issued 8-29-31 and perhaps only 3 examples of this model were built by the Aeronautical Corp. of America at Cincinnati, Ohio. Taylor Stanley was president; Conrad G. Dietz was V.P. and general manager; Robt. B. Galloway was chief engineer.

Listed below are specifications and performance data for the "Cadet" model C-1 as powered with the 36 h.p. Aeronca E-113 engine; length overall 20'0"; height overall 7'6"; wing span 29'0"; wing chord 50"; total wing area 115 sq.ft.; airfoil Clark Y; wt. empty 426 lbs.; useful load 274 lbs.; payload with 8 gal. fuel 50 lbs. (usually a parachute or baggage); gross wt. 700 lbs.; max. speed 95; cruising speed 80; landing (stall) speed 45; climb 650 ft. first min. at sea level; ceiling 12,500 ft.; gas cap. 8 gal.; oil cap. 3 qts.; cruising range at 2.5 gal. per hour 240 miles; price listed alternately as $1695. and $1595. for landplane, $2095. for seaplane. Factory data was skimpy or not available in detail, so some of this data could not be completely verified.

The fuselage interior was neatly arranged for the seating of one on a wide bench type seat; a covered baggage compartment with al-lowance for up to 50 lbs. was just behind the seat-back. A parachute when carried was part of the baggage allowance. A large curved windshield offered ample protection, and transformed the open cockpit into a snug semi-cabin. Appointments were greatly improved with the addition of several pilot aids, but to what extent is doubtful. Although the complete airframe was beefed-up considerably at numerous points for higher stresses to an overall safety factor of 8.5 as mentioned previously, we cannot verify if this factor was for all attitudes. The clipped wing was of considerably shorter span, braced with heavy-gauge streamlined steel wire. The larger wing (36 ft. span) of the "Scout" could also be mounted to the "Cadet" fuselage as an alternate. Metal streamlined wheel pants usually shrouded the 16x7-3 Goodyear "airwheels", but were listed as an option. The color scheme was two-toned with a bright vermillion and maroon finish, using several extra coats of dope. A priming choke, ignition switch, oil pressure gauge, oil temperature gauge, altimeter, tachometer, fuel shut-off, fire extinguisher, and extra strong safety belt were standard equipment. Wheel pants, navigation lights, and aux. fuel tank were optional. The next "Aeronca" development was the deluxe model C-2-N as described in the chapter for ATC # 448 of this volume.

Listed below are only "Cadet" entries that appeared in registration records;

X-11290: Cadet C-1 (# A-122) E-113
NC-11417;   "   (# A-151)   "

Serial # A-151 later modified to C-2-N; two other examples of C-1 were reported as disassembled, crated, and put into storage.

AERONCA "DELUXE SCOUT", C-2-N

Fig. 160. Aeronca deluxe "Scout" with 36 h.p. Aeronca engine was model C-2-N.

The new model C-2-N was a rare and relatively unknown cousin to the perky little "Aeronca" standard C-2, of which more than 100 examples had already been built. Modifications to the later C-2 examples had progressively shown improvement in the landing gear, the tail group, the fuselage, and cockpit cut-out, with slight hidden improvements throughout the airframe itself; for any sizeable improvements to the utility, performance, and general behavior, there was naught else to do but increase the power. As a deluxe sport version of the familiar C-2 "Scout", the model C-2-N was quietly introduced as a companion craft that harbored all the latest improvements thus far, plus the installation of the "bigger" Aeronca engine. The six to ten h.p. increase doesn't seem like much to get all enthused about, but in this case it was; the Aeronca E-113 engine of 36 h.p. furnished ample reason for enthusiasm by providing a pleasant little surge of new bright-eyed performance and bushy-tailed behavior. One must remember that in an airplane that already thrived happily and admirably on low horsepower, the extra 6 to 10 "horses" was quite a kick in the pants.

The Aeronca model C-2-N "Deluxe Scout" was a single-place wire-braced high-winged monoplane that was essentially a high-perform-ance version of the familiar standard C-2 "Scout". Fashioned with all the progressive improvements that added to comfort, utility, and ease of operation, the C-2-N was also fitted with an extra jolt of power. Powered with the bigger 2 cyl. Aeronca E-113 (or E-113-A) engine of 36-40 h.p., the C-2-N translated this extra bit of muscle into noticeable gains throughout its whole performance range. Higher speeds were, of course, noticeable, take-offs were a hop-hop and away, climb-out was increased by a happy rate, and the sharper response greatly emphasized the inherent maneuverability. With all this performance coupled to very low operating costs, the C-2-N posed as the ideal light airplane for the sporting pilot who operated on a very modest budget. Several of the C-2-N might have originally left the factory as such, but actually, any standard C-2 "Scout" was eligible for this up-grading modification and installation of the bigger E-113 engine. The type certificate number for the model C-2-N was issued 8-29-31 and some 4 or more examples of this model were either manufactured or modified by the Aeronautical Corp. of America on Lunken Airport in Cincinnati, Ohio.

Listed below are specifications and performance data for the Aeronca model C-2-N as

Fig. 161. Aeronca model C-2-N operated well on Edo floats.

powered with the 36 h.p. Aeronca E-113 engine; length overall 20'0"; height overall 7'6"; wing span 36'0"; wing chord 50"; total wing area 142 sq.ft.; airfoil Clark Y; wt. empty 426 lbs.; useful load 274 lbs.; payload with 8 gal. fuel 50 lbs. (usually in the form of baggage); gross wt. 700 lbs.; max. speed 85; cruising speed 70; landing speed 36; climb 650 ft. first min. at sea level; ceiling 16,500 ft.; gas cap. 8 gal.; oil cap. 3 qts.; cruising range at 2.5 gal. per hour 210 miles; price approx. $1695. at factory.

Among the many improvements incorporated into this version was a reshaped fuselage that was wider by 6 in., the seat was now wider with a deeper upholstered cushion, and a more comfortable back-rest; behind the seat was a covered baggage compartment with allowance for up to 50 lbs. A parachute when carried was part of this allowance. For an extra 2 hour cruising range, a 5 gal. fuel tank could be mounted in the baggage compartment; in this case, no baggage was allowed. A large curved windshield offered maximum protection and actually transformed the open cockpit into a semi-cabin affair; a small narrow skylight in the cabin roof offered some vision upwards. The stiff-legged tripod landing gear was fitted with Goodyear 16x7-3 "airwheels"; streamlined pants to encase the wheels were optional. The model C-2-N

was also eligible as a seaplane on Edo twin-float gear. Various color schemes were optional and several extra coats of dope were applied for a more durable and a more handsome finish. The standard color scheme was a duo-tone blue fuselage with yellow striping, and the wings were a bright orange. The model C-2-N was still offered into 1933, but a lack of interest finally halted production; work continued on the ever-popular two-seated C-3. Prophetic of the times, this ad appeared in May of 1933: For sale, Aeronca C-2-N, ship has less than 100 hours since new, 40 h.p. engine less than 10 hours total time, airplane and engine still like new, sell for $700.00 cash. Production of the C-3 meanwhile continued on into 1937. A rather unusual development in the "Aeronca" line were the low-winged models LA and LB as described in the chapter for ATC # 596.

Listed below are the only known C-2-N entries as gleaned from registration records:

NC-643W; C-2-N (# 23) Aeronca E-113.
NC-11417;   "   (# A-151)   "
NC-13083;   "   (# A-247)   "
NC-13089;   "   (# A-253)   "

Serial # 23 first as standard C-2; ser. # A-151 first as Cadet C-1; ser. # A-247 also on floats; ser. # A-253 first as standard C-2 Scout.

Fig. 162. Alexander "Flyabout" model D-2 with 45 h.p. Szekely engine.

As a companion model in the little "Flyabout" series, Alexander Aircraft had introduced the model D-2, an improved version that enjoyed the benefits of slightly more horsepower. Although the increase was only 8 h.p., the "Flyabout" used the increase very wisely to gain much more verve in its all-round performance. Powered now with the 3 cyl. Szekely SR-3-0 engine of 45 h.p., the "Flyabout" D-2 was nearly a go-anywhere airplane, and complained very little about what it was asked to do, or where it operated from. As an example, one D-2 operated quite successfully in the high mountains around Bishop, Calif.; born and reared in the mountains of Colorado, the D-2 was quite happy on the higher ground and thinner air. Offering practical closed-in comfort for better weather protection, and quite happy to operate from the higher altitudes, the D-2 was more popular in the western part of the U.S.A. than elsewhere. Arranged in the companionship of side-by-side seating and equipped with dual controls, the "Flyabout" was largely used for student-pilot instruction, or by aspiring pilots bent on building up cheap solo-time. Coming onto the flivver-plane scene rather late, the "Flyabout" had missed some of the early enthusiasm, but it was still being offered in limited production when many other of the early light-planes had long

been discontinued. Every inch an "Eaglerock" the little "Flyabout" had hardy innards and upheld a fine tradition right to the very end.

Drained financially and emotionally because of persistent attempts to fully develop the revolutionary "Bullet", and hampered too by the general slump in the aircraft market, Alexander Aircraft was slowly failing and seriously thinking of withdrawing from aircraft manufacture. Late 1931 surely looked like the end of the road for Alexander. Out of loyalty to the company and to the breed of airplanes it had always built, former employees headed by Proctor Nichols had formed Aircraft Mechanics, Inc.; this to keep the venture alive and to keep the bloodline from thinning out. Manufacture of the "Flyabout" was continued and several improved "Eaglerock" biplane models were still offered on a limited basis. Several of the "Flyabout" were built during 1932, but it was the service and repair business that actually kept the operation solvent. As an approved repair station "Aircraft Mechanics" also offered service, parts and repairs, to any "Eaglerock" built since 1926. By mid-1933 things were at low ebb, materials and supplies from the former Alexander factory were being sold off at greatly reduced prices; used "Eaglerock" and "Flyabout" were being offered at a great sacrifice. With an easing of the

Fig. 163. Flyabout was first cabin airplane in the flivver-plane class.

Fig. 164. Ample dimension of D-2 designed for two people and a puppy. D-2 shown operated in Canada.

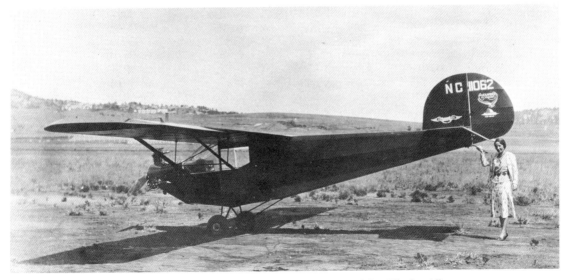

Fig. 165. Young lady dramatizes light weight of the "Flyabout."

general depression in a year or so, Aircraft Mechanics offered a new and improved "Flyabout" for 1935; a trickle of profit held the organization together for several more years.

The Alexander "Flyabout" model D-2 was a squatty high-winged cabin monoplane that was rather distinctive among other craft in the light-plane class. Fully enclosed in an honest-to-goodness cabin, occupants were treated with the companionship of side by side seating. Interior dimensions allowed ample room for two people and a puppy, with some baggage allowance for all three. Large area windows, special windshield framing and an overhead skylight offered excellent visibility in all directions, alleviating that cooped-up feeling. Stout of frame and quite practical in its mechanical makeup, the "Flyabout" was ideal for the flier who was bent on flying hard and often. Powered with the 3 cyl. Szekely SR-3-0 engine of 45 h.p., the model D-2 delivered performance that belied its "flivver" appearance. Breaking ground easily in a scant few hundred feet, climbing out at a snappy angle, and literally wafting back to earth at a snail's pace the "Flyabout" pilot was not necessarily limited to airports; a level pasture or a small clearing would do just as well. Of good aerodynamic proportion the "Flyabout" had a good feel, more like that of a larger ship, with ability and response that made it a delight to fly. A veritable miser in its operating economy the D-2 was also a boon to the owner-pilot who was forced to operate on a very small budget. The type certificate number for the "Flyabout" model D-2 was issued 9-5-31 and at least 14 examples of this model were built into 1932. About a dozen early examples of the D-2 were manufactured by the Alexander Aircraft Co. at Colorado Springs, Colo.; all subsequent examples were built or assembled from stock by Aircraft Mechanics, Inc., also of Colorado Springs. Proctor W. Nichols was president and chief engineer; W. F. Theis was V.P.

Listed below are specifications and performance data for the "Flyabout" model D-2 as powered with the 45 h.p. Szekely engine; length overall 21'7"; height overall 5'9"; wing span 37'10"; wing chord 60"; total wing area 175 sq.ft.; airfoil (NACA) M-6; wt. empty 590 [589] lbs.; useful load 392 [399] lbs.; payload with 7 gal. fuel 173 [180] lbs.; gross wt. 982 [988] lbs.; max. speed 90 [93]; cruising speed 77 [80]; landing (stall) speed 32; climb 600 ft. first min. at sea level; climb to 4250 ft. in 10 min.; ceiling 13,000 ft.; gas cap. 7 gal.; oil cap. 1.5 gal.; cruising range at 3 gal. per hour 175 miles; price $1590. at factory field; figures listed in brackets for 1935 model of D-2.

The construction details and general arrangement of the "Flyabout" model D-2 was typical to that of the model D-1 as described in the chapter for ATC # 439 of this volume. The main difference in the model D-2 was, of course, the mounting of the 3 cyl. Szekely engine on a welded steel tube detachable mount. Cabin interior dimensions were 60 in. long x 30 in. wide x 41 in. high on all examples through 1934; 1935 models had cabin width increased by 6 inches. Dual joy-stick controls were provided. Side windows slid open for ventilation and a cabin heater was optional. A small baggage bin behind the seatbacks had allowance for 3 lbs., or just barely enough for a tool kit; in 1935 the allowance was increased to 10 lbs. The stiff-legged landing gear of 54 in. tread used 16x7-3 low-pressure Goodyear airwheels; wheel brakes were later optional. Cabin entry was an easy step from the ground through a large door on the left-hand side; a modified windshield, extra large side-windows, and an overhead skylight provided excellent vision in all directions. An extra cabane of bracing near upper end of wing struts stiffened the wing at this point to avoid deflection during severe aileron loads. The horizontal stabilizer on examples through 1934 was adjusted for load trim on the ground only; 1935 models offered trim adjustment from the cockpit in flight. Careful streamlining at various points later accounted for a 3 m.p.h. increase in the cruising speed, which directly accounted for better fuel economy. A wooden propeller, dual controls, and Goodyear airwheels were standard equipment. Wheel brakes, a cabin heater, and custom colors were optional.

Listed below are "Flyabout" D-2 entries as gleaned from registration records through 1934:

NC-528Y; Model D-2 (# 3002) Szekely 45.

NC-11061;	"	(# 3003)	"
NC-11062;	"	(# 3004)	"
NC-11070;	"	(# 3005)	"
NC-11077;	"	(# 3006)	"
NC-11079;	"	(# 3007)	"
NC-11080;	"	(# 3008)	"
NC-11084;	"	(# 3009)	"
NC-11085;	"	(# 3010)	"
NC-11093;	"	(# 3011)	"
NC-11094;	"	(# 3012)	"
NC-12502;	"	(# 3013)	"
NC-12503;	"	(# 3014)	"
NC-12504;	"	(# 3015)	"
NC-12533;	"	(# 3016)	"

Serial # 3002, 3003, first as model D-1; ser. # 3015 unverified; this approval for ser. # 3002 and up; this approval expired 9-30-39.

Fig. 166. "Eaglet" model B-31 with 45 h.p. Szekely engine was improved offering for 1931-32.

After a rather slow start that was plagued by lack of finances and a management shuffle, the American Eagle "Eaglet" finally got off into fairly good production. Throughout 1930, some 78 or more examples were produced and delivered to various parts of the country, and enthusiasm for the "Eaglet" was running fairly high. The "Eaglet" model B-31 was to be the improved offering for 1931-32; because of the comparative success and popularity of the previous model 230 (see USCA/C, Vol. 4) the new version was basically the same, and

changed over but very little. For increased utility in private-owner service, and for better performance, the B-31 was improved in some detail and power available was raised to 45 h.p. by installation of the Szekely SR-3-0 engine. Standing somewhat taller now, with just a faint look of putting on some extra weight, the new B-31 tried gamely to elbow its way into some country-wide favor, but never made the grade. Through no fault of its own we might add, because the new "Eaglet" was a fine little airplane, and compared favorably with other light-planes

Fig. 167. Added horsepower made B-31 a better "Eaglet."

Fig. 168. Several early "Eaglet" were modified to B-31 specs.

of the period. Things at home in the company were not yet in a complete harmony, the market was steadily slipping to newer lows, so the model B-31 couldn't help but find itself represented in very small number. Looking wistfully around the new "Eaglet" also found itself as the last of the prolific "American Eagle" line that first took to the air back in 1926.

In the summer of 1931, with very little work going on and the B-31 "Eaglet" not approved as yet, American Eagle had plenty of factory space that was being unused or was entirely vacant. Victor Roos consented happily when Benny O. Howard, the racing-plane genius, offered rental money for space to build two more of his racing airplanes. As sister-ships to the famous "Pete", the new racing airplanes became the now-famous "Mike" and "Ike". Early in 1932, "Aeromarine" was offering brand-new crated 9 cyl. Salmson AD-9 engines for $300.00 each, while they last! No doubt that is why so

many prototype and home-built aircraft were powered with the unusual AD-9 shortly thereafter; even the B-31 "Eaglet" was modified in several examples to mount the sweet-running and sweet-sounding AD-9 of 40 h.p. With "Eaglet" production finally petering out to nothing, and with no other plans in process to take up the tremendous slack, American Eagle-Lincoln was practically out of business and the plant was nearly vacant by 1933. Oddly enough, in a display of faith and tenacity, the B-31 was still listed for production into 1935 and the ATC was still active until 11-30-36. Rights to the "Eaglet" were eventually sold to American Eaglecraft of Fort Worth, Texas.

The "Eaglet" model B-31 was a light parasol-type monoplane with seating for two in tandem; because of its conventional configuration it didn't have that look of a "flivver-plane", even though it certainly was. Tall enough to eliminate stooping, the B-31 was easy to get in and out of;

Fig. 169. "Eaglet" also available with 9 cyl. Salmson engine as model 231.

Fig. 170. Manufacture of "Eaglet" was later revived as American "Eaglecraft."

everything about it was somewhat toy-like by comparison with larger ships, but pilots were eager to fly it and they enjoyed it. Powered now with the 3 cyl. Szekely SR-3-0 engine of 45 h.p., the new "Eaglet" still was no "tiger" by any means, but its performance over earlier versions was greatly improved, while still offering flying pleasure for two on just a few dollars per hour. Slightly heavier now with the added muscle of a more powerful engine, the B-31 was somewhat less demanding to certain technique, and perhaps a little more predictable in its behavior. Typical of the basic "Eaglet" series, the B-31 didn't ask too much of a pilot, and could be flown well in just a few hours of instruction. The new "Eaglet" carried a higher price-tag, but proportionately, it was a lot more airplane for the money. The type certificate number for the "Eaglet" model B-31 was issued 9-11-31 and probably no more than 9 or 10 examples of this model were manufactured by the American Eagle-Lincoln Aircraft Corp. on Fairfax Field in Kansas City, Kansas. Victor Roos was president and general manager; E. E. Porterfield was sales manager to his resignation in Aug. of 1931, being then replaced by J. S. Chick who had been asst. sales manager; M. P. Crews was chief engineer.

Listed below are specifications and performance data for the "Eaglet" model B-31 as powered with the 45 h.p. Szekely SR-3-0 engine; length overall 21'7"; height overall 8'4"; wing span 34'4"; wing chord 60"; total wing area 164.4 sq.ft.; airfoil NACA (M-series); wt. empty 509 lbs.; useful load 413 lbs.; payload with 10.5 gal. fuel 170 lbs.; gross wt. 922 lbs.; max. speed 90; cruising speed 75; landing speed 30; climb 700 ft. first min. at sea level; ceiling 14,500 ft.; gas cap. 10.5 gal.; oil cap. 5 qts.; cruising range at 3 gal. per hour 240 miles; price $1575. at factory field.

The construction details and general arrangement of the model B-31 was basically typical to that of the model 230 as described in the chapter for ATC # 380 of USCA/C, Vol. 4. The heavier empty weight of the B-31 cannot be completely accounted for, but a longer legged landing gear and a larger capacity fuel tank were responsible in part. Fuel capacity was increased to 10.5 gal. for more cruising range; the tank was also mounted high in the fuselage just ahead of the front seat. Solo flying was permitted from the front seat only. The increased useful load was, of course, absorbed by the extra fuel capacity, and no baggage was allowed. The landing gear was equipped with rubber shock-rings, and wheels were either 16x7-4 or 16x7-3 Goodyear "airwheels"; no brakes were provided. Goodrich "semi-airwheels" were optional. A Flottorp wooden propeller, dual controls, Pyrene fire extinguisher bottle, first-aid kit, altimeter, tachometer, oil pressure gauge, fuel level gauge, switch, choke, fuel shut-off, and log books were standard equipment.

Listed below are "Eaglet" model B-31 entires as gleaned from registration records:

X-531Y;	Model B-31 (# 1068)	Szekely 45.
NC-550Y;	" (# 1074)	"
NC-589Y;	" (# 1101)	"
NC-596Y;	" (# 1102)	"
NC-595Y;	" (# 1103)	"
NC-597Y;	" (# 1104)	"
NC-598Y;	" (# 1105)	"
NC-599Y;	" (# 1106)	"
NC-12522;	" (# 1107)	"
;	" (# 1108)	"
NC-12559;	" (# 1109)	"
;	" (# 1110)	"
NC-17007;	" (# 1111)	"

Serial # 1068 first as model A-31 with Continental A-40 engine; ser. # 1074 first as model 230; ser. # 1106 also as model 231 with Salmson 40 engine; ser. # 1108 was exported; ser. # 1109 mfgd. 1933; ser. # 1110 not listed; ser. # 1111 mfgd. 1935; approval expired 11-30-36, rights sold to American Eaglecraft of Fort Worth, Texas.

Fig. 171. Northrop "Alpha 4" gains speed with streamlined landing gear "boots." Modification available to all previous "Alpha."

Introduced to those in aviation as the first practical, all-metal, low-winged cabin monoplane in this country, the Northrop "Alpha" fairly bristled with innovations in aircraft design and construction. As put into service the revolutionary "Alpha" still lacked one or two items in its design to make it one of the most outstanding airplane developments of 1930. The first of these shortcomings was the fixed undercarriage which contributed largely to parasitic drag and hampered the "Alpha" in realizing its fullest potential as a highspeed transport. John K. Northrop was well aware of this fact early in the program and several methods were studied in effort to do away with this problem of drag, but it was not all that simple. The retractable landing gear was of course the logical answer, and several arrangements were calculated and studied, but the retractable gear was still in its infancy and posed many problems. Deciding that mechanical problems and weight penalties actually outweighed the advantages of the folding gear, Northrop turned to the idea of streamlining the landing gear legs which would remain fixed. The calculated difference between the fully retractable landing gear and the highly streamlined fixed gear was not of enough consequence to take on all the added problems. As designed for the "Alpha 4" the landing gear was now of two separate cantilever legs that were fully encased in rather large streamlined

"boots"; this system reduced drag considerably and still retained all the advantages of the reliable fixed gear. After test and approval it was simply the matter of recalling those "Alpha" already in service back to the factory for modification; the prototype of the "Alpha 4" was reworked at the Northrop plant in Calif., and the rest were modified at the Stearman plant in Wichita, Kans. Because of the consolidation of Northrop's plant in Calif. with that of Stearman in Wichita the "Alpha" were technically listed as Stearman, a name which they carried somewhat unhappily.

The Stearman-Northrop "Alpha 4" was a low-winged cabin monoplane of cantilever all-metal construction, and most of the airplanes in this new series were modified from existing airplanes already in service. (Refer to ATC #381 of USCA/C, Vol. 4). The interior of the new model was primarily arranged in coachstyle to seat 6 passengers, but a 3-passenger or 5-passenger configuration was also available; an open cockpit for the pilot was aft of the cabin section. In the combination 3 or 5 place version, balance of the payload could be adjusted for greater allowance of baggage-cargo, or more fuel for extended cruising range. Already arranged in good aerodynamic proportion for high efficiency and maximum performance, the highly streamlined landing gear on the "Alpha 4" boosted speeds by nearly 10 m.p.h. Had the pilot's open cockpit been faired over with a streamlined canopy, the new "Alpha" could well have been judged as the ultimate in a small high-speed transport. Powered with the 9 cyl. Pratt & Whitney "Wasp" SC1 engine of 450 h.p. the "Alpha 4" used every horsepower wisely and delivered exceptional utility in combination with high performance. Despite some increases in weight allowance, the new "Alpha" still operated admirably out of the smaller fields, and the already excellent flight characteristics were perhaps slightly improved. Easy to service and easy to maintain the "Alpha" was popular on the flight-line. With seating configurations adjustable into 3, 5, or 7 places the "Alpha 4" was versatile to the extent that a full load could be dispatched in the best combination available. Most of the "Alpha 4" were in service on the TWA line where they amassed an excellent operational record. The type certificate number for the Stearman-Northrop "Alpha" model 4 was issued 9-10-31 and some 11 or more examples were modified or built to the new specifications. As increased traffic and more cargo tonnage outmoded the seating capacity of the "Alpha 4" they were all converted into cargo-carriers for transcontinental air-express service.

Listed below are specifications and performance data for the "Alpha 4" as powered with the 450 h.p. "Wasp" SC1 engine; length overall 28'5"; height overall (tail up) 9'0"; wing span 43'10"; wing chord at root 100"; wing chord at tip 66"; total wing area 312 sq. ft.; airfoil Clark Y; wt. empty (average) 2800 lbs; useful load 1900 lbs.; payload with 100 gal. fuel 1055 lbs.; payload with 116 gal. fuel 959 lbs.; gross wt. 4700 lbs.; max. speed 177; cruising speed 155; landing speed 62; climb 1200 ft. first min. at sea level; ceiling 19,000 ft.; gas cap. max. 116 gal.; oil cap. 10 gal.; cruising range at 24 gal. per hour 650 miles; no price for conversion or factory-new airplane was announced for this series.

The construction details and general arrangement of the "Alpha 4" were typical to that of the earlier models 2 and 3 as described in the chapter for ATC #381 of USCA/C, Vol. 4. With a useable volume of 120 cu. ft. the cabin interior was adaptable to various arrangements; the all-passenger version seated 6, and optional seating of 3 or 5 allowed the balance of payload in varying amounts of baggage-cargo. Increased weight allowances suggested the need for more wing area, so the overall span was increased by two feet. The most significant change in the Model 4 was, of course, the "booted" cantilever landing gear. With a wheel tread of 9 feet, each oleo-spring leg was fastened independently to outer ends of the center stub-wing; these were then completely faired by large streamlined metal boots. Low pressure semi-wheels were 9.50x12 and brakes were standard equipment. A swiveling tail wheel was sometimes covered with a metal fairing. An adj. metal propeller, electric inertia-type engine starter, navigation lights, a battery, and fire extinguisher were also standard equipment. Radio installation, landing lights, and parachute flares were optional. The next development in the Stearman-Northrop "Alpha" was the cargo-carrying model 4-A as described in the chapter for ATC #461 of this volume.

Listed below are "Alpha 4" entries as gleaned from registration records:

NC-127W Alpha 4 (#2) Wasp 450.
NC-999Y;   "   (#4)   "
NC-933Y;   "   (#5)   "
NC-942Y;   "   (#6)   "
NC-947Y;   "   (#7)   "
NC-961Y;   "   (#8)   "
NC-966Y;   "   (#9)   "
NC-985Y;   "   (#10)   "
NC-986Y;   "   (#11)   "
NC-992Y;   "   (#12)   "
NC-994Y;   "   (#17)   "

Seven of the "Alpha 4" were modified from earlier models 2 and 3; four aircraft were originally built as model 4 (ser. #10, 11, 12, 17); eight of those listed were later converted to model 4-A.

Fig. 172. Nicholas-Beazley NB-8G with 80 h.p. "Genet" engine.

After redesigning the gaunt, pot-bellied "Barling" NB-3 into a smoother, more buxom version called the NB-4, Nicholas-Beazley found themselves with a ship that was left begging for customers. Already toying with a few "experimentals" because of the NB-4's poor showing right from the start, they selected Tom Kirkup's homely little "parasol" for further development; as shown on the manufacturer's roster it was the NB-8. Previous N-B models

had been slanted more to the general-purpose market since therein lie the greatest interest, but because of changes in the overall picture since the onslaught of the depression they decided to stake a claim in the new market that was more favorable to the light-plane. As a light two-place sport-trainer monoplane the NB-8 design was a happy compromise that offered the most airplane for the least amount of money. The NB-8 had made its debut quietly and rather

Fig. 173. View of NB-8G shows early configuration, note stiff-legged landing gear.

Fig. 174. Wings of NB-8G folded to width of just over 10 feet.

shyly, but then went on to captivate all that were properly introduced to her; she was like that. One could hardly say that the NB-8 was a pretty airplane because every line and every dimension was almost as a detriment to its looks; spindly-legged, with its broad wing perched too high atop its squat fuselage it looked altogether unwieldy. But, its homely charm lie in inner traits of personality and behavior that could win you over much quicker than the curves and dimension of outward beauty. Because of her gentle nature the NB-8 was widely used as a primary trainer and instructors will swear to it that nearly every student-pilot had a "crush" on her. For those "sports" that liked to "rubber-neck" around the sky without paying too much attention to their flying, the NB-8 was like a chariot from heaven. Wherever pilots gathered the NB-8 was quickly recommended by all those who flew her, but word-of-mouth advertising takes time; even at that at least 57 were built

into 1932, and perhaps 20 of these were still flying actively in 1939. One or two have been restored in recent years, and are probably fly-ing yet.

As designed by Tom Kirkup the earliest NB-8 development was powered first with the 36 h.p. Aeronca engine, and then the 45 h.p. Szekely engine, but apparently these under-powered combinations were unsuitable. A big jump all the way to 80 h.p. by installing the Armstrong-Siddeley "Genet" engine was quite unusual, but it must have been what the basic NB-8 design needed, because the new combi-nation was nearly perfect. It is very likely that any other engine of like horsepower would have served just as well, but it has been said that Nicholas-Beazley struck a good bargain for the "Genet" engine, so these were used. The Fairchild Airplane & Engine Co. had ex-clusive distributing rights for the A-S "Genet" here in the U.S., but the take-over of Fairchild

Fig. 175. Prototype NB-8 shown with 3 cyl. Szekely engine. Low performance discouraged this combination.

Fig. 176. Coupe-top optional on NB-8G for cold weather. High parasol-mounted wing was cradle for gentle flight and exceptional stability.

by the Aviation Corp. found them with a large inventory of 57 engines and spare parts to dispose of. No doubt these were all purchased along with the distributing rights by N-B at a greatly reduced price. The "Genet" engine was actually manufactured in England and now were being distributed here in the U.S. by N-B; developing 80 h.p. at 2310 r.p.m. its price at this time was $750.00 crated for delivery at Marshall, Mo. Introduced with the "Genet" engine early in 1931 the NB-8G was first certificated on a Group 2 approval numbered 2-353 for about 25 airplanes; the approved type certificate (ATC) was issued later in the year allowing increased gross weight and the optional installation of a coupe-top canopy. Sales held up well throughout most of 1931, but going into 1932 the sales had fallen to such an extent that production had to be halted. Some complete airframe assemblies were probably still on

hand, and at least one ship was put together in 1935. On May 2 of 1938 the N-B Airplane Div. was sold to Air Associates, Inc.

The Nicholas-Beazley model NB-8G was a light open cockpit "parasol" monoplane with side-by-side seating for two. Because of odd arrangement and ample dimension the NB-8G was certainly not typical of most parasol monoplanes, and was not blessed particularly with beauty of line or form. We can venture to guess that Tom Kirkup had much else on his mind when laying out this design. Primarily developed as a training craft it was widely used by small flying-schools; its inherent safety and rugged character was a boon to operators who were therefore able to operate more frequently and more cheaply. A west coast operator offered "Learn to fly for $75.00," and still made a profit. Although most often referred to as a trainer the NB-8G had certain qualities that were also ideal

Fig. 177. Side view of NB-8G is not one of its better angles.

for the sportsman; not the flip-'em-over and wring-'em-out type of sport, but more for the one who occasionally day-dreamed while absorbing the scenery, or one who liked to snoop around and drop into little out-of-the-way places. As powered with the 5 cyl. A-S "Genet" engine of 80 h.p. the NB-8G had sufficient muscle to deliver a commendable performance when spurred on to it, but she would much rather take it easy. Very easy to fly and possessing some remarkable flight characteristics in the hands of a good pilot, the NB-8G was always a lady and had gentleness enough to put up with anybody. It is easy to imagine that there are hundreds of pilots who were once very fond of the NB-8G, and they must have memories to prove it. The type certificate number for the NB-8G was issued 9-18-31 and altogether at least 57 examples of this model were manufactured by the Nicholas-Beazley Airplane Co., Inc. at Marshall, Mo. Russel Nicholas was president; Chas. M. Buckner was V.P.; Howard Beazley was secretary; Tom A. Kirkup was chief engineer; and R. M. "Duke" Ressler, formerly asst. sales manager, was now sales mgr. and chief pilot.

Listed below are specifications and performance data for the Nicholas-Beazley model NB-8G as powered with the 80 h.p. "Genet" Mark 2 engine; length overall 20'3"; height overall 7'9"; wing chord 60"; total wing area 184.5 sq.ft.; airfoil RAF-34; wt. empty 682 (717) lbs.; useful load 493 lbs.; payload with 21 gal. fuel 182 lbs.; gross wt. 1175 (1210) lbs.; figures in brackets for amended allowance; max. speed 110; cruising speed 83; landing speed 39-41; climb 750 ft. first min. at sea level; ceiling 18,000 ft.; gas cap. 21 gal.; oil cap. 2 gal.; cruising range at 4.5 gal. per hour 400 miles; price $1790. at factory in 1931, lowered to $1490. as of 7-33, and reduced to $1345. as of 9-34.

The fuselage framework was built up of welded chrome-moly steel tubing into a rigid Pratt truss, lightly faired to shape with wooden formers and fairing strips, then fabric covered. The open cockpit was deep and well protected with easy entry from the ground by way of large door on the right side. Side-by-side seating offered ample stretch-room, visibility was excellent to all sides, and dual controls were provided. For cold weather protection a detachable coupe-top canopy was available; a baggage compartment of 4 cu. ft. capacity was allowed 12 lbs. but installation of canopy cancelled baggage allowance. The wing framework was built up of laminated spruce spar beams with plywood-gusseted spruce truss-type wing ribs; the leading edge was covered with plywood sheet and the completed framework was covered with fabric. The fuel tank was mounted in center-section panel of the wing, which in turn was mounted high above the fuselage on a cabane of steel tube struts. Later models had a trailing edge cut-out in center-section for visibility up and backward. Ailerons on earliest models

were "balanced" by Flettner-type tabs, but later models used the Friese-type offset hinge. The folding wings pivoted about the lower end of the vee-type bracing struts and the rear spar fitting to an overall width of 10 ft. 4 in. The long-legged landing gear of 72 in. tread used oil-draulic shock absorbing struts; wheels were 16x7-3 Goodyear "airwheels" and no brakes were provided. Earliest models used a stiff-legged landing gear with no shock struts and upper end of landing gear leg was variously mounted at base of front center-section strut or upper longeron at firewall station. The fabric covered tail-group was built up of welded steel tubing; both vertical fin and horizontal stabilizer were adjusted for trim on the ground only. Later models had a novel bungee-cord mechanism to adjust for trim at the control stick. Wing rigging included an angle of incidence at 3 deg. for early models, and 2 deg. for late models; dihedral was 1½ deg. for all. A wooden propeller, speed-ring engine cowl, exhaust collector ring, dual controls, fire extinguisher, fuel gauge, seat cushions, first-aid kit, and log books were standard equipment. A coupe-top enclosure and engine starter were optional.

Listed below are NB-8 entries as gleaned from registration records:

X-436V; NB-8   (# K-1) Szeke. 45
NC-503 Y; NB-8G (#K-2) Genet 80.
NC-517 Y;   "   (# K-3)   "
NC-525 Y;   "   (# K-4)   "
NC-524 Y;   "   (# K-5)   "
NC-541 Y;   "   (# K-6)   "
NC-542 Y;   "   (# K-7)   "
NC-543 Y;   "   (# K-8)   "
NC-544 Y;   "   (# K-9)   "
NC-545 Y;   "   (# K-10)   "
NC-558 Y;   "   (# K-11)   "
NC-559 Y;   "   (# K-12)   "
NC-560 Y;   "   (# K-13)   "
NC-561 Y;   "   (# K-14)   "
NC-562 Y;   "   (# K-15)   "
NC-574 Y;   "   (# K-16)   "
NC-575 Y;   "   (# K-17)   "
NC-576 Y;   "   (# K-18)   "
NC-577 Y;   "   (# K-19)   "
NC-578 Y;   "   (# K-20)   "
NC-580 Y;   "   (# K-21)   "
NC-581 Y;   "   (# K-22)   "
NC-582 Y;   "   (# K-23)   "
NC-583 Y;   "   (# K-24)   "
NC-584 Y;   "   (# K-25)   "
NC-11063;   "   (# K-26)   "
NC-11064;   "   (# K-27)   "
NC-11065;   "   (# K-28)   "
NC-11066;   "   (# K-29)   "
NC-11067;   "   (# K-30)   "
NC-11071;   "   (# K-31)   "
NC-11072;   "   (# K-32)   "
NC-11073;   "   (# K-33)   "
NC-11074;   "   (# K-34)   "
NC-11075;   "   (# K-35)   "
NC-11087;   "   (# K-36)   "

continued on next page

NC-11088;	”	(# K-37)	”
NC-11089;	”	(# K-38)	”
NC-11090;	”	(# K-39)	”
NC-11091;	”	(# K-40)	”
NC-11095;	”	(# K-41)	”
NC-11096;	”	(# K-42)	”
NC-11097;	”	(# K-43)	”
NC-11098;	”	(# K-44)	”
NC-11099;	”	(# K-45)	”
NC-12505;	”	(# K-46)	”
NC-12506;	”	(# K-47)	”
NC-12507;	”	(# K-48)	”
NC-12508;	”	(# K-49)	”
NC-12509;	”	(# K-50)	”
NC-12510;	”	(# K-51)	”
NC-12514;	”	(# K-52)	”
NC-12515;	”	(# K-53)	”

NC-12516;	”	(# K-54)	”
NC-12517;	”	(# K-55)	”
NC-12518;	”	(# K-56)	”
NC-12527;	”	(# K-57)	”
NC-15498;	”	(# K-)	”

Serial # K-4 thru # K-15, K-17 thru # K-22, # K-24 thru # K-30 on Group 2 approval 2-353; ser. # K-16, K-23, K-31 and up on ATC # 452; ser. # K-35, K-38, K-42, K-45, K-55 unverified; ser. # K-56 also as NB-8 Spl. with either Lambert 90 or Velie 65, had Genet 80 in 1933; An NB-8G was delivered to Honduras late in 1933; last NB-8G was assembled from left-over parts in 1935 by L. C. Short, this a/c may have been NC-15498; ser. no. for NC-15498 unknown; approval for NB-8G expired 5-2-38 due to sale to Air Associates, Inc.

Fig. 178. Waco model PCF with 170 h.p. Jacobs LA-1 engine.

Following up on the relative success of the model QCF, Waco Aircraft introduced an interesting companion model. Typical of the earlier QCF in just about every respect the new model PCF, however, did not share in the same success and remained a rather rare version in the F-series lineup. Powered with the 7 cyl. Jacobs LA-1 engine of 170 h.p. the PCF was undoubtedly a good match for any similar ship with this amount of power. Matched evenly with the popular QCF (ATC # 416), and perhaps even a mite better in some respects, the PCF tried earnestly for some recognition of its merits, but it just did not come. Waco Aircraft actually did very little to promote this model so its scarcity cannot be attributed to any fault of the airplane. Of the 3 or so examples that were finally built of this model, one was operated by the Aeronautics Dept. of the State of Pennsylvania. Fitted with deluxe features such as wheel pants, lower wing-root fairings, landing lights, and metal propeller, this craft made the rounds of Pennsylvania airports. Designed also to take the "sweat" out of operating from short, rough airfields, the PCF perhaps minimized some of the legendary horror of flying over the fickle Pennsylvania country-side. At this time the PCF and many other models on the Waco roster were available on the time payment plan; the delivered price also included any "check rides" or instruction necessary for the new owner to operate and fly his new airplane safely.

The Waco model PCF was a compact open cockpit biplane with seating arranged for a pilot and two passengers. As an all-purpose biplane similar to the model QCF the basic design of the PCF was identical except for the powerplant installation and any modifications necessary for this particular combination. Actually, one would be hard put to recognize the difference between the two with just a casual glance. Powered with the 7 cyl. Jacobs LA-1 engine of 170 h.p. the all-round performance of the new PCF was comparable to that of the highly touted QCF; had these two models been introduced at the same time a selection of one over the other would surely have been dominated by engine preference alone. With no handed-down lore to go on and very little printed fact we can only assume then that the PCF shared all the fine qualities that had made the QCF such a great favorite. With inherent traits in its design that also fostered sure-footed and nimble flight characteristics the PCF was listed as being eligible and suitable for aerobatic instruction in the Federal CPTP program. The type certificate number for the model PCF was issued 10-2-31 and it is doubtful if any more than 3 examples of this model were built by the Waco Aircraft Co. at Troy, Ohio. It is perhaps of interest to note here that at least 215 aircraft companies were reported as still doing business in 1930; by the end of 1931 this number had fallen to 110 companies. Despite the continued hope and optimism projected by those in the aircraft industry the lingering "depression" was steadily taking its grim toll.

Listed below are specifications and perform-

Fig. 179. PCF in service with Aero. Dept., State of Penna. Wheel pants and lower wing fillets were optional features.

ance data for the Waco model PCF as powered with the 170 h.p. Jacobs LA-1 engine; length overall 20'6"; height overall 8'9"; wing span upper 29'7"; wing span lower 27'5"; wing chord upper & lower 57"; wing area upper 130.4 sq.ft.; wing area lower 111 sq.ft.; total wing area 241.4 sq.ft.; airfoil Clark Y; wt. empty 1328 lbs.; useful load 972 lbs.; payload with 40 gal. fuel 530 lbs.; gross wt. 2300 lbs.; max. speed (with speed-ring cowl) 125; cruising speed 108; landing (stall) speed 42; climb 900 ft. first min. at sea level; climb to 7500 ft. in 10 mins.; ceiling 15,000 ft.; gas cap. 40 gal.; oil cap. 4 gal.; cruising range at 9.5 gal. per hour 430 miles; price at factory field approx. $4500., depending on the equipment included.

The construction details and general arrangement of the PCF were typical to that of the model QCF as described in the chapter for ATC # 416 of this volume. The data particularly applicable to the model PCF was as follows. Max. allowable baggage was 90 lbs.; a 15 lb. tool-kit was stowed in dash-panel compartment of the front cockpit, and the main baggage compartment in the turtle-back section behind the rear

cockpit had allowance for 75 lbs. Two parachutes at 20 lbs. each, when carried, were part of the baggage allowance. The gaping hole of the front cockpit could be closed off with a metal panel when not in use. The lower wing root on deluxe versions of this model were streamlined into the fuselage junction with a large metal fairing fillet. Low pressure 6.50x10 semi-airwheels with brakes were standard equipment; metal wheel pants were optional. A Hartzell wooden propeller, Heywood air-operated engine starter, speed-ring engine cowl, a compass, and tail wheel were standard equipment. A metal propeller, electric engine starter, navigation lights, landing lights, a battery, dual controls, and 7.50x10 wheels with brakes were optional. The next development in the model F series was the 210 h.p. UBF as described in the chapter for ATC # 473 of this volume.

Listed below are model PCF entries as gleaned from registration records:
NC-11476; Model PCF (# 3557) Jacobs 170.
NC-11483; 		" 		(# 3563) 		"
NS-12439; 		" 		(# 3574) 		"
Approval for PCF expired 10-15-33.

Fig. 180. PCF amid autumn setting in Pennsylvania.

Fig. 181. Sikorsky S-40 with 4 "Hornet" engines was largest amphibian in the world.

The Sikorsky "Clipper" model S-40 was a big airplane, in fact the world's largest amphibian type, a grand and majestic flying monster that was 17 tons of miscellaneous steel and duralumin framework. With its 4 big "Hornet" engines going full blast it had more power than the average railway locomotive, and its 3 tons of fuel were gulped down at the rate of 125 gallons per hour. Designed to carry up to 45 passengers with a generous allowance for their baggage, and a crew, it also stowed away nearly a ton of mail and air-express packages. The plush interior of the cabin was elegantly divided into separate compartments that were connected by wide aisles; it also boasted of 8 foot ceilings and big picture windows for a grand view. Conversion of the wheel-shod S-40 into a flying boat, by removal of the undercarriage allowed another ton for payload or extension of cruising range; Sikorsky was looking way ahead and felt the big S-40 was an important step towards the development of a practical airplane for trans-oceanic service. Designed to the stringent specifications laid down by Pan American Airways the keel for the big hull of the ocean-going S-40 was laid in the latter part of 1930, and by Jan. of 1931 it was ready for water trials and preliminary flight testing. Ceremoniously christened by Mrs.

Herbert Hoover as the "American Clipper" the first S-40 was flown by Chas. "Lindy" Lindbergh on its inaugral two-day flight from Miami to Colombia in So. America. The return trip flight was made in 12 hours of the same day. Rushing completion the next example of the S-40 was christened the "Caribbean Clipper" and another the "Southern Clipper". At this time the big S-40 reigned as the flagships of more than 100 airplanes in the Pan American fleet, and the northern terminus was a huge marine base at Dinner Key just outside of Miami, Florida. Operated generally as flying boats the S-40 flew the long route to Barranquilla in So. America, and to the Panama Canal Zone. The longest non-stop overwater flight regularly operated in the world was the 600 mile hop from Kingston in Jamaica to Barranquilla, Colombia. Back in 1932 the Sikorsky S-40 was the ultimate in intercontinental air travel, and as such was the original of the world-famous Pan American "Clipper Ships" that followed.

The Sikorsky model S-40 was a large 4-engined parasol monoplane of the basic flying-boat type with seating arranged for 38 passengers and a crew of 6. Basically similar to the normal Sikorsky "Amphibian" concept, except that it was about 3 times as large, the S-40 was

Fig. 182. As a "flying boat" the S-40 carried 1800 lbs. additional useful load.

the largest airplane in the U.S.A., the largest "amphibian" in the world at this time, and its 114 foot wing towered nearly 24 feet above the ground. Its cabin interior was wider than that of a Pullman car, and appointments were actually better and much more comfortable. The large stubby vee-bottom hull contained all the accommodations for passengers, baggage and crew, and the outboard tip-floats were almost as big as the hull of an average small flying boat. It is remarkable that Sikorsky elected to stick with the spidery boom-and-strut arrangement for an

airplane so large, but it does prove at least that this maze of framework was actually much more durable than it looked. The large retractable undercarriage made a practical land-plane of the S-40, but the wheeled gear was soon discarded in favor of more useful load; the elimination of its parasitic drag also boosted the cruising range. As powered with 4 big Pratt & Whitney "Hornet B" engines of 575 h.p. each the S-40 was a thundering spectacle that struck crowds with awe wherever it went, and people would travel for miles just to see it arrive or de-

Fig. 183. Passengers boarding "Caribbean Clipper;" S-40 was pride of the Pan American fleet.

Fig. 184. View of 4-engined S-40 dramatizes progress of travel.

part. With the 4 big "Hornet" engines hung under the wing in a line abreast there was a never-ending maze of struts that were required for their mounting, and the problem of engine controls and all the miscellaneous plumbing must have been an engineering challenge. A fully loaded take-off from the water was about 20 seconds, and all-round water characteristics were very good; the stout hull was classed as an ocean-going vessel, but it is very doubtful if all that superstructure fastened on top of the hull would weather very much storm. The S-40 could hardly be described as dainty or nimble, but control was rather light for a ship so large; behavior in the air was sure-footed and solid, and everyone enjoyed a comfortable ride. The type certificate number for the model S-40 was issued 10-17-31 and 3 examples of this model were manufactured by the Sikorsky Aviation Corp. at Bridgeport, Conn.

Listed below are specifications and performance data for the Sikorsky model S-40 as powered with 4 "Hornet B" engines of 575 h.p. each; length overall 76'8"; height overall on wheels 23'10"; wing span 114'0"; wing chord 16'; total wing area (including lift struts) 1875 sq.ft.; airfoil Sikorsky GS-1; wt. empty 24,748 [22,980] lbs.; useful load 9252 [11,020] lbs.; wts. in brackets for flying boat; payload variable according to fuel load; gross wt. 34,000 lbs.; max. speed 134 [138]; cruising speed 115 [117]; figures in brackets for flying boat; landing speed 65; climb 712 ft. first min. at sea level; ceiling 12,000 ft.; gas cap. normal 800 gal.; gas cap. max. 1040 gal.; oil cap. max. 80 gal.; max. cruising range at 125 gal. per hour 900 miles; price $139,000. at factory. Over 3000 lbs. of overwater equipment such as anchors, mooring gear, radio, life vests, air rafts, and escape gear was deductable from useful load; baggage, mail,

and air-express cargo deductable from passenger payload. Performance on any 3 engines; max. speed 115; cruising speed 99; climb 340 ft. first min; ceiling 5200 ft.

The huge two-step hull was a built-up framework of variously shaped duralumin sections covered with riveted "Alclad" metal sheet; all seams were sealed with fabric and marine glue. Divided into 7 water-tight compartments the hull was 11 feet high, 10'5" wide, and over 58 feet long. The anchors and mooring gear hold was in bow of the hull, and the large pilot's compartment was the nerve-center for all operations, and the mounting of radio. The third compartment had 4 passenger seats on one side which could be removed to stow extra baggage and mail; a large hatch was provided for loading and unloading. The other side of this compartment had a rest-room with couch and chair. The fourth compartment had plush accommodations for 16 passengers, and the next compartment had passenger seating for 8; the sixth compartment was a smoking room with 3 lounging chairs. The smoking room was also provided with 2 toilet-rooms, and passenger entrance into the main cabin was by way of a large hatchway and stairs into this room. The last compartment in the stern was provided with folding bunks for the crew. The huge wing framework in 3 sections was built up of dural truss-type spar beams with dural channel truss-type wing ribs; the leading edges were covered with dural metal sheet and the completed framework was covered mostly with fabric. As a "parasol" type the large wing was mounted high above the hull on a system of struts and braced to horizontal outriggers with struts and steel tie-rods; engine nacelles were hung below the wing and tied into the wing-bracing trusses. Four fuel tanks of 140 gal. each were mounted in the center portion of the wing,

Fig. 185. Sikorsky S-40 "Clipper" was link to South American continent.

and a 240 gal. fuel tank was mounted in each outer float; fuel was transferred from floats to wing tanks by engine-driven pumps. The huge retractable landing gear of 17 ft. tread was two separate tripod units using oleo-spring shock absorbing struts; large wire wheels and multiple-disc "Sikorsky" brakes were standard equipment. Removal of the landing gear and the tail wheel allowed 1800 lbs. o f additional useful load. The fabric covered twin-tailed tail group was of construction similar to the wing and was mounted on two large booms extending back from the rear wing spar; all movable controls were of aerodynamic balance and the horizontal stabilizer was adjustable in flight. Each engine was equipped with a combination hand-crank and electric inertia-type starter; priming and engaging controls were in the cockpit. Metal propellers, engine starters, wheel brakes, dual controls, speed-ring engine cowlings, batteries,

navigation lights, fire extinguishers, anchors, and mooring gear were standard equipment. Life vests, air rafts, tank for fresh water, first-aid kit, and survival gear were optional. A later development of the existing S-40 was the model S-40-A as described in the chapter for ATC # 562. The next Sikorsky development following the S-40 was the model S-42 as described in the chapter for ATC # 544.

Listed below are S-40 entries as gleaned from Pan American Airways records:

NC-80V;   Model S-40 (# 2000-X) 4 Hornet B.

NC-81V;   ''   (# 2001)   ''

NC-752V;   ''   (# 2002)   ''

Ser. # 2000-X contracted for on 12-20-29 and delivered 10-10-31 for $139,000.; ser. # 2001 delivered 11-26-31 for $137,000.; ser. # 2002 del. 3-30-32 for $137,000.; all examples operated in the Caribbean.

Fig. 186. The 1932 Taylor "Cub" model E-2 with 37 h.p. Continental A-40 engine.

It is rather difficult to discuss the Taylor "Cub" without reflecting on the great significance this airplane has had in aviation history. The "Cub" has been flying the country over and the world over from 1930 to this very day, and even to the layman who knows nothing at all of airplanes, any small airplane is a "Cub". As airplanes go down in history in recognition of their contribution to aviation development the "Cub" will always be near the top of the list. Starting out demurely as a debutante with no reputation at all, the infectious nature of the Taylor "Cub" soon won it a host of friends from coast to coast, and finally the world over. What was this magic spell that the "Cub" held, why did it keep on flourishing when other typical light-planes had come and gone? Why did pilots always smile gently when they spoke of the Taylor "Cub"; perhaps the only reasonable explanation was a combination of things called the "Cub" personality. To say that the "Cub" was entirely without fault would be grossly in error, but the remarkable thing was that pilots learned to forgive her little shortcomings as readily as she forgave theirs. A pokey little damsel that took her own time and could not be hurried was always happy in her element, and certainly expected the same from all that flew her; a

smart Cub-pilot soon learned to relax and enjoy himself, and the flight as much as she. The first year for the Taylor "Cub" E-2 was no rousing success, but it did manage to represent itself in many parts of the country, and it made many lasting friends. Everyone flocked around the first "Cub E-2" to be delivered in a small California town, and the beaming owner offered all a ride; little did he realize it, but he was kept busy flying all that day. As the word got around the "Cub E-2" became very popular with the small flying-school operator; often just one airplane was the entire fleet, and these were kept busy from dawn to dusk, as weather permitted. One "Cub E-2" as the sole equipment of this particular flying-school had 38 students assigned to her, and they kept her busy flying all week long. In time, there were many "Cubs" of various description, but here we are only concerned with the model E-2. The Taylor "Cub" model E-2 was powered with the 4 cyl. (flat four) Continental A-40 engine of some 37 h.p., and in comparison with other light-planes of the period it fell slightly short on several counts. It was not distinctive in shape as the "Aeronca" or the Curtiss-Wright "Junior", not as comfortable as the Alexander "Flyabout" nor was it flashy and sporty as the Buhl "Bull

Fig. 187. The prototype "Cub" with 9 cyl. Salmson AD-9 engine; C. G. Taylor on left, Bud Havens on right.

Pup"; it was not even pretty by any means, but once you made friends and started courting her you were hooked into a lasting love-affair. Starting out modestly in 1931 and holding up well through the crucial period of 1932-33 sales took a sharp jump in 1934-35. In the 5-year period of production on the "Cub E-2" nearly 350 were built, and at least 230 of these were still flying actively in 1939. Occasionally, you may see one or two that are flying even yet.

Development of the "Cub" largely revolves around the efforts of one man, one C. Gilbert Taylor, who has been labeled variously as a genius, an aeronautical wizard, to an eccentric. Any man with strong convictions and the fortitude to implement them can either be called genius or eccentric, depending on point of

view; aviation history will bear out that C. G. Taylor was a wizard and was much closer to genius. As many others did back in the early twenties, C. G. Taylor started out by trying to make a better airplane of the Curtiss "Jenny"; one version he had modified could carry four with nothing but an OX-5 engine up front. Of great mechanical aptitude, Taylor realized the many shortcomings of outdated war-surplus airplanes and dabbled in the development of better airplanes, airplanes utilizing better materials and methods of construction, of better aerodynamic makeup, and consequently of much better performance. One of the most significant developments in these early days by Taylor was the "Chummy" of 1928. Seating two side-by-side and powered with an air-cooled Siemens-Halske engine the "Chummy"

Fig. 188. Bud Havens and Mary Babb ready for hop in 1931 "Cub."

Fig. 189. 1934 Model of "Cub" E-2 shown over Bradford, Pa.

was a parasol-type monoplane with semi-cabin protection for the occupants; performance of this model was of the best for this day and age. From his operation at Rochester, N. Y. Taylor had moved to Bradford, Penna. where he secured financing, but production of the "Chummy" was stifled because of the creeping depression. Always with a trick or two up his sleeve, Taylor began development of the "Cub" concept, hoping to enter the stream of prosperity that was then flowing in the lightplane market. Organizing the Taylor Aircraft Co. with Wm. T. Piper, a name that later became synonomous with the "Cub", they had a prototype ready to fly in 1930. The first engine installed in the new "Cub" was the 2 cyl. Brownback (Light) "Tiger Kitten" of 20 h.p. but this engine would just barely fly the plane with the pilot alone. The little 9 cyl. (French) Salmson AD-9 of 40 h.p. finally flew the airplane with excellent results, but it was inadviseable to use this engine because of uncertain deliveries from abroad. After several other experiments the new 4 cyl. Continental A-40 engine of 35-37 h.p. was the final choice and proved to be a compatible mating with the "Cub". By Dec. of 1930 Taylor was already appointing dealers in various parts of the country. The "Cub E-2" was first certificated on a Group 2 approval numbered 2-358 (issued 6-15-31) for the first 14 airplanes; the ATC was issued later in the year. Proudly shown at the Detroit Air Show for 1932 as its first formal showing, Taylor also had several demonstrators on the field to entice prospective buyers. Riding out the lean years of 1932-33 with just enough production to break

even, 1934 was a better year for the "Cub E-2", and in 1935 over 200 were built. Petering off to only 7 built in 1936 the stalwart "Cub E-2" was finally discontinued in favor of the new model J-2.

The Taylor "Cub" model E-2 was basically an open-sided parasol monoplane with seating for two in tandem. A large curved windshield transformed the open cockpit into a semi-cabin, but this did not lessen the sporty atmosphere of flying out in the open; later models were available with a detachable enclosure to take the bite out of cold weather flying. Retaining some of the square corners and boxy features of the earlier "Chummy", the "Cub" was fairly large and impressed everyone as being a real airplane instead of just a "flivver". Very little more than a powered glider the "Cub E-2" taught hundreds the art of flying well on minimum power; good "Cub" pilots soon learned to coax extra useful performance out of the airplane by good pilotage. The E-2 was a happy-go-lucky airplane that didn't mind whether it was flown gingerly by a timid student or precisely by an expert, adjusting her mood easily to the tempo; mild-mannered and generally of placid nature, the "Cub" was however known to pull a small practical joke now and then. Powered with the 4 cyl. Continental A-40 engine of 37 h.p. the model E-2 had no power reserve to speak of, but the design was ingeniously arranged to coax good performance out of minimum power. Take-off runs were generally less than 200 ft., climb-out was pretty good for the first minute or so, and a waft of breeze held landing speeds down to about 25 m.p.h. Very

Fig. 190. Mary Babb approves of winter enclosure for 1934 "Cub;" feature was optional.

easy to fly, the "Cub" was fairly light on the controls with good response, and behaved well in all basic flight maneuvers. Pilots that normally flew heavier airplanes found the "Cub" full of surprises when flying it for the first time, but nearly all came down happier for the experience. Relatively docile and completely trustworthy, students and instructors alike felt at ease with the "Cub E-2", so naturally it was a great favorite at flying schools. Owner-pilots of the "Cub E-2" did not usually charge off into the blue on extensive cross-country trips, nor thrill those below with acrobatic shenanigans, they were content to enjoy the simple pleasures and the splendor of flight on a few dollars per hour. Had it not been for the likes of the "Cub" a great many could not have flown at all. Coming along rather late, and after the flivver-plane spree of 1930-31 the "Cub E-2" had a better chance to establish itself as a real airplane, that despite its light weight could boast of efficiency, strength and safety. The type certificate number for the "Cub" model E-2 was issued 11-7-31 and over 300 examples of this model were manufactured by the Taylor Aircraft Corp. at Bradford, Pa. C. Gilbert Taylor was president, general manager, and chief engineer; Wm. T. Piper was secretary-treasurer; and "Bud" Havens was company pilot. Walter C. Jamouneau was demonstrating the "Cub" around the country in 1934 and by 1935 had been appointed chief engineer. Mary Alice Babb took care of all the office work, and T. V. Weld later became sales manager.

Listed below are specifications and performance data for the Taylor "Cub" model E-2 as powered with the 37 h.p. Continental A-40-2 engine; length overall 22'3"; height over all 6'6"; wing span 35'3"; wing chord 63"; total wing area 184 sq.ft.; airfoil USA-35B; wt. empty 525 (532) lbs.; useful load 400 lbs.; payload with 9 gal. fuel 170 lbs.; gross wt. 925 (932) lbs.; wts. in brackets for 1935 model; max. speed 78; cruising speed 65; landing speed 28-30; climb 450 ft. first min. at sea level; ceiling 12,000 ft.; gas cap. 9 gal.; oil cap. 3 qts., later raised to 4 qts.; normal cruising range at 2.5 gal. per hour 220 miles; price $1325. at factory field in 1931-32-33, raised to $1425. in 1934-35. Gross wt. allowance increased to 970 lbs. on later models with empty wt. averaging at 556 lbs.

The Warren-truss fuselage framework was built up mainly of welded 1025 steel tubing with chrome-moly steel tubing and fittings at points of greater stress; the frame was lightly faired to shape and fabric covered. The cockpit was well protected by a large Pyralin windshield and a detachable enclosure was optional; entry was by way of a large let-down door on the right side. The cabin enclosure was not noticeably "faster" but it did make for a "cleaner" airplane, and kept gusts out of the cockpit during certain maneuvers. The interior was sparsely furnished and lacking in solid comforts, but was adequate for a craft of this type. Early models had no provision for baggage, but later models were allowed 5 lbs. The wing framework in two halves was built up of solid spruce spar beams with wing ribs riveted together of drawn aluminum alloy sections; the leading edges were covered with dural metal sheet and the completed framework was covered with fabric. Vee-type streamlined steel tubes braced the wing to lower fuselage fittings. Wing rigging started out with 1 deg. of incidence and ¾ deg. of dihedral with later models

Fig. 191. 1935 Model of "Cub" E-2 shown here as rebuilt 30 years later.

increasing incidence to 1¼ deg. and dihedral was flattened to 3/8 deg. The fuel tank was mounted high in the fuselage using a float-type fuel level gauge. The split-axle landing gear of 56 in. tread had faired vees on each side and used two spools of rubber shock-cord to snub the bumps; wheels were Goodyear 16x7-3 or 7.00x4 and no brakes were provided. 8.00x4 Goodyear airwheels with brakes were later optional. The "Cub E-2" was eligible on skis also. The fabric covered tail-group was built up of welded 1025 steel tubing and formed sheet steel sections; the fin was ground adjustable and the horizontal stabilizer was adjustable in flight. A wooden propeller and dual controls were standard equipment. A detachable enclosure and wheel brakes were later optional. Standard color schemes were variously as red and silver, blue and silver, yellow and black, yellow and blue. The next "Cub" development was the Aeromarine-powered model F-2 as described in the chapter for ATC # 525.

Listed below is a partial listing of "Cub E-2" entries as gleaned from registration records:

NC-11674; Cub E-2 (# 26) Cont. A-40.

NC-12607;	" (# 27)	"
NC-12608;	" (# 28)	"
NC-12609;	" (# 29)	"
NC-12610;	" (# 30)	"
NC-2414 ;	" (# 64)	"
NC-2434 ;	" (# 65)	"
NC-2761 ;	" (# 67)	"
NC-2780 ;	" (# 68)	"
NC-2994 ;	" (# 69)	"
NC-2999 ;	" (# 70)	"
NC-9376 ;	" (# 72)	"
NC-9377 ;	" (# 73)	"
NC-746N ;	" (# 79)	"
NC-743N ;	" (# 80)	"
NC-747N ;	" (# 81)	"
NC-798N ;	" (# 82)	"
NC-951V ;	" (# 83)	"
NC-2119 ;	" (# 84)	"
NC-2120 ;	" (# 85)	"
NC-2126 ;	" (# 86)	"
NC-2169 ;	" (# 88)	"
NC-14310;	" (# 91)	"
NC-14312;	" (# 93)	"
NC-14327;	" (# 94)	"

This approval for ser. # 26 and up; NC-12626 was ser. # 31 and numbers ran consecutively to NC-12630 which was ser. # 35; NC-12664 was ser. # 36 and numbers ran consecutively to NC-12668 which was ser. # 40; NC-12695 was ser. # 41 and numbers ran consecutively to NC-12698 which was ser. # 44; NC-13115 was ser. # 45 and numbers ran consecutively to NC-13120 which was ser. # 50; NC-13143 was ser. # 51 and numbers ran consecutively to NC-13147 which was ser. # 55; NC-13175 was ser. # 56 and numbers ran consecutively to NC-13179 which was ser. # 60; NC-2394 was ser. # 61 and numbers ran consecutively to NC-2396 which was ser. # 63; NC-14328 was ser. # 95 and numbers ran consecutively to NC-14332 which was ser: # 99; ser. # 40 modified to model F-2; ser. # 66, 74, 77, 78, 87, 89, as model F-2 on ATC # 525; ser. # 71, 75, 76, 87, 90, 92, not listed; this approval expired 3-24-37.

A.T.C. # 456
(12-16-31)
HEATH "PARASOL", LNB-4

Fig. 192. Heath LNB-4 with 27 h.p. Heath B-4 engine.

A newcomer to the ranks of "approved aircraft", but with a five-year operational history already to its credit, the diminutive Heath "Parasol" finally made its debut into the select circle. As a popular home-built airplane, flying in all parts of this country and even abroad, the little "Parasol" was certainly well known and very well liked. After a reorganization of the company and a subsequent move from Chicago to Niles, Mich. the Heath "Parasol", like some country bumpkin was all dressed up in a brand new outfit and groomed for government approval. Still basically similar to models built previous,the approved Heath was first offered as the model LNB-4, a single-place open cockpit monoplane powered with the 4 cyl. Heath B-4 inline engine. Putting on some weight and some cross-section here and there the LNB-4 was much more buxom and in general appeared very much larger, but the changes were of some benefit to its behavior and to its performance. As the lowest-priced approved airplane in this country the new "Parasol" held yet another distinction in that it was the only airplane that could be built at home from factory-made assembly kits into an airplane that was eligible for government (ATC) license. Of course, all work had to be done at intervals under the watchful eye of the government inspector. As a cheap and economical airplane that was fun to own and fun to fly, the Heath LNB-4 offered many the chance to play sportsman on a low budget, or to build up low-cost time towards a more advanced pilot license.

The happy heart of the LNB-4 was the Heath B-4 engine, an upright 4 cyl. air-cooled powerplant that was basically similar to the tried and proven Heath-Henderson, a conversion of the popular Henderson motorcycle engine. That is, it was more popular for small airplanes than it ever was in motorcycles. Extensively redesigned to conform to requirements for aircraft engines the Heath B-4 developed 25 h.p. at 2800 r.p.m. giving very reliable service with reasonable care. Weighing about 115 lbs. without a propeller the Heath B-4 engine could be purchased separately for $300.00. When properly tuned and in good running order the Heath B-4 was perhaps the smoothest running engine one could hope to have up front; whether purring like a kitten, or humming like a honey-bee, it was a delightful and memorable sound.

The background development of the Heath model LNB-4 naturally centers around one Edward Bayard Heath who assembled his first home-built airplane back in 1908 and flew it successfully in 1909. A rather small man of likeable personality Ed Heath fervently believed in a future for the light airplane and built several types that earned him national recognition. Since his baptism into aeronautics Heath had made aviation as his way of life, living it almost day and night. Surrounding himself with surplus war-time airplanes (World War I) and parts of all description Ed Heath ran a "trading post" for many years, and also operated a successful flying school. The first Heath "Parasol" as designed by Ed Heath and Clare Lindstedt was

Fig.193. Metal-framed ailerons on earlier LNB-4 changed to wooden frames on later models.

introduced in 1926 and was met early with great interest. Soon available in kit form for fabrication or for assembly by the so-called home-builder the simple "Parasol" skyrocketed into popularity because it intrigued those of mechanical aptitude and offered them a cheap way to fly. Progressively improved as time went by, the "Super Parasol" of 1930-31 was the finest airplane in its class; national and international records can prove this. Despite the crippling business depression that forced many others to close their factory doors, the flivver-type "Parasol" was holding steadily in national and international popularity. In fact, the "hard times" were a boon to his business. A disciple of constant development and improvement, Ed Heath experimented almost constantly and almost always did the test-flying himself. In Feb. of 1931 a structural failure during a test-flight of an experimental low-wing airplane resulted in a fatal crash with Ed Heath going down to his death, a tragic end to a brilliant career. It must have been the secret hope of Ed Heath to see his little "Parasol" someday become a full-fledged "certificated aircraft", but he didn't live to see it. The death of Ed Heath brought about a reorganization of the Heath Airplane Co. into the new Heath Aircraft Corp. which moved the operation from Chicago in May of 1931 to larger quarters in Niles, Mich.

The Heath model LNB-4 was a light open cockpit parasol-type monoplane with seating for one only. The LNB-4 was not technically listed as the "Parasol", but for many years the "Heath Parasol" was as one word, so just from habit it was hard for the new LNB-4 to escape this familiar title. Formally introduced at the Detroit Air Show for 1932 its exhibit drew large crowds of interested people. As a single-place airplane the LNB-4 was naturally destined to be used mostly for sport, but some owners who had learned to fly on other light airplanes used the Heath to build up inexpensive solo time towards a pilot's license. As developed in this new version, the familiar "Parasol" was now larger, taller, nearly 200 lbs. heavier, and faired out to a well-rounded buxom form. Much of this "frost-

ing" as it were, helped to make the new LNB-4 less like a "flivver" and more like a regular airplane. To this treatment the new "Parasol" reacted with some mixed feelings; it was definitely faster because of better streamlining, but the added weight was a cumbersome burden that was some detriment to its former spritely nature. As powered with the 4 cyl. Heath B-4 engine of 25 h.p. the LNB-4 was still able to deliver a commendable performance but the edge was taken off slightly by the added weight. Increased wing area got it off the ground with a surprisingly short run, and any normal pasture was a suitable landing field. Climb-out, because of the high power-loading, was somewhat slow, and it would take nearly an hour to reach its ceiling, but that was of little matter to the average "Heath" pilot. Easy to fly, delightfully responsive, and quite honest in its behavior, the LNB-4 "Parasol" was strictly for fun. As one owner put it: "The only thing wrong with the "Heath" was that the cockpit was too narrow to contain the big grins of pilots who flew it for the first time"! The type certificate number for the model LNB-4 was issued 12-16-31 and at least 6 examples of this model were manufactured by the Heath Aircraft Corp. at Niles, Mich. into 1933. It is not known how many were sold in kit form. Gen. John V. Clinnin was president; Walter A. Clinnin was V.P.; James F. Morrison was secretary-treasurer; R. J. Byrnes was sales manager; and Chas. W. Morris was chief engineer.

Listed below are specifications and performance data for the Heath model LNB-4 as powered with the 25 h.p. Heath B-4 engine; length overall 17'3"; height overall 6-2"; wing span 31'3"; wing chord 54"; total wing area 135.5 sq.ft.; airfoil Clark Y; wt. empty 450 lbs.; useful load 250 lbs.; crew wt. 170 lbs., plus 16 lbs. baggage; gross wt. 700 lbs.; max. speed 73; cruising speed 62; landing speed 32, climb 350 ft. first min. at sea level; ceiling 9000 ft.; gas cap. 9 gal.; oil cap. 6 qts.; cruising range at 2.4 gal. per hour 215 miles; price $1074. at factory in 1932, lowered to $925. in 1933. Low down payment (⅓) and easy monthly payment plan was available. The home assembly kit less engine was available

Fig. 194. Willis Kysor approves of LNB-4 with a smile.

for $499. early in 1932, lowered to $399. in July of 1932.

The fuselage framework was built up of welded steel tubing, heavily faired with wooden formers and fairing strips to a well-rounded shape, then fabric covered. The cockpit was deep, well protected by a large Pyralin wind-shield, and neatly upholstered in Fabrikoid; easy entry was by way of a large door on the left side. A small baggage bin of .5 cu. ft. capacity had allowance for up to 16 lbs. The inline Heath B-4 engine was neatly cowled and well baffled for better streamlining and proper airflow. The wing in two halves was built up of solid spruce

Fig. 195. Heath LNB-4 on skis for winter flying.

spar beams with spruce and plywood truss-type wing ribs; the leading edges were covered with dural metal sheet and the completed framework was covered with fabric. A high-altitude wing of 169 sq. ft. area was available for operation in high mountainous areas. A 4.5 gal. fuel tank was mounted in the root end of each wing half, and 2 small skylights provided vision overhead. Metal-framed narrow chord ailerons spanned full length of each wing half, being directly controlled by push-pull struts coming out of the cockpit. The wing was perched high atop a cabane of inverted-vee steel tube struts with N-type wing bracing struts on each side. The wing placement offered good visibility and excellent pendulum stability. The split-axle landing gear of 48 in. tread used Rusco rubber shock absorbing rings; wheels were 16x4 disc type and brakes were optional. 7.00x4 low pressure tires on one-piece wheels and disc brakes were also optional. The fabric covered tail-group was built up of welded steel tubing; both fin and horizontal stabilizer were adjustable for trim on ground only. Wing rigging used 4 deg. angle of incidence and dihedral was 2 deg. A Heath wooden propeller, and fire extinguisher bottle were standard equipment. A metal propeller, engine starter, and wheel brakes were optional for $90.00 extra. A complete kit of factory-made assemblies, minus the engine and propeller, were available to the home-builder for $499.00. A Heath hardwood propeller was $25.00 and the Heath B-4 engine was priced at $300.00 crated for delivery. The next Heath development was the model LNA-40 as described in the chapter for ATC # 487 of this volume.

Listed below are LNB-4 entries as gleaned from registration records:

-10738;LN	(#149)	Heath B-4.	
NC-10739; LNB-4	(# 150)	"	
NC-10740;	" (# 151)	"	
;	" (# 154)	"	
;	" (# 156)	"	
;	" (# 157)	"	
;	" (# 158)	"	
;	" (# 159)	"	
NC-13153;	" (# 1000)	"	

This approval for ser. # 150, 154, 156, 157, 158, 159, and up; this approval expired 12-1-35 due to sale to Howard E. Anthony (Heath Aviation Co.) of Benton Harbor, Mich.; this listing represents a poor showing of factory-built examples, but many of the LNB-4 were built up from factory kits by owners who then listed them as Spencer-Heath, the so-and-so "Parasol", etc. using their own "manufacturers serial number"; these were not listed here.

A.T.C. # 457
(1-25-32)
STINSON, MODEL R

Fig. 196. Stinson "Model R" with 215 h.p. Lycoming engine; new series was significant step in "Stinson" development.

Stinson Aircraft had achieved great success with their basic "Junior" design for over four years, but it had finally reached its market peak. Progressively improved during this time, the "Junior" kept getting better and better, but to gain any more performance or utility now called for some changes. Still using the basic "Junior" concept several innovations were added to it to increase performance, comfort, and utility in a machine that still looked very much like a "Junior", but there the similarity ended. Somewhat of a milestone in Stinson design, the new craft was simply labeled the "Model R". The fuselage took on much deeper proportion for more head and leg room, the efficient engine cowling was blended into fuselage lines as more of a built-in instead of an add-on, and the most conspicuous change was, of course, the landing gear. What could be called a stub-wing was built into the bottom of forward fuselage serving as attach points for the wing-bracing struts, and also the landing gear; it is easy to see that a folding undercarriage was planned for this series early in the design stages. The retracting gear was not introduced on the "Model R" as discussed here, but was introduced later on the "Model R-3". Previewed

early in 1932 the Model R was powered with the 9 cyl. Lycoming R-680 engine of 215 h.p. and was specifically offered as a truly deluxe cabin transport for the private owner. Handsomely restyled both inside and out the "R" offered roomy comfort, quiet, numerous operational aids, and a noticeable boost in operational performance. Coming fully equipped for much less than $6000. it posed as just about the best cabin airplane bargain in the country at this time. Oddly enough, many prospective customers for this new airplane had just recently bought the Model S, so only a few had reason or means to make a change to the improved Model R. Ben Lyon, a Hollywood movie-actor who often starred in aviation movies, also flew for sport; his latest pride was the Model R. Sportfliers and business-houses showed the greatest interest in the new Model R, but its national acceptance fell far short as compared to previous "Junior-types". Confronted with perhaps the leanest period (1932-33) in aircraft sales it is commendable that at least 30 of these were built and sold.

The Stinson "Model R" was a high-winged cabin monoplane with seating arranged for four. Cabin dimensions were now increased up

Fig. 197. Eddie Stinson stands proudly in front of Model R.

and across for more room, upholstery was padded deeper, and cabin walls were thickly lined for more quiet. The basic changes in the new "R" were custom items that people often asked for in the previous "Junior" types, so these items and more were all incorporated into the new series; the Model R was strictly deluxe in every sense. As the first in this new series the Model R was powered with the 9 cyl. Lycoming R-680 engine of 215 h.p. which was neatly encased in a NACA-type low-drag cowling that was carefully blended into fuselage lines; all exterior lines were a good bit "cleaner" now and performance increases were noticeable in some instances. In general, the Model R handled and performed as well as any of the "Stinson" monoplanes with perhaps the feel and ride of a much bigger ship. Delivering a smooth, quiet ride regardless of conditions or the weather, the "R" was ideal for extended

Fig. 198. "Stinson R" aimed at luxury and prestige for a bargain price.

cross-country travel; business-houses and sport-fliers found this much to their liking. The Model R was a lot of good airplane for the money, but the $1000. hike over the price of the Model S was a hurdle it found hard to jump; even then it sold fairly well in view of the times. Stinson Aircraft sold 139 of their four-place monoplanes in 1931, or about 90% of such airplanes built by all the other companies; Stinson was not to do as well in the next two years. The type certificate number for the Model R was issued 1-25-32 and at least 30 examples of this model were manufactured by the Stinson Aircraft Corp. at Wayne, Mich. On Jan. 26 of 1932 the whole world was saddened by the death of "Eddie" Stinson; demonstrating the new Model R over Chicago, Stinson was forced to a landing that resulted in a mortal injury.

Listed below are specifications and performance data for the Stinson model R as powered with the 215 h.p. Lycoming R-680 engine; length overall 26'1"; height overall 8'9"; wing span 43'3"; wing chord 75"; total wing area 235 sq.ft.; airfoil Clark Y; wt. empty 2225 lbs.; useful load 1100 lbs.; payload with 55 gal. fuel 560 lbs. (3 pass. at 170 lb. each & 50 lb. baggage); gross wt. 3325 lbs.; max. speed 130; cruising speed 110; landing speed 52; climb 675 ft. first min. at sea level; ceiling 12,500 ft.; gas cap. 51-56 gal.; oil cap. 4-5 gal.; cruising range at 12.4 gal. per hour 450 miles; price $5595. at factory field; delivered to west coast for $5962.

The fuselage framework was built up of welded chrome-moly steel tubing, rounded off with formers and fairing strips, then fabric covered. Adjustable front seats were individual and rear seat was of the bench type; a large rectangular door and a convenient step on either side offered easy entry. Cabin walls were thickly lined with Balsam Wool for sound-proofing and insulation, and all windows were of shatter-proof glass; cabin comfort was assured by ample heat and ventilation. The baggage compartment with allowance for 50 lbs. was behind the rear seat. Dual wheel controls, a complete set of Pioneer instruments, and numerous operational aids were also provided. The large vee-type windshield extended further forward and offered better visibility. The semi-cantilever wing framework was built up of solid spruce spars that were routed to an I-beam section with stamped-out duralumin wing ribs; the leading edges were covered with dural metal sheet and the completed framework was covered in fabric. The stub-wing of welded chrome-moly steel tubing was built integral to the fuselage and served as attach points for the wing-bracing

struts and also the landing gear. The semi-cantilever landing gear of 96 in. tread was fitted with oleo-spring shock absorbing struts; wheels were 8.50x10 and self-energizing brakes were standard equipment. A parking brake was also provided. A 5.00x4 tail wheel was fitted and all wheels were shrouded with streamlined "pants". The larger fabric covered tail-group was built up of welded steel tubing; the rudder was aerodynamically balanced and the horizontal stabilizer was adjustable in flight. An adj. metal propeller, an exhaust collector-ring, NACA-type engine cowl, wheel pants, electric engine starter, battery, navigation lights, wheel brakes, parking brake, cabin heater, dual wheel controls, and Pioneer instruments were standard equipment. Standard color scheme was black and red with other color combinations optional. A 73 gal. fuel capacity was also optional. The next development in the R-series was the "Model R-2" as described in the chapter for ATC # 489 of this volume.

Listed below are Model R entries as gleaned from registration records:

NC-12147; Model R (# 8501) R-680.
NC-12148;   "   (# 8502)   "
NC-12149;   "   (# 8503)   "
NC-12150;   "   (# 8504)   "
NC-12151;   "   (# 8505)   "
NC-12152;   "   (# 8506)   "
NC-12153;   "   (# 8507)   "
NC-12154;   "   (# 8508)   "
NC-12155;   "   (# 8509)   "
NC-436M;   "   (# 8511)   "
NC-12159;   "   (# 8513)   "
NC-10874;   "   (# 8514)   "
NC-10861;   "   (# 8515)   "
NC-10876;   "   (# 8516)   "
NC-437M;   "   (# 8517)   "
NC-440M;   "   (# 8518)   "
NC-12139;   "   (# 8519)   "
NC-439M;   "   (# 8520)   "
NC-12124;   "   (# 8523)   "
NC-438M;   "   (# 8524)   "
NC-12138;   "   (# 8525)   "
NC-479M;   "   (# 8527)   "
NC-12125;   "   (# 8528)   "
NC-12134;   "   (# 8529)   "
NC-12888;   "   (# 8530)   "
NC-12189;   "   (# 8531)   "
NC-446M;   "   (# 8532)   "
NC-12197;   "   (# 8533)   "

This approval for ser. # 8501 and up; ser. # 8503 unverified; ser. # 8510, 8522, 8526 not listed; ser. # 8500, 8512 and 8521 as Model R-2; last 3 or 4 a/c mfgd. 1933; this approval expired 2-1-34.

A.T.C. # 458
(2-12-32)
STEARMAN "CLOUDBOY", 6-H

Fig. 199. Stearman model 6-H with 170 h.p. Kinner engine; rating later raised to 190-210 h.p.

Following the successful development of the 300 h.p. model 6-D, Stearman Aircraft decided to split the power difference and brought out two models of the "Six" in the 200 h.p. range. One of these as discussed here was the 6-H version of the standard "Cloudboy" series. Typical of the series the model 6-H was perhaps unusual only in the fact that it was powered with the big 5 cyl. Kinner C5 (R-715) engine of 210 h.p. Earlier examples of this engine were rated 190 h.p. at 1800 r.p.m., but later designated as the C5 and rerated, this engine developed 210 h.p. at 1900 r.p.m. With each "jug" (cylinder) developing over 40 h.p. the widely spaced "wallops" (firing strokes) produced an uncomfortable roughness that occasionally wrought havoc to various parts of the average airframe. The Stearman 6-H was indeed tough and stood up well to this pounding abuse; NC-786H was delivered to Hanford Air Lines and used for varied service into 1934. Both known examples of the 6-H were subsequently modified into the 6-L. In 1935 one 6-H (probably NC-564Y) was equipped with a "hood" and full panels of Kollsman instruments for blind-flight training. Not particularly a successful model, the short-lived 6-H, however, must have left many lasting and mixed impressions on those who flew it. The Army Air Corps equivalent to the commercial

6-H was the Kinner-powered YPT-9C.

The Stearman model 6-H was an open cockpit biplane with seating arranged for two in tandem. Designed primarily for the advanced stages of pilot training the 6-H took a spot about midway in the complete 6-series lineup. Powered with the big "hairy" 5 cyl. Kinner C5 engine of 210 h.p. the 6-H had ample muscle available to perform very well, and there was constant reminder up front that the bit "Kinner" was making it possible. The 6-H was a he-man type of craft, so flight characteristics and general behavior were not necessarily conducive to a smooth, relaxed ride, but close attention to pilotage produced very good results. Built rugged and kept simple it was hoped that the "Cloudboy" would find some favor amongst the civilian flying schools, but the prevailing economic situation stifled any interest that might have developed. The type certificate number for the model 6-H was issued 2-12-32 and 1 example of this model was converted from another existing "Stearman Six"; X-564Y was manufactured originally as the model 6-H. A good indication of the way things were going in the aircraft industry in the closing days of 1931, was the fact that only 67 approved type certificates were issued in that year. Bemoaning the circumstances, of course, many manufacturers did

Fig. 200. Stearman model 6-H; military counterpart was YPT-9C.

not fully realize that the worst was yet to come.

Listed below are specifications and performance data for the Stearman model 6-H as powered with the 210 h.p. Kinner C5 engine; length overall 23'11"; height overall (tail up) 9'7"; wing span upper 32'0"; wing span lower 28'0"; wing chord upper & lower 60"; wing area upper 150.3 sq.ft.; wing area lower 121.9 sq.ft.; total wing area 272.2 sq.ft.; airfoil N-22; wt. empty 1810 [1893] lbs.; useful load 666 [834] lbs.; payload with 38 [66] gal. fuel 230 [229] lbs.; gross wt. 2476 [2727] lbs.; wts. in brackets show amended wt. allowance for 66 gal. fuel; max. speed 119; cruising speed 100; landing (stall) speed 47 [52]; climb 880 [828] ft. first min. at sea level; ceiling 15,200 [14,650] ft.; gas cap. normal 38 gal.; gas cap. max. 66 gal.; oil cap. 5 gal.; cruising range at 12 gal. per hour 300-500 miles; price not announced. Payload includes 1 pass. at 170 lbs., 2 parachutes, and 20 lb. baggage.

The fuselage framework was built up of welded chrome-moly steel tubing in a rigid truss form lightly faired to shape and fabric covered. The Army-type cockpits were quite large and well accessible, with the protection of large 3-piece safety-glass windshields. Dual controls were provided and metal bucket-type seats were adjustable for height. A small baggage bin with allowance for 20 lbs. was located in the turtle-back section behind the rear cockpit. The robust wing framework was built up of heavy-sectioned spruce spar beams with spruce and mahogany plywood truss-type wing ribs; the leading edges were covered with dural metal sheet and the completed framework was covered in fabric. A gravity-feed fuel tank of 38 gal. cap. was mounted in the center-section panel of the upper wing; this assembly was supported above the fuselage by two N-type struts of streamlined steel tubing. An auxiliary fuel tank of 28 gal. cap. was mounted high in fuselage ahead of front cockpit. The four Friese-type ailerons were connected together in pairs by a streamlined push-pull strut. N-type interplane struts were of heavy gauge streamlined steel tubing, and interplane bracing was of heavy gauge steel wire. The stout outrigger landing gear of 85 in. tread used "Aerol" (air-oil) shock absorbing struts; wheels were 30x5 and Bendix brakes were standard equipment. A swivel-mounted tail wheel was attached to very end of fuselage for a longer wheelbase. The fabric covered tail-group was built up of welded 4130 steel tubing; the fin was ground adjustable and the horizontal stabilizer was adjustable in flight. A metal propeller, hand crank inertia-type engine starter, dual controls, and wheel brakes were standard equipment. Navigation lights, landing lights, battery, 28 gal. aux. fuel tank, and extra instruments were optional. The next development in the Stearman 6 was the model 6-L as described in the next chapter of this volume.

Listed below are the only known model 6-H entries per registration records:

NC-786H; Model 6-H (# 6001) Kinner C5.
NC-564Y;   "   (# 6009)   "

Ser. # 6001 originally as 6-A; ser. # 6009 originally built as 6-H later converted to 6-A and 6-L; approval for 6-H expired 2-15-34.

A.T.C. # 459
(2-18-32)
STEARMAN "CLOUDBOY", 6-L

Fig. 201. Stearman 6-L trainer at Boeing School of Aeronautics.

Perhaps one of the more practical versions of the "Stearman 6" biplane, the model 6-L was powered with the popular 9 cyl. Lycoming R-680 engine; dependable, exceptionally smooth-running, and developing 215 h.p. the Lycoming engine was a compatible mate for the versatile "Cloudboy". This particular mating produced a very likeable combination. Developed especially for the advanced stages of pilot training, the 6-L was later in use on the flight-line of the Boeing School of Aeronautics. Development of the model 6-L and its subsequent use by the Boeing school had much to do with the development of the famous Boeing "Kaydet" as used in training schools during the World War 2 period. Born and bred as an all-round training airplane the model 6-L was eligible for use in aerobatic and secondary stages of flight-training in the Civilian Pilot Training Program (CPTP) Of the 6 commercial models that were finally built in the 6-series, two examples have survived the ravages of time and neglect, and both have been carefully rebuilt to the model 6-L specifications. Standing proudly in all its splendor, the NC-788H, as shown here, is no doubt in better condition than when new. As

the final development in the Stearman 6 training plane series the model 6-L also had a counterpart in the Army Air Corps as the YPT-9B. One final version was built in the 6-series, but it was more of a special sport-plane than a trainer; as the model 6-C with a 330 h.p. Wright R-975C engine, it was approved on a Group 2 memo # 2-457. All that were concerned with the "Six" and the YPT-9 must have had an interesting time creating and recreating all these different versions; it certainly speaks well for the versatility of the "Stearman 6" design.

The Stearman model 6-L was an open cockpit biplane with seating arranged for two in tandem. Developed especially for the secondary stages of pilot-training, the 215 h.p. Lycoming furnished optimum power for a satisfactory all-round performance. Every airframe had its best combination, and this seemed to be about the best combination for the Stearman 6. With spirited response and cooperative behavior, the 6-L was especially a suitable airplane for aerobatic training in the CPTP program. Whereas many airplanes had definite feminine character and better enjoyed being treated as ladies, the "Six" was more like a tom-boy that enjoyed

Fig. 202. 3 "Stearman 6" prepare to leave factory; two YPT-9B in background, and YPT-9C in foreground.

the rough-and-tumble. The type certificate number for the model 6-L was issued 2-18-32 and some 3 examples of this version were converted from other models of the "Stearman 6". Manufactured by the Stearman Aircraft Div. of the United Aircraft & Transport Corp. at Wichita, Kansas. J. E. Shaefer was now president and treasurer; Mac Short was V.P. and chief engineer. As of about April of 1932, Stearman was sharply curtailing its plant activities, a move dictated by the relentless depression. All Stearman biplanes would still be on the production list, but built only on customer order. As of this particular date the Northrop "Alpha" and the "Beta" would also be discontinued from the production list. During the prevailing economic conditions of this particular period the plant acted primarily as a service-center for Stearman, Northrop, and Hamilton airplanes. The engineering department headed by Mac Short, continued almost in force in effort to develop new designs. Some of these were for commercial operators and private owners; the military market both here and abroad was also more thoroughly investigated. Later in the year of 1932, Stearman took on some of Boeing's work by fabricating landing gears, tail wheel assemblies, and other small parts for the Model 247 airliner. Thus, the Stearman Div. managed to survive through the worst of it while marking time for better days ahead.

Listed below are specifications and performance data for the Stearman model 6-L as powered with the 215 h.p. Lycoming R-680 engine; length overall 23'8"; height overall (tail up) 9'7"; wing span upper 32'0"; wing span lower 28'0"; wing chord upper & lower 60"; wing area upper 150.3 sq.ft.; wing area lower 121.9 sq.ft.; total wing area 272.2 sq.ft.; airfoil N-22; wt. empty 1880 (1952) lbs.; useful load 671 (797) lbs.; payload with 38 gal. fuel 235 lbs.; payload with 59 gal. fuel 235 lbs.; gross wt. 2551 (2749) lbs.; wts. in brackets as amended for 59 gal. fuel & extra eqpt.; max.

speed 120; cruising speed 100; landing (stall) speed 47 (52); climb 875 (820) ft. first min. at sea level; ceiling 15,000 (14,500) ft.; gas cap. normal 38 gal.; gas cap. max. 63 gal.; oil cap. 5 gal.; cruising range at 12 gal. per hour 300-500 miles; price not announced.

The construction details and general arrangement of the model 6-L were typical to that of the 6-H as described in the previous chapter (ATC # 458). Other pertinent data as follows. A baggage bin with allowance for up to 25 lbs. was in turtle-back section behind the rear cockpit. Two parachutes at 20 lbs. each were part of payload. Main fuel tank of 38 gal. cap. was mounted in center-section panel of the upper wing; direct-reading fuel gauges were visible from either cockpit. An auxiliary fuel tank of 25 gal. cap. was mounted high in fuselage just ahead of the front cockpit. Four metal-framed ailerons were covered with corrugated dural metal sheet; the unusual aileron actuation was transmitted through streamlined push-pull tubes that were fastened to a point ahead of the aileron hinge line. There was a large cut-out in trailing edge of the upper wing for visibility upward and better access to the front cockpit. The lower wings had a wing-walk on either side, and they were neatly faired in at the fuselage junction; lower wing-tips had hand-holds to assist in ground handling. 30x5 wheels with Bendix brakes were standard equipment; brake pedals were provided in both cockpits. A metal propeller, hand crank inertia-type engine starter, exhaust collector ring, dual controls, and fire extinguisher were standard equipment. Extra instruments, navigation lights, landing lights, battery, 25 gal. aux. fuel tank, and first-aid kit were optional. The final development in the "Stearman 6" was the 330 h.p. Wright powered model 6-C as on Group 2 approval numbered 2-457; the next immediate Stearman development was the "Sportster" model 80 as described in the chapter for ATC # 504.

Fig. 203. Beautiful reproduction of 6-L was "grand champion" at national meet.

Listed below are model 6-L entries as gleaned from registration records:

NC-786H; Model 6-L (#6001) Lycoming 215.
NC-788H;   "   (# 6003)   "
NC-795H;   "   (# 6004)   "

Ser. # 6001 was the only example that was converted to each successive development in the 6-series, namely 6-A, 6-F, 6-D, 6-H, 6-L; ser. # 6009 (NC-564Y) also as 6-L at one time; approval for 6-L expired 9-30-39.

Fig. 204. Two-seated model KBA with 100 h.p. Kinner K5 engine; first example in sport-plane series.

Although the popular "Waco" models F and F-1 were largely used by private pilots for sport-flying, both models basically retained the flavor and aptitude of an all-purpose airplane; both somehow had the looks and behavior of an airplane that had to work occasionally to earn its keep. To catch the fancy of those that were looking for an airplane designed especially for sport, Waco Aircraft developed the "Model A" a craft more attuned to the unique and special needs of the flying sportsman or the business-man pilot. With companionable seating for two and ample room for scads of personal baggage, the first version of this series of sport-craft was announced in Feb. of 1932 as the model KBA. Powered with the Kinner K5 engine of 100 h.p. the KBA was the cheapest model in this prolific series, but actually proved less desirable than the up-coming models that enjoyed the installation of more horsepower. In the program of development for the A-series, the prototype model KBA airplane (X-12435) was alternately used as a test-bed in the mounting of various engines. Popular engines with a power spread from 110 h.p. to 210 h.p. were used in the makeup of the models RBA, IBA, PBA, TBA, the rare BBA, and the UBA; the latter being the ultimate in this "sport" series. Although scarce in the number built of its own kind, the model KBA served quite well to spring-board the progressive development of

this interesting series of Waco airplanes.

The Waco model KBA was an open cockpit biplane arranged with the chummy seating of two side-by-side in the sporty atmosphere of a single open cockpit. For those wishing to enjoy their flying in relative "indoor comfort", a detachable coupe-top was available. In limiting the seating capacity to two, ample allowance was provided for up to 136 lbs. of personal luggage or other sport-type gear for extended travel or just outdoor fun. Inheriting the notable "Waco" characteristics of outstanding short-field performance also, the Model A was an airplane one could put down most anywhere as whim or necessity dictated. Powered with the 5 cyl. Kinner K5 engine of 100 h.p. the model KBA did have some limitations in its all-round performance, but its easy, pleasant nature and dutiful character could provide the tops in flying enjoyment. Economical to operate and of sturdy airframe requiring very little maintenance, the KBA posed well as the ideal for the low-budget sportsman. With a firm belief that the new KBA would be warmly received on the aircraft market, Waco Aircraft soon realized that those people who could afford to fly for sport at all, were interested in more powerful airplanes with better performance. This fact actually didn't hold any disappointment because Waco already had other models in the making that held up where the KBA had failed. Whether in error or not we could not determine, but this version was first listed repeatedly as the model KCA; in Waco coded designations, this would signify that it probably had the "C" wings of 1931 in experimental prototype and later changed to "B" wings of 1932 in subsequent production models. The type certificate number for the model KBA was issued 2-24-32 and only one example of this model was built by the Waco Aircraft Co. at Troy, Ohio.

Listed below are specifications and performance data for the Waco model KBA as powered with the 100 h.p. Kinner K5 engine; length overall 21'11"; height overall 8'8"; wing span upper 29'6"; wing span lower 27'5"; wing chord upper & lower 57"; wing area upper 130 sq.ft.; wing area lower 111 sq.ft.; total wing area 241 sq.ft.; airfoil Clark Y; wt. empty 1259 lbs.; useful load 726 lbs.; payload with 32 gal. fuel 341 lbs. (1 pass. at 170 lb., 2 parrachutes, 136 lbs. baggage); gross wt. 1985 lbs.; max. speed 101; cruising speed 86; landing (stall) speed 40; climb 590 ft. first min. at sea level; ceiling 10,500 ft.; gas cap. 32 gal.; oil cap. 3-3½ gal.; cruising range at 6.5 gal. per hour 380 miles; price $3585. at factory field.

The fuselage framework was built up of welded chrome-moly steel tubing, faired to shape with wooden formers and fairing strips, then fabric covered. The wide cockpit with side-by-side seating had comfortable form-fitting seats with a large entry door on left-hand side; deep and well arranged, the cockpit was well protected by a large windshield. A detachable coupe-top weighing 20 lbs. was optional for cold-weather flying. A large luggage bin forward of the cockpit had allowance for up to 100 lbs. and was accessible through a large door on left-hand side; a long locker in the turtle-back section, with allowance for 36 lbs., had ample room for golf clubs, guns, fisghing rods, and other sporting gear. Both lockers had locking-type doors. The wing framework was built up of solid spruce spar beams with spruce and plywood truss-type wing ribs; the leading edges were covered with dural metal sheet and the completed framework was covered in fabric. Two gravity-feed fuel tanks were mounted in the center-section panel of the upper wing; float-type fuel gauges were visible from the cockpit. The rugged landing gear of 71 in. tread used "Waco" oleo-spring shock absorbing struts; low pressure semi-airwheels were 6.50x10 and wheel brakes were optional A 10x3 tail wheel was provided for better ground handling. The fabric covered tail-group was built up of welded steel tubing; the horizontal stabilizer was adjustable in flight. A Hartzell wooden propeller, and Heywood engine starter were standard equipment. A metal propeller, coupe-top for cockpit, navigation lights, dual controls, and wheel brakes were optional. The next development in the Model A series was the Jacobs-powered PBA as described in the chapter for ATC # 464 of this volume.

Listed below is the only KBA entry in registration records:

NC-12435; Model KBA (# 3585) Kinner K5.

A.T.C. # 461
(2-25-32)
STEARMAN-NORTHROP "ALPHA",
4-A

Fig. 205. Model 4-A was cargo-carrying version of Northrop "Alpha;" note where new metal strip blocks out windows.

Already operating successfully in an all-passenger version, or the combination passenger-cargo version, it was evident that the "Alpha" could do well especially as an all-cargo version. The continued gradual increase in cargo tonnage and especially the popularity of air-express shipments, had much to do with changing the "Alpha's" role and extending its useful life for several more years. Range of the "Alpha" and its high cruising speed were ideal for perishable shipments, or those that were urgently needed from distant points in the least possible time. Freshly cut Calif. gardenias were shipped out of San Francisco daily to florists in New York on a 23-hour schedule. Other exotic payloads included silk-worms, medicinal

Fig. 206. Alpha 4-A were equipped with de-icer boots for winter operation.

Fig. 207. 4-A were equipped with night-flying equipment and radio for around the clock service.

serum for emergency cases, fresh orchids, vials of costly perfume, and even boxes of false eyelashes. Of course, all loads were not made up of such interesting shipments; auto parts, textile goods, and misc. packages were most always the average load. To perform efficiently in high-speed transport required the use of several new aids, so it befell the "Alpha" to test many of these in actual service. The use of aircraft radio was yet in its relative infancy, and the "Alpha" did much to perfect its improvement. On the eastern division of the TWA line it was the "Alpha" that had the first commercial installation of the Goodrich "de-icer boot"; these inflatable rubber boots prevented the formation of ice on the wings. An encounter with icing conditions on many flights that first winter proved

that the "boots" on the "Alpha's" leading edges removed ice successfully and prevented schedules from being cancelled because of wintry weather. The "Alpha" we speak of here in such complimentary fashion, is the Stearman-Northrop model 4-A, an adaptation of the passenger-carrying "Alpha 4" discussed previously. All of the "Alpha" in use by TWA were eventually converted into the all-cargo model 4-A and most were still operating actively into 1935.

The Stearman-Northrop "Alpha" model 4-A was a single-place low-winged all-metal monoplane specifically arranged for hauling cargo and air-express shipments. As an adaptation of the "Alpha 4" the model 4-A was stripped of its passenger seating, windows were removed and blocked out, and its 120 cu. ft. volume

Fig. 208. Loading cargo in 4-A on trip to points east; coast-to-coast schedule was 23 hours.

capacity was fitted with bins and tie-downs for various cargo loads. A generous increase in gross weight allowance provided for 1250 lbs. of cargo, and the installation of various operational aids. As the "Alpha 4-A" stood on the ramp ready to go, it was equipped with the latest known navigational and operational devices; this to maintain schedules day or night. The pilot still sat in an open cockpit where he had to "bundle up" against the elements, but most of the old-time pilots preferred it that way despite the discomfort. Powered with the 9 cyl. Pratt & Whitney "Wasp" SC1 engine of 450 h.p. the "Alpha 4-A" handled a sizeable payload out of all sorts of airfields and maintained unusually high cruising speeds for nearly 6 hours at a time. Pilots that flew the "Alpha" enjoyed their work, and were quick with praise for the airplane's compatibility even in the severest service. Easy to service and easy to maintain, the "Alpha" was also a favorite with line-mechanics. The type certificate number for the "Alpha 4-A" was issued 2-25-32 and at least 10 of the "Alpha" were converted to the all-cargo specifications. All modifications were performed at the Stearman plant in Wichita, Kans. As of about April in 1932 manufacture of the "Alpha" and also the "Beta" sport models, were formally discontinued; plant facilities however, were still available as a service-center for the service and repair of Northrop airplanes.

Listed below are specifications and performance data for the Stearman-Northrop "Alpha" model 4-A as powered with the 450 h.p. "Wasp" SC1 engine; length overall 28'5"; height overall (tail up) 9'0"; wing span 43'10"; wing chord at root 100'; wing chord at tip 66"; total wing area 312 sq.ft.; airfoil Clark Y; wt. empty (average) 2650 lbs.; useful load 2450 lbs.; crew wt. 220 lbs.; payload with 148 gal. fuel 1250 lbs.; gross wt. 5100 lbs.; max. speed 177; cruising speed 155; landing speed 65; climb 1100 ft. first min. at sea level, ceiling 17,500 ft.; gas cap. 148 gal.; oil cap. 12 gal.; cruising range at 24 gal. per hour 900 miles; no prices were announced.

The construction details and general arrangement of the "Alpha 4-A" were typical to that of the "Alpha" described in the chapter for ATC # 381 and the conversions described in the chapter for ATC # 451. To convert the "Alpha 4" into an all-cargo carrier, the passenger's cabin was stripped of all its seating and all but two of the windows were removed; bins and tie-downs were arranged to handle various cargo loads. The plush upholstery was removed and replaced with various linings of a more serviceable nature. The pilot's cockpit was provided with ventilation and a heater; the seat was adjustable to various positions for better visibility or sitting comfort. For day and night operation, the 4-A was equipped with all of the latest aids; these included complete night-flying gear, radio equipment, de-icing equipment, and special instruments. Radio equipment and all instruments were readily accessible from the cabin interior for service and repair. Goodrich de-icer boots were installed on leading edges to prevent formation of ice on the wings and empennage. The oleo-spring landing gear used 6-ply 9.50x12 semi-airwheels with brakes; each landing gear leg was fully encased in a large streamlined metal fairing. Crew wt. allowance included pilot, parachute, and 30 lbs. of personal baggage. An adjustable metal propeller, electric inertia-type engine starter, a battery, generator, navigation lights, landing lights, parachute flares, special instruments, radio equipment, fire extinguisher, and first-aid kit were standard equipment. The next Northrop development was the "Gamma" 2-D as described in the chapter for ATC # 549.

Listed below are "Alpha 4-A" entries as gleaned from registration records:

NC-127W; Alpha 4-A (# 2) Wasp 450.
NC-11Y;	"	(# 3)	"
NC-999Y;	"	(# 4)	"
NC-933Y;	"	(# 5)	"
NC-947Y;	"	(# 7)	"
NC-961Y;	"	(# 8)	"
NC-985Y;	"	(# 10)	"
NC-986Y;	"	(# 11)	"
NC-993Y;	"	(# 16)	"
NC-994Y;	"	(# 17)	"

This approval for ser. # 2 through # 17 if modified to conform; this approval expired 3-1-34.

A.T.C. # 462
(2-25-32)
LOCKHEED "ORION", 9-B

Fig. 209. Lockheed "Orion" model 9-B with 575 h.p. Wright "Cyclone" engine; combination was built to order of Swiss line.

The swift Lockheed "Orion" pulled up her wheels and established itself quickly as the fastest transport airplane in the world, so it is natural that news of its daily feats created some interest even in Europe. The Swiss Air Transport Co., Ltd. better known as "Swissair" was at this time interested in buying some new high-speed equipment, so they sent one of their top men to the U.S.A. to have a look around. Evaluating the various transport airplanes available here, the Swiss emissary ordered two of the Lockheed "Orion" specifying only they be powered with 575 h.p. Wright "Cyclone" engines. Slightly modified from those already put into service, this "Orion" became technically known as the model 9-B. Painted a brilliant red, these two "Orion" were the first American transport airplanes exported to Europe for use by a foreign airline. Initiating express flights to Munich and Vienna in May of 1932, their normal schedules were at least 60 m.p.h. faster than any others on the continent. Continually clipping off minutes from their advertised schedules, the "Red Orion" were the sensation of European aviation in that year. In 1933 some promotional survey-flights to Italy, North Africa, Turkey, and Austria demonstrated what was possible with the speedy "Orion" which set city-to-city speed records all the way around. Settling down to fast express round-trip runs from Zurich to Vienna, the two "Rote Orion" (Red Orion) were kept in active service until 1935, when larger airplanes of more capacity became a necessity. In 1936

the two "Orion" 9-B were sold quietly to the Republican Air Force of Spain during the waging of a civil war there. Their three-year performance record was no doubt the instigation of using American-built transport airplanes on many of the foreign airlines afterwards.

The Lockheed "Orion" model 9-B was an all-wood low-winged cabin monoplane with seating arranged for up to seven. Basically typical of the earlier "Orion" 9, the 9-B had the advantage of nearly a year's progress in this design concept, plus the installation of added horsepower. More or less custom-built to the needs of "Swissair" the 9-B was one of the more rare "Orion" models, but it certainly distinguished itself as one of the finest. The fast-flying "Orion" was setting a world-wide standard of performance for the high-speed air transport; former schedules from Zurich to Vienna were 4 hrs. & 20 mins. and the Cyclone-powered 9-B cut this down easily to an amazing 2 hrs. & 30 mins. The 9-B was listed as a 7-place airplane, but it normally carried 5 because it was quite a squeeze to get 6 passengers into the cabin comfortably. As powered with the big Wright "Cyclone" R-1820-E engine of 575 h.p. the 9-B inherited generous performance increases that established it as a rather outstanding airplane. Tucking in its retractable landing gear to eliminate a good portion of the parasitic drag, the 9-B had the habit of getting out quickly and getting there faster. Operational data was not available, but it is reasonable to

Fig. 210. 9-B in "Swissair" service was fastest transport in the world.

assume that this particular version surely must have shared all the good qualities that made the "Orion" such a favorite amongst operators and pilots. The type certificate number for the model 9-B was issued 2-25-32 and only 2 examples of this model were manufactured by the Lockheed Aircraft Co. at Burbank, Calif. Carl B. Squiers was general manager; Richard A. Von Hake was chief engineer; James Gerschler and Richard W. Palmer were project engineers; and Marshall Headle was test pilot. In Oct. of 1931 the Detroit Aircraft Corp. went into receivership, and Lockheed Aircraft was naturally included; it was the only division of this corporation that was still showing a profit. Under receivership, Lockheed continued with a small skeleton crew and 4 airplanes were built in that time, including the two 9-B for "Swissair". In Jan. of 1932, the Lockheed operation and all its assets were up for sale. Teetering on the brink of extinction, a group of aviation pioneers bought up Lockheed and all it stood for, so that it could continue to flourish.

Listed below are specifications and performance data for the Lockheed "Orion" model 9-B as powered with the 575 h.p. Wright "Cyclone" R-1820-E engine; length overall 28'4"; height overall 9'4"; wing span 42'10"; wing chord at root 102"; wing chord at tip 62"; total wing area (including fuselage) 294 sq.ft.; airfoil at root Clark Y-18; airfoil at tip Clark Y-9.5; wt. empty 3570 lbs.; useful load 1830 lbs.; payload with 100 gal. fuel 985 lbs.; gross wt. 5400 lbs.; max. speed 225; cruising speed 195; landing speed 65; climb 1450 ft. first min. at sea level; ceiling 22,000 ft.; gas cap. max. 116 gal.; oil cap. 9-10 gal.; cruising range at 32 gal. per hour 580 miles; price not announced.

The construction details and general arrangement of the model 9-B were typical to that of the model 9 as described in the chapter for ATC # 421 of this volume. The major change in the model 9-B was, of course, the installation of the big "Cyclone" engine; the NACA cowl was of larger diameter and slightly of deeper chord. The front-mounted collector ring normally used on the "Cyclone" was exchanged for one with stacks that curved backwards into two long tail-pipes. Most of the "Orion" had 4 windows down each side of the cabin, but the 9-B only had 3; this points to a cabin arrangement for 4 passengers. A large baggage compartment was to the rear of cabin area and accessible through a door on the outside. The 9-B also had the large fin and rudder which was characteristic of all the later "Orion". The streamlined extension of the pilot's canopy was also longer than on earlier types. An adjustable metal propeller, electric engine starter, navigation lights, a battery, wheel brakes, and a swiveling tail wheel were standard equipment. The next "Orion" development was the model 9-E as described in the chapter for ATC # 508.

Listed below are model 9-B entries as gleaned from registration records:

X-12231; Model 9-B (# 189) Cyclone 575.
X-12232;   "   (# 190)   "

Ser. # 189-190 also as CH-167 and CH-168; later registered as HB-LAH and HB-LAJ.

A.T.C. # 463
(2-26-32)
CURTISS-WRIGHT "SPORT", 16-E

Fig. 211. Curtiss-Wright model 16-E with 5 cyl. Wright R-540 engine was top of the line in sport-trainer series.

There had been a sharp falling off in activity by the average air-service operator in late 1931, consequently, there was less and less need for the so-called all-purpose type of airplane; a greater emphasis was now being placed by most manufacturers on the sport-trainer type and the

Fig. 212. Staunch airframe of 16-E aimed at carefree service.

Fig. 213. Three-seated 16-E offered utility with high performance.

higher powered sport plane. Owing to a gradually receding market, the production of the Curtiss-Wright models 12-Q, 12-K, 12-W, 16-K, and 16-W was discontinued, confining production only to the new 16-E "Light Sport", and 3 models of the "Sportsman-Speedwing" series. The new 16-E "Light Sport" was basically a 16-series airframe that was improved here and there just a little, and then spiced up considerably by installation of the 165 h.p. Wright R-540 engine. Formally shown to the public at the annual Detroit Air Show for 1932, it drew considerable comment, and several orders were placed. Leveled especially at the sportsman-pilot, its sphere of prospective customers was rather small, so a two-place version in slightly modified form was later developed as a military-type primary trainer for export. The sport-type 16-E that operated here in the U.S.A. were pretty well scattered around the country and its

arrival at an airport was bound to create a flurry of interest; well-liked and standing up well to hard service the 16-E piled up many years of active service. Basically typical of the earlier "Travel Air" 12-series and more so of the 16-series the Model 16-E was hailed as the best version of the combined series, and was still being produced into 1935.

The Curtiss-Wright "Sport" model 16-E was a light open cockpit biplane with seating arranged for three; the front cockpit was actually a little tight for two larger people, so it was generally used as a two-place airplane. Quite often it was also used as a single-place airplane with the front windshield removed and the cockpit covered over with a metal panel. Leveled especially at the sportsman, the "Sport" 16-E had the appeal of good looks, a good performance, and numerous aids to make its operation more enjoyable. As powered with the 5 cyl.

Fig. 214. Export-trainer version of 16-E developed for foreign countries.

Wright R-540 engine of 165 h.p. the 16-E was a lively airplane throughout its entire performance range. Stout of frame and rugged of character, the 16-E handled somewhat like a bigger airplane and responded with more enthusiasm to a good firm hand. Later examples were powered with the Wright R-540-E engine of 175 h.p. for a slight improvement in the performance range. Finished well, appointed well, and equipped quite well, the "Sport" was good value for the money; with slight modification to the fuselage frame it was also available as a twin-float seaplane. The type certificate number for the "Sport" model 16-E was issued 2-26-32 and only 10 examples of this model show up in registration records of the period. The prototype example of the 16-E was developed by Travel Air in Wichita, but all subsequent examples were manufactured by Curtiss-Wright Airplane Co. at Robertson (St. Louis), Mo. Early in 1932 Walter Beech resigned as president of C-W to devote more of his time in the development of a revolutionary high-speed transport airplane; the unusual negative-stagger cabin biplane later became known as the Beech "Stagger-Wing". The Curtiss-Wright Div. at St. Louis held its working force to nearly 200 during 1932, but occasionally raised that to 290 or 300 to complete several rush orders. There was much experimentation at Curtiss-Wright during this period, and the new Cyclone-powered "Condor" transport was already being developed.

Listed below are specifications and performance data for the "Light Sport" model 16-E as powered with the 165 h.p. Wright R-540 engine; length overall 20'6"; height overall 8'10"; wing span upper 28'10"; wing span lower 26'4"; wing chord upper & lower 48"; wing area upper 113 sq.ft.; wing area lower 93 sq.ft.; total wing area 206 sq.ft.; airfoil Clark Y-15; wt. empty 1340 (1360) lbs.; useful load 810 (790) lbs.; payload with 33 gal. fuel 412 (392) lbs.; figures in brackets for later model; gross wt. 2150 lbs.; max. speed (front cockpit closed off) 135; cruising speed 115; landing speed 50; climb 1000 ft. first min. at sea level; ceiling 16,500 ft.; gas cap. normal 33 gal.; oil cap. 4 gal.; cruising range at 10 gal. per hour 350 miles; price $4600. at factory field.

The construction details and general arrangement of the model 16-E were typical to that of the 12-series and 16-series as described elsewhere in this volume. The pilot's cockpit had an adjustable bucket-type seat that was shaped for a parachute pack; a streamlined head-rest was optional. The front cockpit had a removable windshield and could be covered with a metal panel when not in use. A baggage bin of 2.5 cu. ft. capacity with allowance for up to 55 lbs. was in the turtle-back section behind the rear cockpit; parachutes at 20 lbs. each were part of the payload allowance. Dual controls, brake pedals, and duplicate instruments were available for the front cockpit also. A 33 gal. gravity-feed fuel tank was mounted in the center-section panel of the upper wing; an extra 20 gal. fuel tank was available for mounting in the front cockpit. The landing gear of 76 in. tread used Hydra-Flex shock absorbing struts; 6.50x10 semi-airwheels were equipped with roller bearings and brakes. A 10x3 tail wheel was standard equipment. All points of wear were fitted with "Zerk" grease fittings, engine cowling was easily removable, and inspection plates were provided at numerous points. A metal propeller, Eclipse electric engine starter, a battery, wiring for navigation lights, dual controls, front cockpit cover, compass, fuel gauge, and a Pioneer air-speed indicator were standard equipment. Brake pedals in front cockpit, duplicate instruments in front cockpit, a head-rest, navigation lights, and custom colors were optional. The next Curtiss-Wright development was the B-14-B "Speed wing" as described in the chapter for ATC # 485 of this volume.

Listed below are model 16-E entries as gleaned from registration records:

NC-12331; Model 16-E (# 3501) Wright R-540
NC-12335;   "   (# 3502)   "
NC-12336;   "   (# 3503)   "
NC-12337;   "   (# 3504)   "
NC-454W;   "   (# 3505)   "
NC-455W;   "   (# 3506)   "
NC-456W;   "   (# 3507)   "
NC-12352;   "   (# 3508)   "
NC-12379;   "   (# 3519)   "
NC-12380;   "   (# 3520)   "

This approval for ser. # 3501 and up; ser. # 3506 later to Alaska; no record of ser. # 3509 through # 3518; this approval expired 9-30-39.

A.T.C. 464
(3-16-32)
WACO, MODEL PBA

Fig. 215. Waco model PBA with 170 h.p. Jacobs LA-1 engine, a popular combination.

On most any airplane model that is offered in numerous versions where the only difference is the powerplant used, there is likely to be one particular version of a basic model series that is more popular than the rest. Of the 6 different versions offered in the sport-type "Waco A" series, the Jacobs-powered PBA, by popular acclaim, was no doubt the most popular. Although not the most powerful, and, certainly not the most economical, the PBA was, however, a satisfying and pleasant blend of top-notch performance and reasonable operating costs. As a true sport airplane for two, the PBA was an ideal vehicle for the sportsman who wished to go places and do things; the versatility of this airplane posed very few limits as to where it could go or what it could do, providing the pilot could handle his part of the mission. Jacobs Aircraft Engines were understandably proud of this particular combination and ordered the first production example as a factory-sponsored demonstrator to show-case their 170 h.p. model LA-1 engine; other examples of the model PBA were well scattered around the country drawing comments of interest. Ollie Davis, sales manager for the Jacobs Aircraft Engine Co., flew the PBA on demonstration tour in the Pacific north-

west for several weeks, lining up plenty of sincere interest for the airplane and the engine. The market for a true sports-plane was rather meager at this time because of a depressed national economy, but the PBA was still well represented in sport-flying circles, and only lack of money on the part of potential customers prevented it from becoming a big hit.

The Waco model PBA was a "convertible" sport-type biplane with side-by-side seating for two. Normally flown in the sporty atmosphere of the open cockpit, a detachable coupe-top canopy was provided to take the sting out of cold wintry winds. The chummy cockpit offered companionship with plenty of elbow room; large compartments to the front and to the rear allowed stowage of numerous articles in personal baggage and all sorts of sporting equipment. With a cruising range of some 4 hours the radius of action for a day's flying fun was quite ample, and remarkable short-field performance allowed spur-of-the-moment visits to all sorts of interesting places. As so ably powered with the 7 cyl. Jacobs LA-1 engine of 170 h.p. the model PBA "Sportsman" had sinewy muscle and forceful drive to turn in a rather exciting performance; trading some top

Fig. 216. Baggage compartments in PBA allowed up to 178 lbs. for luggage and sporting gear.

speed for more useful performance, and added safety, the PBA was not reluctant to drop in almost anywhere and fly back out again. As often dandied up with coupe-top, speed-ring engine cowling, a metal propeller, wheel pants, and wing-root fairings the PBA posed a striking picture and pride of ownership must have run pretty high among PBA owners. The type certificate number for the model PBA was issued 3-16-32 and at least 6 examples of this model were manufactured by the Waco Aircraft Co. at Troy, Ohio.

Fig. 217. View of PBA shows wide entry door and side-by-side seating.

Listed below are specifications and performance data for the Waco model PBA as powered with the 170 h.p. Jacobs LA-1 engine; length overall 21'2"; height overall 8'8"; wing span upper 29'6"; wing span lower 27'5"; wing chord upper & lower 57"; wing area upper 130 sq.ft.; wing area lower 111.5 sq.ft.; total wing area 241.5 sq. ft.; airfoil Clark Y; wt. empty 1369 lbs.; useful load 788 (881) lbs.; payload with 40 gal. fuel 348 (440) lbs.; payload 1 pass. at 170 lbs. & 178 lbs. baggage; gross wt. 2157 (2250) lbs.; figures in brackets for amended wt. allowance; 2250 lb. gross wt. allowed 92 lbs. for 2 parachutes & extra equipment; max. speed 120; cruising speed 103; landing speed 40-42; climb 900-850 ft. first min. at sea level; ceiling 15,000 (14,500) ft.; gas cap. 40 gal.; oil cap. 4 gal.; cruising range at 9.5 gal. per hour 400 miles; price $4285. at factory field.

The construction details and general arrangement of the model PBA were typical to that of other models in the "Waco A" series as described elsewhere in this volume. The single cockpit was well padded and neatly upholstered; dual joy-stick controls were provided to allow flight from either seat. Large doors were on either side with convenient handholds in upper wing to improve exit or entry. The coupe-top canopy was built up of small diameter steel tubing to offer little interference or loss of visibility; attached or detached in 30 mins. the coupe-top was optional for $195.00 extra. Large cutouts in upper wing and in lower wing-roots offered increased visibility upward and downward. Two fuel tanks of 20 gal. capacity each were mounted in center-section panel of the upper wing; float-type fuel gauges were visible from the cockpit. Baggage allowance for up to 142 lbs. and rear compartment had allowance for 36 lbs. The rear compartment was dimensioned for articles of greater length such as golf bags, guns, and fishing rods; the front compartment was dimensioned for suit-cases and traveling bags. Amended allowance of 2250 lb. gross allowed 92 lbs. for two parachutes and extra equipment. The oleo-equipped landing gear of 71 in. tread used 6.50x10 wheels fitted with 7.50x10 low-pressure tires; wheel brakes were standard equipment. The wing panels were finished in silver dope and fuselage color was optional. A wooden propeller, Heywood engine starter, speed-ring cowl, navigation lights, hot-shot battery, compass, dual controls, wheel brakes, cockpit cover, and engine cover were standard equipment. A metal propeller, coupe-top canopy, wing-root fairings, wheel pants, landing lights, and parachute flares were optional. The next development in the "Waco A" series was the Kinner-powered model IBA as described in the chapter for ATC # 465 of this volume.

Listed below are model PBA entries as gleaned from registration records:

NC-12435; Model PBA (# 3585) Jacobs 170.
NC-12445;   "   (# 3597)   "
NC-1244;   "   (# 3598)   "
NC-12466;   "   (# 3609)   "
NC-13038;   "   (# 3610)   "
NC-13054;   "   (# 3611)   "

This approval for ser. # 3585 and up- ser. # 3597 as Jacobs Engine Co. demonstrator; this approval expired 4-1-34.

A.T.C. # 465
(3-16-32)
WACO, MODEL IBA

Fig. 218. Waco model IBA with 125 h.p. Kinner B5 engine; shown with coupe-top enclosure.

The "Waco" model A series was first introduced with the KBA; as a chummy two-seater biplane it was quite modestly powered with the 100 h.p. Kinner K5 engine. In effort to offer the sport-flier just about any power combination imaginable, Waco Aircraft prepared several different versions of the "Model A" with horsepower ranging from the economical 100 to the breath-taking 210. The model IBA with its 125 h.p. Kinner B5 engine was primarily economy-minded to offer the sportsman more flying time for dollars spent. Like other models in this prolific series, the IBA was specifically designed to fit the unique and special needs of the flying sportsman; seating was limited to only two, but there was ample room and weight allowance for scads of personal baggage, for golf clubs, guns, fishing poles, and the like. Designed carefully to translate each and every horsepower into useful performance, the model IBA offered the sportsman a fairly broad selection of places to land in, and with a little coaxing could usually come out with room to spare. Particularly ideal for the low-budget sportsman or business-man, the IBA featured a long cruising range, penny-pinching economy, and a modest delivered price. Built to fit a specific need, the IBA was soon faced with the realization that those who could afford to fly strictly for the sport of it were not necessarily budget-minded, and usually hied away to the more expensive models.

The Waco model IBA was a light open cockpit sport-type biplane with the friendly arrangement of side-by-side seating for two. Normally flown in the sporty atmosphere of the open cockpit, a detachable coupe-top canopy was available for cold-weather protection. As one of seven different models in the series, the IBA was particularly suited to extended cross-country travel, or just plain outdoor fun. Built wisely to withstand more than the normal amount of abuse or misuse, the rugged framework assured many hours of carefree operation. As powered with the 5 cyl. Kinner B5 engine of 125 h.p. the IBA offered a noticeable increase in all-round performance over the KBA while still holding economy of operation to a rather low level. Of easy-going, pleasant nature, and of dutiful character, the IBA was tops in low-cost flying enjoyment. As the third entry in the "Waco A" lineup for 1932, the modest IBA was held to small number, but it proved itself popular to those that had a chance to fly it, and recorded many years of active service. The type certificate number for the model IBA was issued 3-16-32 and perhaps no more than 3 examples of this model were manufactured by the Waco Aircraft Co. at Troy, Ohio.

Listed below are specifications and performance data for the Waco model IBA as powered with the 125 h.p. Kinner B5 engine; length overall 21'11"; height overall 8'8"; wing span upper 29'6"; wing span lower 27'5"; wing chord upper & lower 57"; wing area upper 130 sq. ft.; wing area lower 111.5 sq. ft.; total wing area 241.5 sq. ft.; airfoil Clark Y; wt. empty 1264 (1302) lbs.; useful load 721 (683) lbs.; payload with 40 gal. fuel 287 lbs. (1 pass. at 170 lbs. & 117 lbs. baggage); gross wt. 1985 lbs.; max. speed 110; cruising speed 93; landing speed 39; climb 700 ft. first min. at sea level; ceiling 13,000 ft.; gas cap. max. 40 gal.; oil cap. 13 qts.; cruising range at 7.5 gal. per hour 450 miles; price $4059 at factory field.

The construction details and general arrangement of the model IBA were typical to that of other "A" models as described elsewhere in this volume. The transparent coupe-top canopy was a light welded steel tube framework covered with Pyralin sheet, and added 20 lbs. to the empty weight; installation or removal of the canopy required about 30 minutes. Large doors provided entry to the cockpit from the wing-walk on either side; the canopy was of ample dimension so as not to hinder entry nor restrict the visibility. The roomy cockpit was deeply upholstered and dual joy-stick controls were provided. The baggage allowance was divided between two compartments; 81 lbs. was allowed in front and 36 lbs. was allowed in the rear bin.

The turtle-back bin was dimensioned to allow stowing of lengthier articles such as golf bags, skeet guns, and fishing poles. Typical of all A-series models, the center-section panel of the upper wing and the lower wing butts had large cutouts for improved visibility upwards and down. Low pressure 6.50x10 semi-airwheels with brakes were standard equipment; metal streamlined wheel pants were optional. Two 20 gal. gravity-feed fuel tanks were mounted in the center-section panel of upper wing; float-type fuel gauges were visible from the cockpit. A Hartzell wooden propeller, Heywood engine starter, navigation lights, hot-shot battery, and dual controls were standard equipment. An adjustable metal propeller, and the coupe-top enclosure were optional. Wheel pants and speed-ring engine cowl were later available for this model. The next development in the "Waco A" series was the Warner-powered model RBA as described in the chapter for ATC # 466 of this volume.

Listed below are model IBA entries as gleaned from registration records:

NC-12435; Model IBA (# 3585) Kinner B5.
NC-12446;   "   (# 3594)   "
NC-12453;   "   (# 3603)   "

This approval for ser. # 3585 and up; this approval expired 4-1-34.

Fig. 219. Waco model RBA with 125 h.p. Warner "Scarab" engine; this combination also very popular.

The Waco biplane and the Warner "Scarab" engine always came together as a very compatible combination and the sport-type model RBA was another good example of this agreeable mating. The highly-popular 7 cyl. "Scarab" as mounted into the chubby frame of the "Waco A" presented in front a small, neat diameter that blended nicely into a plump, well-proportioned dimension; be it for line or dimension, or a combination of both, the RBA was perhaps the best-looking model in this sportster series. Outperformed, of course, by several other models in this particular series (such as the TBA, PBA, UBA) the RBA, however, was quite popular for its smooth delivery of a relatively fine performance at a reasonably low level of expenditure. Designed especially as a convertible sport-biplane for the private owner of more modest means, the model RBA seemed to have all the makings of a very successful future, but it was groomed for a market that was rapidly dwindling, and finally did not exist at all. Waco Aircraft developed the basic "Model A" into a very diverse line of models, perhaps to have something suitable for everybody, but if the average sport-flier of this time was able to buy an airplane strictly for sport-use, it is most likely the RBA would have been the more practical for the largest number. The operational record of the RBA has been dimmed somewhat by the passage of time, but at least one has been restored carefully to fly again in recent years.

The Waco model RBA was an open cockpit sport biplane with side-by-side seating for two. By limiting the seating to a pilot and one passenger, ample room and weight allowance was provided for a large stack of personal baggage, various sporting gear, and extra fuel for extended range. Perhaps flown most often in the wind-blown atmosphere of the open cockpit, the RBA, like all others in the A-series, was a "convert-bile" and could be fitted with a coupe-top enclosure for comfort in colder weather. Having no mission to fulfill other than answering to the varied whims of a sporting pilot the RBA had practically go-anywhere utility that did have some limits, but was more than sufficient for the average sportsman-pilot. As powered with the 7 cyl. Warner "Scarab" engine of 110-125 h.p. the model RBA delivered fine performance in a seemingly effortless fashion. Inheriting all of the notable characteristics of the "Waco" biplane, the RBA was easy to fly well, a rewarding pleasure to operate, and pride of ownership was actually a large part of the owner's enjoyment. Reliable and relatively economical, the Warner-powered RBA was ideal for cross-country jaunts of considerable mileage, or for impromptu visits to any number of interesting places. The type certificate number for the

Fig. 220. More than 30 years old, this RBA still provides enjoyable sport-flying.

model RBA was issued 3-16-32 and at least 4 examples of this model were manufactured by the Waco Aircraft Co. at Troy, Ohio.

Listed below are specifications and performance data for the Waco model RBA powered with the 110-125 h.p. Warner "Scarab" engine length overall 21'7"; height overall 8'8"; wing span upper 29'6"; wing span lower 27'5"; wing chord upper & lower 57"; wing area upper 130 sq. ft.; wing area lower 11.5 sq. ft.; total wing area 241.5 sq. ft.; airfoil Clark Y; wt. empty 1260 lbs.; useful load 725 lbs.; payload with 40 gal. fuel 290 lbs.; gross wt. 1985 lbs.; max. speed 107-114; cruising speed 90-98; (higher speeds with rerated 125 h.p. engine & speed-ring cowling); landing speed 39; climb 630-700 ft. first min. at sea level; ceiling 12,800 ft.; gas cap. 40 gal.; oil cap. 13 qts.; cruising range at 7.2 gal. per hour 475 miles; price $4195. at factory field.

The construction details and general arrangement of the RBA were typical to that of other models in the "Waco A" series as discussed elsewhere in this volume. The baggage allowance for the RBA was divided between two compartments; a maximum of 95 lbs. was allowed in front and 36 lbs. was allowed in the rear bin. Two parachutes at 20 lbs. each were part of the bag-

gage allowance. The oleo-equipped landing-gear of 71 in. tread was fitted with 6.50x10 low pressure semi-airwheels with brakes; streamlined metal wheel pants were optional. The 40 gal. fuel supply was divided between two gravity-feed tanks mounted in the center-section panel of the upper wing; float-type fuel gauges were visible from the cockpit. A Hartzell wooden propeller, Heywood engine starter, navigation lights, hot-shot battery, and dual controls were standard equipment. An adjustable metal propeller, speed-ring engine cowl, coupe-top enclosure and wheel pants were optional; optional equipment added approx. 60 lbs. to the empty weight. The next development in the "Waco A" series was the model TBA as described in the chapter for ATC # 474 of this volume.

Listed below are model RBA entries as gleaned from registration records:

NC-12435; Model RBA (# 3585) Warner 110-125.
NC-12442;   "   (# 3592)   "
NC-12444;   "   (# 3593)   "
NC-13041;   "   (# 3595)   "

This approval for ser. # 3585 and up; this approval expired 4-1-34.

Fig. 221. Waco model UEC with 210 h.p. Continental engine; four-seater for 1932 featured better performance.

Jubilant over the comparitively enthusiastic welcome received by the first of the cabin-bi-plane series, the QDC of 1931, Waco Aircraft soon prepared a new and somewhat better version for 1932. Studded with little improvements that enhanced its comfort, its utility, its appearance, and performance, the new model UEC also took on a substantial power boost, and offered all of this for the same delivered price. It is easy to see why the relative success of this particular version was quickly assured, even in the face of a very limp market. Powered with the new 7 cyl. Continental R-670 engine of 210 h.p. the UEC performed its various duties with an extra vigor, over an extended range, and with a characteristic utility that only had a few limitations. Men of business took to the UEC quickly, flying-service operators found it a useful addition to their flight-line, and those that flew for sport or family fun were intrigued by its adaptability to chore or base of operation. Versatility describes the UEC in one word. For specialized services, one UEC was converted to an air-borne ambulance plane, at least one was operating as a seaplane on "Edo" floats, and several were in government service. The heart of the UEC was, of course, the new Continental R-670 engine, a fine example in the great strides being made in aircraft engine development during this period; the UEC was the first airplane to be certificated with this new engine, and the R-670 was to remain a familiar fixture in the future "Waco" lineup.

The Waco model UEC was a light cabin bi-plane with seating arranged for four. Adhering rather closely to the earlier QDC design, the new UEC was quite similar, but considerable improvement was clearly evident at many points. Among the more noticeable changes was a new windshield form, a slight modification to the large rear-view windows, a cleaning up of upper wing root attachments, wing-root fairings for the lower wings, and the new wing cellule now used a large tension-compression strut instead of the more normal criss-cross steel wires. The nose-section was lengthened slightly, and a number of louvers provided better venting for the engine compartment. Even with the engine shrouded in a circular speed-ring cowling, and wheels encased in oval streamlined wheel-pants, the UEC was no curvacious thing of beauty, but its likeable personality came through strong enough to easily overshadow this small failing.

Typical of all "Waco" designs, the UEC was practically a go-anywhere airplane, and a very enjoyable airplane to ride in or to fly; cost per seat-mile was quite reasonable and built-in reliability added hours to the owner's pleasure. The popularity of the model UEC naturally promoted its longevity so many were still flying actively for years to come. The type certificate number for the model UEC was issued 3-24-32 and some 40 examples of this model were manufactured by the Waco Aircraft Co. at Troy, Ohio.

Listed below are specifications and performance data for the Waco model UEC as pow-

Fig. 222. Model UEC on Edo floats.

Fig.223.Versatility of UEC adaptable to work or play.

ered with the 210 h.p. Continental R-670 engine; length overall 24'8"; height overall 8'6"; wing span upper 33'2"; wing span lower 28'2"; wing chord upper & lower 57"; wing area upper 134 sq.ft.; wing area lower 111 sq.ft.; total wing area 245 sq.ft.; airfoil Clark Y; wt. empty 1670 lbs.; useful load 1030 lbs.; payload with 50 gal. fuel 525 lbs.; gross wt. 2700 lbs.; max. speed (with speed-ring & wheel pants) 133; cruising speed 116; landing speed 49; climb 1000 ft. first min. at sea level; ceiling 15,000 ft.; gas cap. 50 gal.; oil cap. 4.5 gal.; cruising range at 12 gal. per hour 450 miles; price $5985. at factory field.

The construction details and general arrangement of the model UEC were typical to that of the earlier QDC as described in the chapter for ATC # 412 of this volume. Exterior changes in the longer fuselage included a longer nose-section with louvered cowling panels, the windshield was divided into more panels for a more rounded form, the rear-view windows were altered slightly for better airflow, and the turtle-back section was faired just a little fuller. The roomy cabin interior was finished in new fabrics, a swing-over wheel provided dual controls, and a large baggage compartment was behind the rear seat; a large cabin-entry door was on left-hand side. The wing cellule was altered slightly, and a heavy-gauge tension-compression bracing strut was used instead of steel wires; a 25 gal. fuel tank was mounted in the root end of each upper wing-half with a float-type fuel gauge for each tank. The patented "Waco" landing gear used splined axles to keep the wheels in line as the "oleo" struts were deflected; 7.50x10 or 8.50x10 semi-airwheels with brakes were standard equipment. A wooded propeller, Heywood engine starter, speed-ring cowl, wheel brakes, tail wheel, dual controls, and wiring for lights were standard equipment. A metal propeller, wheel pants, navigation lights, landing lights, and parachute flares were optional.

The next development in the Waco cabin bi-plane was the Kinner-powered model OEC as described in the chapter for ATC # 468 of this volume.

Listed below are model UEC entries as gleaned from registration records:

NC-12452;	Model UEC	(# 3605)	Cont. 210.
NC-12455;	"	(# 3621)	"
NC-12456;	"	(# 3622)	"
NC-12457;	"	(# 3623)	"
NC-12458;	"	(# 3624)	"
NC-12459;	"	(# 3625)	"
NC-12461;	"	(# 3626)	"
NC-12462;	"	(# 3627)	"
NC-12464;	"	(# 3634)	"
NC-12470;	"	(#3635)	"
NC-12465;	"	(# 3636)	"
NC-12471;	"	(# 3637)	"
NC-12472;	"	(# 3638)	"
NC-12473;	"	(# 3639)	"
NC-12468;	"	(# 3641)	"
NC-12475;	"	(# 3642)	"
NC-13030;	"	(# 3643)	"
NC-13031;	"	(# 3644)	"
NC-13034;	"	(# 3645)	"
NC-13036;	"	(# 3650)	"
NC-13033;	"	(# 3651)	"
NC-13037;	"	(# 3654)	"
NC-13035;	"	(# 3655)	"
NC-13039;	"	(# 3656)	"
NC-13040;	"	(# 3657)	"
NC-13043;	"	(# 3658)	"
NC-13044;	"	(# 3659)	"
NC-13045;	"	(# 3675)	"
NC-13047;	"	(# 3676)	"
NC-13048;	"	(# 3677)	"
NC-13050;	"	(# 3678)	"
NS-74Y;	"	(# 3679)	"
NC-13052;	"	(# 3680)	"
NC-13055;	"	(# 3682)	"
NC-13056;	"	(# 3683)	"
NS-38;	"	(# 3684)	"
NS-11;	"	(# 3685)	"
NC-13059;	"	(# 3686)	"
NC-13060;	"	(# 3687)	"
NC-646N;	"	(# 3694)	"

Ser. # 3636 and 3644 on Edo floats; ser. # 3684 (NS-38) later as NC-18613; ser. # 3685 (NS-11) later as NC-18631; ser. # 3679 (NS-74Y) with N.Y. Conservation Dept.; UEC on floats eligible for approval on Group 2 memo # 2-418.

A.T.C. # 468
(3-24-32)
WACO, MODEL OEC

Fig. 224. Waco model OEC with 210 h.p. Kinner C5 engine; shown in prototype.

The four-place Waco model OEC was developed right along with the Continental-powered model UEC and the only difference between them was the choice of engines; hung onto the nose-section of the OEC in a very conspicuous manner, was the big 5 cyl. Kinner C5 engine of 210 h.p. Kinner Motors stuck fervently to the 5 cyl. configuration for their engines and advertised on occasion that an engine such as the C5-210 actually offered better visibility, that is, because there were less cylinders up there to block the view ahead. Relatively cheaper than other big engines of similar horsepower the 5 cyl. C5-210 blossomed out on several different airplane types, but its use never became extensive nor very popular. H. C. Lippiatt, a star "Travel Air" salesman for years, changed over to selling "Waco" airplanes in 1932, and the third OEC to come off the line was used by him as a demonstrator up and down the west coast. With a special talent for selling "Travel Air" airplanes, Lippiatt also became a star "Waco" salesman. Offered as a companion model to the UEC the Kinner-powered OEC compared favorably in most every respect, but only a few were built. Designed especially for the private-owner

to use for business or for sport the model OEC was offered continually throughout the year of 1932, but it had made a rather poor showing.

The Waco model OEC was a light cabin biplane with seating arranged for a pilot and three passengers. Basically, the OEC was typical of the model UEC except for its engine installation and some slight modifications necessary to this particular airframe-engine combination. The new OEC was formally introduced to the flying public at the annual Detroit Air Show for 1932 and it attracted its share of interest perhaps because of the big 5 cyl. engine on its nose. Waco Aircraft presented most of its complete line for 1932 at the week-long exhibition and was assured by the response that this should be a good year. For Waco Aircraft it was a pretty good year.

As powered with the 5 cyl. Kinner C5-210 engine of 210 h.p. the OEC literally stomped with the extra power, and delivered a rather exceptional all-round performance, but the strong jolts of the big engine coursing through its airframe were hardly conducive to peace of mind or smiles of relaxation. As fitted with a special speed-ring engine cowl and streamlined wheel pants, the OEC cruised easily at 120 m.p.h.; and

Fig. 225. OEC at Kinner factory hangar;
H. C. Lippiatt in foreground.

Fig. 226. Speed-ring and wheel pants on OEC
were optional extras.

its radius of operation was extended to four hours. The type certificate number for the model OEC was issued 3-24-32 and perhaps only 3 examples of this model were manufactured by the Waco Aircraft Co. at Troy, Ohio.

Listed below are specifications and performance data for the Waco model OEC as powered with the 210 h.p. Kinner C5-210 engine; length overall 24'9"; height overall 8'6"; wing span upper 33'2"; wing span lower 28'2"; wing chord upper & lower 57"; wing area upper 134 sq.ft.; wing area lower 111 sq.ft.; total wing area 245 sq.ft.; airfoil Clark Y; wt. empty 1667 lbs.; useful load 1033 lbs.; payload with 50 gal. fuel 528 lbs.; gross wt. 2700 lbs.; max. speed (with speed-ring cowl & wheel pants) 133; cruising speed 118; landing speed 49; climb 1000 ft. first min. at sea level; ceiling 15,000 ft.; gas cap. normal 50 gal.; oil cap. 4.5 gal.; cruising range at 12 gal. per hour 450 miles; price $5885. at factory field.

The construction details and general arrangement of the model OEC were typical to that of the QDC, UEC, and BEC as described elsewhere in this volume. The big Kinner engine was fastened to a removable engine mount and cowling panels were louvered to vent the engine compartment. A baggage compartment with allowance for up to 43 lbs. was in the turtleback section behind the rear-view windows with access from the outside. A small tool-kit compartment under the rear seat had allowance for

14 lbs. The OEC was also eligible for conversion to an ambulance-plane. The wing cellule of the OEC was also braced with a tension-compression strut instead of the criss-cross steel wires. Normal fuel capacity was 50 gal. (2 tanks in upper wings at 25 gal. each); 20 gal. tanks for a 40 gal. capacity were optional. Serial # 3620 was eligible with 66 gal. fuel capacity; two 25 gal. tanks in upper wing roots and a 16 gal. tank in butt-end of lower right wing. Fuel from lower tank was transferred to upper tanks by hand-operated wobble pump. 7.50x10 or 8.50x10 semi-airwheels with brakes were standard equipment; streamlined metal wheel fairings were optional. A wooden propeller, a Heywood engine starter, navigation lights, hot-shot battery, swing-over or Y-type dual control wheels, wheel brakes, compass, and tail wheel were standard equipment. A metal propeller, speed-ring engine cowl, wheel pants, ambulance equipment, metal wing root fairings, landing lights, and parachute flares were optional. The next development in the Waco cabin biplane was the rare model BEC as described in the chapter for ATC # 472 of this volume.

Listed below are model OEC entries as gleaned from registration records:
NC-12440; Model OEC (# 3576) Kinner C5.
NC-12451;   "   (# 3604)   "
NC-12467;   "   (# 3620)   "
This approval for ser. # 3576 and up; this approval expired 4-1-34.

A.T.C. # 469
(3-25-32)
REARWIN "JUNIOR", 4000

Fig. 227. Rearwin "Junior" model 4000 with 40-50 h.p. "Aeromarine" engine.

There was very little choice in aircraft engines for the light-plane during this period, so when a promising powerplant did come along it was at least worth a try. The 3 cyl. "Poyer" of 40 h.p. was tested by Rearwin earlier, but the engine suffered development pains, so they shelved that project and decided to give the new 3 cyl. "Aeromarine" a try. The 3 cyl. "Aeromarine" engine had not yet been installed in an approved airplane, so tests proceeded cautiously. Designed well and built well, the "Aeromarine" AR-3 developed 40 to 50 h.p., it also behaved itself quite well and was considered as a good powerplant. As used by Rearwin in the "Junior" the AR-3 developed 40 h.p. at 2050 r.p.m. with a restriction plug in the induction system and single ignition. The mating of this engine with the Rearwin "Junior" be-

Fig. 228. "Junior 4000" makes way for altitude as it displays the classic shape for lightplanes of this period.

Fig. 229. Winter enclosure on 4000 was optional extra.

came the model 4000 and several examples of this model were built. With modification to the carburetor and with twin-ignition the AR-3 engine developed 50 h.p. at 2150 r.p.m.; most of the earlier installations were modified later to enjoy this power increase. With "Juniors" coming off the line occasionally, and no ready sales for them in sight, Rearwin created a purpose for some of these airplanes by opening up a flight-training school. A solo-course was offered for $75.00 and a private-pilot course was offered for $175.00; Rae Rearwin's two young sons were among the first to be taught how to fly at the new school. As his own customer, Rearwin could only use a small portion of his production, and orders for airplanes were painfully slow in coming, so formal production of the "Junior" was suspended later in 1932. The design was still held active however, and one "Junior" was built in 1933 and another in 1934. Of the "Junior" model 4000 that were built and sold nearly all were used for sport-flying, but a Texas rancher used his almost daily to patrol his large holdings. Only 1650 commercial airplanes were sold in 1931, and the light open cockpit monoplane dominated the market for the first time.

The Rearwin "Junior" model 4000 was a trim light parasol-type monoplane with open cockpit seating for two in tandem; normally it was flown with open sides, but a cozy detachable enclosure could be fitted in wintry weather. Basically similar to the earlier "Junior" 3000 except for its engine installation, the model 4000 also stood tall and rather spindly, but it didn't seem to have that flivver-plane look about it. Huskiest and heaviest of the so-called light-weights the Rearwin "Junior" allotted its extra weight to a rugged airframe and extra fuel capacity for more range. As powered with the 3 cyl. de-rated Aeromarine AR-3 engine of 40 h.p. the model 4000 compared favorably in all-round performance, but with the modified 50 h.p. engine it left most of the puddle-jumpers (Aeronca, Cub, etc.) in its

prop-wash. Easy-going and friendly, the 4000 still offered an hour's flying time for just a few dollars, and pilots found association with this airplane generally a happy one. Introduced abruptly to a market that barely existed, the "Junior 4000" posed anxiously and waited for customers that came few and far between. The type certificate number for the model 4000 was issued 3-25-32 and some 8 examples of this model were manufactured by Rearwin Airplanes, Inc. on Fairfax Field in Kansas City, Kansas.

Listed below are specifications and performance data for the Rearwin "Junior" model 4000 as powered with the 50 h.p. Aeromarine AR-3 engine; length overall 22'3"; height overall 7'6"; wing span 36'0"; wing chord 60"; total wing area 179.5 sq. ft.; airfoil (NACA) M-series; wt. empty 605 (617) lbs.; useful load 433 (423) lbs.; payload with 12 gal. fuel 180 (170) lbs.; gross wt. 1038 (1040) lbs.; wts. in brackets with 12 lb. enclosure; max. speed (with enclosure) 91; cruising speed 76; landing speed 30; climb 700 ft. first min. at sea level; ceiling 16,000 ft.; gas cap. 12 gal.; oil cap. 6 qts.; cruising range at 2.8 gal. per hour 240 miles; price $1880. at factory field without enclosure. The following data pertains to model 4000 as offered in 1935; length overall 21'8"; height overall 7'3"; wing span 36'0"; wing chord 60"; wing area 179 sq. ft.; wt. empty (with 28 lb. enclosure) 635 lbs.; max. speed 92; cruising speed 80; landing speed 35; climb 650 ft. first min. at sea level; ceiling 15,000 ft.; cruising range 240 miles; no price announced. Aeromarine AR-3 rated 50 h.p. at 2150 r.p.m., weighing 145 lbs.; price $560.00 crated for delivery.

The fuselage framework was built up of welded chrome-moly and 1025 steel tubing, lightly faired to shape and fabric covered. One elongated open cockpit seated two in tandem; there was a large windshield in front and a smaller windshield for the rear seat, but a detachable full enclosure was optional. A

Fig. 230. "Junior 4000" popular for pilot-training or economical sport-flying.

large rectangular door offered easy entry to either seat. The wing framework in two halves was built up of laminated spruce spar beams with spruce and birch plywood truss-type wing ribs; the leading edges were covered with plywood sheet and the completed framework was covered in fabric. The center-section was mounted high above the cockpit on steel tube struts, and the wings were braced to the lower fuselage by streamlined steel tube struts. The split-axle landing gear of 72 in. tread used a spool of rubber shock-cord or Rusco rubber compression-rings to absorb the shock; 16x7-4 Goodyear airwheels without brakes were standard equipment. Tail skid was of the steel spring-leaf type. The fabric covered tail-group was built up of welded steel tubing and channel sections; horizontal stabilizer was adjustable in flight. A wooden "Aeromarine" propeller, dual joy-stick controls, and individual windshields were standard equipment. A light (12 lb.) or heavy (28 lb.) detachable winter enclosure

was optional. The next development in the Rearwin "Junior" was the model 3100 as described in the chapter for ATC # 481 of this volume.

Listed below are "Junior" 4000 entries as gleaned from registration records:

NC-508Y;	Model 4000 (# 202-A)	Aeromarine AR-3
NC-557Y;	" (# 212)	"
NC-11058;	" (# 215)	"
NC-11060;	" (# 217)	"
NC-12524;	" (# 220-A)	"
NC-12543;	" (# 221-A)	"
NC-12555;	" (# 222-A)	"
NC-12558;	" (# 223-A)	"

This approval for ser. # 202-A and up; ser. # 202-A first as model 3001 with Poyer engine; ser. # 212 and # 215 first as model 3000; ser. # 219 and up eligible with 12 lb. or 28 lb. enclosure at 1066 lbs. gross wt.; ser. # 222-A mfgd. 1933; ser. # 223-A mfgd. 1934; this approval expired 11-5-36.

Fig. 231. Pilgrim model 100-B with 575 h.p. Wright "Cyclone" engine; 6 examples in service
with American Airways.

The Pilgrim model 100-A was already in American· Airways service as the new 100-B was being developed. Incorporating a few little details of aerodynamic and structural refinement, the main difference between the two aircraft was the engine installed. Instead of the "Hornet" B" as mounted in the 100-A the new 100-B mounted the Wright "Cyclone" R-1820-E engine of 575 h.p. Otherwise the same in every respect, the 100-B stood shoulder to shoulder with the 100-A and also distinguished itself in commendable daily service. As the identity of these two "Pilgrim" models was primarily established by the engine installed, it is interesting to note that in 1934 American Airways converted 3 of the Hornet-powered 100-A into Cyclone-powered 100-B, and 2 of the Cyclone-powered 100-B into the Hornet-powered 100-A. The reason for this switch is not clear, but it was during overhaul time, and whether by design or coincidence, this is the way it turned out. The Pilgrim model 100-B was built in a batch of ten airplanes; six of these were delivered to American Airways, and four were delivered to the Army Air Corps as the Y1C-24, a ten-place utility transport. By mid-1932 the "Pilgrim" had replaced much of the older equipment, so American Airways had a big clearance sale; offered at bargain prices, this surplus equipment included about 15 different types of airplanes, mostly of smaller capacity which had outlived their usefulness on the line. By 1935 larger and faster equipment was being put into service on American Airways routes so the "Pilgrim" were being side-lined one by one; in June of 1935 at Cleveland, Ohio, all of the 100-A and 100-B were up for sale at prices ranging from $2200.00 and up.

Happily enough, all sold quickly and were scattered to all parts of our hemisphere; in truth, the most interesting part of "Pilgrim" lore and history was accumulated after they left airline service.

The Pilgrim model 100-B was a high-winged cabin monoplane of large and buxom proportion that had seating arranged for ten; as a transport for passengers, mail, and express-cargo, it was primarily designed for the shorter routes. Nine passengers were seated quite comfortably in the main cabin section while passenger baggage was stowed in the plane's bulging belly; a large compartment under the pilot's cabin floor had ample allowance for mail and cargo. The elevated pilot's station high up in front gave him a clear, commanding view during take-offs and landings, and pilots were ready with praise for this thoughtful feature; as used later in the "bush country" pilots found this feature often made the difference between the success or failure of a flight. As powered with the 9 cyl. Wright "Cyclone" R-1820-E engine of 575 h.p. the 100-B converted this power into rather amazing performance. The broad, swept-back wing could lift large payloads out of small fields that often were little more than a grassy pasture, and its rugged structure allowed the tackling of almost any chore. All components were readily accessible for repairs or service thereby cutting operating costs and reducing time away from the flight-line. "Bush pilots" who were often their own mechanics, enjoyed the ease of maintenance and were thankful for the rugged structure that soaked up abnormal amounts of abuse. Not a bit fussy or critical, even under the most trying conditions, it is not hard to understand

Fig. 232. Pilgrim 100-B converted to 100-A by installing "Hornet" engine.

why pilots put such an unwavering trust into the ability of the 100-A or the 100-B. Capable, reliable, and extremely cooperative, it was adored by the pilots who actually jumped at the chance to fly the "Pilgrim". The type certificate number for the model 100-B was issued 3-25-32 and 10 examples of this model were manufactured by American Airplane & Engine Corp. at Farmingdale, L.I., N.Y. Richard H. Depew, sales engineer for the corporation, resigned in June of 1932 to join a large eastern firm distributing the novel "autogiro". Inheriting the design for a ten-

place low winged all-metal transport from Fairchild, "American Airplane" experimented further in the development of this design, but turned it over to "General Aviation" late in 1932 when "American" withdrew from the aircraft manufacturing field. Starting out as the Fairchild "Model 150" this design eventually became the "General GA-43".

Listed below are specifications and performance data for the Pilgrim model 100-B as powered with the 575 h.p. Wright "Cyclone" engine; length overall 38'0"; height overall

Fig. 233. YIC-24 was Army version of 100-B; Army version had no belly compartments.

Fig. 234. Load capacity and short-field performance of Pilgrim 100-A and 100-B ideal for service in "the bush."

12'3"; wing span 57'0"; wing chord 8'4"; total wing area 459 sq.ft.; airfoil Goettingen 398; wt. empty 4437 lbs.; useful load 3313 lbs.; payload with 150 gal. fuel 2153 lbs. (9 pass. at 170 lb. each & 623 lb. mail-baggage-cargo); gross wt. 7750 lbs.; max. speed 136; cruising speed 118; landing (stall) speed 65; climb 800 ft. first min. at sea level; ceiling 13,600 ft.; gas cap. 150 gal.; oil cap. 12 gal.; cruising range at 32 gal. per hour 510 miles; no price was announced. The following details were given for Army-version (Y1C-24) of 100-B; 10 place; length overall 39'2"; wing span 57'5"; gross wt. 7070 lbs.; max. speed 136; folding wings; 4 were procured in 1932.

The construction details and general arrangement of the model 100-B were typical to that of the 100-A as described in the chapter for ATC # 443 of this volume. The capacity for baggage-mail-cargo was divided among 5 different compartments; forward compartment under pilot's cabin floor was allowed 476 lbs., compartment under front passenger seat in main cabin was allowed 60 lbs., and 3 belly compartments were allowed 70 lbs. each. Toilet and lavatory equipment was provided to rear of main cabin section; approx. 2.5 gals. of water were provided for a small wash-basin. The 150 gal. fuel supply was divided among 3 tanks; one 55 gal. tank and a 20 gal. reserve tank were mounted in the root end of the right wing half, and a 75 gal. tank was mounted in the root end of the left

wing half. The landing gear was fitted with 36x8 wheels and brakes, or 35x16-6 Goodyear airwheels with brakes; a 12x5-3 tail wheel was full swivel. The 100-B was also eligible with skis. Area of the vertical fin was increased by 2 sq.ft., but all other surfaces remained the same. All of the 100-B were eligible also as one-place cargo carriers, with passenger seats removed and replaced with freight bins and cargo tiedown straps. An adjustable metal propeller, speed-ring engine cowl, electric engine starter, a battery, generator, a two-way radio, navigation lights, landing lights, parachute flares, cabin heaters, toilet and lavatory equipment, 18 lb. tool kit, 3 fire extinguishers, and first-aid kits were standard equipment. Some of the "Pilgrim" freighter-version were later equipped with the 715 h.p. Wright "Cyclone" engine for work in "the bush".

Listed below are model 100-B entries as gleaned from registration records:
NC-737N; Model 100-B (# 6701) Cyclone 575.
NC-738N;   ”   (# 6702)   ”
NC-739N;   ”   (# 6703)   ”
NC-740N;   ”   (# 6704)   ”
NC-741N;   ”   (# 6705)   ”
NC-742N;   ”   (# 6706)   ”
The four Y1C-24 delivered to Army Air Corps in 1932 were most likely ser. # 6707-6708-6709-6710; approval for 100-B expired 4-1-33; ser. # 6701 and # 6703 as model 100-A in 1934.

A.T.C. # 471
(3-26-32)
KELLETT "AUTOGIRO", K-3

Fig. 235. Kellett K-3 in picturesque setting high over Los Angeles.

The new model K-3 was another version of the "Kellett" sport-type autogiro; offered as a "convertible" it could be flown with open cockpit for summer enjoyment, or with coupe-top canopy in wintry weather. Formally shown to the public at the annual Detroit Air Show for 1932, it drew its fair share of interest and was hailed as a considerable improvement over the earlier K-2. Mounting the big 5 cyl. Kinner C5 engine of 210 h.p. it promised nearly double the rate of climb and much better control for hemmed-in landings; with the streamlined detachable coupe-top installed, its maximum speed was up to 110 m.p.h. Favored by the world-wide interest in the "autogiro," one example of the Kellett K-3 was delivered to a sportsman-pilot in Buenos Aires of Argentina as the first autogiro to be delivered to South America. Another example of the K-3 accompanied Cmdr. Byrd on his second expedition to the South Pole; used occasionally throughout the year it proved its worth on special missions. One wintry day the K-3 was taking off from the camp-grounds on Little America for a routine mission, but an extreme tail-heavy condition caused by snow that had drifted into its fuselage rear had upset its balance and it crashed back to the ground. Damaged quite extensively, it was not repaired, but it had already proven that operation of an auto-

giro under trying conditions and in extremely cold weather was quite practical. The Kellett model K-3 with its relative abundance of power reserve was among the first to be used for towing "sky-ads"; attached to a 400 foot cable trailing from the autogiro was a banner some 100 to 200 feet long with 9 foot letters spelling out the message. The autogiro was still of sufficient novelty to attract attention thus making the towed banner an excellent advertising media. Several advertising campaigns had been conducted over eastern cities in 1932, and this was soon to become a lucrative business. With its relatively high performance the Kellett K-3 was primarily offered as a sport-type machine, but its inherent utility forced it into all sorts of utilitarian chores.

The Kellett model K-3 was a sport-type autogiro with side-by-side seating for two; as a "convertible," it could be flown as open cockpit, or flown with the coupe-top enclosure that was removed or installed in a matter of minutes. To provide the power reserve and the higher performance necessary in a sport-type autogiro, the K-3 was powered with the big 5 cyl. Kinner C5-210 engine. This combination allowed fully loaded take-offs in still air of less than 165 feet, the climb-out was nearly doubled, and top speed was greatly improved. There was now

Fig. 236. View reveals aerodynamic arrangement of Kellett K-3; rotor turned at 130 r.p.m. at cruising speed.

better control for landings into hemmed-in places, and the average landing roll hardly exceeded 35 to 50 feet. Just generally speaking, the Kellett K-3 was not a machine recommended for amateurs, but a good pilot could take to it easily and harness its spirit into an exceptionally good performance. The flush of newness was beginning to wear off the autogiro to some extent, and several years of operation was beginning to separate some of the myth from reality; it was by now the conclusion that the "autogiro" was a wonderful machine, but it required

a complete understanding and a special technique to bring out its full potential. The type certificate number for the Kellett model K-3 was issued 3-26-32 and perhaps 6 or more examples of this model were manufactured by the Kellett Aircraft Corp. at Philadelphia, Penna. W. Wallace Kellett was president; C. T. Ludington was V.P.; W. Laurence LePage was V.P. of engineering; R. G. Kellett was secretary-treasurer; and Guy Miller was test pilot. A reorganization took place in April of 1932 and the firm's name was changed to the Kellett Autogiro Corp.; refinanc-

Fig. 237. Kellett K-3 dubbed "Snowman" with Byrd expedition to South Pole.

Fig. 238. Kinner C5 engine of 210 h.p. provided K-3 with high performance.

ing was provided to enlarge the marketing program and to study new autogiro developments. Downtown office quarters were also moved out to the factory on the Philadelphia airport.

Listed below are specifications and performance data for the Kellett model K-3 as powered with the 210 h.p. Kinner C5 engine; length overall (fuselage only) 19'6"; height overall 12'7"; rotor dia. 41'0"; rotor blade chord 23"; rotor disc area 1320 sq.ft.; rotor speed 130 r.p.m. at cruise; fixed-wing span 26'0"; wing chord 54"; fixed-wing area 100 sq.ft.; wing airfoil RAF-30; wt. empty 1647 lbs.; useful load 653 lbs.; payload with 35 gal. fuel 235 lbs. (1 pass. at 170 lb. & 65 lb. baggage); gross wt. 2300 lbs.; max. speed 110; cruising speed 90; landing speed 15-20; climb 980 ft. first min. at sea level; ceiling 10,000 ft.; gas cap. 35 gal.; oil cap. 5 gal.; cruising range at 13.5 gal. per hour 250 miles; price $8135. at factory field. Amended allowance later increased useful load to 753 lbs. and gross wt. to 2400 lbs.

The construction details and general arrangement of the model K-3 were typical to that of the K-2 as described in the chapter for ATC # 437 of this volume. The most significant change in the model K-3 was the installation of the big Kinner C5 engine; complete with exhaust collector-ring, the C5 weighed 420 lbs. and the price was $2250. The spacious cockpit was well upholstered and a 7-inch spring-filled seat cushion ironed out the jar of hard landings; the detachable coupe-top weighing some 24 lbs. was fabricated from riveted dural metal sheet using Pyralin windows. The baggage compartment of 5.5 cu.ft. capacity with allowance for up to 65 lbs. was behind the seat back; two parachutes at 20 lbs. each were part of the baggage allowance. The usually wide landing gear of 144 in. tread used oleo-spring shock absorbing struts of 10 in. travel; 7.50x10 semi-airwheels with brakes were standard equipment. An adjustable metal propeller, Heywood engine starter, navigation lights, hot-shot battery, wheel brakes, dual controls, and tail wheel were standard equipment. The coupe-top enclosure was $370.00 extra. The next development in the Kellett autogiro was the model K-4 as described in the chapter for ATC # 523.

Listed below are model K-3 entries as gleaned from registration records:

NC-10767; Model K-3 (# 2) Kinner C5.
NC-12605;   "   (# 12)   "
NC-12671;   "   (# 14)   "
NC-12691;   "   (# 16)   "
NC-12633;   "   (# 17)   "
NC-12615;   "   (# 18)   "
NC-13151;   "   (# 20)   "

This approval for ser. # 2, 12, 14 and up; ser. # 2, 12, 17, 18, first mfgd. as model K-2 and modified into model K-3; ser. # 13, 15, 19 unknown, one may have been shipped to So. America; this approval expired 9-30-39.

A.T.C. # 472
(4-1-32)
WACO, MODEL BEC

Fig. 239. Waco model BEC with 5 cyl. Wright R-540 engine similar to airplane shown; BEC was extremely rare type.

Occasional mention and some veiled rumors is all that is known about the "Waco" model BEC; Waco Aircraft did have a few rare models and several one-of-a-kind in its lineup to now, but this one is perhaps the rarest of them all. We know that there really was a model BEC at one time, but it's going to be hard to prove it. Using Waco designation structure we can dissect this airplane into 3 of its major components to see in mind's-eye just what it would be like. The model designation "BEC" tells us (B) that it was a 5 cyl. Wright R-540 engine, and (E) the E-type wing cellule of 1932 mounted on the current C-type fuselage; the four-place cabin model UEC has already been described (ATC # 467), so we can picture the BEC as being typical of the UEC in general except for its engine installation. The reason for such a combination as the BEC is hard to determine unless it was largely in the interests of operating economy; performance-wise this airplane must have been pretty much of a burden for the 165 h.p. engine. Putting the "Wright 5" in the earlier and lighter DC airframe would have been much more logical. So here we have a rare and somewhat unusual airplane that was assembled with some purpose in mind, but what that purpose might have been has never been demonstrated nor explained sufficiently to leave its mark. It is

quite logical to assume that at least one example of the model BEC must have been built, at least for certification tests, but record of it in pertinent listings does not even exist.

Designation structure of the various "Waco" models had meaningful and definite purpose to identify a particular airplane as to its various major components, the components that went together to make up the airplane as a complete assembled unit; from this system it is entirely possible to tender a reasonably accurate description. Thus we know that the model BEC was a light cabin biplane with seating arranged for four. As fitted with the improved E-type wing cellule, we have an airplane, at least from the firewall back, that now resembles the UEC. Installation of the 5 cyl. Wright R-540 engine of 165 h.p. (coded as B) into what we have to now, makes up the completed unit as the BEC. To carry our conjecture further it is logical to assume that this airplane must have traded its performance potential for economy of operation; to a certain economy-concious customer this would not be an unlikely trade. By a direct comparison with the earlier QDC, which also mounted a 165 h.p. engine, it is doubtful if the BEC had ability to perform as well. The type certificate number for the model BEC was issued 4-1-32 and at least one example of this model must have been built by the Waco Aircraft Co. at Troy, Ohio.

Listed below are calculated specifications and performance data for the Waco model BEC as powered with the 165 h.p. Wright R-540 engine; length overall 24'10"; height overall 8'6"; wing span upper 33'3"; wing span lower 28'2"; wing chord upper & lower 57"; wing area upper 134 sq.ft.; wing area lower 111 sq.ft.; total wing area 245 sq.ft.; airfoil Clark Y; wt. empty 1650 lbs.; useful load 1000 lbs.; payload with 50 gal. fuel 500 lbs.; gross wt. 2650 lbs.; max. speed 120; cruising speed 100; landing speed 49; climb 650 ft. first min. at sea level; ceiling 13,000 ft.; gas cap. 50 gal.; oil cap. 4 gal.; cruising range at 9.8 gal. per hour 450 miles; price not announced. These figures were calculated by making comparison of earlier QDC with the UEC and OEC.

The construction details and general arrangement of the model BEC were probably typical to that of the UEC and OEC as described previously in this volume. Some of the changes in the new 1932 EC combination (fuselage-wing) as compared to the earlier DC combination brought on some extra weight, but this was slight penalty for all that was included. Being of the EC (1932) combination it is quite likely that the model BEC shared all these improvements with only the deliberate swapping of some performance in exchange for operating economy, and extended range. A fuel capacity of 50 gal. was divided into two tanks, one 25 gal. tank mounted in the root end of each upper wing half; it is quite likely that the BEC operated often with less than full fuel capacity. A wooden propeller, speed-ring engine cowl, Heywood engine starter, wheel brakes, and dual wheel controls were among standard equipment for the 1932 EC series.

There was no listing for the model BEC in any of the registration records, so it is quite likely that the BEC may have been converted to UEC or OEC specifications following certification testing. The next Waco development was the 3-place model UBF as described in the chapter for ATC # 473 of this volume.

A.T.C. # 473
(4-1-32)
WACO, MODEL UBF

Fig. 240. Waco model UBF with 210 h.p. Continental engine; factory named it "Tourist."

As a development from the earlier Waco model QCF, (ATC # 416) the new UBF was basically a three-place open cockpit all-purpose biplane, a stubby machine of high performance and exceptional utility. With spirited nature and a sturdy frame designed to handle some of the more specialized chores of the flying-service operator, there was still a playful streak down deep in its makeup that appealed to those who flew only for the sport of it. To some sportsman the three-seated carrying capacity was of more consequence, and others often flew it as a one-seater with the front cockpit covered over. When covered with a metal panel, the front cockpit became a nice large baggage compartment. One of the few ships to be "named" by Waco

Fig. 241. UBF primarily leveled at sportsman, but utility was easily adapted to all-purpose service.

Fig. 242. UBF as "Texaco 17" was familiar sight across country.

Aircraft, the UBF was known as the "Tourist", and later (1933) leveled especially at sportsman and men of business. The "Texaco # 17" of the Texas Co. was one of the more prominent business-owned airplanes and was seen all over the central and eastern part of the country with Hal Henning as pilot. Other examples of the UBF were operated by flying-service operators for the various chores that required high performance, but some were known to be "hopping passengers" during leaner periods of the year. In March of 1934 two XJW-1 (a sky-hooked version of the UBF) were placed into Navy Service on the "U.S.S. Macon", a huge dirigible. Shuttling to and from the "Macon" while in full-flight, the XJW-1 acted as utility aircraft on various prosaic missions. After loss of the U.S.S. Macon in 1935 the XJW-1 were "unhooked" and served in utility duties at regular Naval air-stations until World War 2. Known in flying circles as the F-2 and F-3 the UBF piled up an enviable service record in many years of active flying; at least one has been restored carefully to fly again in recent years.

The Waco model UBF was an open cockpit biplane with seating arranged for three. Designed primarily for the specialized chores of the flying-service operator, its rather high performance and exceptional utility actually became more attractive in time to the needs and liking of the sportsman-pilot. Normally flown as a three-seater the front cockpit could be covered over and flown as a single-seater with provision then for large amounts of baggage and extra fuel for an extended range. Stubby and deep-chested, the UBF had its useful load tightly

grouped and therefore was not penalized by any excess weight nor cumbersome dimension. With no need to be choosy as to chore or place of operation, the UBF operated quite happily out of small pasture-strips or any suitable clearing; to further increase its utility, the UBF was also eligible as a three-seated seaplane on Edo twin-float gear. As powered with the 7 cyl. Continental R-670 engine of 210 h.p. the UBF had an exceptional performance throughout the whole range of flight; take-offs were sometimes less than 100 feet, climb-out could be held to a breath-taking rate, and landings were always nice and easy. Sure-footed and extremely nimble, the UBF was a pleasure to fly, and despite its capability of high performance, it still showed considerate traits in its manner. The three-place all-purpose biplane was by now a dying breed, and it would not be far out of line to say that the 1932-33 model UBF was perhaps one of the best. The type certificate number for the model UBF was issued 4-1-32 and at least 11 examples of this model were manufactured by the Waco Aircraft Co. at Troy, Ohio.

Listed below are specifications and performance data for the Waco model UBF as powered with the 210 h.p. Continental R-670 engine; length overall 20'9"; height overall 8'9"; wing span upper 29'6"; wing span lower 27'5"; wing chord upper & lower 57"; wing area upper 130 sq. ft.; wing area lower 111.5 sq. ft.; total wing area 241.5 sq. ft.; airfoil Clark 6; wt. empty 1376 (1380) lbs.; useful load 924 (920) lbs.; payload with 40 gal. fuel 484 (480) lbs.; payload with 55 gal. fuel 390 lbs.; gross wt. 2300 lbs.; max. speed (with speed-ring &

Fig. 243. Navy version of UBF (XJW-1) equipped with sky-hook for service with dirigible U.S.S. Macon.

wheel pants) 132; cruising speed 116; landing speed 42; climb 1500 ft. first min. at sea level; ceiling 15,800 ft.; gas cap. 40-55 gal.; oil cap. 4-5 gal.; cruising range at 13 gal. per hour 340-460 miles; price $5025. at factory field. With gross wt. of seaplane at 2635 lbs. performance suffered accordingly.

The construction details and general arrangement of the model UBF were typical to that of other "Waco F" models as described elsewhere in this volume. The front cockpit of the F-2 series was improved slightly for more room, and larger windshields offered better weather protection; entry door was on the left side. Front cockpit could be covered neatly with a detachable metal panel when not in use. The baggage allowance of 65 lbs. was divided among two compartments; front cockpit bin was allowed 15 lbs. (tool kit) and rear compartment in turtleback of fuselage was allowed 50 lbs. The "Model F" for 1932-33 were fitted with "B" wings (also used on Model A) which were a slight improvement over the "C" wings of 1931. Two fuel tanks of 20 gal. each were mounted in the fuselage just behind firewall. The patented "Waco" landing gear used 6.50x10 wheels fitted with 7.50x10 low-pressure tires; wheel brakes and a parking brake were standard equipment. As a seaplane the UBF was fitted with Edo M-2665 twin-float gear; baggage allowance was 77 lbs. (14 lbs. front and 63 lbs. rear compt.) which included 20 lbs. for anchor and rope. Payload of seaplane could be increased 60 lbs. to include 3 parachutes. As a single-seater landplane, "Texaco # 17" was fitted with 70 gal. fuel supply (2 tanks in center-section at 20 gal. each, and 2 tanks in fuselage at 15 gal. each); 140 lbs. baggage was allowed in panel-covered front cockpit and rear cockpit was equipped with a heater. For standard land-

plane a wooden propeller speed-ring engine cowl, Heywood engine starter, navigation lights, hot-shot battery, wheel brakes, parking brake, tool kit, engine cover, and cockpit covers were standard equipment. An adjustable metal propeller, landing lights, parachute flares, wing-root fairing, wheel pants, cockpit heater, extra 15 gal. fuel tank, and 8 in. streamlined tail wheel were optional. For seaplane an adjustable metal propeller, speed-ring cowl, Heywood engine starter, navigation lights, hot-shot battery, aux. fin, tool kit, engine cover, and cockpit covers were standard equipment; an extra 15 gal. fuel tank was optional. Standard color scheme was silver wings with either gray, black, silver, or vermillion fuselage optional. Color combinations other than standard available on order. The next development in the F-2 series was the model PBF as described in the chapter for ATC # 491 of this volume.

Listed below are model UBF entries as gleaned from registration records:

NC-12443; Model UBF (# 3606) Cont. 210.
NC-12447;   "   (# 3607)   "
NC-12454;   "   (# 3608)   "
N C-13026;   "   (# 3615)   "
 NC-155Y;   "   (# 3618)   "
NC-12437;   "   (# 3646)   "
NC-13027;   "   (# 3660)   "
NC-13071;   "   (# 3689)   "
NC-11274;   "   (# 3690)   "
NC-13074;   "   (# 3691)   "
NC-13075;   "   (# 3692)   "
NC-13419;   "   (# 3762)   "
NC-13444;   "   (# 3763)   "
NC-13442;   "   (# 3766)   "

This approval for ser. # 3606 and up; ser. # 3618 first as "Texaco # 17"; ser. # 3691 on Edo floats; ser. nos. for XJW-1 unknown; this approval expired 9-30-39.

A.T.C. # 474
(4-1-32)
WACO, MODEL TBA

Fig. 244. Waco model TBA with new 160 h.p. Kinner R5 engine was extremely rare type.

In the program of development for the "Waco" sport-type Model A series, it is somewhat unusual that one particular airplane (X-12435) was used repeatedly as the prototype version for each successive model With the final development of at least seven different models in this series, perhaps Waco Aircraft should be commended and credited with using practical money-saving tactics. Basically similar from the firewall station back, each different version of the "Model A" varied only in its engine installation and whatever modifications would be necessary to a particular combination. This particular development in the "Waco A" was the fifth model (TBA) and it required only the removal of the previous engine with its mount and cowling, and replacing it with the 5 cyl. Kinner engine of 160 h.p. With a new engine mount, some reformed cowling sections, and the Kinner R5 installed, this model became known as the TBA. After required tests and final certification for this version, it appears that the Kinner R5 engine was removed, and the airplane once again went on to become something else. The model TBA had its identity for a brief period, then became nothing more than an entry in the records.

As another version in the prolific Waco sport-model A-series, the TBA was also an open cockpit biplane with side-by-side seating for two; normally flown in the wind-swept atmosphere of the open cockpit, all versions could be fitted with a detachable coupe-top canopy for cold-weather comfort. With large luggage compartments both fore and aft, there was ample allow-ance for personal baggage and all sorts of sport-type gear, enough for extended cross-country travel or just outdoor fun. In inheriting all of the notable "Waco" characteristics, it is quite likely that the model TBA performed very well to the tune of its 160 h.p. As powered with the 5 cyl. Kinner R5 engine of 160 h.p. it is logical to assume also that the TBA was perhaps nearly the equal of the popular Jacobs-powered PBA which mounted 170 h.p. The Kinner R5 was a relatively new engine and its mounting in the TBA was the first approved installation; another soon after this was in the Pitcairn sport-type "Autogiro". For the next several years the R5 was used mostly in Kinner-built airplanes so the Kinner Airplane & Motor Co. became its own best customer. The type certificate number for the model TBA was issued 4-1-32 and only 1 example of this model was manufactured by the Waco Aircraft Co. at Troy, Ohio.

Listed below are specifications and performance data for the Waco model TBA as powered with the 160 h.p. Kinner R5 engine; length overall 21'6"; height overall 8'9"; wing span upper 29'6"; wing span lower 27'5"; wing chord upper & lower 57"; wing area upper 130 sq.ft.; wing area lower 111.5 sq.ft.; total wing area 241.5 sq.ft.; airfoil Clark Y; wt. empty 1307 lbs.; useful load 780 lbs.; payload with 40 gal. fuel 340 lbs. (1 pass. at 170 lbs., 2 parachutes & 130 lbs. baggage); gross wt. 2087 lbs.; max. speed 116; cruising speed 98; landing speed 40; climb 800 ft. first min. at sea level; ceiling 14,500 ft.; gas cap. 40 gal.; oil cap. 4 gal.; cruising range at 9.5 gal. per hour 400 miles; price $4490. at factory field. The Kinner R5 engine developed 160 h.p. at 1975 r.p.m.; price was $1985. complete with exhaust collector ring.

The construction details and general arrangement of the model TBA were typical to that of other models in the "Waco A" series as described elsewhere in this volume. The baggage allowance of 150 lbs. was divided between front and rear compartments; 2 parachutes at 20 lbs. each were part of the baggage allowance. The coupe-top canopy added 20 lbs. to the empty weight; price of the coupe-top was $195.00 installed. The landing gear of 71 in. tread used patented oleo shock absorbing struts; 7.50x10 semi-airwheels with brakes were standard equipment. Tail wheel was 10x3 with full swivel. The 40 gal. fuel supply was divided between two tanks mounted in center-section panel of the upper wing. A wooden propeller, Heywood engine starter, navigation lights, hot-shot battery, and dual controls were standard equipment. A metal propeller, Eclipse electric engine starter, coupe-top canopy. landing lights, parachute flares, wheel pants, and lower wing-root fairings were optional. The next development in the Waco model A series was the UBA as described in the chapter for ATC # 479 of this volume.

Listed below is only known TBA entry as gleaned from registration records:

NC-12435; Model TBA (# 3585) Kinner R5.

This same airplane also modified into model BBA with installation of Wright R-540 engine, model BBA not approved; approval for model TBA expired 4-1-34.

Fig. 245. The "Fairchild 24" model C-8 with 95 h.p. Cirrus Hi-Drive engine, aimed at making sport-flying a pleasure.

Kreider-Reisner (Fairchild) developed the new Model C-8 as a running-mate to their popular "Fairchild 22", a new and clever design that would appeal to the cabin-plane advocates as strongly as the "Twenty Two" did to the open cockpit enthusiasts. Clearly of kin in more ways than one, the new "Fairchild 24" (24-C8) presented a smart appearance with features that were rarely incorporated into one small airplane. Seating two in the companionship of side-by-side seating, the comfortable cabin offered plenty of room, excellent visibility, and none of the skimpy interior treatment usually associated with a small light airplane. By installation of the 4 cyl. inverted inline Cirrus (A.C.E.) "Hi-Drive" engine, the 24-C8 gained further advantage in visibility over and around the nose, and the completely cowled-in engine was quickly accessible for maintenance or servicing. Developed primarily for the private owner-flier who would use the airplane more or less for recreation, the new 24-C8 was a well-studied combination of practical utility and good performance. Introduced formally at the annual Detroit Air Show for 1932, the new "Twenty Four" attracted much interest, and gave hint of promise that this new concept would become increasingly popular as time went on. Looking back now to the perky little 24-C8 of 1932 it is hard to realize that its success spawned the development of at least 17 different "Model 24"

over a period of some 15 years. It is also surprising that one of the venerable 24-C8, nearly 35 years old, had been restored to active flying in more recent years.

The new "Fairchild 24" (Kreider-Reisner) model C-8 was a light high-winged cabin monoplane with side-by-side seating for two. The model 24-C8 as shown, was a comparitively large airplane for just two people, but this was purposely planned to avoid skimping on room, and to offer an airplane one could walk around or get into comfortably without assuming a permanent crouch. Developed primarily as a light sport-type airplane for the owner-flier ranks, the model 24-C8 had features particularly suitable for pilot-training also. As powered with the 4 cyl. Cirrus "Hi-Drive" engine of 95 h.p. the model C-8 had power reserve for an impressive performance in the economy so appreciated by the average owner-flier. Arranged in good aerodynamic proportion with an airframe of ample dimension, the new "Twenty Four" was a comfortable airplane in every respect, comfortable to be in, and comfortable to operate. By the same token, its modest operating expenses made it a comfortable airplane to own. Introduced during a time of pinch-penny and hesitant buying, the 24-C8 had no opportunity to create a very large following, but its sensible design laid firm ground-work for variations of this model that followed. The type certificate number for the

Fig. 246. Dimension for comfort was one of many features in new "Twenty Four."

Fairchild model 24-C8 was issued 4-2-32 and 10 examples of this model were manufactured by the Kreider-Reisner Aircraft Co., Inc. at Hagerstown, Maryland, a division of the Fairchild Aviation Corp.

Listed below are specifications and performance data for the Fairchild model 24-C8 as powered with the 95 h.p. Cirrus "Hi-Drive" engine; length overall 23'2"; height overall 7'0"; wing span 35'8"; wing chord 66"; total wing area 170 sq.ft.; airfoil (NACA) N-22; wt. empty 1030 lbs.; useful load 570 lbs.; payload with 24 gal. fuel 236 lbs.; gross wt. 1600 lbs.; max. speed 114; cruising speed 95; landing speed 44; climb 700 ft. first min. at sea level; ceiling 12,000 ft.; gas cap. 24 gal.; oil cap. 2.5 gal.; cruising range at 6.2 gal. per hour 330 miles; price originally quoted as $3360. at factory, raised to $3450. in mid-1932.

The fuselage framework was built up of welded chrome-moly steel tubing, faired to shape with wooden formers and fairing strips, then fabric covered. Cabin width was 40 in. at the seat providing ample room for two big people; a large door and convenient step on either side provided easy entry. Visibility forward and to the sides was excellent with a large overhead skylight providing visitility upwards and back. A baggage compartment with allowance for up to 40 lbs. was behind the seat-back, and dual joystick controls were provided. The wing framework in two halves was built up of spruce I-beam spars with spruce and plywood Pratt-truss wing ribs; the leading edges were covered with dural metal sheet and the completed framework was covered in fabric. The root ends of each wing-half were tapered and rounded off where they fastened to the fuselage for better visibility; a 12 gal. gravity-feed fuel tank was mounted in the root end of each wing. The robust outrigger landing gear of 110 in. tread used oleo-spring shock absorbing struts, and was a part of the wing bracing truss; 6.50x10 semi-airwheels with brakes were standard equipment. A full-swivel 8x4 tail wheel was provided for better ground handling. The fabric covered tail-group was

Fig. 247. Model C-8 initiated "Fairchild 24" concept that flourished for 15 years.

Fig. 248. Head-on view shows minimum head-resistance of inline engine; visibility also improved.

similar to that of the "Twenty Two" both in shape and construction; the horizontal stabilizer was adjustable in flight. A wooden propeller, dual joy-stick controls, wheel brakes, and a tail wheel were standard equipment. Goodyear 19x9-3 airwheels with brakes, or the Fairchild sport-type landing gear with wheel pants were optional. Standard color schemes were same as for the "22"; other two-tone combinations were optional. The next development in the "Fairchild 24" was the Warner-powered model 24-C8A as described in the chapter for ATC # 497 of this volume.

Listed above are model 24-C8 entries as gleaned from registration records:

X-12631;   24-C8 (# 2000) Hi-Drive 95.
NC-12661;   ''   (# 2001)   ''
NC-12675;   ''   (# 2002)   ''
NC-13108;   ''   (# 2003)   ''
NC-13109;   ''   (# 2004)   ''
NC-13110;   ''   (# 2005)   ''
NC-13111;   ''   (# 2006)   ''
NC-13112;   ''   (# 2007)   ''
NC-13168;   ''   (# 2008)   ''
NC-13191;   ''   (# 2009)   ''

This approval for ser. # 2001 and up; reg. no. for ser. # 2004 unverified; model C-8 also tried with Wright-Gipsy engine but no further development beyond tests; approval for 24-C8 expired 9-30-39.

A.T.C. # 476
(4-3-32)
BELLANCA "PACEMAKER", E

Fig. 249. Bellanca "Pacemaker" model E with 420 h.p. Wright R-975-E2 engine.

In development of the popular "Pacemaker" series, G. M. Bellanca mixed in carefully the desirable proportions of lifting capacity, safety, speed, and performance into a blend of mechanical assemblies that made up into an outstanding airplane. Entries in the record-books and enthusiastic pilot-reports have easily confirmed that this was so. Working around this basic design since 1927, each "Bellanca" monoplane as it rolled out on the line was perhaps somewhat better than the one just before it; there really was no cause for radical change in a good basic design, so each was only improved in some detail as a contribution toward making the "Bellanca" a better airplane. The new "Pacemaker" model E for 1932 reflected well the continuous upgrading of this basic design, and as a result was to now the finest version in this series. Outwardly at a glance there appears to be but little change in the new "Model E" over the previous "Pacemaker"; the changes were mostly so subtle as to be practically unnoticeable, but they were there and served their purpose well. Installation of the latest operational aids, a greater fuel capacity for extended cruising range, and a generous increase in useful load allowance added up to hundreds of pounds, so the "Pacemaker E" was a heavier airplane empty and at loaded gross weight. Some of the early examples of the Model E were still powered with the 330 h.p. Wright engine, but only until the 420 h.p. engine was

made available. Upon installation of the new 9 cyl. Wright R-975-E2 engine of 420 h.p. the "Pacemaker E" surged with new-found performance and almost acted like a "Skyrocket". Three examples of this model were operated nationally by the Dept. of Commerce, Aero. Branch, and one was operated by the Des Moines Register & Tribune, a newspaper that had long been an enthusiastic booster for the development of aviation. The "Model E" was only built in small number, but it was a significant example in the progressive development of the "Pacemaker" series.

The Bellanca "Pacemaker" model E was a high-winged cabin monoplane with seating arranged for six. Basically, the "Model E" was still quite similar to earlier examples in the "Pacemaker" series, but the desire to make a good airplane better did have its noticeable effects. Quite definitely slanted towards the needs of big-business, the "E" offered maximum utility with an unusually high performance, an appealing combination for the sportsman-pilot. To now this was the best "Pacemaker" yet, and its appearance across the country was met with great interest. As first powered with the 330 h.p. engine the Model E was somewhat burdened with extra weight, but it really came to new life with the 420 h.p. engine. As powered with the new 9 cyl. Wright R-975-E2 engine, developing 420 h.p. at 2150 r.p.m., the "Pacemaker E" showed terrific gains in every respect,

Fig. 250. More powerful engine unleashed extra performance in model E.

and its overall performance was nearly comparable to the thundering "Skyrocket". To offset higher wing loadings caused by the extra weight, the wing area was increased, and the streamlining properties of the modified speed-ring engine cowl and tear-drop wheel pants added considerably to the top speed. Experiments with the engine cowl of deeper chord showed gains in speed and improvement of airflow, so most all of the Model E were later seen with this deeper type of cowl. Many of the changes and the improvements made at the factory to successive airplanes were available to earlier airplanes also, so it was not unusual to see a "Bellanca" with perhaps 1 or 2 years of service already to its credit suddenly blossom out with new lines and added finery. Maneuverability and general behavior of the new "Pacemaker E" was sharpened consider

ably and most pilots considered it a treat to fly. Some structural improvements added to the safety factor, to in-flight comfort, and to carefree operation over extensive periods of time. All that the "Pacemaker E" had to offer added up to a considerable amount of money, and money in this amount was not so easily available, so sales for the Model E were necessarily small. The type certificate number for the "Pacemaker" model E was issued 4-3-32 and it is difficult to determine just how many examples were built; only 7 show up in the aircraft registry for 1932-33. Manufactured by the Bellanca Aircraft Corp. at New Castle, Dela.

Listed below are specifications and performance data for the Pacemaker model E as powered with the 420 h.p. Wright R-975-E2 engine; length overall 27'10"; height overall 8'4"; wing span 47'6"; wing chord 79"; total

Fig. 251. Pacemaker E in service with Dept. of Commerce.

Fig. 252. Striking view of model E shows typical Bellanca design improved only in detail.

wing area 291 sq. ft.; airfoil "Bellanca" (modified R.A.F.); wt. empty 2706 lbs.; useful load 1950 lbs.; payload with 120 gal. fuel 1000 lbs. (5 pass. at 170 lb. each & 150 lb. baggage); gross wt. 4657 lbs.; max. speed (with speed-ring cowl & wheel pants) 150; cruising speed 125; landing speed 55; climb 1100 ft. first min. at sea level; ceiling 20,000 ft.; gas cap. 120 gal.; oil cap. 8 gal.; cruising range at 24 gal. per hour 700 miles; price was variable.

The construction details and general arrangement of the "Pacemaker E" were typical to that of the earlier CH-300 and CH-400, except for the following: The new modified landing gear of 90 in. tread used "Aerol" (air-oil) shock absorbing struts; 9.50x10 semi-air-wheels with brakes were encased in streamlined metal wheel pants. A new 5x4 tail wheel with shock absorbing strut required a cut-out in bottom of rudder to permit swivel. The Wright engine was tightly shrouded with a "speed-ring" cowl, and the long engine exhaust tail-pipe was provided with a heater-muff for cabin heat. All windows were of shatter-proof glass except two side-windows at the pilot station which were of Pyralin and slid back for ventilation or emergency exit. The interior was sound-proofed, insulated, and tastefully upholstered in fine fabrics; optional interior arrangements were available. Most of the Model E were later equipped with the new Switlik chair-pack parachutes which were fastened into the seat as part of the cushioning and upholstery, to be removed from the seat only in emer-

gency. The baggage allowance of 150 lbs. was divided with 30 lbs. in an upper cabin compartment and 120 lbs. in the main compartment at the rear; a toilet compartment was available to the rear of the cabin and its installation was deducted from the payload. Gravity-feed wing tanks of 60 gal. capacity were mounted in the root end of each wing half; extra seating was allowable with an equivalent reduction in fuel weight. An adjustable metal propeller, speed-ring engine cowl, electric engine starter, battery, navigation lights, cabin heater, wheel pants, and tail wheel were standard equipment. Landing lights, parachute flares, a generator, and Lear radio equipment were optional. The next Bellanca development was the "Skyrocket D" as described in the chapter for ATC # 480 in this volume.

Listed below are "Pacemaker E" entries as gleaned from registration records:
NC-10762 Model E (# 202) Wright 420.
NC-10763;   "   (# 203)   "
      ;   "   (# 204)   "
   NS-5Y;   "   (# 205)   "
   NS-6Y;   "   (# 206)   "
   NS-7Y;   "   (# 207)   "
NC-13187;   "   (# 218)   "
This approval for ser. # 202 and up; except for ser. # 218 all first had 330 h.p. Wright engine; ser. # 205 later modified to "Skyrocket D"; ser. # 204, 208, 209, 210, 211, 212, 213, 214, 215, 216, 217 unknown; ser. # 218 later eligible at 4843 lbs. gross wt.; approval for Model E expired 4-15-34.

A.T.C. # 477
(4-4-32)
STATES, MODEL B-4

Fig. 253. The States model B-4 with 125 h.p. Kinner B5 engine; former tunnel-type cowling was discarded.

The "States" model B-3 had made a fair showing in 1931, and attracted a modest following of owners who became steadfast boosters. The outlook for 1932 was not as rosy, but the sport-plane market was still fairly active in the low-priced bracket, which encompassed the "States" parasol monoplane. In developing the new model B-4 for the sport-plane market States Aircraft could see reason for only very little change, but the nature and behavior of the new monoplane was spiced with added power. As powered now with the 125 h.p. Kinner engine the model B-4 still inherited all the basic features of this design, and the power boost only served to put a finer edge on its behavior. At least one example of the B-4 was built in modest quarters just outside of Chicago in the corner of a rented building; shortly after States Aircraft decided to vacate this area and try for greener pastures that were beckoning down in Texas. The company moved and located in Center, Tex. during July-Aug. of 1933 in a 100x200 ft. steel building on the edge of the city's new airport. In Oct. of 1933, the company was awarded a Dept. of Commerce certificate as an Approved Repair Station, and this eventually became the bulk of their business. Bud Downs, Adam Bialorski, and Jos. Isvolt came down from Chicago with the company with Leo Childs and Frasaer Baggett, both Texas men, joining the firm on its location in Center. J. B. Sanders, owner of the airport land, was the firm's general manager. Sketchy records seem to indicate that up to 10 airplanes were built at this new facility, but it is doubtful if all these were the "States" monoplane. Among some of the more notable jobs done by States at Center, Tex. was repair to the 1931 winner of the endurance-flight record; not otherwise identified it is believed to be the Packard-powered "Bellanca". All 6 of the above-mentioned men worked at various duties in the factory or the repair shop, and it appears that Leo Childs acted somewhat in the engineering capacity; Leo Childs previously had his own operation at Galveston, Tex. After reasonable success with the combined manufacturing-repair business, States Aircraft closed its doors in 1937 for reasons unknown; what took place beyond that time is also unknown. We do know that "type certificates" were still active for the "States" monoplane into 1939.

The "States" model B-4 was an open cockpit parasol-type monoplane with seating for two in tandem. Developed primarily for low-budget sport flying, the B-4 garnered its appeal not so much from performance, but more from the carefree operation offered by its simplicity and inherent strength. Rugged in frame throughout the fuselage was particularly deep for weather protection, and there was ample stretch-room for even the biggest pilot. Visibility was good in most any direction, and the high-mounted wing provided a handy walk-around for entry, exit, or servicing. As clearly shown, everything about the "States" was robust, from the thick wing and deep fuselage down to the spraddle-legged undercarriage. As a go-just-about-anywhere airplane, the "States" allowed generous deviation from normal grounds, out to where the punishment would be higher in exchange for more en-

Fig. 254. States B-4 was leveled at the sportsman, but often used for pilot-training.

joyment. As powered with the 5 cyl. Kinner B5 engine, the new model B-4 did not transform this basic design to any great extent, but performance increases would be noticeable throughout the entire range. Power reserve was available as a satisfying bonus. When stacked against all the other parasol monoplanes of this period, it is doubtful if the "States" could come away with any particular honors, but it was a very good example of compromise that swapped some performance for more safety and utility. The type certificate number for the model B-4 was issued 4-4-32 and at least 2 examples of this model were manufactured by the States Aircraft Corp. at Chicago Hts., Ill. prior to July of 1933 and at Center, Tex. into 1937.

Listed below are specifications and performance data for the States model B-4 as powered with the 125 h.p. Kinner B5 engine; length overall 22'0"; height overall 7'10"; wing span 32'0"; wing chord 72"; total wing area 180 sq.ft.; airfoil Clark Y; wt. empty 1098 lbs.; useful load 555 lbs.; payload with 24 gal. fuel 220 lbs. (1 pass. at 170 lbs., 2 parachutes at 20 lbs each, 10 lbs. baggage); gross wt. 1653 lbs.; max speed 115; cruising speed 97; landing (stall) speed 38; climb 850 ft. first min. at sea level; ceiling 15,000 ft.; gas cap. 24 gal.; oil cap. 3 gal.; cruising range at 7.2 gal. per hour 290 miles; Wts. listed are with metal propeller; price not announced, probably just under $4000.

The construction details and general arrangement of the States model B-4 were typical to that of the B-3 as described in the chapter for ATC # 349 of USCA/C, Vol. 4. The only noticeable difference in the makeup of the B-4 was the discarding of the intricate venturi-type cowling around the Kinner engine; the engine cowling on the model B-4 was now of the more normal type for simplicity and ease of service. On the later "States", including the model B-4, a streamlined steel tie-rod was added to the wing-bracing truss for greater strength. The wide-tread landing gear used low-pressure 22x10-4 Goodyear airwheels; wheel brakes were optional. A metal propeller, wiring for navigation lights, Goodyear airwheels, steel spring-leaf tail skid, and dual joy-stick controls were standard equipment. An engine starter, wheel brakes, navigation lights, and custom colors were optional. No doubt model B-3 were elibible for modification into model B-4.

Listed below are States model B-4 entries as gleaned from registration records:
NC-12902; Model B-4 (# 109) Kinner B5.
NC-12984;   "   (# 110)   "
       ;   "   (# 111)   "
       ;   "   (# 112)   "
NC-11984;   "   (# 113)   "
Ser. # 109 mfgd. Chicago Hts.; ser. # 110 probably mfgd. Texas 1933; ser. # 113 mfgd. Texas 1934. Approval expired 9-30-39.

Fig. 255. Pitcairn model PA-18 with 160 h.p. Kinner R5 engine; shaft forward of pylon was rotor starter.

In developing the earlier sport-type model PAA-1, Pitcairn Aircraft offered this craft hopefully to fit the more modest requirements of the average private-owner and sportsman. For sport-flying of a general nature, the modestly powered PAA-1 offered economy of upkeep and operation, but naturally in exchange for much less performance. To some extent this combination at first showed promise of being the ideal machine, but actually the PAA-1 was sorely underpowered to the extent that performance suffered badly, and the flight technique required under these aggravated conditions was more than the average amateur pilot cared to cope with. To offset these shortcomings, Pitcairn had developed the new PA-18 for 1932 which now had several aerodynamic improvements, some mechanical improvements, and the mind-easing benefit of some horsepower reserve. The improved combination of better streamlining, more rotor blade area, more effective controls, and the

much-needed boost in horsepower was all translated into quicker take-offs, better climb, and certainly much better slow-speed performance. Formally shown at the annual Detroit Air Show for 1932, the plumpish PA-18 created considerable interest among autogiro prospects and several were ordered for early delivery. In the main, the PA-18 was used mostly for general sport-flying, but its peculiar versatility was also adapted to many specialized uses. A novel use of the PA-18 was later demonstrated by the towing of a trailing sky-sign over a prominent football game; flying into the teeth of a fairly good breeze, the autogiro was able to maintain position over the stadium area for nearly an hour. The best part of fying an autogiro for sport, or for hire, was the fun of "just moseying around" to enjoy the vistas normally missed in flying a speeding airplane. In this new form, the Pitcairn model PA-18 sparked considerable interest among the nation's sportsmen, and also in-

Fig. 256. Designed for sport the PA-18 was said to be best-liked of the Pitcairn "autogiro."

spired the modification for most of the previous PAA-1 and PA-20 to a similar combination as the PA-18 that was later called the PA-24. One of the more popular "autogiro" of this period, the model PA-18, served in a multitude of duties and remained on the active scene for many years afterward.

The Pitcairn model PA-18 was a sport-type autogiro with open cockpits arranged to seat two in tandem. Typical of its bigger (PCA-2) sistership, the stubby PA-18 was more or less a copy in scaled-down fashion. Primarily developed for the amateur sport-flier, the PA-18 embodied the latest developments in autogiro knowledge with equipment and appointments designed to enhance the pleasures of flying in a machine of this type. As powered with the new 5 cyl. Kinner R5 engine of 160 h.p. performance of the PA-18 was considerably improved overall, and especially during critical low-speed maneuvering. Stable and very capable, the PA-18 was perhaps the best in a small autogiro and its chance for a better future was stifled only by economic circumstance. The type certificate number for the model PA-18 was issued 4-7-32 and 18 or more examples of this model were manufactured by Pitcairn Aircraft, Inc. on Pitcairn Field in Willow Grove, Penna.; as of Jan. in 1933, the firm name was changed to the more appropriate Pitcairn Autogiro Co. Earlier in 1932 R. B. C. Noorduyn, formerly with Anthony Fokker and more recently as V.P. of Bellanca Aircraft, was appointed as the executive engineer at Pitcairn Aircraft to help in development of

new autogiro designs; most notable among these new wind-mill craft was a cabin-type transport with seating for 4 or 5. An accounting for this period shows that 51 of the autogiro were built in 1931 and 46 of these were sold; the unsold autogiro were retained by manufacturers to continue with development and testing programs.

Listed below are specifications and performance data for the Pitcairn model PA-18 as powered with the 160 h.p. Kinner R5 engine; fuselage length overall 19'5"; height overall (tail up) 11'4"; rotor blade dia. 40'0"; rotor blade chord 18.6"; rotor blade area 117 sq.ft.; fixed-wing span 21'3"; fixed-wing chord 36"; fixed-wing area 55 sq.ft.; fixed-wing airfoil Clark Y; wt. empty 1344-1354 lbs.; useful load 556 lbs.; payload with 30 gal. fuel 180 lbs.; gross wt. 1900-1910 lbs.; max. speed 100; cruising speed 85; landing speed 20-25; climb 700 ft. first min. at sea level; ceiling 12,000 ft.; gas cap. 30 gal.; oil cap. 3.5 gal.; cruising range at 9.5 gal. per hour 250 miles; price $6750. at factory (with instruction) in 1932; price reduced to $4940. (no instruction) in 1933. Amended allowance later raised gross wt. to 1950 lbs.

The construction details and general arrangement of the model PA-18 were in many instances typical to that of the models PAA-1 and PA-20 as described in the chapter for ATC # 433. The fuselage framework was built up of welded 4130 and 1025 steel tubing, heavily faired to a rounded shape with formers and fairing strips, then fabric covered. A large door on left side provided entry to the front cockpit. Both seats were

Fig. 257. PA-18 designed to overcome poor showing of earlier PAA-1.

fitted with thick resiliant cushions, and large built-up windshields were of shatter-proof glass; dual joy-stick controls were provided. A small baggage locker was in the turtle-back section behind rear cockpit. The 30 gal. fuel supply was divided between a 25 gal. tank and a 5 gal. reserve tank, both mounted high in forward fuselage. The spidery oleo-spring landing gear of 10 ft. tread used 6.50x10 semi-airwheels; wheel brakes, a parking brake, and tail wheel were standard equipment. The fixed wing was built up of spruce box-type spar beams with spruce truss-type wing ribs and covered in fabric; the fixed wing was wire-braced in conjunction with the landing gear truss. The fabric covered tail-group was built up of welded 4130 and 1025 steel tubing; auxiliary fins were mounted on horizontal stabilizer for improved directional control, and horizontal stabilizer was adjustable for trim in flight. The rotor system was similar to that of the PAA-1 and PA-20 except for some structural variation. All exposed airframe fittings, and most of the cockpit hardware were nickel-plated against corrosion. A fixed metal propeller, Heywood engine starter, a battery, navigation lights, seat cushions, dual controls, wheel brakes, parking brake, tail wheel, and rotor blade starter were standard equipment.

A custom finish in a variety of color combinations was optional upon order at no extra cost. The next development in the Pitcairn autogiro was the model PA-24 as described in the chapter for ATC # 507.

Listed below are model PA-18 entries as gleaned from registration records:

Registration	Model	Serial	Engine
NC-12663;	Model PA-18	(# G-62)	Kinner R5.
NC-12676;	"	(# G-63)	"
NC-12677;	"	(# G-64)	"
NC-12678;	"	(# G-65)	"
NC-12679;	"	(# G-66)	"
NC-12680;	"	(# G-67)	"
NC-12681;	"	(# G-68)	"
NC-12682;	"	(# G-69)	"
NC-12683;	"	(# G-70)	"
NC-12684;	"	(# G-71)	"
NC-12685;	"	(# G-73)	"
NC-13131;	"	(# G-74)	"
NC-13189;	"	(# G-75)	"
NC-13190;	"	(# G-76)	"
NC-2435;	"	(# G-77)	"
NC-2437;	"	(# G-78)	"
;	"	(# G-79)	"
NC-2491;	"	(# G-80)	"

This approval for ser. # G-62 and up; reg. no. for ser. # G-71 unverified; ser. # G-72 and #, G-79 unknown; this approval expired 9-30-39.

A.T.C. # 479
(4-23-32)
WACO, MODEL UBA

Fig. 258. Waco model UBA with 210 h.p. Continental engine; sporty combination drew glances of envy.

To catch the roving fancy of the clientele that were looking for an airplane designed specifically for high-performance sport flying, Waco Aircraft proudly introduced the two-seated model UBA. The stubby model UBA as powered with a 210 h.p. Continental engine was,the top of the line in the A-series, and perhaps the most efficient sport-plane of this type. Quite capable even with the prompting of a timid hand, the chesty UBA became a breath-taking machine in the hands of a good pilot; breaking ground often in less than 100 feet, and landing in almost the same distance, the UBA had the knack to bring out the show-off in any man. Although there were not many sport-fliers or play-boy pilots willing to plunk down nearly $5000. for an airplane of this type, the UBA was, however, actively represented throughout the country. The Eclipse Aviation Corp. (starters, generators, etc.) operated a UBA for business promotion in the east, the Thomas Fruit Co. (bananas) operated one here and there out of Missouri, and at least one example operated in and out of California. A rather special "Waco," the UBA always drew admiring glances and complimentary comment; this did not show up on the company's ledger as sales, but it did strengthen the memory of "Waco" tradition. Starting way down in the power range, Waco Aircraft introduced the "Model A" sport rather cautiously in hopes of selling a good number of the cheaper models while they worked up gradually to the higher-powered versions; with each model in this series built more or less to

some specific need, or a preference, it soon became evident that those who could fly strictly for sport had no need to be budget-minded, and spent their money on the more expensive models. Altogether the "Waco A" series made a rather poor showing in volume, and the higher-powered models sold better than the cheaper models, a peculiar phenomenon of this troubled period.

The Waco model UBA was a "convertible" sport biplane with side-by-side seating for two. Normally flown in the open cockpit configuration during the summer months, a detachable coupe-top canopy could be easily fitted to ward off the sting of wintry weather. By limiting the seating capacity to a pilot and one passenger, ample room and weight allowance was provided for heaps of personal baggage and all sorts of sporting gear. Having no mission to fulfill other than answering to the spontaneous whims of a sporting pilot, the UBA had practically go-anywhere utility that was almost without limit. As powered with the 7 cyl. Continental R-670 engine of 210 h.p. the UBA had all-round performance that certainly could warm the heart of any good man. Operating in and out of even the tiniest fields with a climb-out that was just short of remarkable, the UBA pilot could drop in just about anywhere, and they often did. Inheriting all the noteable features and characteristics of the "Waco" biplane, the UBA was rather easy to fly well, response was sharp, and maneuverability was one of its better features. Of particularly rugged frame and hardy character, the

Fig. 259. Les and Martie Bowman; Martie delivered UBA from Troy, O. to Calif. UBA was top of the line in sport series.

UBA was a pleasure to operate, and pride of ownership was actually a large part of the owner's enjoyment. When dandied up with a metal propeller, speed-ring cowl, coupe-top canopy, and streamlined wheel pants, the UBA cut quite a figure among airplanes parked out on the line. The type certificate number for the model UBA was issued 4-23-32 and at least 6 examples of this model were manufactured by the Waco Aircraft Co. at Troy, O. From experience with the sport A-series during 1932, Waco Aircraft introduced only 2 versions for 1933, and both of these mounted engines of higher power.

Listed below are specifications and performance data for the Waco model UBA as powered with the 210 h.p. Continental R-670 engine; length overall 21'0"; height overall 8'9"; wing span upper 29'6"; wing span lower 27'5"; wing chord upper & lower 57"; wing area upper 130 sq. ft.; wing area lower 111.5 sq. ft.; total wing area 241.5 sq. ft.; airfoil Clark Y; wt. empty 1409 (1401) lbs.; useful load 841 (899) lbs.; payload with 40 gal. fuel 401 (459) lbs.; gross wt. 2250 (2300) lbs.; figures in brackets for amended wt. allowance; max. speed (speed-ring cowl, canopy, wheel pants) 132; cruising speed 115; landing speed 42; climb 1500 ft. first min. at sea level; ceiling 15,800 ft.; gas cap. 40 gal.; oil cap. 4 gal.; cruising range at 12.5 gal. per hour 345 miles; price $4895. at factory field.

The construction details and general arrangement of the model UBA were typical to that of other models in the A-series as described elsewhere in this volume. The strengthening of certain fuselage members in the station behind firewall allowed gross weight increase to 2300 lbs. The detachable coupe-top canopy could be installed or removed in about 30 minutes; price was $195.00 extra. The baggage allowance of 165 lbs. was divided among two compartments; front compartment was allowed 128 lbs. and rear compartment in turtle-back section was allowed 36 lbs. Two fuel tanks of 20 gal. each were mounted in center-section panel of the upper wing; an extra 20 gal. tank could be installed in upper fuselage above front baggage compartment. Two parachutes, when carried, were part of the baggage allowance. The patented landing gear of 71 in. tread used 6.50x10 wheels fitted with 7.50x10 low-pressure tires; wheel brakes were standard equipment. Skis were optional for winter operation. A wooden propeller, compass, dual controls, wheel brakes, and 10x3 tail wheel were standard equipment. An adjustable metal propeller, lower wing-root fairings, metal wheel pants, coupe-top canopy, landing lights, parachute flares, extra 20 gal. fuel tank, and skis were optional. Standard color scheme was silver for wings, with gray, black, silver, or vermillion fuselage optional. The next development in the "Waco A" was the model PLA as described in the chapter for ATC # 502.

Listed below are model UBA entries as gleaned from registration records:

NC-12435; Model UBA (# 3585) Cont. 210.
NC-12449;   "   (# 3600)   "
NC-12463:   "   (# 3601)   "
NC-12469;   "   (#3602)   "
NC-13032;   "   (# 3612)   "
NC-13046;   "   (# 3613)   "

This approval for ser. # 3585 and up; this approval expired 5-1-34.

Fig. 260. Handsome Bellanca "Skyrocket D" with supercharged "Wasp" engine.

Efficient performance of the "Bellanca" design to this point had been proven in just about any flight endeavor, and each successive version was blessed with the same inherent qualities, plus many of the little improvements that were continually being added as airplanes were coming off the assembly line. Guiseppe Bellanca, like a maestro conducting a symphony, spent most of his time at the factory, hovering nearby like a happy mother-hen, and it was not at all unusual for him to suggest slight changes here, and some improvement there, every day; this making each "Bellanca" that came off the line perhaps just a little bit better than the ones before it. On occasion, significant changes of a more extensive nature fostered the evolution into another model, and this was the case of the "Skyrocket" model D. While at first glance the Model D would appear virtually unchanged, it did harbor a number of changes that were calculated to further increase efficiency, performance, and convenience of operation. The heart of the thundering "Skyrocket D" was the super-

charged Pratt & Whitney "Wasp" SC-1 engine which was rated 450 h.p. at 6000 feet, offering sea level performance at cruising altitude. Standing just a bit taller with a shade more wing span, the Model D was about 300 lbs. heavier when empty, with the gross weight increased by a similar amount. At sea level or thereabouts, the Model D would perhaps be comparable to any good Bellanca CH-400, but at 6000 ft. or better it showed its tail to all of them. Other benefits woven into the "Skyrocket D" came mainly as operational aids and other conveniences that were standard equipment now instead of being added later on to undermine useful load capacity. Built in very small number, the owner's roster was shared by the Dept. of Commerce (Aero. Branch) and several nationally-known business houses. Catering to a very particular clientele, the "Skyrocket D" was custom-built and tailored exactly to the owners wishes; everything from the cabin interior arrangement to the color scheme was the customer's option. It is fact that the "Skyrocket D" was actually

Fig. 261. Deluxe version of "Skyrocket D" capable of 170 m.p.h. despite boxy appearance.

Fig. 262. Skyrocket model D operated by Standard Oil Co. of Kansas.

not very well known as such, but it did share a significant spot in the development of "Bellanca" airplanes.

The Bellanca "Skyrocket" model D was a custom-built high winged cabin monoplane with seating normally arranged for six. Despite its rather compact-looking proportion for an airplane of this type, the improved Model D offered ample room in the cradle of good comfort. Classed as a light passenger transport and designed to operate with maximum efficiency, the Model D could not very well forget that it was a "Skyrocket", and behaved much more like a sport-type airplane than an obedient air-carrier. Ordinarily there was not much to get excited about in a large cabin monoplane such as this, but the "Skyrocket D" has to be an exception to this because it certainly was not an ordinary airplane. As powered with the 9 cyl. Pratt & Whitney "Wasp" SC-1 engine of 450 h.p. (at 6000 ft.) the "Skyrocket D" had the unusual ability to get better as it gained altitude with its maximum ability available in the vicinity of 6000 feet; this, of course, was possible because of the supercharged "Wasp" engine. As fitted with streamlined wheel pants and a low drag "speed-ring" engine cowl, the Model D could top-off at 170 m.p.h. (at 6000 ft.) or cruise along easily at 145 m.p.h.; relatively speaking, this hardly seems likely for a boxy-looking cabin monoplane, but the wizardry of "Bellanca" design is what made it all possible. Otherwise, the Model D still shared all the inherent qualities of earlier "Skyrocket" (CH-400) versions that were such popular favorites the country over. The type certificate number for the "Skyrocket" model D was issued 4-27-32 and about 6 or 7 examples of this model were manufactured by the Bellanca Aircraft Corp. At New Castle, Delaware.

Listed below are specifications and performance data for the "Skyrocket" model D as powered with the "Wasp" SC-1 engine; length overall 27'11"; height overall 8'5"; wing span 47'6"; wing chord 79"; total wing area (including struts) 291 sq. ft.; airfoil "Bellanca" (modified R.A.F.); wt. empty 2920 lbs.; useful load 1980 lbs.; payload with 120 gal. fuel 1010 lbs. (5 pass. at 170 lb. each & 160 lb. baggage); gross wt. 4900 lbs.; max. speed (at 6000 ft.) 170; cruising speed (at 6000 ft.) 145; landing speed 60; climb 1250 ft. first min. at sea level; service ceiling 24,000 ft.; gas cap. 120 gal.; oil cap. 8 gal.; cruising range at 25 gal. per hour 700 miles; price at factory variable.

The construction details and general arrangement of the "Skyrocket" model D were typical to that of the model CH-400 as described in the chapter for ATC # 319 of USCA/C, Vol. 4. The most apparent change in the Model D was the new landing gear which was slightly different in makeup and geometry to offer an increase in structural strength and better streamlining. "Aerol" (air-oil) shock absorbing struts were used in conjunction with 9.50x12 semi-airwheels for softer landings; the wheels were encased in streamlined metal wheel pants and Autofan wheel brakes were standard equipment. The wing was basically the same except for a 1 ft. 2 in. increase in overall span which was divided among the two wing tips; one fuel tank of 60 gal. cap. was mounted in the root end of each wing half. The roomy cabin interior was arranged and fitted to the customer's order with the addition of such standard niceties as cabin heat, cabin ventilation, cabin lights, soundproofing, night-flying equipment, dual controls, and an unusually complete set of engine and flight instruments. Toilet equipment and provisions for the installation of radio were optional. An adjustable metal propeller, electric engine starter, a battery, generator, speed-ring engine cowl, wheel pants, cabin heater, navigation lights, landing lights, flares, dual controls, an artificial horizon, compass, and a 5x4 tail wheel were standard equipment. The next Bellanca development was the big "Aircruiser" as described in the chapter for ATC # 563.

Listed below are "Skyrocket D" entries as gleaned from registration records:

NC-12656; Model D (# 633) Wasp SC-1.
NC-12657;   "   (# 634)   "
NC-12658;   "   (# 635)   "
NC-13155;   "   (# 636)   "
   XRE-3;   "   (# 637)   "
    NS-3;   "   (# 638)   "
   NS-5Y;   "   (# 205)   "

This approval for ser. # 205, 633 and up; ser. # 205 first as Pacemaker E; ser. # 637 delivered to U.S. Navy as XRE-3; ser. # 638 later as NC-18613; this approval expired 4-1-34.

A.T.C. #481
(5-6-32)
REARWIN "JUNIOR", 3100

Fig. 263. Rearwin "Junior" model 3100 with new 50 h.p. Szekely engine.

When the improved 3 cyl. Szekely engine was announced, Rearwin Airplanes was the first to try it in a new version of the "Junior" monoplane. Also a typical 3 cyl. engine, the new Szekely SR-3-55 had a higher compression ratio, operated at a higher r.p.m., and was improved somewhat internally for a little more reliability. With this new 50 h.p. engine installed, the Rearwin "Junior" became the model 3100, and more or less a companion model to the Aeromarine-powered model 4000 just previously released. Although 5 horsepower is not very much to get excited about, it did mean something to a small airplane such as the "Junior"; in comparison with the 45 h.p. model 3000 there should have been some noticeable difference in performance and useable utility. With its 5 h.p. boost and a more reliable engine, the model 3100 was clearly a better airplane. One previously built model 3000 was converted into the model 3100 by an installation of the new improved engine; it is likely that many owners of the "Junior" 3000 would have wished to do likewise, but Szekely Motors were hard hit financially about this time and finally had to discontinue manufacture. Formal production of the Rearwin "Junior" series was also suspended later in 1932. The next several years at Rearwin Airplanes were spent in the designing and developing of new models; several of these models were introduced later during a slight upswing in the nation's economy. In a sense the "depression", by now a firmly-rooted household word, was still very much with us even in 1934-35, but things were looking somewhat better, and people were beginning to buy airplanes again.

The Rearwin "Junior" model 3100 was a light parasol-type monoplane with seating arranged for two in tandem; normally flown with open sides, a detachable enclosure was available for colder weather. Basically, all of the Rearwin "Junior" were alike except for the engines installed, so the model 3100 was closely akin to the 3000 and the 4000. As powered with the new 3 cyl. Szekely SR-3-55 engine of 50 h.p. the model 3100 promised some improvement over the earlier (45 h.p.) model 3000 and was more on a par with the 50 h.p. model 4000. Both Rearwin Airplanes and Szekely Motors were feeling the steady pinch of a skidding market, so it is hard to wager a guess as to what the future would have had in store for the new 3100 and the 4000. The model 3100 was quite rare, and it was also the last development in the Rearwin "Junior" series. The type certificate number for the model 3100 was issued 5-6-32 and 2 examples of this model were manufactured by Rearwin Airplanes, Inc. on Fairfax Field in Kansas City, Kansas. It seemed almost as a useless gesture, but Hart Bowman, reputed to be one of the first successful airplane salesmen in this country, became sales manager for Rearwin Airplanes in Jan. of 1933.

Listed below are specifications and performance data for the "Junior" model 3100 as powered with the 50 h.p. Szekely SR-3-55 engine; length overall 21'8"; height overall 7'6" wing span 36'0"; wing chord 60"; total wing area 179 sq. ft.; airfoil (NACA) M-series; wt. empty (with 28 lb. enclosure) 633 lbs.; useful load 438 lbs.; payload with 12 gal. fuel 185 lbs. (1 pass. at 170 lb. & 15 lb. baggage); gross wt. 1071 lbs.; max. speed (with enclosure) 92; cruising speed 76; landing speed 35; climb 640 ft. first min. at sea level; ceiling 14,500 ft.; gas cap. 12 gal.; oil cap. 6 qts.; cruising range at 2.9 gal. per hour 240 miles; price was not announced.

The construction details and general arrangement of the model 3100 were typical to that of models 3000 and 4000 as described in chapters for ATC # 434 and # 469 of this volume. For the "Junior" model 3100 (ser. # 219) and subsequent airplanes a new and better enclosure was developed weighing 28 lbs., so as compared to the earlier flimsy enclosure of only 12 lbs. the new enclosure was stiffer and more practical. The "Junior" of 1932 was also to have been available with the 3 cyl. Jacobs L-3 engine of 55 h.p., but this version was apparently never developed. A CAA directive stated that Szekely engines in the models SR-3-L and SR-3-45 would no longer be eligible for installation in aircraft approved after 12-22-32; this then limited the choice of Szekely engines to the SR-3-55 of 50

h.p. Standard equipment on the model 3100 included a wooden propeller, steel spring-leaf tail skid, 16x7-4 Goodyear airwheels, individual windshields, a baggage compartment with allowance for 15 lbs., and dual joy-stick controls. A detachable winter enclosure was optional. The next Rearwin development to be certificated was the "Sportster" model 7000 as described in the chapter for ATC # 574 issued in 1935.

Listed below are "Junior" model 3100 entries as gleaned from registration records:
NC-11059;   Model 3100   (# 216)   SR-3-55.
NC-12513;   "   (# 219)   "
This approval for ser. # 219 and up; ser. # 216 modified into 3100 from earlier 3000; this approval expired 11-5-36.

A.T.C. # 482
(5-6-32)
GENERAL-WESTERN "METEOR", P-2-S

Fig. 264. Meteor model P-2-S with 100 h.p. Kinner K5 engine.

The General-Western "Meteor" model P-2-S was an interesting newcomer to the sport-trainer field, a husky sport-type airplane that had many practical design features in its favor. Arranged as a parasol-monoplane for convenience, the stout semi-cantilever wing also offered strength and good pendulum stability. Sport monoplane advocates have often voiced a distinct preference for the parasol-type machine, perhaps because the configuration promoted more desirable flight characteristics in a light airplane. The "parasol" also offered excellent visibility during many of the critical stages of a flight, and was a handy machine to get around to during servicing or maintenance. As a craft specifically designed for sport-flying the "Meteor" was of husky build, but not to the point that it would be hampered by its own strength. Fairly long moment arms assured gentle but firm response with overall aerodynamic makeup that was attuned towards a sporty nature. Sport flying of these early times was usually an exhuberant way of enjoying the pleasures of guiding a good airplane through flight, and moods could often approach that of being reckless; the "Meteor" was game enough to join these moods of fun, and was stout enough to withstand the extra stresses. Bearing the soft rounded lines that were a well-known trademark of Albin K. Peterson, its designer, the "Meteor" was quite handsome in a rather feminine way, but it was easy to find and to bring out the lurking tom-boy in its nature. Developed primarily as a sport-trainer the model P-2-S was a good sport-type airplane first, but it did have suitable characteristics for the training of pilots also. The model P-2-S "Sportster" was the sport version of the "Meteor" and thereby was bedecked with interior appointments and other niceties more apt to appeal to the private-owner flier. Built in rather, small number and rarely seen outside of the west-coast area, at least one of the "Meteor" survived the ravages of storage and time to fly again in 1955.

Early in 1930 the General-Western Aero Corp., Ltd. was organized in Los Angeles, Calif. with one million dollars in capital assets; plans were then announced for the manufacture of the newly-designed Q-10, a ten-place twin-engined amphibious airliner. With circumstances strongly against such a venture at that time, the ambitious project tried, but never did get off the ground. Later that year a reorganization was effected with L. F. Vremsak as president, and with Albin K. Peterson as treasurer and chief engineer. In Dec. of 1930 the prototype of a new sport-plane had been built by the new General-Western firm at Burbank, Calif.; as a cheaper companion model to the sport-plane it was also to be offered in a trainer version. As first introduced, the new airplane was occasionally called the "Bantam", soon changed to the "Phantom",

Fig. 265. P-2-S a fine example of typical sport-plane of this period.

and finally to the "Meteor". By 1932 the company had moved its facility from Burbank to the General-Western airport at Goleta, a suburb of Santa Barbara, Calif.; general offices were finally moved to the airport also.

The General-Western "Meteor" model P-2-S was an open cockpit parasol-type monoplane with seating arranged for two in tandem. The P2-S was finished off neatly in fine interior appointments, and equipped with numerous operational aids. Much of the standard equipment on the P-2-S (Sportster) were items that the average sport-flier found almost necessary, so these were included as standard and not as options to be bought and installed later. The handsome "Meteor" was a stout well-built airplane that assured carefree service, a high performance, and long range, a combination of features that would appeal to any sportsman-pilot. Powered with the popular 5 cyl. Kinner K5 engine of 100 h.p. the P2-S had power reserve to deliver a good per-

formance with ample ability to operate in and out of the smaller airfields; it was pretty much a fun airplane. Flight characteristics were firm and responsive with a good solid feel through all the maneuvers; the "Meteor" was not developed to excel in acrobatic flying, but it was capable of a rather impressive display. Represented in a very small number, the "Meteor" did not leave very much lore behind, but pilots did speak of it fondly. The "Meteor" (as P-2) was first approved on a Group 2 memo numbered 2-285 (issued 10-13-30) for one airplane. The type certificate number for the model P-2-S was issued 5-6-32 and about 5 examples of this model were manufactured by the General-Western Aero Corp., Ltd. at the Goleta airport.

Listed below are specifications and performance data for the "Meteor" Model P-2-S as powered with the 100 h.p. Kinner K5 engine; length overall 24'2", height overall 7'10"; wing span 32'0"; wing chord at root 72"; wing chord at tip

Fig. 266. P-2-S on factory field; factory in background.

Fig. 267. P-2-S shown was converted to "duster" with 220 h.p. Continental engine; view at
Bellflower, Calif. in 1953.

54"; total wing area 163 sq. ft.; airfoil Goetting-
en 398; wt. empty 1137 lbs.; useful load 613
lbs.; payload with 32 gal. fuel 228 lbs. (1 pass. at
170 lb. & 58 lb. baggage); gross wt. 1750 lbs.;
max. speed 115; cruising speed (.9 power) 105;
landing (stall) speed 42; climb 800 ft. first min.
at sea level; ceiling 13,500 ft.; gas cap. 32 gal.;
oil cap. 3 gal.; cruising range at 7 gal. per hour
420 miles; price $3280. at factory field as an-
nounced April of 1932.

The fuselage framework was built up of
welded 4130 steel tubing, heavily faired with
wooden formers and fairing strips to a well-
rounded shape, then fabric covered. The cockpits were deep and well protected by large
Fiberloid windshields; bucket seats were
shaped for a parachute pack. The interior was
upholstered with leather, floor-boards were
reinforced with dural metal sheet, and dual joy-
stick controls were provided. Convenient entry
steps were provided for each cockpit, but the
lack of a door hampered entry to the front seat. A
baggage bin of 4 cu. ft. cap. and allowance for
up to 58 lbs. was located high in the cowl just
ahead of front windshield; two parachutes at 20
lbs. each, when carried, were part of the baggage
allowance. The tapered semi-cantilever wing
was built up of spruce and plywood box-type
spar beams with spruce and plywood truss-type
wing ribs; the leading edges were covered with
dural metal sheet and the completed framework
was covered with fabric. The fuel tank was
mounted in the thick central portion of the wing;

a float-type fuel gauge was visible from either
cockpit. The wing was perched high atop a cabane of steel tube struts, and braced to the lower fuselage longerons; all struts were of heavy
gauge and of streamlined section. The split-
axle landing gear of 70 in. tread used rubber
compression-ring shock absorbers; Goodyear
20x9-4 "airwheels" with brakes were standard
equipment. A tail skid was normally used, but a
tail wheel was optional. The fabric covered tail-
group was built up of welded 4130 steel tubing;
the fin was ground adjustable and the horizontal
stabilizer was adjustable in flight. A metal propeller, complete set of instruments, fire extinguisher, and first-aid kit were also standard
equipment. A Heywood engine starter and tail
wheel were optional. The next development in
the "Meteor" was the model P-2-T trainer as
described in the chapter for ATC # 488 of this
volume.

Listed below are all Meteor P-2 entries as
gleaned from registration records:

X-188W;	Model P-2	(# 101)	Kinner K5.
NC-958Y;	"	(# 102)	"
NC-12254;	"	(# 103)	"
NC-12260;	"	(# 104)	"
NC-12238;	"	(# 105)	"
NC-12294;	"	(# 106)	"

This approval for ser. # 104 and up; reg. no. for
ser. # 103 unverified; ser. # 105 mfgd. 9-6-32;
ser. # 106 mfgd. 1933, later converted to "duster"; approval expired 3-21-35 due to sale to Air
Transport Mfg. Co., Ltd.

Fig. 268. Handsome view of Fairchild 22-C7B with 125 h.p. Menasco C4 engine.

As the third version in the popular "Fairchild 22" series, the model C-7-B (22-C7B) was developed especially by Kreider-Reisner to meet the strictest demands of the more advanced pilot, and yet have all the agreeable qualities required for normal operation by the average amateur pilot. Continuing with the neat slender lines made possible by use of the "inline" engine, this particular model proved again the versatility of this basic design; the basic "Twenty Two" also had the habit of hiding several talents that were brought to the fore by application of more power. As powered with the new 4 cyl. Menasco "Pirate" inverted inline engine of 125 h.p. the 22 C7B continued to offer the features that contributed most to the durability and utility of an airplane, and the "plus" above it all was the promise of a snappy live-wire performance. As shown here in good likeness, this new "Twenty Two" was every bit as trim and girlish as its earlier sister-ships, but was purposely bedecked in casual finery that suggested the subtle poise of a true sport-plane. One of the more handsome of the "parasol monoplanes" this was also a rugged, good-performing airplane at a fairly sensible price. By anyone's standard of comparison, the Fairchild 22-C7B was an attractive choice for a cheaper sport-type airplane, but the market for this type of airplane was naturally limited at this time. Most of the few that were built were well scattered about the U.S.A., and later one was exported to Manila in the Phillipine Islands.

The Fairchild 22 model C-7-B was an open cockpit parasol-type monoplane with seating arranged for two in tandem. Basically typical of the earlier Rover-powered C-7 and the Cirrus-powered C-7-A it is easy to guess that the Menasco-powered C-7-B was developed strictly for sport use. Along with the generous increase in horsepower, were several other interior and exterior features that added up to practical enjoyment and cause for beaming pride of ownership. Posing on its new streamlined sport-type landing gear with its wing perched high off the ground, the 22-C7B was a very handy airplane; getting in or out was easy enough, servicing or maintenance were uncomplicated, and the range of visibility was excellent on the ground or in the air. As powered with the Menasco C4-125 engine of 125 h.p. the 22-C7B had plenty of pepper in its performance and a natural willingness to do just as bid. Light on the controls with a pleasant response, it was well capable of acrobatics whether guided with precision or merely herded by exhuberance. Stout of frame and rugged of character, the "Twenty Two", especially in this version, was a pleasant playmate for the sporting pilot. In view of its many inherent features that offered utility, carefree operation, and exciting recreation, the 22-C7B was a lot of airplane for the money invested. The type certificate number for the Fairchild (Kreider-Reisner) model 22-C7B was issued 5-9-32 and at least 8 examples of this model were manufactured by the Kreider-Reisner Aircraft Co., Inc. at Hagerstown, Md.; a division of the Fairchild Aviation Corp. Sherman Fairchild was president; Louis

Fig. 269. Dainty appearance of 22-C7B belies its rugged character and extra strength.

E. Reisner was V.P.; and George Hardman was chief engineer.

Listed below are specifications and performance data for the Fairchild 22-C7B as powered with the 125 h.p. Menasco "Pirate" engine; length overall 21'11"; height overall 8'0"; wing span 31'10"; wing chord 66"; total wing area 170 sq. ft.; airfoil (NACA) N-22; wt. empty 1010 lbs.; useful load 590 lbs.; payload with 30 gal. fuel 218 lbs. (1 pass. at 170 lb. & 48 lb. baggage, or 2 parachutes); gross wt. 1600 lbs.; max. speed 125; cruising speed 106; landing speed 45; climb 1050 ft. first min. at sea level; ceiling 18,000 ft.; gas cap. 30 gal.; oil cap. 3 gal.; cruising range at 7.5 gal. per hour 400 miles; price $3450. at factory. Gross wt. allowance later increased to 1750 lbs. when equipped with metal propeller, sport-type landing gear, engine starter, and battery; some of the performance suffered proportionately.

The construction details and general arrangement of the Fairchild 22-C7B were typical to that of the models 22-C7 and 22-C7A as described elsewhere in this volume. Normal improvements of the "Fairchild 22" during 1932-33 included the following in general, and the 22-C7B in particular: Bucket-type seats were fitted for a parachute pack, windshields were of the 3-piece sport type, and instrument panels were mounted in rubber. Brake pedals were standard in rear cockpit and optional for installation in front cockpit. Duplicate instruments in front cockpit and dual joy-stick controls were also optional. All airframe fittings were enameled if internal and cadmium plated if external; all movable control surfaces and control operating mechanisms were mounted on grease-packed ball bearings, 34 in all. Fuel tanks of terne plate were mounted in the fuselage (21 gal.) and (9 gal.) in center portion of the one-piece wing; a float-type fuel level gauge was visible from either cockpit. The optional one-piece or two-piece wing was now fitted with a leading edge "spoiler strip" to eliminate float and was also handy as a tell-tale "stall" warning. The optional sport-type landing gear of 91 in. tread had faired center-vees and the 6.50x10 semi-airwheels were encased in streamlined

Fig. 270. Experimental version of 22-C7B with 120 h.p. "Gipsy" III engine; combination
slated for Canada.

Fig. 271. Deluxe version of 22-C7B with sport-type landing gear and custom color scheme.

metal wheel pants; wheel brakes were standard equipment. "Fairchild" oleo-spring shock absorbing struts of 8 in. travel were optional for both standard and sport-type landing gear; Goodyear 19x9-3 airwheels with brakes were also optional. The fabric covered tail-group was still similar in construction and general shape, but area of the rudder was increased for better slow-speed control. The horizontal stabilizer was adjustable in flight from either cockpit. The final finish of the completed airplane consisted in 4 coats of clear dope, 2 coats of aluminum dope, and 3 coats of color pigmented dope; the last 3 coats were hand-rubbed and finally waxed to a high shine. Standard color schemes were International-Orange fuselage with Ivory wing, or Insignia-Blue fuselage with Army-Navy Yellow wing. Other two-tone combinations were $40.00 extra. A wooden propeller, wiring for lights, wheels brakes, and steel spring-leaf tail skid were standard equipment. A Curtiss-Reed metal propeller, electric engine starter, battery, navigation lights, streamlined sport-type landing gear, 19x9-3 Goodyear airwheels with brakes, brake pedals in front cockpit, duplicate instruments in front cockpit, dual controls, landing lights, parachute flares, and 8x4 tail wheel were optional extras. The next Fairchild 22 development was the Gipsy-powered 22-C7D as described in the chapter for ATC #503.

Listed below are model 22-C7B entries as gleaned from registration records:

NC-12670; Model 22-C7B (# 1500) Menasco 125.
NC-13104;   "   (# 1501)   "
       ;   "   (# 1502)   "
       ;   "   (# 1503)   "
NC-13165;   "   (# 1504)   "
NC-13166;   "   (# 1505)   "
NC-13167;   "   (# 1506)   "
       ;   "   (# 1507)   "
NC-14V;   "   (# 1508)   "

This approval for ser. # 1500 and up; reg. no. for ser. # 1502, 1503, 1507 unknown; ser. # 1500 later modified to C7-F with Warner 145; this approval expired 7-1-35.

A.T.C. # 484
(5-12-32)
STINSON, MODEL U

Fig. 272. 3 New Lycoming transport-type engines power graceful "Stinson U."

With the inheritance of Century and Century-Pacific Air Lines, and also the 24 Stinson "Tri-Motor" (Model T) that came with the deal, American Airways began replacing much of their single-engined equipment with the acquired tri-motors. To cope with the continuing increase in passenger traffic on the American Airways system, Stinson Aircraft was already developing a new larger, faster, and more comfortable tri-motor that was to replace the faithful Model T. Introduced in mid-1932 as the Model U "Airliner," the new tri-motor was still very much of recognizable Stinson configuration but many structural, mechanical, and aerodynamic improvements were evident. Actually a sesqui-plane (wing and a half) because of the thick lower stub wing, the new "Tri-Motor" mounted the recently developed Lycoming transport-type engines of 240 h.p. each; much "cleaner" in the aerodynamic sense, despite its increase in bulk, the "Model U" offered gains in operating efficiency and performance. At least 16 of the new "Airliner" were hurriedly put into service on various American Airways route; One example went to the Phillipine Islands for airline service among the sugar centers; Transamerican Airlines operated one initially on alternate routes between Buffalo, Cleveland, Detroit, and Chicago; Eastern Air Transport operated a special Wright-powered version for evaluation on their eastern seaboard system; One example of the tri-motored "U" was specially fitted also as an 8-place deluxe "club plane"; plush accommodations were to the executives' order of the "San Francisco Examiner", a Hearst newspaper. A big, beautiful airplane that was studded with an array of mechanical, and aerodynamic refinements, the "Model U" offered more payload at better speeds over that of the "Model T" (SM-6000-B) but the increases were quite small in comparison to the rapidly mounting demands; as a consequence, its actual service life on major routes was quite short as it was replaced by still larger and faster equipment. A good indication of what was taking place on the nation's airlines is illustrated by the fact that as of July in 1932 some 580 aircraft were operated by the various lines; one year later in July of 1933, the number of aircraft operated had dropped to 544, but all the lines were handling considerably more business.

The Stinson tri-motored "Model U" was basically a transport-type high-wing monoplane

Fig. 273. Tri-motored "Stinson U" used on frequent schedule from New York to Boston.

with seating arranged for ten passengers and a crew of two. Often called a sesqui-plane or sesqui-wing, the lower stub-wing was arranged to offer bracing for the main wing, to offer mounts for the outboard engines, and also attachment for the landing gear; compartments for the stowage of baggage and cargo were also provided in the thick stub-wing on either side. Primarily arranged as a coach-type transport for 10 passengers the "U" was also available in various other interior combinations. For combination loads of passengers and mail-cargo either one or two of the front seats in main cabin could be removed and replaced with auxiliary cargo bins. Initially operated by a crew of two, the co-pilot was later dispensed with and his station was used to mount

Western Electric two way radio-telephone equipment and other navigational aids. As powered with 3 of the 9 cyl. Lycoming R-680-BA engines of 240 h.p. each, the Model U had sufficient power reserve to continue flight in the case of failure to one engine; fully loaded, normal flight on any two engines could be maintained to a ceiling of 7000 ft. Performance on all 3 engines was very good and flight characteristics were favorably comparable to the earlier Stinson tri-motor, but distribution of useful load was more critical and did have either favorable or unfavorable effect on flight attitudes. In general, the Model U was not as popular among pilots as the older Model T. Because of its failing to provide sufficient capacity for the rapid increases in passenger

Fig. 274. Stinson U as deluxe club-plane for executives of San Francisco "Examiner."

Fig. 275. Coach-style interior of Model U; front seats quickly replaced with mail-bins.

traffic and cargo tonnage, plus the fact that it was soon outmoded by new designs in airline transports, the Model U was relatively un-successful on the major routes. By 1936 most of the "Tri-Motor U" were either shunted onto secondary lines or in unscheduled service by flying-service operators. The type certificate number for the Stinson tri-motored Model U was issued 5-12-32 and 23 examples of this model were manufactured by the Stinson Aircraft Corp. at Wayne, Mich. In the winter of 1932 B. D. DeWeese (V.P. & gen. mgr. at Stinson) was flown to the west coast in a Model U for demonstration to Western Air Express, but the demonstration did not promote a sale to the airline. However, the sale of an 8-place deluxe "club plane" to the San Francisco "Examiner" did result.

Listed below are specifications and performance data for the Stinson tri-motored Model U as powered with 3 Lycoming R-680-BA engines of 240 h.p. each; length overall 45'3"; height overall 12'6"; main wing span 66'2"; main wing chord 105"; stub-wing span 14'3"; stub-wing chord 84"; main wing area 460 sq. ft.; stub-wing area 54 sq.ft.; total wing area 514

Fig.276. Retired from American Airways this Stinson U flew charter and sight-seeing flights out of Detroit.

sq.ft.; area including wing struts 574 sq.ft.; airfoil (main wing) Goettingen 398; wt. empty 6230-6300 lbs.; useful load 3070-3100 lbs.; payload with 140 gal. fuel 1795-1825 lbs.; gross wt. 9300-9400 lbs.; max. speed 145; cruising speed 123; landing speed 60; climb 900-850 ft. first min. at sea level; ceiling 14,500-14,000 ft.; gas cap. normal 140 gal.; gas cap. max. 160 gal.; oil cap. 12-15 gal.; cruising range at 40 gal. per hour 440-500 miles; price $22,900. at factory field, reduced to $19,500. late in 1932.

The fuselage framework was built up of welded chrome-moly steel tubing, faired to shape with formers and fairing strips, then fabric covered. Forward portion of the fuselage to leading edge of wing was covered in metal panels. The main cabin walls were lined with ply-metal for sound-proofing and insulation; upholstery was in fine durable fabrics. Ten seats were arranged in the main cabin with lavatory facilities aft of the main entry door; all windows were of shatter-proof glass and individual fresh-air vents and a reading light were provided at each seat. One or two of the front passenger seats in the main cabin were removable to provide aux. cargo bins. Pilot's cabin normally seated two with dual wheel controls, but co-pilot station was sometimes used to mount two-way radio gear. Two baggage compartments of 58 cu. ft. total capacity were in the stub-wing with allowance for 335 to 400 lbs.; a fuselage compartment just behind and below pilot station was allowed 200 lbs., and aux. cargo bins that had replaced a passenger seat were allowed 170 lbs. each. The wings were built up of welded chrome-moly steel tube girder-type spar beams with wing ribs, built up of dural tubing; the leading edges were covered with dural metal sheet and the completed framework was covered in fabric. A 70 or 80 gal. fuel tank was mounted in root end of each main wing half; the upper main wing was braced to end of stub wing by heavy-gauge duralumin struts. Outboard engine nacelles were mounted to extremities of the stub-wing and each engine was shrouded with an NACA-type low-drag cowling; each landing gear unit was "sprung" by two large "Aerol" struts and fastened to underside of engine nacelles. The 12.50x14 wheels fitted with low-pressure tires

were encased in streamlined pants and provided with hydraulic brakes. The fabric covered tail-group was built up of welded steel tubing; movable control surfaces had aerodynamic balance, and both fin and horizontal stabilizer were adjustable for trim in flight. Metal propellers, exhaust collector-rings, electric engine starters, wheel brakes, batteries, generator, lavatory compartment, reclining chairs, tail wheel, fire extinguishers, and wheel pants were standard equipment. Night-flying equipment and Western Electric two-way radio telephone were optional. The next development in the Stinson tri-motor was the low-winged "Model A" as described in the chapter for ATC # 556.

Listed below are Model U entries as gleaned from registration records:

X-432M; Model U (# 9000) 3 Lyc. 240.

NC-12113;	"	(# 9001)	"
NC-12114;	"	(# 9002)	"
NC-12115;	"	(# 9003)	"
NC-12116;	"	(# 9004)	"
NC-12117;	"	(# 9005)	"
NC-12118;	"	(# 9006)	"
NC-12119;	"	(# 9007)	"
NC-12120;	"	(# 9008)	"
NC-12121;	"	(# 9009)	"
NC-12122;	"	(# 9010)	"
NC-12127;	"	(# 9011)	"
NC-12126;	"	(# 9012)	"
;	"	(# 9013)	"
X-12129;	"	(# 9014)	"
NC-12133;	"	(# 9015)	"
NC-12136;	"	(# 9016)	"
NC-12137;	"	(# 9017)	"
NC-12192;	"	(# 9018)	"
NC-12193;	"	(# 9019)	"
NC-12194;	"	(# 9020)	"
NC-12195;	"	(# 9021)	"
;	"	(# 9022)	"
NC-12196;	"	(# 9023)	"

This approval for ser. # 9001 and up; ser. # 9000 on Group 2 memo numbered 2-413; ser. # 9014 as model U-1 with 3 Wright 270 h.p. engines; ser. # 9020 unverified; ser. # 9022 unknown; ser. # 9023 as 8 pl. deluxe club-plane for "San Francisco Examiner"; this approval expired 5-15-34.

Fig. 277. Curtiss-Wright model B-14-B with 330 h.p. Wright R-975-E engine; this example operated by Dept. of Commerce.

The Curtiss-Wright model B-14-B was a high-performance biplane developed purposely for the well-to-do sportsman; as shown in its splendor at the Detroit Air Show for 1932 it was difficult to imagine an airplane of this type being hitched to all-purpose duties for some flying-service operator. Patterned quite closely after the earlier A-14-D "Sportsman" (ATC # 442) this new version had the advantage of more power and all that goes with it; hidden under the shroud of the big NACA cowling as a surprise were two more engine cylinders, an added punch that unleashed some 60 to 90 more horsepower. Naturally, the extra drive of a 300-330 h.p. Wright engine turned everything on to make the B-14-B a rather outstanding airplane. Curtiss-Wright had already discontinued their cheaper training biplanes of 1931, and decided to go along with the rising demand for higher-priced sporting airplanes in 1932, but there was actually not enough demand to go around to the various builders. Dropping the earlier "Sportsman" label for the 14-series, and changing it more fittingly to "Speedwing", Curtiss-Wright had also built a 420 h.p. version of this charger (B-14-R)

for "Casey" Lambert to play around with. The exceptional performance of the "Speedwing" type, and especially the B-14-R, prompted Curtiss-Wright engineers to develop the two-seated "Osprey". The "Osprey" biplane was a versatile jack-of-all-trades, but basically offered as a cheap military fighter-bomber to small foreign countries that were rearming on a small budget. Meanwhile, the model B-14-B was built in only 2 examples; the Curtiss-Wright Flying Service used one as a demonstrator, and the one seen more frequently was the black and orange single-seater operated by the Bureau of Air Commerce. As a custom-built airplane finished and fitted to order, the "Speedwing" was still offered into 1936.

The Curtiss-Wright "Speedwing" model B-14-B was an open cockpit sport-biplane with seating arranged for three. There actually was ample room for the seating of 3, but the "Speedwing" was most often seen with the front cockpit covered to take advantage of the gain in speed. The turbulence caused by a gaping open cockpit at 150 to 170 m.p.h. was of considerable consequence, so the 'pit was normally covered. From

Fig. 278. Certain angles of "Speedwing" reflect its "Travel Air" lineage.

its big, round NACA cowling in front, down its tapering fuselage to its slender wings, the "Speedwing" reflected the feeling of speed in its every line. Built especially for the sportsman
~~...~~ some meas-
~~...~~ ind
~~...~~ yl.
~~...~~ he
~~...~~ er-
~~...~~ ght
~~...~~ he
~~...~~ er-
~~...~~ so
~~...~~ a

happy association with this machine. Although of "Travel Air" lineage, by a very loose connection, the C-W "Speedwing" was certainly no "Travel Air" either in the air or on the ground. Most "Travel Air" bitten pilots resented or even scoffed at the suggestion of kinship. Be it known here now that the "Speedwing" was more of a kin to the Rearwin "Ken-Royce". The type certificate number for the "Speedwing" model B-14-B was issued 6-1-32 and perhaps no more than 2 examples of this model were manufactured by the Curtiss-Wright Airplane Co. at St. Louis, Mo. With the resignation of Walter Beech early in 1932, Ralph S. Damon became president

Fig. 279. B-14-B as modified for extra speed; speed was its stock in trade.

Fig. 280. B-14-B led to development of "Osprey," a fighter-bomber for export.

and George A. Page, Jr. was transferred to the St. Louis Div. as chief engineer. A reason for excitement at the plant during this time was the development of the new "Condor" T-32 transport. Oddly enough, in May of 1933 Curtiss-Wright still had a small stockpile of rebuilt Curtiss OX-5 engines, guaranteed like new in a crate for $45.00 each. Needless to say, there was no stampede for this bargain offering.

Listed below are specifications and performance data for the "Speedwing" model B-14-B as powered with the 300 h.p. Wright R-975-E engine; length overall 23'2"; height overall 9'1"; wing span upper 31'0"; wing span lower 23'7"; wing chord upper 60"; wing chord lower 48"; total wing area 248 sq.ft.; airfoil (NACA) N-9; wt. empty 2008 lbs.; useful load 1059 lbs.; payload with 66 gal. fuel 454 lbs.; gross wt. 3067 lbs.; max. speed (front cockpit covered) 177; cruising speed 150; landing speed 57; climb 1600 ft. first min. at sea level; ceiling 18,700 ft.; gas cap. 66 gal.; oil cap. 5 gal.; cruising range at 16 gal. per hour 575 miles; price $13,500. at factory field. Model B-14-B also eligible with Wright R-975-E engine rerated to 330 h.p.; performance was gained in proportion.

The construction details and general arrangement of the B-14-B were typical to that of the model A-14-D as described in the chapter for ATC # 442 of this volume. The rear cockpit was protected by a large Triplex shatter-proof windshield, and fitted with a cockpit heater. Baggage allowance of up to 148 lbs. was divided among 2 compartments; lower compartment was allowed 100 lbs. and upper compartment was allowed 48 lbs. The upper compartment allowance was cut to 8 lbs. if radio gear was installed. A 43 gal. fuel tank was mounted high in the fuselage ahead of front cockpit, and a 23 gal. fuel tank was mounted in center-section panel of upper wing. A metal fillet streamlined lower wing roots at fuselage function. The landing gear of 81 in. tread used Hydra-Flex shock absorbing struts that were encased in streamlined metal cuffs; 8.00x10 semi-airwheels with brakes were standard equipment. 8.50x10 semi-airwheels with brakes were optional. An adjustable metal propeller, electric engine starter, navigation lights, battery, cockpit heater, dual controls, front cockpit cover, clock, compass, bank and turn indicator, fuel gauges, rate of climb indicator, airspeed indicator, tachometer, oil pressure & oil temperature gauges, altimeter, and instrument panel lights were standard equipment. Landing lights, parachute flares, radio, and wheel pants were optional. The next Curtiss-Wright development was the "Condor" T-32 transport as described in the chapter for ATC # 501.

Listed below are B-14-B entries as gleaned from registration records:

NC-12332; Model B-14-B (# 2010) Wright 300.
NS-1A;   "   (#2011) Wright 330.

This approval for ser. # 2010 and up; ser. # 2011 with Bureau of Air Commerce; this approval expired 9-30-39.

A.T.C. # 486
(6-1-32)
CONSOLIDATED "FLEETSTER",
17-AF

Fig. 281. "Fleetster" model 17-AF with 575 h.p. Wright "Cyclone" engine; extended capacity provided seating for ten.

As a small high-performance airliner, the fast-flying Consolidated "Fleetster" had blazed many trails in our hemisphere. Oddly enough, its normal theater of operations had been far to the south and far to the north of us in South America and in Alaska. As a new and improved development in the "Fleetster" series, the sleek model 17-AF broke this precedent to serve briefly here in the U.S.A. Formerly known as the New York, Philadelphia, & Washington Airways, the "Ludington Airlines" added a "Fleetster" 17-AF to their fleet of airplanes in June of 1932. Washington and New York City which were 205 air-miles apart were now within 80 minutes of each other, and 4 round-trips were scheduled daily. This fast service became quite popular among the dignitaries and the "Fleetster" was kept rather busy. Douglas Fairbanks and Mary Pickford, both famous movie-stars and also man and wife, were preparing to board the Ludington "Fleetster" at Washington to fly to New York; asking nonchalantly how many the plane carried, Fairbanks bought tickets for all the seats so he and his wife would be alone together on the flight. One-way fares were $13.25 and round-trip fare was $22.50; this was an increase of some 15% over rates on the regular hourly service in the Stinson "Tri-Motors". Two more of the ten-place 17-AF were built for Ludington Airlines, and after short service these were acquired by Pan American Airways System in June of 1933; the first Ludington "Fleetster" was also acquired in June of 1933 and all 3 were operated by Pan Am into 1934. One of these "Fleetster" was then put into service by Pacific-Alaska Airways and the other two were sold to Amtorg.

This then was the last of "Fleetster 17" production, but an interesting variation was delivered to the U.S. Navy as the XBY-1, a cigar-shaped attack and dive-bomber that was designed to operate from an aircraft-carrier.

The sleek Consolidated "Fleetster" model 17-AF was a cigar-shaped high winged cabin monoplane designed expecially for fast, frequent schedule on the shorter routes; seating was arranged for 9 passengers and a pilot. The new 17-AF was basically similar to earlier models in the 17-series, and especially the 17-2C, but several changes had been made to improve its performance; the most apparent was the longer wing, the spindly low-drag landing gear, and a bubble-type canopy for the pilot. Other changes were structural and some changes were made to interior arrangement. As it stood taller on its big, fat "airwheels", the 17-AF was also longer, empty weight had been increased by some 300 lbs., there was nearly a 700 lb. boost in the useful load, and increased wing area helped to hold up the 1000 lb. boost in the gross weight. As powered with the big 9 cyl. Wright "Cyclone" R-1820-E engine of 575 h.p. or the R-1820-F of 650 h.p. the "Fleetster" 17-AF had an impressive performance and a remarkable ability that was unusual among craft of this type. Conspicuously void of external wing bracing and other drag-producing assemblies, the 17-AF was a "smoothie" that could sustain a top speed of better than 180 m.p.h.; and cruise easily at 160; speed was actually the economic justification for air travel and the "Fleetster" had plenty of it. Designed for efficient and profitable operation in airline service, and to cater to the comforts

Fig. 282. Fleetster brought New York City within 80 minutes of nation's capital.

and conveniences of the air traveler, the large circular fuselage offered plenty of room and ample allowance for payload. As a "hot ship" the "Fleetster" handled quite nicely in the air and pilots enjoyed flying it. The type certificate number for the "Fleetster" model 17-AF was issued 6-1-32 and only 3 examples of this model were manufactured by the Consolidated Aircraft Corp. at Buffalo, New York. Rueben H. Fleet was president; Larry D. Bell was V.P. and general manager; and R. P. Whitman was asst. to general manager. Except for an order of the parasol type model 20-A this was the end of "Fleetster" production. The "Fleet" trainer biplane was still in small production and Consolidated expanded more of its manufacture to the military types.

Listed below are specifications and performance data for the "Fleetster" model 17-AF as powered with the 575 h.p. Wright "Cyclone" R-1820-E engine; length overall 34'2"; height overall 9'7"; wing span 50'0"; wing chord at root 105"; wing chord at tip 69"; total wing area 361.5 sq.ft.; airfoil Goettingen 398; wt. empty 3639 lbs.; useful load 2640 lbs.; payload with 90 gal. fuel 1830 lbs. (9 pass. at 170 lb. each & 300 lbs. baggage); gross wt. 6279 lbs.; max. speed 180 [190]; cruising speed 155 [160]; landing speed 60; climb 1000 [1250] ft. first min. at sea level; ceiling 18,000 [20.000] ft.; gas cap. 90 gal.; oil cap. 12 gal.; cruising range at 32 [35] gal. per hour 380 [360] miles; figures in brackets for 17-AF with R-1820-F engine; price $24,500. at factory. Amendment later allowed 17-AF as 9

Fig. 283. Beautiful lines of "Fleetster" aimed at reducing "drag."

Fig. 284. XBY-1 was development of "Fleetster" for Navy as attack-bomber.

place with 200 gal. fuel at 6500 lbs. gross wt.

For the most part,the construction details and general arrangement of the 17-AF were typical to that of models 17 and 17-2C as described in the chapters for ATC # 291 and # 369. The large main cabin was arranged with 3 wide seats each accommodating 3 across; occupants of the front seat faced backward, and all other occupants faced forward. A conveniently placed door on either side provided entry to any seat. The baggage compartments of 60 cu. ft. total capacity and with allowance for up to 300 lbs. were fore and aft of the main cabin area. The pilot's station seated only one and was placed high in the fuselage slightly ahead of the wing. The spindly-looking semi-cantilever landing gear was wire-braced and used "Aerol" (air-oil) shock absorbing struts; large low-pressure 30x13-6 Goodyear airwheels were fitted with hydraulic brakes. A 45 gal. fuel tank was mounted in the wing flanking each side of the fuselage. The cantilever wing was typical to the all-wood construction on earlier Model 17, but the span was

increased by 5 feet. Fuel load, passenger seating, and baggage allowance could be altered to various suitable configurations; the 9 passenger configuration with 300 lb. baggage allowance and 90 gal. fuel was as used by Ludington Airlines. A metal propeller, electric inertia-type engine starter, battery, generator, navigation lights, parachute flares, hydraulic wheel brakes, fire extinguisher, and tail wheel were standard equipment. A ground adjustable metal propeller, 200 gal. fuel supply, 14 gal. oil cap, and installation of Wright R-1820-F engine were optional. The next Consolidated development was the parasol-winged "Fleetster" model 20-A as described in the chapter for ATC # 494 of this volume.

Listed below are model 17-AF entries as gleaned from registration records:

NC-703Y; Model 17-AF (# 1) Cyclone 575.
NC-704Y;   "   (# 2)   "
NC-705Y;   "   (# 3)   "

This approval for ser. # 1-2-3 only.

A.T.C. # 487
(6-3-32)
HEATH "PARASOL", LNA-40

Fig. 285. Heath "Parasol" model LNA-40 with 37 h.p. Continental A-40 engine.

As a popular home-built airplane seen flying here and there in all parts of rural America, the bouncy little Heath "Parasol" was certainly well known to all and very well liked by home-builders and amateur pilots. Now as a newcomer to the exalted ranks of "approved aircraft", the flivver-type Heath made its bashful debut into the so-called select circle, but oddly enough, failed to gain very much by it. Still basically similar to models developed in the previous five years, the approved Heath was first offered with the 25 h.p. Heath B-4 engine as the model LNB-4, and now in a new development as the LNA-40. Posing as the LNA-40 the plump little "Parasol" was powered with the Continental A-40, a flat-four air-cooled engine of some 37 h.p. Up to this point in its career a converted 4 cyl. motorcycle engine was usually hung in the mounts of the "Parasol", so installation of the "Continental" was quite a treat and it responded to the mating happily and favorably. Billed as the lowest-priced approved airplane in the U.S. the new Heath also held another distinction in that it was the only approved airplane that could be built at home from factory-made assembly kits and be eligible for license. As developed in this new LN-version, the familiar airframe was now taller with much more wing, control surfaces were much bigger, and the open-cockpit fuselage was faired to a more buxom form; all this altered but certainly did not hide its former identity.

Actually, much of this padding and dimensional increase helped to make the new Heath less like a "flivver" and more like a regular airplane. As a single-seater, the LNA-40 had to be strictly for fun, or for building up cheap solo-time towards a commercial pilot license. There were literally thousands of prospective buyers for the new Heath in any of its 3 different versions, but prevailing economic conditions left everybody just wishing and not buying. Those who could scrape together the necessary dollars seemed to prefer to buy the "kit" and build it themselves instead of buying the airplane ready-made at the factory; the handsome saving could then be converted into a lot of flying time. Still offered into the late thirties, the LNA-40 as a type was represented in small number, but the home-built Heath "Parasol" of all description were likely to be seen anywhere.

The Heath model LNA-40 was a light open cockpit parasol-type monoplane with seating for one only; as a single-seater this craft was naturally destined to be a sport-type airplane. Each year the National Air Races (NAR) were like a mecca for sport-fliers, and each year since 1926 the Heath made its appearance; the events for 1931 saw only two Heath participants but their efforts were a credit to the type. In the 115 cu. in. free-for-all event one C. Duke Mueller flying an experimental LNA-40 special with clipped wings, romped in first at 91.2 m.p.h.; Merrill Lambert flying a somewhat similar ship

Fig. 286. 1936 Version of LNA-40 built in Benton Harbor, Mich.

came in third. In the events for 1932 several Heath made an appearance and the competition couldn't help but notice. Art Davis flying a clipped wing LNA-40 (?) in the 115 cu. in. free-for-all event, crossed the line first at 88.9 m.p.h.; later in the 200 cu. in. free-for-all event he led them all across the line at 101.5 m.p.h. E. F. Gallagher flying a standard LNA-40 (?) finished the 510 cu. in. handicap event in 8th spot at about 60 m.p.h.; a few days later Gallagher floated into 4th place in a precision landing contest. Any wins at the NAR were naturally used as bally-hoo for the Heath, but the biggest stunt of all was the landing of an LNA-40 on the roof-top of a building, but of course they

failed to film the ingenious "arresting tear" that was used to shorten the landing roll, or the sloping ramp that was built over the parapet just in case the "Parasol" was not airborne yet when it reached the edge. C. Duke Mueller in the same clipped-wing he used at the NAR in 1931 was the daring pilot for this stunt. As powered with the 4 cyl. Continental A-40 engine of 37 h.p. the LNA-40 was a delightfully spry machine that was fun to fly and easy to own, but factory-made examples of this version were coming off in very small number; the "assembly kits" were more popular. The type certificate number for the Heath model LNA-40 was issued 6-3-32; from scant record available it is difficult to determine just

Fig. 287. Flight in LNA-40 was happy experience.

Fig. 288. Exciting view of SNA-40 after landing on 300 ft. roof-top of building.

how many examples of this model were built. Hanging on into 1933 the Heath Aircraft Corp. finally began to falter and was reorganized with additional financing as the International Aircraft Corp. of Niles, Mich. The manufacturing facility and company officers remained without change. The models built thru 1933-34-35 were generally called International-Heath.

Listed below are specifications and performance data for the Heath model LNA-40 as powered with the 37 h.p. Continental A-40-2 engine; length overall 17'3"; height overall 6'2"; wing span 31'3"; wing chord 54"; total wing area 135.5 sq.ft.; airfoil Clark Y; wt. empty 465 lbs.; useful load 235 lbs.; crew wt. & extras 174 lbs.; gross wt. 700 lbs.; max. speed 80; cruising speed 68; landing speed 32; climb 500 ft. first min. at sea level; ceiling 14,000 ft.; gas cap. 9 gal.; oil cap. 4 qts.; cruising range at 2.9 gal. per hour 200 miles; price $1224. at factory in 1932, lowered to $1085. in 1933-34.

The construction details and general arrangement of the model LNA-40 were typical to the LNB-4 as described in the chapter for ATC # 456 of this volume. The only significant difference in the LNA-40 was the mounting of the Continental A-40 engine; the engine nacelle was completely cowled in, but engine cylinders were exposed to the cooling air. The cockpit was roomy, deep, well protected by a large Pyralin windshield, and neatly upholstered in Fabrikoid; entry direct from the ground was by way of a large door on the left side. A 4.5 gal. fuel tank was mounted in root end of each wing half, and 2 small skylights provided vision overhead. A "high altitude" wing of 169 sq. ft. area was available for operation in high moun-

tainous areas, and a "clipped wing" was available for sport and racing. The landing gear of 48 in. tread used "Rusco" rubber shock-absorber rings; disc type 16x4 wheels were available with brakes. Goodyear 7.00x4 low pressure tires on one-piece aluminum wheels with disc brakes were also optional. Both vertical fin and horizontal stabilizer were adjusted for "trim" on ground only. A wooden propeller, and fire extinguisher bottle were standard equipment. A complete kit of factory-made assemblies, minus engine and propeller, were available to the home-builder for $499.; the Continental A-40 engine could be purchased from Heath for $450. The next Heath development was the CNA-40 mid-wing as described in the chapter for ATC # 495 of this volume.

Listed below are Heath LNA-40 entries as gleaned from registration records:

X-11313;	LNA-40	(# 152)	Cont. A-40
X-11399;	"	(# 160)	"
NC-12814;	"	(# 161)	"
NC-12874;	"	(#)	"
NC-12970;	"	(#)	"
NC-13197;	"	(# 1002)	"
NC-13658;	"	(# 1003)	"
NC-15792;	"	(#)	"

This approval for ser. # 160 and up; ser. # 152 as LNA-40 Spl. (SNA-40) with clipped wings; ser. # 160 modified to standard LNA-40 by International-Heath; ser. nos. for NC-12874, NC-12970, NC-15792 unknown; International-Heath started serial numbering at # 1000; approval expired due to sale to Howard E. Anthony on 12-1-35 (Heath Aviation Co.) of Benton Harbor, Mich.

A.T.C. # 488
(6-15-32)
GENERAL-WESTERN "METEOR",
P-2-T

Fig. 289. Model P-2-T was trainer version of "Meteor;" prototype shown.

The General-Western "Meteor" model P-2-T (Trainer) was a converted model of the (Sportster) P-2-S. Developed as a training-plane version of the "Meteor," the model P-2-T was still basically identical to the P-2-S, but was stripped of all finery not necessary to its role in the training of pilots. Bare of interior upholstery, minus wheel brakes, and other such niceties of no consequence to the student-pilot, the P-2-T gained the advantage of 100 lbs. less weight and $330.00 less in delivered price. The weight advantage was translated into slightly better performance, and the price advantage would certainly be of some consequence to pinch-penny operators during these lean times. The model P-2-T trainer was apparently developed in anticipation of a demand for an airplane of this particular type, but it does not seem likely that any examples of this version were built and sold as such. Actually, it would be but simple matter to convert any P-2-S into a P-2-T simply by removing or leaving off certain items of equipment. With the bottom of "the great depression" just ahead (1933) activity at General-Western Aero consisted mostly of operating a flying school (using "Meteor" monoplanes, of course), and an aircraft repair shop; tooling for the manufacture of the "Meteor" was gathering dust. In 1935 the Air Transport Mfg. Co. acquired the "Meteor" designs and made a concerted effort to revive the airplane, however, they met with very little suc-

cess. It was no coincidence either that the "Kreutzer" light tri-motor was another design acquired by Air Transport; both airplanes (Meteor & Kreutzer) were designed by Albin K. Peterson and he was also an official of the newly-organized company. One example of the General-Western "Meteor" was converted to a "crop duster" sometime in 1953, and proved the parasol monoplane as particularly suitable for this type of work. Doubling the power with installation of a 220 h.p. Continental engine, the converted "duster" carried an 800 lb. payload and swooped over the fields of cotton with the agility of a bird.

The General-Western "Meteor" model P-2-T was an open cockpit parasol monoplane with seating for two in tandem. Basically typical of the sport-type P-2-S it would be difficult to positively identify the P-2-T trainer as such because differences between the two were all in equipment, or lack of it. Stripped of non-essentials, the trainer version was 100 lbs. lighter and a good deal cheaper. As a pilot-training airplane, the P-2-T had several useful features in its favor, mainly because of the high parasol-mounted wing. Good visibility was its better feature allowing direct vision during the critical moments of a take-off or landing, also in the airport pattern, or during the practice of basic maneuvers. To a student this was of great help. The weight advantage boosted the power reserve for added

Fig. 290. Stout wing was typical of strength built into "Meteor" airframe.

safety in the tight spots, and allowed a better climb-out on the way to the practice area. As powered with the 5 cyl. Kinner K5 engine of 100 h.p. the P-2-T was probably a little more lively than the P-2-S, and probably somewhat more tolerant of the beginner's mistakes. The type certificate number for the model P-2-T was issued 6-15-32 but the aircraft registry listed no P-2-T as such. The General-Western flying school at Goleta used the "Meteor," of course, and it is likely they may have modified their school ships to the P-2-T specification. The General-Western Aero Corp., Ltd. by this time had the plant and offices on the factory airport in Goleta, Calif. L. F. Vremsak was president and general manager; Ed W. Stow was V.P.; A. J. Roberts was treasurer; Stewart Klingelsmith was secretary; and Albin K. Peterson was chief engineer. The Air Transport Mfg. Co., Ltd. of Glendale, Calif. bought design rights to the "Meteor" in 1935 and made effort to revive its manufacture but without much success. E. L. Hollywood was president and general manager; Albin K. Peterson was V.P. and chief engineer; and A. T. Hay, Jr. was sales manager.

Listed below are specifications and performance data for the "Meteor" model P-2-T as powered with the 100 h.p. Kinner K5 engine; length overall 24'2"; height overall 7-10"; wing span 32'0"; wing chord at root 72"; wing chord at tip 54"; total wing area 163 sq.ft.; airfoil Goettingen 398; wt. empty 1069 lbs.; useful load 581 lbs.; payload with 30 gal. fuel 208 lbs. (1 pass. at 170 lbs. & 2 parachutes); gross wt. 1650 lbs.; max. speed 115; cruising speed (90% power) 105; landing (stall) speed 40; climb 900 ft. first min. at sea level; ceiling 14,000 ft.; gas cap. max. 30 gal.; oil cap. 3 gal.; cruising range at 7 gal. per hour 400 miles; price $2950. at factory field in 1932.

The construction details and general arragement of the model P-2-T were typical to that of the P-2-S as described in the chapter for ATC # 482 of this volume. Modifications to the P-2-T consisted mostly of leaving out several appointments, and items of equipment. The cockpit interior was bare of upholstery, and the instrument panel was equipped with only bare necessities for local operation. Dual joy-stick controls and parachute-type bucket seats were provided. The fuel cap. was held to a max. of 30 gal., but operation would usually be carried on with less. A baggage compartment of 1.5 cu. ft. capacity with allowance for up to 38 lbs. was located in the top cowl just ahead of the front windshield; no baggage was allowed when two parachutes were carried. The formed dural metal sheet turtle-back was removable for inspection or maintenance to various assemblies in the rear fuselage. Lift-handles on lower longerons were provided for ground handling. The split-axle landing gear of 70 in. tread used rubber compression-rings as shock absorbers; big roly-poly 20x9-4 Goodyear airwheels also helped to absorb much of the shock. No wheel brakes were provided. The steel tube tail skid was sprung with rubber shock-cord. A Storey wooden propeller, and short exhaust stacks were standard equipment. Of the 6 "Meteor" built into 1933 none have actually been listed as a P-2-T, so no listing is entered here; see P-2-S listing on ATC # 482.

A.T.C. # 489
(6-27-32)
STINSON, MODEL R-2

Fig. 291. Stinson model R-2 enjoyed advantage of increase in horsepower.

As a companion offering in the new Stinson R-series, the "Model R-2" was basically typical of the "Model R" except for slight detail changes and a boost in power. Stinson Aircraft intended the Model R-2 especially for light transport duty, so it was equipped as if it were a small airliner. Interior appointments were still rather plush with all the conveniences for maximum comfort, but all was of a more durable nature as would be fitting in a carrier for public use. Perhaps the most significant change in this model was the increase in power that was furnished by the Lycoming R-680-BA "transport type" engine of 240 h.p. The trend now toward higher power output called for increased compression ratios, higher operating r.p.m., fuels of higher octane rating, and better dissipation of engine heat. As redesigned for transport use, the new Lycoming R-680-BA engine had its compression ratio increased to 6.5 to 1 as compared to 5.3 to 1 on the earlier R-680, and fuel of 80 octane rating was now required. Improved fin area and design of cylinder heads was also featured for better cooling. First introduced into service on the tri-motored "Model U" the R-680-BA engine was also used in the Model R-3. In the lineup of "Stinson R" monoplanes the model R-2 would be rather difficult to single out as such because all of its distinguishing features were more oꜰ less under cover, but it did offer better performance and rather plush workaday utility. Despite of what it had to offer at a reasonable price it did not

attract many customers, so it joined the band of rare Stinson models.

The Stinson model R-2 was a high-winged cabin monoplane with seating arranged for three passengers and a pilot. Basically typical of the earlier Model R, the R-2 was, however, fitted in the livery of a transport airplane. It was the intent of Stinson Aircraft to offer the Model R-2 as a specially fitted airplane for use as a chartered air-taxi, a small airliner on intermediate lines, or as a company-owned transport in the field of business. The Standard Oil Co. of Indiana operated an R-2 on various company chores requiring speedy transport of men and equipment. As powered with the new 9 cyl. Lycoming R-680-BA engine of 240 h.p. the Model R-2 operated with functional ability and rather high performance. Very well equipped with numerous operational aids, the R-2 was also available with a full complement of night-flying gear for 24 hour standby service. As rolled out of assembly the R-2 was ready to put into any service without resorting to the purchase of numerous "optionals". Whatever the underlying reason, it remains that all of the R-series were scarce in number, but the newer concept surely led the way for the highly popular "SR" monoplanes that Stinson developed in the next few years. The type certificate number for the Model R-2 was issued 6-27-32 and no more than 2 or 3 examples of this model were manufactured by the Stinson Aircraft Corp. at Wayne, Mich. L. B. Manning was now president; Wm. A. Mara was V.P.; B. D. DeWeese was general manager; and A. H. Saxon was chief engineer.

Listed below are specifications and performance data for the Stinson model R-2 as powered with the 240 h.p. Lycoming R-680-BA engine; length overall 26'2"; height overall 8'9"; wing span 43'4"; wing chord 75"; total wing area 235 sq.ft.; airfoil Clark Y; wt. empty 2227 lbs.; useful load 1098 lbs.; payload with 55 gal. fuel 568 lbs. (3 pass. at 170 lb. each & 58 lb. baggage); gross wt. 3325 lbs.; max. speed 133; cruising speed 112; landing speed 52; climb 700 ft. first min. at sea level; ceiling 13,000 ft.; gas cap. 55 gal.; oil cap. 4 gal.; cruising range at 13 gal. per hour 450 miles; price $5995. at factory field.

The construction details and general arrangement of the Model R-2 were typical to that of the Model R as described in the chapter for ATC # 457 of this volume. Because of its specific development for transport use, the R-2 was fitted with interior appointments of more durable nature; other interior niceties included assist ropes and ash-trays at each seat. Improved cabin heat and ventilation allowed cabin comfort under varying conditions, and heavy sound-proofing allowed normal conversation during flight. The pilot's seat was adjustable, and a reclining back for right front seat was optional. The Lycoming R-680-BA "transport type" engine offered extra power, and its mounting in rubberized bushings eliminated much of the vibration normally transmitted to the airframe. The baggage compartment with allowance for 58 lbs. was behind the rear seat. Low-pressure 8.50x10 semi'airwheels were fitted with self-energizing brakes, tail wheel was 5.00x4, and all wheels were encased in streamlined metal "pants". Wing rigging on the R-2 employed no incidence, and dihedral was at 1.5 deg. A 27 gal. fuel tank was mounted in the root end of each wing half, and a 1 gal. tank was mounted in the fuselage; fuel level gauges were mounted in the cabin. An adjustable metal propeller, NACA-type engine cowl, electric engine starter, a battery, exhaust collector-ring, cabin heater, wheel pants, navigation lights, wheel brakes, parking brake, and tail wheel were standard equipment. Landing lights, parachute flares, and radio equipment were optional. The next development in the Stinson R-series was the revolutionary Model R-3 as described in the chapter for ATC # 493 of this volume.

Listed below are Model R-2 entries as gleaned from registration records:

X-12178: Model R-2 (# 8500) Lyc. 240.
    NS-40;   "   (# 8512)   "
NC-447M;   "   (# 8521)   "

This approval for ser. # 8521 and up; ser. # 8500 and 8512 first as model R modified to R-2; this approval expired 7-1-34.

A.T.C. # 490
(8-18-32)
KINNER "SPORTSTER,"
K-100

Fig. 292. Kinner "Sportster" model K-100 with 100 h.p. Kinner K5 engine.

The sale of "Kinner" engines had dropped from a total of 291 in the year of 1931 to only 93 engines sold during the first 10 months of 1932. This downward trend in sales clearly had much to do with Kinner Motors deciding to build airplanes, and help develop their own engine market. Kinner's formal entry into the aircraft manufacturing business was the low-winged "Sportster" K-100, a trim-looking open monoplane for two with side-by-side seating; powered with the Kinner K5 engine of 100 h.p. Its relative simplicity was matched by its sturdiness, and its reliable performance. Offered with wings that folded alongside for ease of storage, the "Sportster K" was primarily developed for sport-flying, but its inherent good manners soon relegated it to the flight-line of numerous pilot-training schools. Used extensively by small flying-schools on the west coast, it eventually migrated eastward; and even Parks Air College, one of the

largest schools in the country, had a bevy of "Sportster K's" on the flight-line introducing the neophyte to the wonders of flying. The companionship of side-by-side seating was very practical for training pilots, and it also instigated buddy-rides among the sport-fliers who found it more pleasant to fly with a friend and share the enjoyment. Accepted into the fold almost immediately, the "Sportster K" was still in good production during 1935. In the intervening time, Kinner expanded its airplane line to at least a half-dozen interesting models, and the popularity of "Kinner Airplanes" was by then well established. Of the undetermined number of "Sporster K's" that were built, at least 35 were still flying actively in 1939. If you were to have one flying now, you'd be surrounded by a circle of envy.

W. "Bert" Kinner was certainly no stranger to aircraft manufacture. In fact, his first aeronautical endeavors were the little "Airster" biplane

Fig. 293. Pleasant rounded lines of "Sportster" typical also of its nature; everyone had a kind word for the "Sportster."

Fig. 294. "Sportster K" became very popular for training and sport.

and the revolutionary "Coupe" monoplane. Greatly intrigued by airplane engines, also, Bert Kinner devoted most of his time in the late twenties to building the popular Kinner power-plant; but his desire to develop and to build aircraft was not entirely lost. Developing a set of folding-wings onto the fuselage of a former "Bolte" sport-plane, Kinner conceived the idea for the low-winged "Sportster," which he had hoped to sell for less than $2000. A redesign of Kinner's prototype by young Max B. Harlow became the "Sportster K," and by the time it was developed sufficiently for certification tests, Bert Kinner had already left Kinner Motors. A previous reorganization of Kinner Motors forced Bert Kinner into some idle time, so this gave him ample opportunity to develop his folding-

wing mechanism. Frequently at odds with management over future policy, Bert Kinner finally took his leave, to travel and to study the skidding aircraft market. Not one to spend his time in idleness, Bert Kinner busied himself with a further refinement of the folding wing, and with the designing and developing of a new "Airster." Meanwhile, Robert Porter, president of Kinner Motors, had flown to the Detroit Air Show for 1932 with his wife, Lillian, in the new Kinner "Sedan," a low-winged, high performance cabin monoplane especially designed for Porter by Lawrence "Larry" Brown. The prototype Kinner "Sportster K," finished in three shades of purple, was already on exhibit during the week-long show, and it stirred plenty of interesting comment.

Fig. 295. "Sportster K" with winter enclosure, to fend off wintry winds.

Fig. 296. Bert Kinner shows folding wing development.

The Kinner "Sportster K" was a light, open cockpit low-winged monoplane with side-by-side seating for two. Its sturdy frame was complimented by the trim of simple lines, and its reliability was enhanced by its relative mechanical simplicity. Primarily designed for the private-owner type of flier, the "Sportster K" was a thoroughly compatible machine that could assure hours of flying pleasure without much of the usual attentive fuss or muss; flying-service operators learned of this quickly and several were enjoying the advantage of having the "Sportster" on their flight-line. Among its many other fine features, the "Sportster K" also became noted for its ability to operate in and out of small airstrips at high altitudes. As a stunt to prove this, one pilot landed the "Sportster" on a small plateau near the top of 14,000 foot Mount Rainier in Washington; the take-off back out was somewhat marginal, but nevertheless successful. Dotting the west coast from north to south, the "Sportster K" finally drifted eastward, where it was also accepted with great interest. As powered with the popular 5 cyl. Kinner K5 engine of 100 h.p., the "Sportster K-100" was an easy-going airplane that was somewhat reluctant to hurry, but delivered its performance in gracious and honest manner. Particularly easy to fly and of unusually good manners, the "K-100" was always described as a very pleasant airplane, especially if treated gently — as a nice lady should be. A cooperative nature and a lanky, stout airframe did permit a certain amount of levity or mistreatment, but an acquired affection for this airplane usually discouraged such action. Finally relegated to all-purpose service because of its willingness to perform any reasonable chore without complaint, the "Sportster K" remained very popular through the years, and is well-remembered even to the present time. The type certificate number for the "Sportster K" was

issued 8-18-32, and an undetermined number of this model was manufactured by the Kinner Airplane & Motor Corp. at Glendale, California. Robert Porter was president and general manager; B. L. Graves, formerly president of Bach Aircraft Co. was V.P.; Max. B. Harlow and Lawrence "Larry" Brown were project engineers. B. W. James was chief engineer in 1935 and B. T. Salmon was chief engineer in 1936.

Listed below are specifications and perfromance data for the 1932-33 "Sportster K" as powered with the 100 h.p. Kinner K5 engine; length overall 23'8"; height overall 7'0"; wing span 39'0"; wing chord 72"; total wing area 202 sq.ft.; airfoil Clark Y; wt. empty 1075 [1119] lbs.; useful load 575 [581] lbs.; payload with 24 gal. fuel 252 [258] lbs.; gross wt. 1650 [1700] lbs. (figures in brackets for late 1933 model); max. speed 104; cruising speed 90; landing speed 37; climb 800 ft. first min. at sea level; ceiling 14,000 ft.; gas cap. 24 gal.; oil cap. 9 qts.; cruising range at 7 gal. per hour 300 miles; price $2490. at factory.

Following data is for 1934-35-36 models of the "Sportster K"; length overall 24'2"; height overall 7'0"; wing span 39'0"; wing chord 72"; total wing area (including fuselage) 227 sq.ft.; airfoil Clark Y; wt. empty 1218 [1257] lbs.; useful load 657 [618] lbs.; payload with 24 gal. fuel 334 [295] lbs. (figures in brackets for 1935-36 models); gross wt. 1875 lbs.; max. speed 105; cruising speed 90; landing speed 45; climb 700 ft. first min. at sea level; ceiling 13,000 ft.; gas cap. 24 gal.; oil cap. 10 qts.; cruising range at 7 gal. per hour 300 miles; price not announced.

The fuselage framework was built up of welded chrome-moly steel tubing, heavily faired to a well-rounded shape, then fabric covered. Upholstered in Fabrikoid, the open cockpit — with side-by-side seating for two — was roomy, deep, and well protected by a large wind-

Fig. 297. 1934 Version of "Sportster K" had several improvements.

shield; the seat was adjustable. Easy entry off the wing-walk was through a large door on either side; a convenient hand-hold on either side offered assistance onto or off the wing-walk. Braced to the fuselage, a wing stub on either side provided attachment for the landing gear and outer wing panels; a baggage compartment with allowance for 40 lbs. on each side was in the wing stub. The wing framework was built up of routed spruce spar beams, with spruce and plywood truss-type wing ribs; the leading edges were covered with dural metal sheet, and the completed framework was covered in fabric. Braced to the fuselage by an inverted vee-type truss, the folding wings pivoted back about a point on the upper fuselage longeron; folded-back width was 9 feet. Of two separate assemblies, the tripod-type landing gear was fastened to the wing stub using Kinner-made oleo-spring shock absorbing struts; 19x9-3 Goodyear airwheels with brakes were standard equipment. A 24 gal. fuel tank was mounted high in the fuselage just behind the firewall; a 3 gal. reserve tank was part of the main tank with on-off controls on the dashboard. Aircraft to ser. # 90 were allowed baggage up to 80 lbs.; aircraft from ser. # 104 and up were allowed baggage up to 162 lbs.; two parachutes at 20 lbs. each were part of the baggage allowance in either case. Aircraft to ser. # 90 had a small wing-root fillet; aircraft from ser. # 104 and up had the large wing-root fillet. The fabric covered tail-group was built up of welded chrome-moly steel tubing; aircraft to ser. # 90 had adjustable horizontal stabilizer, and aircraft from ser. # 104 and up had fixed horizontal stabilizer with "tabs" for fore-aft trim. A wooden propeller, Heywood engine starter, navigation lights, hot-shot battery, 19x9-3 Goodyear airwheels with brakes, a parking brake, 8 in. swiveling tail wheel, dual joy-stick controls, chrome-plated exhaust collector-ring, tail-pipe, a Pyrene fire extinguisher, compass, first-aid kit, log books, and fuel gauge were

standard equipment. A metal propeller, an Eclipse electric engine starter, and coupe-top canopy (13 lbs.) were optional. Wings were rigged at 0 deg. incidence and 4.5 deg. of dihedral. The next development in the Kinner "Sportster" series was the model B, as described in the chapter for ATC # 516.

Listed below are "Sportster K" entries as gleaned from registration records:

NC-12235;	Sportster K	(# 1)	Kinner K5.
NC-12276;	"	(# 2)	"
NC-12281;	"	(# 4)	"
NC-12295;	"	(# 6)	"
NC-12296;	"	(# 8)	"
NC-12290;	"	(# 10)	"
NC-12299;	"	(# 20)	"
NC-218Y;	"	(# 22)	"
NC-222Y;	"	(# 24)	"
NC-228Y;	"	(# 26)	"
NC-234Y;	"	(# 28)	"
NC-235Y;	"	(# 30)	"
NC-13700;	"	(# 40)	"
NC-13701;	"	(# 42)	"
NC-13751;	"	(# 44)	"
NC-13707;	"	(# 64)	"
NC-13709;	"	(# 66)	"
NC-13750;	"	(# 68)	"
;	"	(# 82)	"
NC-13779;	"	(# 90)	"
NC-13798;	"	(# 104)	"
NC-13799;	"	(# 118)	"
NC-14211;	"	(# 124)	"
NC-14213;	"	(# 126)	"
NC-14218;	"	(# 136)	"
NC-14225;	"	(# 142)	"
NC-14233;	"	(# 146)	"
NC-14237;	"	(# 150)	"
NC-14238;	"	(# 162)	"
NC-14264;	"	(# 164)	"

Ser. # 28 later modified to Sportster B; reg. no. for ser. # 82 unknown; above listing as of Jan. 1935; this approval expired 2-16-39.

Fig. 298. Waco model PBF with 170 h.p. Jacobs LA-1 engine.

The three-seated model PBF was, perhaps, to be the last of the so-called "Waco" all-purpose biplanes. Other "Waco" three-seaters followed the PBF for several years afterward, but the later examples were held to more specialized duties, and generally were considered as sport-type airplanes. Basically, the model PBF was offered to the trade as an all-purpose biplane that could earn most of its keep- but it, too, was used quite often just for sport, and occasionally as a trainer. The 7 cyl. "Jacobs 170" engine, as mounted in the PBF, seemed to be the ideal powerplant for the three-place "Waco" F-2 series biplane; in all-purpose use, experience had proven that too little power was many times a handicap, and surplus power was a needless extravagance. The ideal combination, in this case, provided a rather high performance, with sufficient power in reserve, at reasonably low operating costs. Maintenance and repair costs were also held to a more reasonable minimum. With less than a year's time between them, the model PBF was still very much typical of the earlier PCF (ATC # 453), but was fitted with the series "B" wings of 1932 and numerous little improvements were added to make this model a much better airplane. Disposition of the four PBFs that were built into 1933 was not investigated beyond the first registration to the Waco Aircraft Co., but it is recorded that the second example off the line was delivered to the State College of Pennsylvania. This institution was one of 89 across the U.S.A. that offered various courses useful to

a proposed career in aeronautics; 21 students enrolled at Penn. State College to learn various phases of aviation, so the PBF and one part-time instructor were kept busy enough in the semester of 1932-33. The models UBF and especially the PBF were the best all-purpose biplanes that Waco Aircraft had built to that time, but even they could see that the day of the classic all-purpose biplane was coming to an end.

The Waco model PBF was a compact, open cockpit biplane with seating arranged for a pilot and two passengers. As an all-purpose biplane, the basic design of the PBF was typical of the earlier QCF and PCF, except for minor improvements that were inevitable in the progressive development of a series. Sensibly arranged, with all of its useful load in a well-distributed, compact form, the stubby PBF did not have to labor under excess weight nor any cumbersome dimension. Like some of its earlier kin, the PBF was never choosy as to chore or place of operation, being entirely as happy working from a small grassy strip. Although of hardy and compatible nature, and quite content to put up with everyday hum-drum if need be, there was still a playful streak in its innards that could be sparked to life with the slightest provocation. As powered with the 7 cyl. Jacobs LA-1 engine of 170 h.p. the PBF was a combination of top-notch performance at a fairly reasonable price. Deft and very nimble, its behavior was, however, tempered with a sprinkling of inherent considerate traits that

Fig. 299. PBF might be considered as last of the "Waco" all-purpose biplanes.

were appreciated by amateur and professional alike. Waco Aircraft bragged on their airplanes and well they should have; but the best testimony came from the pilots that flew them. "Waco" pilots did not swagger, perhaps, like a "Travel Air" or "Stearman" pilot would; but that contented smile of theirs was more effective than the swagger. The type certificate number for the model PBF was issued 8-20-32, and at least four examples of this model were manufactured by the Waco Aircraft Co. at Troy, Ohio. The Jacobs Aircraft Engine Co. (formerly of Camden, N. J.) had moved all its operations to Pottstown, Penna., where it had acquired more space and better manufacturing facilities; the new plant was formerly used by the Light Mfg. & Foundry Co., which had been manufacturing the "Brownback" engines.

Listed below are specifications and performance data for the Waco model PBF as powered with the 170 h.p. Jacobs LA-1 engine; length overall 20'10"; height overall 8'9"; wing span upper 29'7"; wing span lower 27'5" wing chord upper and lower 57"; wing area upper 130.5 sq.ft.; wing area lower 111 sq.ft.; total wing area 241.5 sq. ft.; airfoil Clark Y; wt. empty 1344 lbs.; useful load 956 lbs.; payload with 40 gal. fuel 516 lbs. (2 pass. at 170 lb. each, 95 lb. baggage, and 81 lb. allowance for equipment extras); gross wt. 2300 lbs.; max. speed 120; cruising speed 102; landing speed 42; climb 850 ft. first min. at sea level; ceiling 14,500 ft.; gas cap. 40 gal.; oil cap. 4 gal.; cruising range at 10 gal. per hour 390 miles; price $4415. at factory field. This model was also planned to mount the 5 cyl. Wright R-540 engine of 165 h.p., but delivered price of the Wright engine was considered excessive.

The construction details and general arrangement of the model PBF were typical of that of other F-series biplanes, as described in this volume. A comparison, perhaps, will disclose an improved outward appearance that was achieved by closer attention to detail. Smart colors were accentuated with appropriate trim in a hand-rubbed, glossy finish. A slight lengthening of the fuselage permitted more room in both cockpits, and larger windshields offered better protection from drafts. A metal panel cover for the front cockpit was optional, to take advantage of the gain in speed. A total baggage allowance of 95 lbs. was divided between two compartments; 15 lbs. was allowed in front and 80 lbs. was allowed in the rear compartment. Two 20 gal. fuel tanks were mounted in the center-section panel of the upper wing; float-type fuel gauges were visible from the rear cockpit. "Spoiler strips" were mounted on the leading edges of the upper wing, to cause a burble at high angles of attack and act as "stall warning". The landing gear was fitted with 6.50x10 wheels mounting 7.50x10 low-pressure tires; wheel brakes and a parking brake were standard equipment. A wooden propeller, speed-ring engine cowl, Heywood engine starter, navigation lights, hot-shot battery, dual controls, a 10x3 tail wheel, compass, engine cover and cockpit covers, tie-down ropes, first-aid kit, log books, and tool kit were standard equipment. A metal propeller, front cockpit panel cover, landing lights, parachute flares, and wheel pants were optional. Standard colors were gray, black, or vermillion fuselage with silver wings; any other two-tone color combinations were optional. The next Waco development was the model UIC cabin biplane, as described in the chapter for ATC # 499 of this volume.

Listed below are model PBF entries as gleaned from registration records:

NC-13029; Model PBF (# 3616) Jacobs 170.
NC-13049;   "   (# 3649)   "
NC-13428;   "   (# 3693)   "
NC-13446;   "   (# 3765)   "

This approval for ser. # 3616 and up; this approval expired 9-1-34.

A.T.C. # 492
(9-1-32)
MONOCOUPE, MODEL 70-V

Fig. 300. The "Monocoupe" 70-V with 65 h.p. Velie engine; loss in performance was traded for economy.

"Monocoupe" history makes practically no mention of the rare model 70-V as such. Developed during the same time that 1932 versions of the "Monocoupe 90" were coming off the line, the 70-V was very much the same except for a few minor differences. With only a rare factory photograph to go on, the visible differences show a more simplified landing gear that led to the setup used on the 90-A, and a larger vertical fin as also used on later models in 1933-34. Of course, the crux of the whole matter was the 5 cyl. Velie M-5 engine that was mounted in the nose, and then shrouded with a low-drag Townend-ring, as if to conceal its presence and identity. One must wonder why the "Velie" was ever mounted in the "Ninety" airframe at this stage of the game, but it has been hinted and rumored repeatedly that a small stockpile of these engines were still lying around the factory and needed getting rid of. Rerated to 65 h.p. at a higher operating r.p.m., the surplus Velie M-5's were to be installed in the so-called 70-V; and they planned to sell them at a relatively lower price than the standard Lambert-powered "Ninety". If this particular combination was to have unloaded the surplus "Velie" engines, it certainly did no such thing; the air-

plane shown here was evidently the only example that was built. The strangled economy of the times prompted many things, some frantic and some futile, but airplane development at the "Monocoupe" factory, however, continued on, as it always did, to perpetuate the ultimate in the small cabin monoplane.

The "Monocoupe" model 70-V was a light, high-winged cabin monoplane with side-by-side seating for two; it was apparently of the same basic airframe as used for the "Model 90" during this period of its production. Some changes were noted, but these were of transitory nature and not particularly identifiable with the 70-V only. In the program laid out for 1932, the Monocoupe Corp. announced plans to offer models ranging up in price from $2395., with various engines ranging upwards from the 65 h.p. Velie; this then serves as a good clue that the 70-V version must have been planned early as a part of the total lineup offered in 1932. Listings and advertisements for 1933 also mention that the standard "Monocoupe" was available with the Velie M-5, the Lambert 90, etc.; no specific mention had ever been made of the model 70-V as such, but apparently it was quickly available for sale should the occasion arise.

As powered with the 5 cyl. Velie M-5 engine of 65 h.p., the standard "Monocoupe 90" airframe must have suffered for the loss of 25 h.p. that it was normally accustomed to (90 h.p.); but the resulting economy of operation and lower purchase price could have been of enough consequence to offset the loss in performance. The type certificate number for the model 70-V was issued 9-1-32, and it is doubtful whether any more than one example of this model were manufactured by the Monocoupe Corp. on Lambert Field in Robertson (St. Louis), Mo.

With factual data or information unavailable on this model from any of the normal sources, the following observations are offered in discussion. With the Velie 65 and Lambert 90 engines of practically identical dimension and weight there would be practically no installation problems, and the airplane itself would only be concerned with the loss of 25 horsepower. By trim-

ming some 90 lbs. off the useful load, performance of the 70-V would at least be comparable to the earlier "Model 113" in some instances, and in some instances it would be better. In this light, the model 70-V does not seem to be such a drastic step backward. With a price-tag of $2395. pinned on the model 70-V, it was still best value anywhere for this type of airplane; but the uncertainty of a market gripped in the strangle of a nation-wide depression cannot be calculated in advance. The next "Monocoupe" development was the classic model D-145, as described in the chapter for ATC # 529.

Listed here is the only known example of the model 70-V:

NC-428N; Model 70-V (# 617) Velie M-5.

Company literature of the period would infer that any "Model 90" would be eligible for this modification.

Fig. 301. Stinson R-3 shows off to emphasize retractable landing gear; model developed as small airliner.

As portrayed here in rare photos, the "Model R-3" was certainly no ordinary Stinson, and (especially if seen gamboling in full-flight) it was a rather dramatic sight. Dramatic in the sense that it was one of the few high-winged monoplanes that tucked its drag-producing landing gear into the belly and out of sight. The intended use of the retractable landing gear was foreshadowed early in the development of the "Model R" series - which had the normal fixed undercarriage, but the thick stub-wing was a positive give-away as to further development plans for this series. As finally announced, there were to be 4 models (the R, R-1, R-2, R-3) in this series; the 215 h.p. Model R had fixed gear, and the R-1 was to be similar but fitted with retracting gear. The 240 h.p. Model R-2 had the fixed gear, and the R-3 was similar but with the retracting gear. As the models were being prepared for certification, it was found advisable to eliminate the model R-1 from the series. The Model R, which was by far the most popular, was primarily intended for the private-owner or the sport-flier, while the models R-2 and R-3 were specifically developed for light transport duties by feeder-lines or charter operators. As normally fitted, the new Model R-3 was a true airliner in a scaled-down fashion, and elimination of landing gear drag added measurably to cruising speeds and operational range. Because of the high-winged configura-

tion, the overall gain by retracting the gear was not nearly so great as expected; but it certainly was a noval effort for improvement of performance in the high wing design. At this particular stage of commercial airplane development, the successful airplanes with retractable landing gears, that disappeared entirely from the airstream, were rare; these could be counted on fewer than the fingers of one hand. As a milestone in progress, then, the Stinson R-3 was certainly a revolutionary airplane, but it lived out its relatively short life without very much success.

The Stinson model R-3 was a high-winged cabin monoplane, with seating arranged for three passengers and a pilot. Typical of the Model R-2, the new R-3 was also intended for transport-type use, and was equipped with appointments and operational aids befitting the role of a small airliner. The R-3 also offered the bonus of higher speeds and greater operational range by retracting its landing gear, certainly a highly significant achievement in a craft of this particular type. Factual operational data on this particular type of landing gear system is not available, but the simple drum and cable system was probably no more bother than just the extra manual labor it foisted on the busy pilot. As powered with the 9 cyl. Lycoming R-680-BA transport-type engine of 240 h.p., the model R-3 delivered very good performance,

Fig. 302. Stinson model R-3 with 240 h.p. Lycoming engine; model not successful but led to popular "Reliant."

which in most listings appears to be rather con-servative; Stinson Aircraft was very proud of the model R-3, but they were not particularly boast-ful about it. There is no reason to believe that the "clean" underside of the R-3 had any appreciable effect on flight characteristics, so we can safely assume that this airplane com-pared favorably with the myriad of "Juniors" that came before it. Although not a particularly successful series when judged by numbers built, the "Stinson R" monoplanes definitely laid some firm ground-work for the SR "Reliant" that followed shortly after. The type certificate number for the Model R-3 was issued 9-1-32, and perhaps no more than three examples of this model were manufactured by the Stinson Aircraft Corporation, a division of the Cord Corporation, at Wayne, Michigan.

Listed below are specifications and per-formance data for the Stinson model R-3 as powered with the 240 h.p. Lycoming R-680-BA engine; length overall 26'2"; height overall 8'6"; wing span 43'4"; wing chord 75"; total wing area 235 sq.ft.; airfoil Clark Y; wt. empty 2290 lbs.; useful load 1210 lbs.; payload with 56 gal. fuel 665 lbs.; payload with 73 gal. fuel 565 lbs.; gross wt. 3500 lbs.; max. speed 138; cruising speed 118; landing speed 62; climb 600 ft. first min. at sea level; ceiling 12,500 ft.; gas cap. normal 56 gal.; gas cap. max. 73 gal.; later also eligible with 90 gal. fuel cap.; cruising range at 13 gal. per hour 470-640 miles; 90 gal. fuel load extended range to nearly 770 miles; oil cap. 5-6 gal.; price $6497. at factory field.

The construction details and general arrange-ment of the Model R-3 were typical of that of the R-2, as described in the chapter for ATC # 489 of this volume. The fashionably durable interior was accented by satin-chrome hardware and polished wood trim; other niceties included assist ropes and ash-trays at each seat. All seats

were deeply padded, and the pilot's seat was adjustable two ways for his convenience and comfort. The baggage compartment was allowed only 50 lbs., but there was ample weight al-lowance in the cabin area for miscellaneous baggage items. The wing framework was typical of Stinson practice, with the use of stainless steel stampings that were spot-welded into truss-type wing ribs. Fuel tanks were mounted in the root ends of each wing-half with capacity varying at 56-73-90 gal., according to range desired. Fuel-level gauges were mounted in-side cabin. The retractable landing gear, which folded upward and inward, was a mechanical system operated manually by the pilot; cables and a drum, in 20 to 1 reduction, retracted or extended the gear by means of a winding crank. Locking pins secured the gear in either up or down position, and tell-tale signals informed the pilot of its position. Low pressure 7.50x10 semi-airwheels with brakes were standard equipment. The engine was mounted in rubber-ized bushings to dampen vibration; a large exhaust collector-ring and tail-pipe eliminated much of the engine noise. An adjustable metal propeller, electric engine starter, a battery, navigation lights, tail wheel, cabin heater, and wheel brakes were standard equipment. Radio equipment, radio shielding, landing lights, and parachute flares were optional. The next development in the Stinson cabin monoplane was the model SR, as described in the chapter for ATC # 510.

Listed below are the only known R-3 entries as gleaned from registration records:
NC-449M; Model R-3 (# 8600) Lyc. 240.
NC-12187;   "   (#   )   "
NC-12131;   "   (# 8602)   "
Ser. no. for NC-449M unverified; ser. no. for NC-12187 unknown; this approval for ser. # 8600 and up; this approval expired 9-1-34.

A.T.C. # 494
(9-15-32)
CONSOLIDATED
"FLEETSTER," 20-A

Fig. 303. Fleetster 20-A winging its way to connect passengers with main line to east and west coast.

Following the basic pattern of the earlier "Fleetster 20" quite closely, the new model 20-A was especially developed by order of (TWA) Transcontinental & Western Air, Inc. Built to the suggested specifications of TWA, the model 20-A was specifically arranged and fitted to handle combination loads in fast shuttle-type service. Placed into service in Oct. of 1932 on a new 272 mile route, the parasol-winged "Fleetster" fleet connected several large northern cities with the main coast-to-coast route. Originating in the motor-capital of Detroit with stops along the way at Toledo and Ft. Wayne, the "Fleetster" arrived at Indianapolis in just under two hours to connect passengers with the main line to California and points west. Mixed in with passenger loads was airmail and miscellaneous air-express shipments. Becoming very familiar from lower Michigan through Ohio and Indiana, the fast-flying 20-As were a rather romantic sight, and people often came to the airports just to watch them come in and leave. Most transport pilots who came up through the open-cockpit biplane days preferred the parasol-monoplane for airline service; exceptional stability made the pilot's job a lot easier, and the extended visibility was welcomed when coming into or leaving crowded terminals. The first significant development of the parasol-monoplane for airline service was the Lockheed "Air Express", and the Fokker F-14 was another good example. As the best of this type developed up to that time, the "Fleetster" 20-A served well for several years and finally rung down the curtain on this particular type of airplane for major airline service.

The roundish Consolidated "Fleetster" model 20-A was a parasol-type cabin monoplane with seating arranged for 6 or 7 passengers and a pilot. Specifically adapted for hauling combination loads, the seating could also be varied to allow 300 to 500 lb. shipments of varied cargo. Previous experience had confirmed that the parasol-winged configuration was especially suitable to this type of service on the shorter routes, requiring numerous stops and frequent changes in passenger load. As shown here, the new model 20-A was still basically similar to earlier examples of the 20-series, but several changes had been made to improve its performance and its utility. The most apparent of several changes was the larger cantilever wing, the spindly low-drag landing gear, and a pro-

*Fig. 304. Pilots liked parasol-wing of 20-A, but passengers did not always
share same feeling.*

tective canopy for the pilot. Other changes were structural, and some changes allowed variation of interior arrangement. Standing much taller now on its big, fat "airwheels," the 20-A was also longer, its empty weight was substantially increased, useful load was increased by a generous amount, and increased wing area helped to hold up the 900 lb. increase in gross weight. Despite these heavier loadings, the "Fleetster 20-A" was faster and all-round performance was actually better. As powered with the big 9 cyl. Pratt & Whitney "Hornet" B1 engine of 575 h.p., the 20-A had impressive performance and a remarkable ability that was quite unusual

among small transport-type aircraft. Conspicuously void of external wing bracing struts and other drag-producing assemblies, the 20-A could sustain top speeds of 175 m.p.h., and cruise quite comfortably at 160. "TWA" advertised 160 m.p.h. schedules, so pilots held to it even if they had to use a few extra r.p.m. Described by pilots as a "hot ship," the "Fleetster 20-A" handled especially well in the air and all enjoyed flying it; passengers often had mixed feelings about the huge wing being suspended on 4 little struts, but generally, most enjoyed the ride. The type certificate number for the "Fleetster" model 20-A was issued 9-15-32

*Fig. 305. Fleetster 20-A with 575 h.p. "Hornet B" engine; 20-A was last of
the "Fleetster" line.*

Fig. 306. Weary and work-worn 20-A still active after second World War.

and 7 examples of this model were manufactured by the Consolidated Aircraft Corp. at Buffalo, New York.

Listed below are specifications and performance data for the "Fleetster" model 20-A as powered with the 575 h.p. "Hornet" B1 engine; length overall 33'9"; height overall 12'0"; wing span 50'0"; wing chord at root 105"; wing chord at tip 69"; total wing area 361.5 sq. ft.; airfoil Goettingen 398 modified; wt. empty 3850 (4160) lbs.; useful load 2950 (2640) lbs.; payload with 190 gal. fuel 1525 (1215)lbs. (7 pass. at 170 lb. each and 335 lb. baggage-cargo, or 6 pass. and 195 lb. baggage-cargo); (figures in brackets for a/c equipped with radio & night-flying gear); gross wt. 6800 lbs.; max. speed 175; cruising speed (80% power) 160; landing speed 62; climb 1050 ft. first min. at sea level; ceiling 18,000 ft.; gas cap. 195 gal.; oil cap. 15 gal.; cruising range at 33 gal. per hour 800 miles; price not announced.

Except for apparent changes, the construction details and general arrangement of the "Fleetster 20-A" were typical of that of the earlier Model 20 as described in the chapter for ATC # 320. Normally, the larger cabin interior was arranged for seven passengers; the wide front bench seated 3 across and occupants faced backwards, four individual seats faced forward with an aisle between them. Entry door to the main cabin was on the right side to the rear. A large baggage-cargo hold with allowance for 300 lbs. was forward of the main cabin with access door on right side. The pilot's cockpit

was protected with a sliding canopy and provided with heat and ventilation. Except for increased area, the all-wood cantilever wing was similar to that of the Model 20; the fuel supply was divided among two 80 gal. wing tanks and a 35 gal. tank in the center-section. In operation on shorter routes, some fuel load was often swapped for increased allowance in baggage and cargo. The spindly-looking semi-cantilever landing gear of 120 in. tread used "Aerol" shock absorbing struts; Goodyear 30x13-6 airwheels were fitted with hydraulic brakes. A 16x7-4 tail wheel was full-swivel, originally encased in a streamlined fairing. These fairings were later discarded in service. All aircraft were later equipped with two-way radio telephone and night-flying equipment. An adjustable metal propeller, electric inertia-type engine starter, a battery, generator, navigation lights, cabin heaters, fire extinguishers, first-aid kits, two-way radio, and night-flying equipment were standard equipment. The next Consolidated development was the 160 h.p. Fleet model 11, as described in the chapter for ATC # 526.

Listed below are Fleetster 20-A entries as gleaned from registration records:

NC-13208; Model 20-A (# 1) Hornet 575.
NC-13209;   ”   (# 2)   ”
NC-13210;   ”   (# 3)   ”
NC-13211;   ”   (# 4)   ”
NC-13212;   ”   (# 5)   ”
NC-13213;   ”   (# 6)   ”
NC-13214;   ”   (# 7)   ”

This approval for ser. # 1 through # 7 only.

A.T.C. # 495
(10-27-32)
HEATH "CENTER-WING," CNA-40

Fig. 307. Heath model CNA-40 with 37 h.p. Continental A-40 engine; shown after landing in street at World's Fair of 1933.

The Heath "Center-Wing" model CNA-40 was developed through a very illustrious ancestry, a lineage of famous mid-wing racing airplanes tracing back to the "Tomboy," the "Baby Bullet," and the Heath "Cannon Ball". Inheriting all of this illustrious background to work with, the Heath Aircraft Corp. developed the CNA-40 mid-wing in 1932 as a companion model to their LNB-4 and LNA-40 parasol monoplanes. Basically similar to either of these except for the wing and its placement, the CNA-40 was also available in the simplified home-assembly kit. After certification (ATC) three of the new "Center-Wings" were flown on a mission of goodwill to the Chicago World's Fair in 1933 and remained for a time on exhibit. The sprawling fair was a gathering of marvels to depict a "Century of Progress". The three little airplanes and their pilots represented the good wishes of the governor and the people of Michigan. Two of the craft used on the missionary flight were finally sold (one had been modified for racing in late 1933), and the prototype of the CNA-40 series remained as a factory demonstrator until sold in

1934. With its shining light more or less hidden under a bushel, the CNA-40 "Center-Wing" was not selling to any extent, but it actually could have done very well. Compared to the chubby "Parasol" the middle-wing version attracted more of the sporty clientele, and some examples were fitted with shorter clipped-wings for racing around the pylons. A small and tidy little ship, the CNA-40 was a charmer that not only looked decidedly handsome, but could also seduce the heart of any pilot in just a few minutes. In 1933 the fourth example off the line was sold — less engine, propeller, tires, tubes, and instruments — to an enthusiast who trucked it home to Dayton, Ohio on a trailer. Two other examples of the "Center-Wing" were reportedly sold to a firm in South America for patrolling pipe-lines. Had more of the CNA-40s been built, it is quite certain they could have been sold in fairly good numbers; the query of nearly all prospects was "how soon can I get one". In the bottom of the great American depression, the International Aircraft Corp. (which was formed in 1933 to continue building Heath airplanes) apparently

Fig. 308. Heath CNA-40 flew when other lightplanes were restricted to the hangar.

found it more profitable to sell stock in the company than to build airplanes; complaints of disgruntled stockholders finally led to a seizure of the firm by the Treasury Department and a subsequent sale to Howard E. Anthony in 1935. Howard Anthony, an ambitious and resourceful engineer, continued production in a facility at Benton Harbor, Michigan as the Heath Aviation Co. until World War 2. To the present date, at least one example of the CNA-40 has withstood the ravages of time and has been restored to fly again; sporting a set of small "racing wings" this craft now poses prettily in a museum of airplanes.

The Heath "Center-Wing" model CNA-40 was an ultra-light open cockpit mid-wing monoplane with seating for one only. As a single-seater this airplane was primarily developed for the sport-flying enthusiast, and was occasionally used for racing around the pylons. Among pilots, an offer to fly the "Center-Wing" was like an invitation to fun and excitement. With a higher wing loading, even in the standard (107 sq. ft.) version the "Center-Wing" could be flown safely in weather that usually grounded such as the "Aeronca" and the "Cub," riding the stiff breezes and turbulent air with the aplomb of an ocean-liner. As powered with the 4 cyl. Continental A-40-2 engine of 37 h.p., the CNA-

40 was a happy sprite that was full of vim and vigor with a snappy response to match. Stable and rather easy to fly, the "Center-Wing" would almost spell out in advance what it was likely to do in case of pilot error, but it certainly did not tolerate carelessness. The clipped-wing version of the CNA-40, with nearly 8 feet cut off the wing span, had to be managed with a lighter and firmer hand, but it was absolutely honest and reveled in speed or mild horse-play. To extend the range on cross-country hops, the "clip-wing" could be throttled way back to about 70 m.p.h. on 1.8 gallons of fuel per hour! With this cruising speed only some 10 m.p.h. above "the stall," it allowed no daydreaming along the way. The CNA-40 with the standard wing had ample area to pull it easily out of small fields, or to get it back in again. The loss in top speed was a fair exchange for the better all-round performance. The type certificate number for the model CNA-40 was issued 10-27-32, and at least 4-or possibly 6-examples of this model were manufactured by the Heath Aircraft Corp. at Niles, Michigan (which had been reorganized into the International Aircraft Corporation. The Heath Aviation Co. of Benton Harbor, Michigan offered the models LNB-4 and CNA-40 in 1936, but production count was not available.

After the untimely death of Ed Heath, one

Fig. 309. Early Heath "Center-Wing" with Heath B-4 engine and wire-braced wings.

Fig. 310. The CNA-40 was fun for one; verdant fields were its habitat.

Fred Seiler, formerly chief engineer at Kreider-Reisner and also chief engineer a short time with Kellett, was called in to manage the Heath company. Initiating the LN series, Seiler called upon Charles W. Morris, a stress engineer from Kellett, to assist him in getting type certificates for the new series. Unfortunately, Fred Seiler crashed fatally during an experimental test-flight in July of 1931, so Morris took over as chief engineer and groomed the LN series through to certification. Morris was largely responsible for design of the LNB-4, the LNA-40, and also designed the CNA-40 mid-wing. Being also a pilot, Charles Morris did much of the test-flying for certification. C. Duke Mueller and Merrill Lambert were also outstanding Heath pilots. With the discouraging sales slump of 1933, Morris shopped around for work and received an order from Curtiss to weld up "Hawk" engine mounts; making up parts for an airplane amusement ride on the midway at the Chicago World's Fair (1933) also helped to keep things going for a while. During this time, a two-place side-by-side parasol monoplane with Velie engine was developed, and Health also built the unusual Herrick Verto-Plane. Upon sale of the company to Howard E. Anthony in 1935, Chas. Morris went to Curtiss in Buffalo, and Anthony continued operation as the Heath Aviation Co. at Benton Harbor, Mich. Following World War 2, Howard Anthony bought up large surplus stocks of wartime electronic equipment and instituted a mail-order business that flourishes to this day, manufacturing the famous "Heath-Kit".

Listed below are specifications and performance data for the Heath model CNA-40 as powered with 37 h.p. Continental A-40-2 engine; length overall 17'3" (16'11"); height overall 4'8" (4'6"); wing span 26'10"; wing chord 54"; total wing area 107.4 sq. ft.; airfoil Clark Y; wt. empty 455 (450) lbs.; useful load 220 (225) lbs.; crew wt. and extras 170 (165) lbs.; gross wt. 675 lbs.; max. speed 87 (93); cruising speed 72 (80); landing (stall) speed 38 (40); climb 500 ft. first min. at sea level; ceiling 12,500 (11,000) ft.; gas

cap. 7 (9) gal.; oil cap. 4 (5) qts.; cruising range at 2.8 gal. per hour 180 (220) miles; price $1095. at factory in 1933-34; figures in brackets for 1936 model as built by Heath Aviation Co. CNA-40 also eligible for ATC when assembled at home from "Heath Simplified Assembly Kit"; "clipped-wing" version (69.6 sq. ft.) max. speed 105; cruising speed 90; landing (stall) speed 60.

The construction details and general arrangement of the CNA-40 were typical of that of the models LNB-4 and LNA-40, except for the following: The fuselage framework of the NCA-40 was similar in detail except for placement of the wing; in the center-wing configuration the panels were fastened to the upper fuselage longerons and braced with N-type steel tube struts from underneath. As against the 135.5 sq. ft. wing area of the "Parasol" the standard "Center-Wing" had 107.4 sq. ft., and the racing panels were trimmed to 69.6 sq. ft.; chord remained the same in either case. Standard rigging of the wing was 3 degrees for angle of incidence and also for dihedral; both settings were usually altered for racing. The cockpit was upholstred in Fabrikoid and protected by a large Pyralin windshield. A flush type step-in in lower fuselage aided in access to top of wing for entry into cockpit. The landing gear used 16x4 aluminum disc-type wheel and brakes were optional; 7.00x4 Goodyear airwheels with brakes were also optional. A wooden propeller, basic engine instruments, springleaf tail skid, seat cushions, and fire extinguisher were standard equipment.

Listed below are CNA-40 entries as gleaned from registration records:

X-11364;	CN	(# 155)	Cont. A-40.
NC-12851;	CNA-40	(# C-50)	"
NC-12881;	"	(# C-51)	"
NC-12882;	"	(# C-52)	"
NC-13532;	"	(# C-53)	"

Ser. # 155 probably experimental prototype for CNA-40 series; ser. # C-50, C-51, C-52 mfgd. 10-32; ser. # C-53 as X-13532 with "Osprey" engine.

Fig. 311. Beech 17-R was hailed as most novel aerodynamic development of the period.

The "Beech" model 17-R was, without doubt, the most outstanding example of aerodynamic novelty in this period. Fairly reeking with sophistication and daring, it is testimony indeed that Walter Beech and his associates had the fortitude to by-pass convention and look far into the future. A marked departure from normal practice — the negatively staggered wings had at first the impact of novelty, but the selection of this configuration had its practical side also. As used on the close-coupled "Beech 17" the negative stagger contributed largely to the pilot's overhead and lateral visibility, and to certain structural advantages that allowed the grouping of load-carrying assemblies into more efficient trusses. Negative stagger in a wing cellule had heretofore been eyed with some suspicion, but wind-tunnel tests on the Beech wing cellule, with its (38%) negative setting, showed an unusually stable lift-curve at angles up to 30 degrees with no tendency to "fall off" sharply. The combination of airfoil choice and wing arrangement produced improvement of airflow for gentle characteristics at higher angles of attack. Streamlined to the highest possible degree with landing gear fairings, a NACA-type engine cowl and the liberal use of fairing fillets, the 17-R was "clean" and exceptionally fast. With a landing speed of some 60 m.p.h. the spread of speed to a maximum of 200 m.p.h. was also quite unusual. Designed primarily as a four-place high speed transport for the businessman the 17-R offered undoubtable prestige and pro-

motional value beside the high performance, but it was more than a year later that Beech Aircraft finally sold their first airplane to a businessman. Saving the prototype airplane for demonstration work, the hurried second example of the 17-R was sold to Loffland Bros. Co. of Tulsa, Okla. in 1933. After modification to landing gear and tail wheel for better ground handling characteristics during take-off and in landing, the first example was finally sold to the Ethyl Corp. in 1934. Pleased but not particularly jubilant over the progress made so far, Walter Beech was confident he had an airplane design of unusual possibilities, and needed only find a way to sell it.

The airplane that was to become the Beech 17-R was actually discussed and planned while Walter Beech was still president of Curtiss-Wright in St. Louis, but the higher-ups in the corporation were not interested in any kind of cabin biplane at this time. Resigning from Curtiss-Wright, Walter Beech went back to Wichita; with most of his money and money from a few local businessmen, he formed the Beech Aircraft Co. in April of 1932. Setting up shop in one corner of the idle Cessna plant, Beech and 8 employees began to shape the revolutionary biplane designed by Ted Wells; its rapid progress spurred everyone on with mounting excitement. By Nov. of 1932 the glistening 17-R was ready for test-flight, and several days later had clocked 201.2 m.p.h. Fulfilling design calculations almost to a tee, such performance in a commercial cabin airplane was unheard-of in 1932. News of

Fig. 312. Every line and curve of 17-R was tailored to speed.

this travelled fast in the airplane fraternity. By 1933 the 17-R was widely known as a "hot airplane" and it was certainly not an airplane that could be sold to just anybody; only two of the model 17-R were built and sold, but the basic design was proven in use, and in its wake was the making of some exciting aviation history.

The Beech model 17-R was a radical innovation in the form of a cabin biplane with seating arranged for 4 or 5. Truly inspired by imagination and the fortitude to look beyond the conventional, the negative-stagger arrangement actually had as much promotional value as it did practical value. Mechanical arrangement of various assemblies bears out the underlying reason for this unconventional configuration, but its shock-value to an ailing industry must have also been of prime consideration. While designs of other companies were just progressive refinements of standard practice, the Beech 17-R was a major break-through that instigated both promise and controversy. Designed primarily as a deluxe

transport for the business-executive it offered cruising speeds that were unmatched by anything on the market; that it also offered luxury, comfort and utility was graphic illustration of the careful planning that went into this design. As powered with the 9 cyl. Wright R-975-E2 engine of 420 h.p., the 17-R reaped sensational benefits from this amount of power to a ratio never before achieved. The "Beechcraft" model 17-R was fast, there was no doubt about that, and its flight characteristics were practically without fault; but like any "hot" airplane it was a worrisome handful on the ground. Widening of the narrow-tread landing gear and several other modifications tamed its ground behavior to a large degree, but it was still "a pilots airplane". Pilots voiced a certain satisfaction in flying this airplane, but they earned it on take-off or landing. The approved type certificate number for the model 17-R was issued 12-20-32 and only 2 examples of this model were manufactured by the Beech Aircraft Co. at Wichita, Kan. Walter

Fig. 313. Beech 17-R was powered with 420 h.p. Wright R-975-E2 engine; note unusual tunnel-type engine cowl.

Fig. 314. Exaggerated view emphasizes unusual arrangement of 17-R.

H. Beech was president; Ted A. Wells was V.P. and chief engineer; and Olive Ann Beech was secretary-treasurer. Among others, it is very probable that Herb Rawdon had a hand in design of the 17-R. The second airplane was actually sold to the Ethyl Corp. in 1934 and operated into 1935, when it crashed to destruction during a severe ice storm. The operational history of these two airplanes was not very long, but certainly quite exciting.

Listed below are specifications and performance data for the Beech model 17-R as powered with the 420 h.p. Wright R-975-E2 engine; length overall 24'2"; height overall 8'8"; wing span upper 34'4"; wing span lower 34'4"; wing chord upper & lower 60"; wing area upper 178 sq.ft.; wing area lower 145 sq.ft.; total wing area 323 sq.ft.; airfoil N-9; wt. empty 2700 lbs.; useful load 1800 lbs.; payload with 145 gal. fuel 695 lbs. (3 pass. at 170 lbs. each & 175 lbs. baggage); gross wt. 4500 lbs.; max. speed 201; cruising speed 175; landing speed 60; climb 1600 ft. first min. at sea level; ceiling 20,000 ft.; gas cap. normal 145 gal.; gas cap. optional 115 gal.; oil cap. 8.5 gal.; cruising range at 24 gal. per hour 960 miles; price $19,000. at factory during 1933, lowered to $17,930. in 1934.

The stubby fuselage framework was built up of welded chrome-moly steel tubing, deeply faired to a streamlined shape with wooden formers and fairing strips, then fabric covered; entire cabin portion was covered in dural metal sheet with wing-root and other fairings as part of the cover. Two welded steel tube trusses across bottom of the fuselage carried major loads of the landing gear, lower wings, fuel tanks, bracing wires, and front occupants. Cabin walls were insulated and the interior was richly upholstered; adjustable individual seats were mounted in front and a deep couch-type seat in back was wide enough to seat three. Large entry doors were provided on either side; a baggage compartment with allowance for up to 175 lbs. was behind rear seat and accessible through a large outside door on right side. Cabin lighting and ventilation were provided; the big formed windwhield and all other windows were of shatter-proof glass. The wing framework in four panels was built up of welded steel tube girder-type spar beams with spruce and plywood truss-type wing ribs; the wing rib spacing was 6 in. to preserve the airfoil form across the span. The leading edges were covered with dural metal sheet and the completed panels were covered in fabric; Friese-type "differential" ailerons with 45 deg. up and 15 deg. down were on the lower wing panels. I-type interplane struts of the racing type were heat-treated steel assemblies, and interplane bracing was of heavy-gauge streamlined steel wire; all fittings and terminals were within the structure. The unusual landing gear was partially retractable (6 in.) and was fully encased in large streamlined fairings; hydraulic shock absorbers and 9.50x12 semi-airwheels with brakes were standard equipment. An electric servo-motor operated the short wheel retraction and extension. A 16x7 tail wheel encased in a metal fairing was mounted rigidly with no swivel. Two fuel tanks were mounted in the deep fairing of the lower fuselage; engine-driven fuel pumps provided fuel transfer with a hand operated wobble-pump for emergency. The fabric covered tail-group was built up of welded chrome-moly steel tubing; horizontal stabilizer was ad-

Fig. 315. Prototype 17-R as modified for Ethyl Corp.; changes tamed its nature.

justed for trim with an electric servo-motor, and a split-rudder fanned out for "drag" during landing. The split-rudder was later abandoned and small "drag flaps" were mounted on underside of upper wings. All movable controls were mounted on ball-bearings and were cable operated. A Lycoming-Smith controllable metal propeller, Eclipse electric engine starter, generator, battery, navigation lights, cabin lights, landing lights, parachute flares, a full complement of engine and flight instruments, fuel pumps, electric servo-motors, and electric fuel gauges were standard equipment. The next development in the Beech model 17 was the thundering A-17-F as described in the chapter for ATC # 548.

Listed below are Beech 17-R entries as gleaned from registration records:
NC-499N; Model 17-R (# 17R-1) Wright 420.
NC-58Y;   "   (# 17R-2)   "

A.T.C. # 497
(1-9-33)
FAIRCHILD 24, MODEL C-8-A

Fig. 316. Fairchild 24-C8A with 125 h.p. Warner "Scarab" engine; shown with standard landing gear.

A keen interest in the recently introduced "Fairchild" 24-C8, prompted Kreider-Resiner Aircraft to develop the new line one step further with a radial-engined version; this was a pleasant variation with a little more power and a slight boost in general owner appeal. As powered with the popular 7 cyl. radial-type Warner "Scarab" engine of 110-125 h.p. the new model 24-C8A offered all the good features of this basic design with the bonus that naturally comes with more horsepower. As shown here, the radial-engined installation in the 24-C8A was perhaps not as "clean" aerodynamically as the slender "inline" installation of the Cirrus-powered 24-C8, nor was visibility quite as good over and around the front, but the difference seemed not enough to be of consequence to anyone. Local enthusiasm was very heartening and suggested the justification for some national bally-hoo. A demonstration tour through the vast south-west with the new Warner-powered "Twenty Four" stirred up much attention and considerable admiration for the sporty cabin monoplane. Most of the comment was leveled at its comparative roominess, its robust-looking construction, and its apparent practical utility for adaptation to many uses. Early deliveries of the 24-C8A were well scattered around the country, and one example even found its way to service in Alaska. Some of the 24-C8A were in use for pilot-training, and a few were used by business-houses, but generally this cabin two-seater was a sport-type airplane that was owned by the so-called sportsman-pilot. Of the 25 examples that were built in this particular

model almost all turned in many years of diversified flying with a good service record.

The Fairchild (Kreider-Reisner) model 24-C8A was a high-winged cabin monoplane with side-by-side seating for two. Because of its generous dimension, its neat interior roominess, its allowance for ample baggage and extra equipment, its ease of entry or exit, and its appeal to the owner-pilot in general, it was somewhat outside the class of the average small airplane; perhaps a more suitable expression would describe it as a "small limousine" for two. Priced in a bracket considerably higher than that of other light two-seaters the "Twenty Four" (24-C8A) was leveled at a somewhat smaller segment of the market, but it did well in spite of this handicap and laid down very firm ground-work for future models in this series. There is vague suggestion that the prototype for the model 24-C8A might have been planned around the 5 cyl. Warner "Junior" engine of 90 h.p., but records do not confirm this. As formally introduced in its prototype the C-8-A mounted the "Scarab" of 110 h.p. and all examples following shortly mounted the rerated "Scarab" of 125 h.p. As powered with the 7 cyl. Warner "Scarab" engine of 125 h.p. the model 24-C8A had ample power in reserve for a delightful performance with some left-over punch for use in the clinches. With no particular stand-out features in its performance, the 24-C8A was more like a good combination of everything; and owner-pilots were quite happy with it. The type certificate number for the model 24-C8A was issued 1-9-33 and at least 25 ex-

Fig. 317. Two-seated 24-C8A became very popular for sport-flying.

amples of this model were manufactured by the Kreider-Reisner Aircraft Co., Inc. at Hagerstown, Md.; a div. of the Fairchild Aviation Corp.

Listed below are specifications and performance data for the Fairchild model 24-C8A as powered with the 125 h.p. Warner "Scarab" engine; length overall 23'5"; height overall 7'0"; wing span 35'8"; wing chord 66"; total wing area 170 sq.ft.; airfoil (NACA) N-22; wt. empty 1183 lbs.; useful load 617 lbs.; payload with 30 gal. fuel 244 lbs. (1 pass. at 170 lb. with 74 lb. allowance for baggage and extra equipment); gross wt. 1800 lbs.; max. speed 124; cruising speed 105; landing (stall) speed 48; climb 900 ft. first min. at sea level; ceiling 16,000 ft.; gas cap. normal 30 gal.; gas cap. max. 40 gal.; oil cap. 3 gal.; cruising range at 7.5 gal. per hour 360 miles; price $3850. at factory. Gross wt. allowance was 1750 lbs. for earliest versions with standard landing gear, increased

Fig. 318. 24-C8A lost some visibility due to "round" engine, but combination
was more popular.

Fig. 319. 24-C8A also available with custom colors and sport-type landing gear.

to 1800 lbs. for installation of sport-type landing gear, metal propeller, and extra equipment; later amendment allowed 1850 lbs. for gross wt. Performance; figures listed here are for 1800 lb. gross wt.; figures for 1750 lb. or 1850 lb. gross wt. would be proportionately higher or lower.

The construction details and general arrangement of the model 24-C8A were typical of the 24-C8, as described in the chapter for ATC # 475 of this volume. The most obvious change in the new 24-C8A was the Warner radial engine that was shrouded in a speed-ring cowling; the engine was mounted in rubber pads to dampen vibration. The large baggage compartment behind the seat-back had allowance for up to 74 lbs. with an additional 50 lb. allowance for two parachutes or extra equipment. Windshield panels were of shatter-proof glass, and door-panels slid open for ventilation. A 15 gal. fuel tank was mounted in the root end of each wing half for 30 gal. normal cap.; larger 20 gal. tanks for a total of 40 gal. cap. were optional. The standard outrigger landing gear of 110 in. tread used oleo-spring shock absorbing struts of 8 in. travel; low-pressure 6.50x10 semi-airwheels with brakes were standard equipment. A streamlined sport-type landing gear with 6.50x10 wheels encased in wheel pants was optional; Goodyear 19x9-3 airwheels were optional for use on either landing gear. A 10x3 tail wheel was standard, but an 8x4 tail wheel was optional; skis were also available for either landing gear. A wooden propeller, wiring for navigation lights, speed-ring engine cowl, 10x3 tail wheel, and standard-type landing gear were normal equipment. A metal propeller, engine starter, battery, navigation

lights, sport-type landing gear, 8x4 tail wheel, Goodyear 19x9-3 airwheels, a 40 gal. fuel cap., extra instruments, and skis were optional. The next development in the "Fairchild 24" was the model 24-C8B as described in the chapter for ATC # 498 of this volume.

Listed below are model 24-C8A entries as gleaned from registration records:

NC-13169; 24-C8A (# 2500) Warner 125.

NC-13170;	”	(# 2501)	”
NC-13171;	”	(# 2502)	”
NS-44;	”	(# 2503)	”
NC-2515;	”	(# 2504)	”
NC-2548;	”	(# 2505)	”
NC-2550;	”	(# 2506)	”
NC-2561;	”	(# 2507)	”
NC-2570;	”	(# 2508)	”
NC-2890;	”	(# 2509)	”
NC-2931;	”	(# 2510)	”
NC-2967;	”	(# 2511)	”
NC-2987;	”	(# 2512)	”
NC-2988;	”	(# 2513)	”
NC-9384;	”	(# 2514)	”
NC-9385;	”	(# 2515)	”
NC-9386;	”	(# 2516)	”
NC-9387;	”	(# 2517)	”
NC-9388;	”	(# 2518)	”
NC-9389;	”	(# 2519)	”
NC-9390;	”	(# 2520)	”
NC-9391;	”	(# 2521)	”
NC-9397;	”	(# 2522)	”
NC-9477;	”	(# 2523)	”
NC-956V;	”	(# 2524)	”
NC-957V;	”	(# 2525)	”

This approval for ser. # 2500 and up; ser. # 2503 with Dept. of Commerce, Aero. Br.; ser. # 2518 to Alaska in 1934; ser. # 2524-2525 mfgd. 1934; this approval expired 9-30-39.

Fig. 320. Fairchild 24-C8B with 125 h.p. Menasco C4 engine; the "24" design was particularly attractive with inline engine.

Closely resembling the earlier Cirrus-powered (A.C.E.) Fairchild 24-C8, the new model 24-C8B — as developed by Kreider-Reisner — was more or less hiding neatly the installation of a 125 h.p. Menasco "Pirate" engine. As shown here, no clearly visible clues will positively identify this version, but there is certain evidence of nearly a year's progress in the refinement of this design. Very much like the first "Twenty Four" (C-8), the 24-C8B had its head-resistance greatly reduced; and visibility was also very good over and around the slender nose. With the self-evident aerodynamic advantage of the inline-engined installation, and also the advantage of a generous boost in horsepower, the 24-C8B could have been at this time the top of the line in this cabin two-seater series. Why Fairchild and Kreider-Reisner did not push this model closer into the limelight of national attention is a moot question; it seems that two examples of this particular model were built and any record beyond that is somewhere in the past. One of these airplanes was still registered to Krieder-Reisner Aircraft into 1935, perhaps for duty around the plant, but final disposition of either or both airplanes is unknown. As an interesting sidelight for the close of the year records will show that some 550 commercial-type airplanes were built in 1932, and about 750 airplanes were sold in that year; this indicates clearly that some 200 airplanes of those sold must have been left-over stocks from 1931. The prospects ahead for 1933 promised to be very similar, if not worse.

The Fairchild (Kreider-Reisner) model 24-C8B was a high-winged cabin monoplane with side-by-side seating for two. Because of the 4 cyl. inverted inline engine installed in this model, it was basically typical of the earlier 24-C8, so most of the apparent difference would be of operational nature. A year's progress in the refinement of this basic design also shows many improvements in airframe detail. The same engine used in the open-seated Fairchild 22-C7B was used in the cabin-type 24-C8B, and both configurations were arranged to appeal strongly to the sporting pilot. As powered with the 4 cyl. inverted air-cooled Menasco "Pirate" C4-125 engine of 125 h.p., the model 24-C8B was perhaps more than a good match for its Warner-powered running-mate the 24-C8A; engine preference in this case would be a deciding factor in the selection of either model. Operational data for the 24-C8B was not available, but it is reasonable to assume that it must have shared all the good features that made the "Twenty Four" series a country-wide favorite. Priced rather high for an airplane of this type at this time, it is well to point out that the 24-C8B was generously equipped with many of the so-called extras as standard equipment. The type certificate number for the model 24-C8B was issued 2-2-33 and only two examples of this model were manufactured by the Kreider-Reisner Aircraft Co., Inc. at Hagerstown, Maryland; a division of the Fairchild Aviation Corp.

In the chapter for ATC # 208 of U.S. CIVIL AIRCRAFT, Vol. 3 it was stated in the last sentence of first paragraph that "Amos" Kreider had retired to take up other interests. Ironically

Fig. 321. 24-C8B typical of earlier 24-C8 except for boost in power.

enough this was only partially true. Perhaps the basis for this statement was the use of some misleading information, and should have been checked out further. Actually, according to Fairchild factory records, Ammon H. Kreider was killed in a mid-air collision over Ford Airport in Dearborn, Mich. on April 13 of 1929; this tragic incident was apparently well hushed in publications of that time and perhaps hardly ever discussed among airmen afterwards. We are sorry to have to mention this at all, but it is pertinent to historical fact.

Listed below are specifications and performance data for the model 24-C8B as powered with the 125 h.p. Menasco "Pirate" engine; length overall 24'1"; height overall 7'0"; wing span 35'8"; wing chord 66"; total wing area 170 sq.ft.; airfoil (NACA) N-22; wt. empty 1156 lbs.; useful load 644 lbs.; payload with 30 gal. fuel 271 lbs. (1 pass. at 170 lbs., 80 lbs. baggage and 21 lb. allowance for extra equipment); gross wt. 1800 lbs.; max. speed 125; cruising speed 106; landing (stall) speed 48; climb 900 ft. first min. at sea level; ceiling 16,000 ft.; gas cap. 30 gal.; oil cap. 3 gal.; cruising range at 7.5 gal. per hour 365 miles; price $3990. at factory, lowered shortly to $3950.

The construction details and general arrangement of the model 24-C8B were typical to that of the 24-C8 and 24-C8A as described earlier in this volume. The air-cooled inverted Menasco "Pirate" engine was neatly cowled and baffled for streamlining and proper cooling; metal cowling panels were quickly removable for repair or service. Windshield panels were of shatterproof glass, and door window-panels slid open for ventilation. The large baggage compartment with allowance for up to 80 lbs. was behind the seat-back; two parachutes at 20 lbs. each, when

carried, were part of the baggage allowance. The cabin interior was neatly upholstered, a large overhead skylight offered visibility upward, and dual joy-stick controls were provided; a cabin heater was optional. Many small improvements were included in the wing structure along with balanced ailerons of an improved design; a 15 gal. fuel tank was mounted in the root end of each wing half. Wing rigging included 1 deg. of incidence and 1.5 deg. of dihedral. The standard outrigger landing gear of 110 in. tread used oleo-spring shock absorbing struts of 8 in. travel; 6.50x10 semi-airwheels with brakes were standard equipment. A sport-type landing gear with faired center-vees and wheel pants was optional; Goodyear 19x9-3 airwheels with brakes were optional with either landing gear. A 10x3 tail wheel was standard, but a Goodyear 8x4 tail wheel was optional. Metal-framed skis for winter-flying were also available. A wooden propeller, dual controls, wheel brakes, compass, wiring for navigation lights, 10x3 tail wheel, a fire extinguisher, and first-aid kit were standard equipment. A metal propeller, engine starter, navigation lights, a battery, 19x9-3 Goodyear airwheels with brakes, 8x4 Goodyear tail wheel, sport-type landing gear, skis, and custom colors were optional. The next Fairchild (Kreider-Reisner) development was the Gipsy-powered model 22-C7D as described in the chapter for ATC # 503.

Listed below are model 24-C8B entries as gleaned from registration records:

NC-13172; 24-C8B (# 3000) Menasco C4.
NC-13173;   ”   (# 3001)   ”

This approval for ser. # 3000 and up; ser. # 3001 still registered to K-R into 1935; this approval expired 9-30-39.

A.T.C. # 499
(3-2-33)
WACO, MODEL UIC

*Fig. 322. View reflects the beauty of Waco model UIC with 210 h.p.
Continental engine.*

In tracing back development of the "Waco" cabin biplane to the QDC of 1931, it is quite remarkable to see the progress made in this series in less than two years' time. Popular right from the start, the "Waco C" cabin-type biplane was making a good name for itself; but as the first novelty began wearing off, many operators were hinting broadly of improvements that would make the airplane even better. Then, as if in one fell swoop, all these improvements were incorporated into one airplane, and it emerged as the remarkable UIC of 1933. From perhaps any angle the new UIC was a beauty; the longer fuselage now had soft rounded lines, the rear-view windows were redesigned for a more graceful contour, and the larger cabin interior promised much more stretch room. The front end of the airplane was its crowning glory; the 210 h.p. Continental engine was now tightly shrouded in a deep-chord NACA cowling, a cowling that sported fancy-looking "blisters" over the rocker-arm boxes to hold down overall diameter. The forward third of the fuselage was, of course, blended into this circular section with a redesigned windshield, a faired landing gear and lower wing fillets; and the finishing touch were the streamlined "wheel pants". So, it is not surprising that the customer could now get at least 10 m.p.h. more in top speed, much more cruising range, an excellent range of visibility,

extra room inside, more conveniences, and better styling, all for the same price of a year ago. It is not surprising also that the model UIC sold faster than it could be built, and some owners of the earlier cabin "Waco" got quickly in line for the new model. At least 70 of the UIC were built and sold in 1933, and the owners' list sounded like a who's who of big-names and dignitaries; they were R. C. "Cliff" Durant, Powell Crosley, Jr., Henry B. Dupont, the lovely Jacqueline Cochrane, Dr. John D. Brock, Gar Wood — the "Silver Fox" of boat-racing, A. Felix Dupont, Jr., David Ingalls, and this to name just a few. The UIC was also harnessed to the needs of business by the Berry Bros. Co., Champion Spark Plug Co., the State of Ohio, Shell Oil Co., Standard Oil of Ohio, the Texas Co., and the Ethyl Corp. to also name just a few. Nearly every state in the U.S.A. had at least one operating within its confines. One was bush-flying in Alaska on floats. Another one, at least, was in Canada on floats; and 12 other foreign countries were reportedly among those on the list of satisfied customers. In summation, it was not difficult to have a high regard for this airplane because it was a fairly remarkable machine.

The Waco model UIC was a cabin-type biplane with seating arranged for four. Extra dimension inside allowed more stretch-room for four large people, and luxurious appointments

Fig. 323. UIC custom-finished in "Berryloid" was operated by Berry Bros. as "Wings of Progress VII."

offered extra comfort and pleasant styling. Window area down the sides, to the rear, and overhead, offered good visibility in all directions, and interior comfort was regulated by ventilation and cabin heat. Restful and relaxing flight was also assured by thickly insulated walls that allowed conversation among passengers now in near-normal tone. Considerably improved over earlier models in this series (Model C) the enthusiasm for the UIC was certainly more than justified. To further increase its utility for work or for play the UIC was easily converted into an ambulance-plane, or mounted on Edo "floats" to operate from water. The listing of owners points to the fact that most examples were used either for business or sport, but the exceptional utility and efficiency of the UIC was easily adapted to many special requirements. As powered with the 7 cyl. Continental R-670 engine of 210 h.p., the model UIC handled its extra weight and dimension very nicely, still giving top-notch performance under most any circum-

Fig. 324. UIC as "Texaco 18" was frequent sight across country.

Fig. 325. Abundant window area in UIC provided excellent visibility.

stance. Burdened only slightly by higher useful loads, the UIC still had the remarkable ability to get in and out of smaller airfields, and it had the pleasant knack of making every pilot look his best in a difficult situation. Typical of the series, the UIC was pleasantly stable, quite easy to fly well, delightfully responsive; and even the most sophisticated owner was stirred with a sense of pride. Extensively equipped, the UIC was delivered "ready to fly — with no extras to buy". To further extol the virtues of this airplane, we might mention that the pattern of the "Waco" cabin biplane remained quite similar to the UIC for the next several years. The type certificate number for the model UIC was issued 3-2-33 and at least 70 examples of this model were manufactured by the Waco Aircraft Co. at Troy, Ohio. Clayton J. Bruckner was president; Lee N. Brutus was V.P.; A. Francis Arcier was chief engineer; and Hugh R. Perry was sales manager.

Listed below are specifications and performance data for the Waco model UIC as powered with the 210 h.p. Continental R-670 engine; length overall 25'2"; height overall 8'6"; wing span upper 33'3"; wing span lower 28'3"; wing chord upper and lower 57"; wing area upper 134 sq.ft.; wing area lower 111 sq.ft.; total wing area 245 sq.ft.; airfoil Clark Y; wt. empty 1690 lbs.; useful load 1110 lbs.; payload with 50 gal. fuel 610 lbs. (3 pass. at 170 lbs. each and 100 lbs. baggage); payload with 70 gal. fuel 490 lbs.; gross wt. 2800 lbs.; max. speed 140; cruising speed 125; landing speed 49; climb 900 ft. first min. at sea level; ceiling 14,400 ft.; gas cap. normal 50 gal.; gas cap. max. 70 gal.; oil cap. 4-5 gal.; cruising range at 12.5 gal. per hour 450-600 miles; price $5985. at factory field. Seaplane on Edo P-3300 twin-float gear; length overall 28'11"; height on water 10'0"; wt. empty 2079 lbs.; useful load 1171 lbs.; payload with 50 gal. fuel 671 lbs.; payload with 70 gal. fuel 551 lbs.; gross wt. 3250 lbs.; max. speed 126; cruising speed 110; landing speed 54; climb 675 ft. first min. at sea level; ceiling 12,000 ft.; cruising range 400-550 miles.

The fuselage framework was built up of welded chrome-moly steel tubing, faired to a well-rounded cross-section with wooden formers and fairing strips, then covered in fabric. Deeply upholstered seats were placed two in front and a double seat in back with convenient entry through a large door on each side. Cabin walls were insulated and neatly upholstered with abundant window area providing visibility in all directions. Cabin vents and heaters provided interior comfort at all times, and front side-windows rolled down for pilot convenience. A throw-over control wheel, dual rudder pedals, and dual brake pedals allowed control from either front seat. Baggage allowance was 100 lbs. and a 15 lb. tool kit was stowed under rear seat; no baggage allowed with 70 gal. fuel. Wing panels were built up of solid spruce spar beams with spruce and plywood truss-type wing ribs; leading edges were covered with dural metal sheet and the completed framework was covered in fabric. A metal-framed, metal-covered aileron was fitted to each wing panel and connected together in pairs with a streamlined push-pull strut; a "spoiler strip" was mounted on upper wings of the seaplane version. A heavy gauge "tension-compression" strut served as interplane bracing instead of the normal criss-cross wires. Upper wing roots were rounded and tapered at fuselage junction for increased visibility; both lower and upper wing roots were faired into fuselage junction with metal fillets. A 25 gal. fuel tank in root end of each upper wing half provided normal 50 gal. capacity, but 35 gal. tanks were available for extended range. A faired landing gear of 90 in. tread was slightly improved over earlier models; 6.50x10 wheels were fitted with 7.50-10 low-pressure tires and brakes were standard equipment. The wheels were neatly encased in streamlined metal wheel pants. The seaplane version was fitted with "Edo" P-3300 twin-float gear; anchor, rope, and tool kit were stowed under rear seat. The fabric covered tail-group was built up of welded steel tubing; elevators had aerodynamic balance and

Fig. 326. Primitive setting of UIC in Canada.

horizontal stabilizer was adjustable in flight. Seaplane version had larger vertical fin with a fin extension under fuselage, and a larger rudder. Standard colors were silver, gray, black, or vermillion fuselage with silver wings; custom colors were optional. A wooden propeller, Heywood engine starter, navigation lights, hot-shot battery, cabin vents and heater, wing fillets, throw-over control wheel, wheel brakes, parking brake, NACA engine cowl, wheel pants, tail wheel, compass, door locks, assist cords, cabin dome light, ash trays, fire extinguisher, first-aid kit, tool kit, and log books were standard equipment. A metal propeller, electric engine starter, 70 gal. fuel cap., Edo P-3300 floats, and radio equipment were optional. Modification as ambulance-plane was $285.00 extra. The next "Waco" development was the two-seated model PLA "Sportsman" as described in the chapter for ATC # 502.

Listed below are model UIC entries as gleaned from registration records:

NC-13061;	UIC	(# 3713)	Cont. 210.
NC-13062;	"	(# 3715)	"
NC-13066;	"	(# 3716)	"
NC-13064;	"	(# 3717)	"
NC-13065;	"	(# 3719)	"
NC-13063;	"	(# 3720)	"
NC-13070;	"	(# 3721)	"
NC-13068;	"	(# 3722)	"
NC-13069;	"	(# 3723)	"
NC-13072;	"	(# 3724)	"
NC-11432;	"	(# 3725)	"
NC-13400;	"	(# 3727)	"
NC-13402;	"	(# 3748)	"
NC-13403;	"	(# 3751)	"
NC-13405;	"	(# 3752)	"
NC-13407;	"	(# 3753)	"
NC-13406;	"	(# 3754)	"
NC-13404;	"	(# 3755)	"
NC-13409;	"	(# 3756)	"
NC-13416;	"	(# 3757)	"
NC-13408;	"	(# 3767)	"
NC-13412;	"	(# 3768)	"
NC-13411;	"	(# 3769)	"
NC-13413;	"	(# 3770)	"
NC-13415;	"	(# 3771)	"
NC-13417;	"	(# 3772)	"
NC-13422;	"	(# 3773)	"
NC-13414;	"	(# 3774)	"
NC-13420;	"	(# 3775)	"
NC-13418;	"	(# 3776)	"
NC-13424;	"	(# 3777)	"
NC-13423;	"	(# 3778)	"
NC-13421;	"	(# 3779)	"
NC-13425;	"	(# 3780)	"
NC-13426;	"	(# 3781)	"
NC-13430;	"	(# 3782)	"
NC-13427;	"	(# 3783)	"
NC-13429;	"	(# 3784)	"
NC-13438;	"	(# 3785)	"
NC-13434;	"	(# 3786)	"
NC-13432;	"	(# 3789)	"
NC-13433;	"	(# 3791)	"
NC-13435;	"	(# 3792)	"
NC-13440;	"	(# 3794)	"
NC-13436;	"	(# 3795)	"
NC-13437;	"	(# 3797)	"
NC-13439;	"	(# 3798)	"
NC-13578;	"	(# 3802)	"
NC-13443;	"	(# 3805)	"
NC-13058;	"	(# 3806)	"
NC-13431;	"	(# 3807)	"
NC-13447;	"	(# 3810)	"
NC-13448;	"	(# 3812)	"
NC-13561;	"	(# 3813)	"
NC-13449;	"	(# 3815)	"
NC-13562;	"	(# 3816)	"
NC-13563;	"	(# 3817)	"
NC-13565;	"	(# 3819)	"
NC-13572;	"	(# 3821)	"
NC-13566;	"	(# 3822)	"
NC-13567;	"	(# 3823)	"
NC-13568;	"	(# 3824)	"
NS-13575;	"	(# 3825)	"
NC-13570;	"	(# 3826)	"

Fig. 327. East or West, the UIC was popular everywhere.

NC-13573; ” (# 3827) ”
NC-13569; ” (# 3828) ”
NC-13577; ” (# 3829) ”
NC-13574; ” (# 3830) ”
NC-13892; ” (# 3832) ”
Serial # 3721 to David Ingalls; ser. # 3723 to R. C. Durant, later to Berry Bros. Co.; ser. # 3754 to Alaska on floats; ser. # 3755 to Powell Crosley, Jr.; ser. # 3757 to Jacqueline Cochrane; ser. # 3771 to Champion Spark Plug Co.; ser. # 3780 to Standard Oil of Ohio; ser. # 3783 to Tex LaGrone; ser. # 3785 to Henry B. Dupont; Ser. #3795 to Ethyl Corp.; ser. # 3813 to Shell Aviation Co. of Calif.; ser. # 3815 to Dr. John D. Brock of K.C.; ser. # 3821 to A. Felix Dupont, Jr.; ser. # 3825 to State of Ohio; ser. # 3826 to Gar Wood; ser. # 3829 to Texas Co. as "Texaco #18"; ser. # 3832 mfgd. 1934.

A.T.C. # 500
(3-16-33)
BOEING, MODEL 247

Fig. 328. The Boeing 247 preparing to load at United air terminal in Burbank.

Successful development of the revolutionary "Monomail" provided the aerodynamic break-through that fostered several other interesting Boeing design concepts; notable among these were the YB-9 "bomber" and, as an evolution from this design, the Model 247 high-speed transport. Inspired by the success of the "Mono-mail" and the possibilities of the twin-engined YB-9, the design-development of the "247" was a logical course; in fact, the transport de-sign was almost completed before the bomber had yet flown. Staring out onto new horizons through the door opened by the "Monomail," the Boeing design-team were looking excitedly into the future and were applying new-found principles in many directions. With design details of the new three-mile-a-minute trans-port circulated secretly among the airlines that made up the Boeing Air Transport System, and subsequently the United Air Lines, decision was quickly made to completely re-equip all lines with the new twin-engined 247 as soon as possible. Sparked by the exciting promise of a new era in airline service, an order for 60 was placed while the new transport was still in the "mock-up" stage. With a first-batch of 15 start-ed by mid-1932, the Model 247 first flew in Feb. of 1933; first delivery was to the eastern division of UAL in April. Several more were delivered to other routes in May, and the entire fleet was delivered and in service by Septem-ber of that year. As the first low-winged, all-metal, twin-engined air transport on the sched-uled airlines - its speed, comfort, and safety

created quite a furor in airline circles, and also were the reasons for its quick public acceptance. Almost quite suddenly all other air transports became obsolete, and the Boeing "Model 247" was to set a fast snow-balling trend for the im-mediate future.

The all-metal Boeing "Model 247" was a low wing twin-engined transport monoplane with seating arranged for 10 passengers, a crew of 3 including a comely stewardess, and stowage for some 400 lbs. of baggage-cargo. Fairly bristling with innovations destined to set a trend, the "247" had an internally braced cantilever wing, the landing gear was retractable, the twin engines were cowled with low-drag speed-rings, and mounted on nacelles built into the wing's leading edge. The smooth all-metal structure also promised efficiency, safety, and durability. Built in relative secrecy, advent of the 247 startled the airline industry with its assemblage of new ideas to fit the future. In regular passenger service by late 1933, the 247 winged its way across the country and lopped off over 7 hours from the previous San Francisco to New York time; the schedule on 247 flights with 7 stops enroute was less than 20 hours. Because of its faster schedules and its attention to passenger comfort, the 247 became an im-mediate success, and all divisions of the United Air Lines system reached new highs in pas-senger and cargo revenues. As the first airliner to be powered with supercharged engines (the 247 mounted two of the new Pratt & Whitney "Wasp" S1D1 rated 550 h.p. at 5000 ft.) turning

Fig. 329. A 247 of Pacific Air Transport at Seattle in 1934; port was northern terminus.

3-bladed fixed-pitch propellers a top speed of better than 180 m.p.h., it soon earned the title of "three-mile-a-minute-transport." Subsequent installation of the new variable-pitch propellers raised cruising speeds by nearly 10 m.p.h. and generally improved the all-round performance. To perform efficiently and reliably in scheduled service, the 247 was equipped with two-way radio gear, the latest navigational devices, night-flying equipment, and various mechanical and aerodynamic aids to lighten the pilot's chore. As a pace-setter, the Boeing 247 shone brightly for at least a year or two, but its accomplishments were soon to be eclipsed by the competition that it had fostered. The type certificate number for the Model 247 was issued 3-16-33 and 61 examples of this model were manufactured by the Boeing Airplane Co. at Seattle, Wash., a div. of the United Aircraft & Transport Corp.

By mid-year of 1932 Boeing began to realize that much of their stores of material and many miscellaneous parts on hand would never again be used by them for aircraft manufacture. To clear out this obsolete inventory more than 200 material and stock items were offered in a big sale at unusually attractive prices. In the rush to fulfill orders on hand for the Model 247, Boeing Aircraft used a 1300 man work-force to meet scheduled deliveries. Stearman Aircraft in Wichita, another division of the "United" combine, was kept busy building landing gears, tail wheels, and other small assemblies for the 247 to help Boeing meet their delivery dates.

Listed below are specifications and performance data for the Boeing model 247 as powered with two "Wasp" S1D1 engines rated 550 h.p. at 5000 ft.; length overall 51'4"; height overall 12'6"; wing span 74'0"; wing chord at root 180"; wing chord at tip 88"; total wing area

Fig. 330. Model 247 against a backdrop of darkness displays concept that set pattern for the "modern" airliners to follow.

Fig. 331. Boeing 247 prototype on early test hop.

(including fuselage) 836 sq.ft.; airfoil Boeing 106 modified; wt. empty 8370 lbs.; useful load 4280 lbs.; payload with 250 gal. fuel 2155 lbs. (10 pass. and 455 lb. mail-baggage); gross wt. 12,650 lbs.; max. speed (5000 ft.) 182; cruising speed (5000 ft.) 161; landing speed 58; sea level take-off 790 ft.; climb 1070 ft. first min. at sea level; climb 830 ft. per min. at 5000 ft.; climb to 8000 ft. in 10 mins.; service ceiling 18,400 ft.; gas cap. max. 265 gal.; gas cap. normal 203 gal.; oil cap. 20 gal.; cruising range at 60 gal. per hour 600 miles; price approx. $50,000. at factory field.

The semi-monocoque fuselage framework in four sections was built up of riveted dural channel members; the four completed sections were then bolted together and covered with smooth riveted aluminum alloy sheet. The main cabin section had 5 seats on each side and a seat for the stewardess at the end of the aisle. The cabin walls were sound-proofed, insulated, and upholstered in gray-green fabric; the passenger chairs upholstered in green whip-cord had reclining backs. Twenty feet long and six feet high, the main cabin was equipped with heating and ventilating vents at each seat, also ash trays, dome lights, and reading lamps. A lavatory and stewardess' pantry were just opposite and aft of the main rear-door entry. All windows were of shatter-proof glass; the last window on the left side was also a knock-out emergency exit panel. The baggage and cargo was divided between two compartments; the compartment in the fuselage nose had 60 cu. ft. capacity and the compartment to the rear of

the main cabin had capacity for 65 cu. ft. Radio-telephone installation was in the upper nose compartment just ahead of the windshield. The pilot's compartment, distinguished by its forward-slanting windshield, seated a pilot and co-pilot, and provided dual controls; seats were adjustable and side windows slid open. The cantilever wing framework was built up of duralumin truss-type spars with tubular dural truss-type wing ribs; the stub wing was built integral with the fuselage and supported the engine nacelles. Outer wing panels were bolted to the stub wing and completed framework was covered with smooth duralumin sheet. Anodizing of all metal skin covering left a gray-ish-looking finish that was normally left un-painted. The fuel tanks, one in each wing stub, were on each side of the fuselage; the right tank had a built-in 70 gal. reserve. The retractable landing gear of 17 ft. 3 in. tread used "Boeing" air-oil shock absorbing struts; wheels were 42x15-16 and hydraulic brakes were standard equipment. The landing gear was retracted into the engine nacelles or extended to down position by electric motors; the full-swivel tail wheel was 16x7-3. The cantilever all-metal tail group was a riveted dural structure; fixed surfaces and movable surfaces were covered with smooth dural metal sheet. The rudder elevator, and aileron used the then-novel trailing edge flaps (trim tabs) for "trimming" airplane during flight. Both elevator and rudder had offset-hinge aerodynamic balance to lighten control forces at pilot's wheel. Stewardess' pantry was stocked to serve light meals while in flight.

Fig. 332. A few 247 retired by United Air Lines were operated by Western Air Express.

Three-bladed metal propellers, electric engine starters, a generator, battery, engine-driven fuel pumps, emergency wobble-pump, night-flying equipment, two-way radio telephone, pressure-type and hand operated fire extinguishers, dual control wheels, and a lavatory were standard equipment. The next development in the Boeing model 247 was the 247-A executive transport version as described in the chapter for ATC # 524.

Listed below are Model 247 entries as gleaned from various records:

NC-13301; 247 (# 1682) 2 Wasp. 550.
NC-13302;   "   (# 1683)   "
NC-13303;   "   (# 1684)   "
NC-13304;   "   (# 1685)   "
NC-13305;   "   (# 1686)   "
NC-13306;   "   (# 1687)   "
NC-13307;   "   (# 1688)   "
NC-13308;   "   (# 1689)   "
NC-13309;   "   (# 1690)   "
NC-13310;   "   (# 1691)   "
NC-13311;   "   (# 1692)   "
NC-13312;   "   (# 1693)   "
NC-13313;   "   (# 1694)   "
NC-13314;   "   (# 1695)   "
NC-13315;   "   (# 1696)   "
NC-13316;   "   (# 1697)   "
NC-13317;   "   (# 1698)   "
NC-13318;   "   (# 1699)   "
NC-13319;   "   (# 1700)   "

NC-13320 was ser. # 1701 and numbers ran consecutively to NC-13329 which was ser.

1710; NC-13330 was ser. # 1712 and numbers ran consecutively to NC-13359 which was ser. # 1741; ser. # 1711 (NC-13300) was manufactured as Model 247-A; last 2 model 247 manufactured were ser. # 1944-45, registered in Germany as D-AGAR and D-AKIN; approx. 32 of the Model 247 manufactured were later modified to 247-D; prototype airplane (ser. # 1682) later modified to 247-E; initial delivery of 247 as follows: 20 to Boeing Air Transport, 23 to National Air Transport, 9 to Pacific Air Transport, 7 to Varney Air Lines - all to United Air Lines on 5-1-34; last two 247 were delivered to Lufthansa (Germany) in 1934.

The closing chapters of this volume give hint and some preview to the marvels to be expected in the next few years. These were times that Douglas introduced the now-famous DC-2, Sikorsky and Martin had built their huge trans-oceanic "Clipper" ships, Lockheed came out with its famous "Electra", the popular Stinson "Reliant" had blossomed out in several beautiful models, and the "Waco" cabin biplane kept getting better and better. Even the Beech "Stagger-Wing" was no longer just a novelty. Air-racing had its influence in bringing out airplanes like the Ryan ST, or the Kinner "Sport-wing", and although private-fliers had perhaps fewer "makes" to choose from, there was no shortage in diverse models that were available. It seems that every year of aviation development since back in the 1920s was brimfull of excitement; generally speaking, the years 1933-34-35 were especially exciting.

APPENDICES

PHOTO CREDITS

Joseph P. Juptner – Fig. 267

James Kuhl Collection - Fig. 197

Louis M. Lowry - Figs. 243, 332

F. C. McVickar - Figs. 233, 323

Charles W. Meyers - Fig. 118

Chas. W. Morris - Figs. 194, 195, 285, 287

National Air & Space Museum - Figs. 83, 166

National Aviation Museum - Figs. 10, 34, 133

Ralph Nortell - Fig. 122

Norman S. Orloff - Fig. 97

Ortho - Kansas City - Fig. 227

Billy Park-Phillips Petroleum Co. - Fig. 73

Edward Peck - Figs. 67, 206

Harold K. Phillips - Fig. 55

Pratt & Whitney Aircraft Div. - Figs. 112, 156

Van Rossem - Fig. 235

Sikorsky Aircraft - Figs. 56, 57, 58, 184, 185

Edgar B. Smith - Figs. 123, 124, 140

Smithsonian Institution - Figs. 33, 35 (National Aeronautical Collection of the Smithsonian Inst.), 38, 59, 62, 63, 89, 98, 99, 104, 146, 161 (National Air Museum).

Spencer & Wyckoff - Figs. 275, 291

Robert W. Thompson - Figs. 308, 310

Frank Turgeon Jr. - Fig. 189

John W. Underwood - Figs. 12, 249, 260 (Sanborn Studio).

Jos. White Collection - Fig. 277

Dick Whittington - Figs. 152, 153, 154, 155

Gordon S. Williams - Figs. 1, 9, 13, 14, 17, 18, 25, 36, 37, 40, 42, 69, 77, 80, 85, 86, 90, 94, 101, 102, 106, 107, 120, 121, 129, 143, 150, 159, 163, 164, 176, 177, 198, 207, 212, 228, 230, 231, 232, 234, 237, 238, 250, 251, 262, 263, 275, 278, 279, 286, 292, 294, 295, 303, 312, 314, 329, 330.

Young Aviation - Fig. 114

BIBLIOGRAPHY

BOOKS:

The Ford Story; Wm. T. Larkins
Revolution in the Sky; Richard Sanders Allen
Boeing Aircraft Since 1916; Peter M. Bowers
Aircraft Year Book (1932-33); Aero. Cham. of Com. of America
Jane's All the World's Aircraft (1931-33); C. G. Grey
Pedigree of Champions; The Boeing Co.
The Gee Bee Story; Chas. G. Mandrake
Staggerwing!' Robert T. Smith
Airways; Henry Ladd Smith
U.S. Army Aircraft; James C. Fahey

PERIODICALS:

Flying   Western Flying
Aviation   American Airman
The Pilot   Popular Aviation
Aero Digest   Lightplane Review
Air Progress   Journal of A.A.H.S.
Air Trails Pictorial   Antique Airplane News

SPECIAL MATERIAL:

Licensed and Identified Aircraft Register of 1932-33-34,
                          by Aero. Cham. of Com. of America, Inc.
Factory brochures and promotional literature.

CORRESPONDENCE WITH FOLLOWING INDIVIDUALS:

Melba Beard   C. G. Taylor   H. Lloyd Child
Chas. F. Schultz   Chas. W. Morris   Peter M. Bowers
Robt. W. Thompson   John W. Underwood   Norman S. Orloff
Harold K. Phillips   John E. Issitt   Erwin C. Eshelman
Edward J. Gardyan   Earl C. Reed   Theron K. Rinehart
Marion Havelaar   Wanda R. Samford

INDEX